D1235664

Jesus Through Middle Eastern Eyes

CULTURAL STUDIES IN THE GOSPELS

KENNETH E. BAILEY

IVP Academic

An imprint of InterVarsity Press
Downers Grove, Illinois

InterVarsity Press
P.O. Box 1400, Downers Grove, IL 60515-1426
World Wide Web: www.ivpress.com
Email: email@ivpress.com

InterVarsity Press® is the book-publishing division of InterVarsity Christian Fellowship/USA®, a movement of students and faculty active on campus at hundreds of universities, colleges and schools of nursing in the United States of America, and a member movement of the International Fellowship of Evangelical Students. For information about local and regional activities, visit intervarsity.org.

The Scripture quotations quoted herein are from the Revised Standard Version of the Bible *(with occasional alterations based upon the author's preferred translation), copyright 1946, 1952, 1971 by the Division of Christian Education of the National Council of the Churches of Christ in the U.S.A. Used by permission. All rights reserved.*

Design: Cindy Kiple

Images: View of Bethlehem by Chernetsov, Nikanor Grigor'evich at Pushkin Museum, Moscow, Russia /The Bridgeman Art Library
        Middle Eastern man: Reza/Getty Images

ISBN 978-0-8308-2568-4

Printed in the United States of America ∞

Library of Congress Cataloging-in-Publication Data

Bailey, Kenneth E.
  Jesus through middle eastern eyes / Kenneth E. Bailey.
      p. cm.
  Includes bibliographical references and index.
  ISBN-13: 978-0-8308-2568-4 (pbk.: alk paper)
  1. Jesus Christ—Biography. I. Title.
  BT299.3.B35 2007
  232.9—dc22

                                                                                            2007031449

P   35   34   33   32   31   30   29   28   27
Y   32   31   30   29   28   27   26   25   24   23   22   21

To

DAVID MARK BAILEY

With Deep Gratitude for his Choice of Hope over Despair

And for His Songs in the Night

With Unfading Love

Contents

Preface

THIS BOOK CAME ABOUT IN STAGES. Some of its chapters were originally transcriptions of professionally recorded video lectures. The meticulous work of transcription was done by my dear friend and colleague, Dr. Dale Bowne, professor of New Testament (emeritus), Grove City College. I am profoundly grateful to him for all his hard work both in transcribing and in commencing the process of transforming lecture-style material into readable prose.

Other chapters are composed of new material on studies of parables that I published nearly three decades ago. The majority of these chapters are presented here for the first time. I am deeply grateful to InterVarsity Press for the privilege of making these findings available to readers interested in examining texts in the light of traditional Middle Eastern culture.

The chapters are a selection. The birth of Jesus, Beatitudes, prayer, women in the ministry of Jesus, dramatic actions and parables are included. The goal is to offer brief glimpses of some of the treasures that await us as Western isolation from Middle Eastern Christian interpretation of the Bible is slowly brought to an end. My purpose is to add new perspectives to our understanding of the text, rather than to rearrange old ones.

I am grateful also to Joel Scandrett, my editor and friend, who has patiently guided this project from beginning to end. Always helpful and insightful, he has wisely urged me to strengthen the work in places of weakness and to clarify the text in places of obscurity. To him I am profoundly indebted.

My debt to my personal copy editor, Sara Bailey Makari, can never be paid. She has broken up my convoluted sentences, straightened my shifting tenses, identified many points of confusion and eliminated excess verbiage. In short, she has contributed enormously to whatever quality the final product may exhibit. Thank you, Sara.

For more than two decades I have had the rare privilege of the sound advice and wise council of an "advisory committee" comprising members of the Presbytery of

Shenango (PCUSA) and more recently of the Episcopal Diocese of Pittsburgh. This highly qualified group of people now includes the Rev. Dr. William Crooks; Rev. Dr. David Dawson; Rev. Dr. Joseph Hopkins; Mr. Thomas Mansell, Attorney at Law; Rev. Pamela Malony; Mr. William McKnight, CPA; and Rev. Dr. Ann Paton. To all these dear friends I wish to express my long-term gratitude and indebtedness.

Many churches and individuals, known and anonymous, have helped support my continuing research efforts. Without their assistance I would not have been able to acquire the resources or complete the work of writing this book. I think particularly of the Eastminster Presbyterian Church, Wichita, Kansas, and Trinity Presbyterian Church, Mercer, Pennsylvania. To all of them I offer my sincere thanks.

The more than ten million Arabic-speaking Christians of the Middle East can trace their origins to the day of Pentecost, where some of those present were from Arabia and heard the preaching of Peter in Arabic. Two bishops from Bahrain attended the Council of Nicaea.[1] Arabic-speaking Christian theologians and exegetes from roughly A.D. 900 to 1400 produced five centuries of the highest quality Christian scholarship, quality that is also found in the present.

For forty years it was the greatest privilege of my life to have been accepted, encouraged, loved, sustained, taught and directed by the living inheritors of that Semitic Christian world. For the good days and the hard days, together through wars and rumors of wars, I would thank them all. This book is but a flawed attempt to learn from their (and our) heritage and through it to try to think more clearly about the life and message of Jesus of Nazareth.

Soli Deo Gloria!
Kenneth E. Bailey

---

[1]Irfan Shahid, *Byzantium and the Arabs in the Fourth Century* (Washington, D.C.: Dumbarton Oaks Research Library and Collection, 1984), p. 330.

Introduction

FOR SIXTY YEARS, FROM 1935-1995, my home was in the Middle East. With a childhood in Egypt and forty years spent teaching New Testament in seminaries and institutes in Egypt, Lebanon, Jerusalem and Cyprus, my academic efforts have focused on trying to understand more adequately the stories of the Gospels in the light of Middle Eastern culture. This book is a part of that continuing endeavor.

The written sources for such a quest are ancient, medieval and modern. As regards *ancient* literature (Aramaic, Hebrew, Syriac and Arabic), I am not solely interested in the Old Testament, the intertestamental literature, and the Dead Sea Scrolls. The post-New Testament Jewish literature (Mishnah, Midrash Rabbah and the two Talmuds) is also important. In addition to Judaica, there is the literature of the Eastern Semitic-speaking churches.

Writing about the importance of the Eastern Christian tradition, John Meyendorff says:

> The idea that the early Christian tradition was limited to its Greek and Latin expressions is still widespread. This assumption distorts historical reality and weakens greatly our understanding of the roots of Christian theology and spirituality. In the third and fourth centuries Syriac was the third international language of the church. It served as the major means of communication in the Roman diocese of the "East," which included Syria, Palestine, and Mesopotamia.[1]

Middle Eastern Christians have been called the forgotten faithful. The world knows that across the centuries there have been Jews and Muslims in the Middle East. For the most part, however, Middle Eastern Christians evaporated from Western consciousness after the Council of Chalcedon in A.D. 451. Few are aware of the existence today of more than ten million Arabic-speaking Christians who

---

[1]John Meyendorff, preface to *Ephrem the Syrian, Hymns*, trans. Kathleen McVey (New York: Paulist, 1989), p. 1.

possess a rich heritage of ancient and modern literature. Speaking a Semitic language, these Christians are a people who live, breathe, think, act and participate in Middle Eastern culture; they are rooted in the traditional ways of the Middle East. Their voices, past and present, need to be heard in biblical studies.

In an attempt to listen to those voices, this set of essays makes use of early Syriac and Arabic Christian literature on the Gospels. Syriac is a sister language to the Aramaic of Jesus. Arabic-speaking Christianity began on the day of Pentecost when some of those present heard the preaching of Peter in Arabic. In the early centuries, Arabic-speaking Christianity is known to have been widespread in the Yemen, Bahrain, Qatar and elsewhere.[2] With the rise of Islam, Arabic gradually became the major theological language for all Eastern Christians. Centuries of high quality Arabic Christian literature remain, for the most part, unpublished and unknown.[3] All of these sources, Syriac, Hebrew/Aramaic and Arabic, share the broader culture of the ancient Middle East, and all of them are ethnically closer to the Semitic world of Jesus than the Greek and Latin cultures of the West.

Out of that earliest period emerged the writings of Ephrem the Syrian and the three classical translations of the Gospel into Syriac: the Old Syriac, the Peshitta and the Harclean, all three of which have been consulted for this book.

Beginning in the eighth century, the early Arabic Christian tradition becomes important. Starting with the early medieval period, the most outstanding Middle Eastern New Testament scholar I have discovered thus far is Abu al-Faraj Abdallah Ibn al-Tayyib al-Mashriqi, most commonly known as Ibn al-Tayyib. This outstanding scholar of Baghdad died in A.D. 1043. Georg Graf describes him as "Philosoph, Arzt, Monch und Priester in einer Person."[4] Indeed, he was a Renaissance man five hundred years before the Renaissance. Fully competent and widely read in Greek, Ibn al-Tayyib was also a trained medical doctor who taught medicine and authored medical texts. As a scholar he translated the New Testament from Syriac into Arabic, authored philosophical and theological works, edited an Arabic version of the Diatessaron and wrote commentaries on the Old and New Testaments.[5] His work on the Gospels is quoted repeatedly in this book.

A second major voice from the medieval period is the Coptic scholar Hibat

---

[2]J. Spencer Trimingham, *Christianity Among the Arabs in Pre-Islamic Times* (London: Longmans, 1979).

[3]Georg Graf, *Geschichte der christlichen arabischen Literatur*, 5 vols. (Vatican City: Biblioteca Apostolica Vaticana, 1944-1953).

[4]Graf, *Geschichte der christlichen arabischen Literatur*, 2:160.

[5]Albert Abuna, *Adab al-Lugha al-Aramiyya* (Literature in the Aramaic Language) (Beirut: Starko Press, 1980), pp. 417-18.

Allah ibn al-'Assal, who in 1252 completed a critical edition of the four Gospels with a full apparatus. His work is an amazing compendium of how the text was translated from Greek, Coptic and Syriac into Arabic over the centuries before his day.[6] Diyunisiyus Ja'qub ibn al-Salibi's (d. A.D. 1171) commentaries on the Gospels have also been consulted.

As regards the *modern period*, I have relied on Ibrahim Sa'id, a prominent Egyptian Protestant scholar who in the twentieth century produced able commentaries in Arabic on *Luke* and *John*. In addition, I have turned again and again to Matta al-Miskin, the Coptic Orthodox scholar who died in 2006. This learned monk, who nearly became the patriarch of his church, spent decades of his monastic life writing commentaries on the New Testament in Arabic. His six large volumes on the Gospels are stunning and unknown outside the Arabic-speaking Christian world.

Beyond the commentaries, ancient and modern, lie the versions. I am convinced that the Arabic Bible has the longest and most illustrious history of any language tradition. The ancient Christian traditions translated the New Testament into Latin, Coptic, Armenian and Syriac. But by the fifth century those translation efforts stopped.[7] Arabic New Testaments have survived from perhaps the eighth and certainly the ninth century. They were translated from Syriac, Coptic and Greek, and continued to be refined and renewed up until modern times.[8] Translation is always interpretation, and these versions preserve understandings of the text that were current in the churches that produced them. They are a gold mine for recovering Eastern exegesis of the Gospels.

These essays not only focus on culture but also on rhetoric. The peoples of the Middle East, ancient and modern, have for millennia constructed poetry and some prose using parallelisms. Known to the West as "Hebrew parallelisms" they are used widely in the Old Testament. But, early in the Hebrew literary tradition, these parallelisms were put together into what I have chosen to call "prophetic homilies." The building blocks of these homilies are various combinations of the Hebrew parallelisms. Sometimes ideas are presented in pairs that form a straight-line sequence and appear on the page in an AA BB CC pattern. At other times, ideas are presented and then repeated backward in an A B CC B A outline. These can be called "inverted parallelism" (they are also named "ring composition" and

---

[6]Kenneth E. Bailey, "Hibat Allah Ibn al-'Assal and His Arabic Thirteenth Century Critical Edition of the Gospels," *Theological Review* (Beirut) 1 (1978): 11-26.
[7]The one exception to this is the Harclean Syriac which was completed in A.D. 614.
[8]I. Guidi, "Le traduzione degle Evangelli in arabo e in ethopico," *Tipografia della Reale Accademia dei Lincei*, vol. CCLXXV (1888): pp. 5-37.

"chiasm"). A third rhetorical style I refer to as "step parallelism" because the parallelisms follow an ABC ABC pattern. Often these three basic styles are combined in a single homily. One finely crafted early example of such a combination of rhetorical styles appears in Isaiah 28, as seen in figure 0.1:

Therefore *hear the word of the LORD*, you scoffers,
who *rule* this people *in Jerusalem*!

Because you have said,

1. a. "We have made a *covenant with death*,
    b. and *with Sheol we have an agreement:*   COVENANT MADE WITH
    c. when the *overwhelming scourge passes through*   Death, Sheol
    d. it will *not come to us;*

2.   a. for we have made *lies* our *refuge*,   REFUGE
        b. and in *falsehood* we have *taken shelter;"*   Shelter made

        therefore thus says the Lord God,
3.   "Behold, I am laying in *Zion* for a *foundation*   BUILDING
        a *stone*, a *tested stone*,   Material
        a *precious cornerstone*, a sure *foundation:*

4.   'He who *believes* [in it—LXX]   INSCRIPTION
            will *not be shaken.*'

5.   And I will make *justice the line*,   BUILDING
            and *righteousness* the plummet;   Tools

6.   a. and *hail* will *sweep away the refuge of lies*,   REFUGE
        b. and *waters* will *overwhelm the shelter.*"   Shelter destroyed

7. a. Then *your covenant with death* will be *annulled*,
    b. and your *agreement with Sheol* will *not stand;*   COVENANT ANNULLED WITH
    c. when the *overwhelming scourge passes through*   Death, Sheol
    d. you will be *beaten down by it.*

Figure 0.1. Isaiah's parable of the two builders (Is 28:14-18)

A number of rhetorical features are prominent in this homily. Among them are:

- The homily has seven stanzas. Those stanzas are *inverted*, with stanza 1 matching 7, stanza 2 matching 6, and stanza 3 matching 5. The center (stanza 4) is the climax, where the prophet calls on the people to *believe* and *not be shaken*. This distinct rhetorical style, with its seven stanzas, is so early and so widely used that it deserves a name. I have chosen to call it the "prophetic rhetorical template." It appears in Psalm 23. Seventeen of these also appear in the Gospel of Mark. By New Testament times therefore, this style was at least a thousand years old.

- Stanza 1 relates to stanza 7 using "step parallelism." When placed side by side these comparisons are evident:

1. a. "We have made a *covenant with death,*
   b. and *with Sheol we have an agreement;*   COVENANT MADE WITH
   c. when the *overwhelming scourge passes through*   Death, Sheol
   d. it will *not come to us;*

7. a. Then *your covenant with death* will be *annulled,*
   b. and your *agreement with Sheol* will *not stand;*   COVENANT ANNULLED WITH
   c. when the *overwhelming scourge passes through*   Death, Sheol
   d. you will be *beaten down by it.*

Clearly, the four statements in stanza 7 match and flatly contradict what is said in stanza 1. Stanzas 1c and 7c are identical.

- A quick glance at stanzas 2 and 6 exhibit the same kind of relationships. Only, in this case, Isaiah is using two ideas in each step of his step parallelism. These ideas have to do with the "refuge and the shelter." In the first, the refuge and shelter are standing. In the second, they are destroyed.

- Stanzas 3 and 5 also match, but in a different way. The first lists the promised new foundation stone. The second describes the building tools to be used. The "line" (the horizontal) will be "justice," and the "plummet" (the vertical) will be "righteousness." To build a stone house the mason must have building materials (3) and the tools with which to build (5). These two stanzas are clearly a match.

- The climax in the center focuses on the promised blessing of faith. The building they have built (the refuge and shelter) will shake and fall. But with faith (in God) they *will not be shaken.* Furthermore, as is usual, the center relates to the beginning and the end. The rulers of Jerusalem have a "covenant with death" (1) that will not stand (7). The one who "believes" (4) will alone be unshaken. The center (4) is composed of two lines and 4a relates to 1 while 4b connects with 7. This can be seen as:

4. a. He who *believes*   (relates to 1 with its "covenant/agreement," which by its very nature demands some level of "belief")

   b. Will *not be shaken*   (relates to 7 where "not stand" and "beaten down" characterize the worthless covenant *that will be shaken*)

This kind of analysis may be seen by some as "interesting" and "artistically satisfying," but is it significant for interpretation? For centuries the church has generally seen most of the texts examined in this book as having a straight-line, "this after that" order. All the rhetorical patterns here displayed may or may not be convincing to you, but even if *some* are judged to be valid, what difference does it make? A few comments on this important question may be helpful.

1. If the author is presenting his or her case using an ABC CBA structure, then half of what he or she has to say about "A" will appear in the first line and the other half must be read in line six. The same is true of the second line (B) and the fifth line (B), which again form a pair. To miss this pairing of ideas is to miss an important part of how the speaker or author is presenting the case.

2. "Inverted parallelism" places the climax in the center, not at the end. As noted, this rhetorical style is often referred to as "ring composition" because the author's mind moves in a circle and returns to the subject with which he or she began. A simple case of this phenomenon appears in Luke 16:13, which is composed in the following manner:

> No man can serve *two masters;*
> > Either he will *hate* the one
> > > and *love* the other,
> > > > or be *devoted* to the one
> > > and *despise* the other.
> You cannot serve *God and mammon.*

By pairing the first and last lines it is clear that the two masters Jesus is discussing are *God* and *material possessions*. Each asserts authority over the life of the believer, and a fundamental choice about who will be allowed mastery must be made. In addition, the climax appears in the center where love and devotion to one master (God) is urged. Logically trained minds assume that the climax always occurs at the end. When this is not the case, the interpreter needs to know how to find it.

3. Where a particular narrative begins and ends can often be determined with much greater certainty when the rhetorical form is uncovered. Paul has a great hymn to the cross which is recorded in 1 Corinthians 1:17—2:2. The Western division for chapter two is in the wrong place. This hymn opens with reference to the preaching of Christ crucified. Christ crucified appears in the middle and again at the end.[9] The rhetorical style identifies the beginning and the end of

---

[9]Kenneth E. Bailey, "Recovering the Poetic Structure of I Corinthians i 17-ii 2: A Study in Text and Commentary," *Novum Testamentum* 17 (October 1975): 265-96.

this masterpiece and allows us to reflect on it as a whole.

4. Rhetorical analysis exposes the smaller sections, which allows them to maintain their integrity rather than to be neglected or broken up into separate verses.

5. Rhetorical analysis delivers the reader from the tyranny of the number system. The text is permitted its own ordering of ideas. The numbers, however useful they are for finding one's place, subtly dictate to the reader, "you *Will* see these ideas or stories as a straight line sequence which follows the numbers." Rhetorical analysis frees us from 1,650 years of dominance by chapter headings and 450 years of subtle control by verse numbers.

6. At times the rhetorical order of the material is an important internal component to help make decisions regarding which Greek reading to select. External evidence regarding which texts are the oldest and most reliable is very important. Internal evidence of the rhetorical styles involved also deserves consideration.

7. The parallels between stanzas (straight line, inverted or step) often unlock important meanings otherwise lost. In Isaiah 28:14-18, Isaiah is discussing the national threat of the coming of the Assyrian army under the dreaded Sennacherib. The leaders who "rule . . . in Jerusalem" (v. 14) had made a covenant with Egypt and were telling the people that everyone was safe as a result. Isaiah was not convinced. The Egyptian world focused on a cult of the dead. Isaiah refers to the covenant with Egypt as a "covenant with death" (read: Egypt). The prophet presents the government's case in stanza 1 and then demolishes it line by line in stanza 7. We need to be able to observe him engaged in his devastating critique.

8. Occasionally in the Gospels there are carefully balanced sets of lines, to which some "footnotes" have been added. This is the case in Luke 12:35-38, where the phrase "in the second or third watch of the night" breaks the balance of the lines. A second "footnote" appears in the second half of Luke 4:25. These explanatory notes can be spotted when the basic rhetorical structure is identified. Such "footnotes" affirm the antiquity of the underlying text.

9. As noted, these rhetorical styles are Jewish and can be traced to the writing prophets and beyond. The reappearance of these same styles in the New Testament makes clear that the texts involved came out of a Jewish, not a Greek world. The case for the historical authenticity of the material is thereby strengthened.

10. All the intelligent people were not born in the twentieth century. When we observe these sophisticated, thoughtful and artistically balanced rhetorical styles, we form a high opinion of their authors.

Rhetorical analysis of biblical texts is like playing the saxophone: it is easy to do poorly.[10] The rhetorical analysis here offered is a start and further refinement is inevitable.

In the West the inspiration of Scripture is rarely discussed as part of biblical studies. Paul Achtemeier observes that the doctrine of inspiration "within the past two or three decades, has been notable more by its absence than its presence. It has been honored by being ignored in many circles."[11] Middle Eastern churches have lived as a minority within a sea of Islam for more than a thousand years. In such a world Scripture's inspiration cannot be avoided. The world of Islam believes that the Qur'an was dictated by the angel Gabriel to the prophet Muhammad in seventh-century Bedouin Arabic, one chapter at a time over a ten year period. The material itself is affirmed to be both uncreated and eternal in the mind of God and cannot be translated. The phrase used to describe this event is "nuzul al-Qur'an" (the descent of the Qur'an). The same verb describes the "descent" of a mountain climber from a high peak. It is a preexistent whole that "comes down" from the heights.

Early illuminated manuscripts of the Gospels often contain a drawing on the first page of an angel dictating to the Gospel author.[12] On the popular level, in certain circles, there is an unspoken yearning for the certainty that comes with the Islamic understanding of inspiration.

But our Greek text does not allow for such a theory. Instead, we are obliged to consider four stages through which our canonical Gospels have passed. These are:

1. the *life and teaching* of Jesus of Nazareth in *Aramaic*

2. the Aramaic *eyewitness testimony* to that life and teaching[13]

3. the *translation* of that *testimony* into *Greek*

4. the selection, arrangement and editing of those *Greek texts* into *Gospels*

---

[10]For a list of eight "words of caution" in the practice of rhetorical analysis, see Kenneth E. Bailey, *Through Peasant Eyes*, in *Poet and Peasant and Through Peasant Eyes* (Grand Rapids: Eerdmans, 1980), pp. xix-xx.

[11]Paul J. Achtemeier, *The Inspiration of Scripture: Problems and Proposals* (Philadelphia: Westminster Press, 1980), p. 14.

[12]This view is as old (2nd cent. B.C.) as the book of Jubilees 2:27; 2:1.

[13]See Richard Bauckham, *Jesus and the Eyewitnesses: The Gospels as Eyewitness Testimony* (Grand Rapids: Eerdmans, 2006).

With these stages in mind, it is necessary to discuss the inspiration of the Gospels as a *process* that took thirty to fifty-plus years to complete. If we are only interested in the first stage, we opt for "a canon within a canon." For the last fifty years I have followed the Western debate over these matters with great care and interest.[14] But to ignore the process and grant significance only to the first stage is to deny the way any significant history is remembered and recorded.

Kenneth Cragg, the distinguished Anglican Islamic scholar, discussed the nature of the Gospels in a sermon preached at All Saints Episcopal Cathedral, Cairo, Egypt, on January 16, 1977. On that occasion he said:

> Much in current Western scientific mentality has been tempted to deny the status of 'fact' (and so of truth) to everything not demonstrable in test-tubes or provable by 'verification'. This instinctive reductionism of many contemporary philosophers sadly prevents them from reckoning with the historical meaning of faith and the deep inter-relation of both event, and mystery.
>
> Let us take help from a parable. November 22 (Texas), 1963. Suppose I say: "A man with a rifle from a warehouse window shot and killed another man in a passing car." Every word here is true (assuming we accept the Warren Commission). But how bleak and meager the facts are – so sparse as to be almost no facts at all. The event is not told at all. But suppose I go further and say: "The President of the United States was assassinated." This is more deeply factual because it is more fully related. The victim is identified, the killing is told as political, and the perspective is truer. But we are still a long way from the meaning of the tragedy. Let us attempt a further statement: "Men everywhere felt that they had looked into the abyss of evil and people wept in the streets."
>
> That third statement tugs at the heart. It is true with a different sort of truth. It pre-supposes what the others state, but goes beyond into dimensions that begin to satisfy the nature of the fearful things that happened. Without something like that third story the event would remain concealed in a part-told obscurity so remote as to be, in measure, false.
>
> Now let us set the Gospels, and the whole New Testament, in the light of this parable. Clearly they are the third kind of statement, deeply involving heart and mind in a confession of experienced meaning – meaning tied intimately to history and to event. That is the way it is with Jesus – not neutrality, bare record, empty chronology, but living participation and heart involvement. For Jesus' story, like all significant history, cannot be told without belonging with the telling in mind and soul.
>
> Christian faith is fact, but not bare fact; it is poetry, but not imagination. Like the arch which grows stronger precisely by dint of the weight you place upon it, so the

---

[14]See Achtemeier, *Inspiration of Scripture.*

story of the Gospels bears, with reassuring strength, the devotion of the centuries to Jesus as the Christ. What is music, asked Walt Whitman, but what awakens within you when you listen to the instrument? And Jesus is the music of the reality of God, and faith is what awakens when we hearken.[15]

In harmony with what Kenneth Cragg has written, and within the perspective of the understanding of inspiration outlined here, these studies will attempt to examine the texts "holistically."

Perhaps the editors of television documentaries are the closest modern counterpart to the compilers/authors of the Gospels. The editor of a television documentary must select, arrange, edit and provide voice-over commentary for all that he or she presents. If that editor is "open minded," there will be a serious attempt to present the subject fairly. The word *fairly* means "in harmony with the editor's deepest perceptions as to the truth about the subject."

Many contemporary commentaries on the Gospels, understandable and rightly, expend enormous energies debating the "primary" or "secondary" nature of the material. Is this or that word or phrase traceable to Jesus or to his Jewish followers or the Greek church? I am convinced that the Gospels are history theologically interpreted. In harmony with what has previously been said about inspiration, I grant that the Spirit of God was given to Jesus (Mk 1:9-11) but also to the church (Acts 2:1-4) that remembered him. Separating, therefore, the exact words of Jesus from the careful editing of the Gospel authors is not the intent of these studies. The theological-historical drama of the text will be examined as a creative whole.

A full-fledged technical commentary is also not the goal of this book. I am aware of opinions other than my own and have followed and engaged in the various strands of debate in the Western New Testament guild over the last half century. This book, however, is not intended to interact with the great volume of current literature on the texts presented, a task that has already been ably accomplished by Joseph Fitzmyer, Arnold Hultgren, I. Howard Marshall and others.[16]

Hopefully, nontechnically trained readers will be able to follow the enclosed discussions with ease. With no presumptuous comparisons intended, the goal is to present a Middle Eastern cultural commentary somewhat patterned after *Read-*

---

[15]Kenneth Cragg, "Who is Jesus Christ?" An unpublished sermon preached by Bishop Cragg at All Saints Episcopal Cathedral, Cairo, Egypt on Sunday, January 16, 1977.

[16]Joseph Fitzmyer, *The Gospel According to Luke*, vol. 2 (New York: Doubleday, 1981); Arland J. Hultgren, *The Parables of Jesus* (Grand Rapids: Eerdmans, 2000); I. Howard Marshall, *The Gospel of Luke* (Exeter, U.K.: Paternoster, 1978).

ings in St. John's Gospel by the former archbishop of Canterbury William Temple.[17] The work of Lesslie Newbigin on John's Gospel also comes to mind.[18]

My intent is to contribute new perspectives from the Eastern tradition that have rarely, if ever, been considered outside the Arabic-speaking Christian world. It is my fond hope that these essays may help the reader to better understand the mind of Christ, and the mind of the Gospel author/editors as they recorded and interpreted the traditions available to them. The reader will decide if I have in any way succeeded.

All of the quotations from Arabic sources recorded in this book are my own translations. It seems pedantic to constantly repeat "my translation" at the end of each of them. I am alone responsible for any errors. However, I do identify where I have translated texts from Hebrew, Aramaic, Greek and Syriac. In the biblical texts quoted, I have worked with the Revised Standard Version and occasionally made my own translations from the Greek. Where I present the rhetorical structure of a text, I use the RSV, but I occasionally revise this translation on the basis of the Greek text.

The texts studied here are grand texts that have inspired the faithful for nearly two millennia. Surely, "fear and trembling" must overtake any interpreter who dares to enter sacred space where candles burn on the altar. May it be so for writer and reader alike.

---

[17]William Temple, *Readings in Saint John's Gospel*, 1st and 2nd ser. (London: Macmillan, 1955).
[18]Lesslie Newbigin, *The Light Has Come* (Grand Rapids: Eerdmans, 1982).

PART ONE

The Birth of Jesus

1

The Story of Jesus' Birth

LUKE 2:1-20

THE TRADITIONAL EVENTS OF THE CHRISTMAS STORY are well-known to all Christians. The birth of Jesus includes three wise men bearing gifts, shepherds in the fields in mid-winter, a baby born in a stable and "no room in the inn." These aspects of the account are firmly fixed in the popular mind. The question becomes: Is there a critical distinction to be made between the text and the traditional understanding of it? Have the centuries added meanings to our understanding of the text that are not there?[1]

A diamond ring is admired and worn with pride, but with the passing of time, it needs to be taken to a jeweler to be cleaned to restore its original brilliance. The more the ring is worn, the greater the need for occasional cleaning. The more familiar we are with a biblical story, the more difficult it is to view it outside of the way it has always been understood. And the longer imprecision in the tradition remains unchallenged, the deeper it becomes embedded in Christian consciousness. The birth story of Jesus is such a story.

The traditional understanding of the account in Luke 2:1-18 contains a number of critical flaws. These include:

1. Joseph was returning to the village of his origin. In the Middle East, historical memories are long, and the extended family, with its connection to its village of origin, is important. In such a world a man like Joseph could have appeared in Bethlehem, and told people, "I am Joseph, son of Heli, son of Matthat, the son of Levi" and most homes in town would be open to him.

2. Joseph was a "royal." That is, he was from the family of King David. The family of David was so famous in Bethlehem that local folk apparently called the

---

[1]For a technical discussion of this text see Kenneth E. Bailey, "The Manger and the Inn: The Cultural Background of Luke 2:7," *Theological Review* 2 (1979): 33-44.

town the "City of David" (as often happens). The official name of the village was Bethlehem. Everyone knew that the Hebrew Scriptures referred to Jerusalem as the "City of David." Yet locally, many apparently called Bethlehem the "City of David" (Lk 2:4). Being of that famous family, Joseph would have been welcome anywhere in town.

3. In every culture a woman about to give birth is given special attention. Simple rural communities the world over always assist one of their own women in childbirth regardless of the circumstances. Are we to imagine that Bethlehem was an exception? Was there no sense of honor in Bethlehem? Surely the *community* would have sensed its responsibility to help Joseph find adequate shelter for Mary and provide the care she needed. To turn away a descendent of David in the "City of David" would be an unspeakable shame on the entire village.

4. Mary had relatives in a nearby village. A few months prior to the birth of Jesus, Mary had visited her cousin Elizabeth "in the hill country of Judea" and was welcomed by her. Bethlehem was located in the center of Judea. By the time, therefore, that Mary and Joseph arrived in Bethlehem they were but a short distance from the home of Zechariah and Elizabeth. If Joseph had failed to find shelter in Bethlehem he would naturally have turned to Zechariah and Elizabeth. But did he have time for those few extra miles?

5. Joseph had time to make adequate arrangements. Luke 2:4 says that Joseph and Mary "went up from Galilee to Judea," and verse 6 states, "*while they were there, the days* were accomplished that she should be delivered" (KJV, italics added).[2] The average Christian thinks that Jesus was born the same night the holy family arrived—hence Joseph's haste and willingness to accept any shelter, even the shelter of a stable. Traditional Christmas pageants reinforce this idea year after year.

In the text, the time spent in Bethlehem before the birth is not specified. But it was surely long enough to find adequate shelter or to turn to Mary's family. This late-night-arrival-imminent-birth myth is so deeply engrained in the popular Christian mind that it is important to inquire into its origin. Where did this idea come from?

---

[2]Some modern translations hide the fact that a number of days passed in Bethlehem before Jesus was born. The original text (along with the King James Version) is precise.

A CHRISTIAN NOVEL

The source of this misinterpretation stems from approximately two hundred years after the birth of Jesus, when an anonymous Christian wrote an expanded account of the birth of Jesus that has survived and is called *The Protevangelium of James*.[3] James had nothing to do with it. The author was not a Jew and did not understand Palestinian geography or Jewish tradition.[4] In that period many wrote books claiming famous people as the authors.

Scholars date this particular "novel" to around the year A.D. 200, and it is full of imaginative details. Jerome, the famous Latin scholar, attacked it as did many of the popes.[5] It was composed in Greek but translated into Latin, Syriac, Armenian, Georgian, Ethiopic, Coptic and old Slavonic. The author had clearly read the Gospel stories, but he (or she) was unfamiliar with the geography of the Holy Land. In the novel, for example, the author describes the road between Jerusalem and Bethlehem as a desert. It is not a desert but rather rich farm land.[6] In the novel, as they approach Bethlehem, Mary says to Joseph, "Joseph, take me down from the ass, for the child within me presses me, to come forth."[7] Responding to this request, Joseph leaves Mary in a cave and rushes off to Bethlehem to find a midwife. After seeing fanciful visions on the way, Joseph returns with the midwife (the baby has already been born) to be faced with a dark cloud and then a bright light overshadowing the cave. A woman by the name of Salome appears out of nowhere and meets the midwife who tells her that a virgin has given birth and is still a virgin. Salome expresses doubt at this marvel and her hand turns leprous as a result. After an examination, Mary's claim is vindicated. Then an angel suddenly "stands" before Salome and tells her to touch the child. She does so and the diseased hand is miraculously healed—and the novel spins on from there. Authors of popular novels usually have good imaginations. An important part of this novel's story line is that Jesus was born even before his parents arrived in Bethlehem. This novel is the earliest known reference to the notion that Jesus was born the night Mary and Joseph arrived in or near Bethlehem. The average Christian, who has never heard of this book, is nonetheless unconsciously influenced by it.[8] The novel

---

[3]Oscar Cullman, "Infancy Gospels," in *New Testament Apocrypha*, ed. Wilhelm Schneemelcher (Philadelphia: Westminster Press, 1963), 1:370-88.

[4]Ibid., p. 372.

[5]Ibid., p. 373.

[6]I lived on that road for ten years, and at that time it ran through flourishing olive orchards.

[7]*The Protevangelium of James* 17:3, in *New Testament Apocrypha*, ed. Wilhelm Schneemelcher (Philadelphia: Westminster Press, 1963).

[8]Curiously, Codex Bezae (5th-6th century A.D.) changes the text to read "as they arrived she brought forth . . ." This change in the Greek text affirms the idea that Jesus was born just as they arrived.

is a fanciful expansion of the Gospel account, not the Gospel story itself.

To summarize the problems in the traditional interpretation of Luke 2:1-7, Joseph was returning to his home village where he could easily find shelter. Because he was a descendent of King David nearly all doors in the village were open to him. Mary had relatives nearby and could have turned to them but did not. There was plenty of time to arrange suitable housing. How could a Jewish town fail to help a young Jewish mother about to give birth? In the light of these cultural and historical realities, how are we to understand the text? Two questions arise: Where was the manger, and What was the "inn"?

In answer to both questions, it is evident that the story of the birth of Jesus (in Luke) is authentic to the geography and history of the Holy Land. The text records that Mary and Joseph "went up" from Nazareth to Bethlehem. Bethlehem is built on a ridge which is considerably higher than Nazareth.[9] Second, the title "City of David" was probably a local name to which Luke adds "which is called Bethlehem" for the benefit of nonlocal readers. Third, the text informs the reader that Joseph was "of the *house* and *lineage* of David." In the Middle East, "the house of so-and-so" means "the family of so-and-so." Greek readers of this account could have visualized a building when they read "house of David." Luke may have added the term *lineage* to be sure his readers understood him. He did not change the text, which was apparently already fixed in the tradition when he received it (Lk 1:2). But he was free to add a few explanatory notes. Fourth, Luke mentions that the child was wrapped with swaddling cloths. This ancient custom is referred to in Ezekiel 16:4 and is still practiced among village people in Syria and Palestine. Finally, a Davidic Christology surfaces in the account. These five points emphasize that the story was composed by a messianic Jew at a very early stage in the life of the church.

For the Western mind the word *manger* invokes the words *stable* or *barn*. But in traditional Middle Eastern villages this is not the case. In the parable of the rich fool (Lk 12:13-21) there is mention of "storehouses" but not barns. People of great wealth would naturally have had separate quarters for animals.[10] But simple village homes in Palestine often had but two rooms. One was exclusively for guests. That room could be attached to the end of the house or be a "prophet's chamber" on the roof, as in the story of Elijah (1 Kings 17:19). The main room was a "family room" where the entire family cooked, ate, slept and lived. The end of the room next to the door, was either a few feet lower than the rest of the floor or blocked off with

---

[9]Nazareth is 1,600 feet above sea level, while Bethlehem is built on a ridge and is 2,250 feet high.
[10]Yizhar Hirschfeld with M. F. Vamosh, "A Country Gentleman's Estate: Unearthing the Splendors of Ramat Hanadiv," *Biblical Archaeology Review* 31, no 2 (2005): 18-31.

heavy timbers. Each night into that designated area, the family cow, donkey and a few sheep would be driven. And every morning those same animals were taken out and tied up in the courtyard of the house. The animal stall would then be cleaned for the day. Such simple homes can be traced from the time of David up to the middle of the twentieth century. I have seen them both in Upper Galilee and in Bethlehem. Figure 1.1 illustrates such a house from the side.

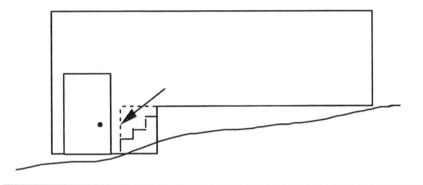

Figure 1.1. Typical village home in Palestine viewed from the side

The roof is flat and can have a guest room built on it, or a guest room can be attached to the end of the house. The door on the lower level serves as an entrance for people and animals. The farmer *wants* the animals in the house each night because they provide heat in winter and are safe from theft.

The same house viewed from above is illustrated in figure 1.2.

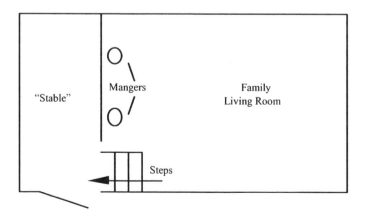

Figure 1.2. Typical village home in Palestine viewed from above

The elongated circles represent mangers dug out of the lower end of the living room. The "family living room" has a slight slope in the direction of the animal stall, which aids in sweeping and washing. Dirt and water naturally move downhill into the space for the animals and can be swept out the door. If the family cow is hungry during the night, she can stand up and eat from mangers cut out of the floor of the living room. Mangers for sheep can be of wood and placed on the floor of the lower level.

This style of traditional home fits naturally into the birth story of Jesus. But such homes are also implicit in Old Testament stories. In 1 Samuel 28, Saul was a guest in the house of the medium of Endor when the king refused to eat. The medium then took a fatted calf that was "in the house" (v. 24), killed it, and prepared a meal for the king and his servants. She did not fetch a calf from the field or the barn, but *from within the house.*

The story of Jephthah in Judges 11:29-40 assumes the same kind of one-room home. On his way to war, Jephthah makes a vow that if God will grant him victory on his return home he will sacrifice the first thing that comes out of his house. Jephthah wins his battle but as he returns home, tragically, and to his horror, his daughter is the first to step out of the house. Most likely he returned early in the morning and fully expected one of the animals to come bounding out of the room in which they had been cramped together all night. The text is not relating the story of a brutal butcher. The reader is obliged to assume that it never crossed his mind that a member of his family would step out first. Only with this assumption does the story make any sense. Had his home housed only human beings, he would never have made such a vow. If only people lived in the house, who was he planning to murder and why? The story is a *tragedy* because he expected *an animal.*

These same simple homes also appear in the New Testament. In Matthew 5:14-15, Jesus says,

> "No one after lighting a lamp puts it under a bushel, but on a stand, and it gives light to all in the house."

Obviously, Jesus is assuming a typical village home with one room. If a single lamp sheds light on *everybody in the house,* that house can only have one room.

Another example of the same assumption appears in Luke 13:10-17 where on the sabbath Jesus healed a woman who "was bent over and could not fully straighten herself." Jesus called to her and said, "Woman, you are *freed* [lit. untied] from your infirmity." The head of the synagogue was angry because Jesus had "worked" on the sabbath. Jesus responded, "You hypocrites! Does not each of you on the sabbath untie his ox or his ass from the manger, and lead it away to water it?" (v. 15). His point being: Today, on the sabbath you untied an *animal*. I "untied" a *woman*. How can you blame me? The text reports that "all his adversaries were put to shame" (v. 17).

Clearly, Jesus knew that every night his opponents had at least an ox or an ass *in their houses*. That morning everyone in the room had taken animals out of houses and tied them up outside. The ruler of the synagogue did not reply, "Oh, I never touch the animals on the sabbath." It is unthinkable to leave animals in the house during the day, and there were no stables. One of the earliest and most carefully translated Arabic versions of the New Testament was made, probably in Palestine, in the ninth century. Only eight copies have survived. This great version (translated from the Greek) records this verse as: "does not every one of you untie his ox or his donkey from the manger *in the house* and take it outside and water it?"[11] No Greek manuscript has the words "in the house" in this text. But this ninth-century Arabic-speaking Christian translator understood the text correctly. Doesn't everybody have a manger in the house? In his world, simple Middle Eastern villagers always did!

The one-room village home with mangers has been noted by modern scholars as well. William Thompson, an Arabic-speaking Presbyterian missionary scholar of the mid-nineteenth century observed village homes in Bethlehem and wrote, "It is my impression that the birth actually took place in an ordinary house of some common peasant, and that the baby was laid in one of the mangers, such as are still found in the dwellings of farmers in this region."[12]

The Anglican scholar E. F. F. Bishop, who lived in Jerusalem from 1922 to 1950, wrote:

> Perhaps . . . recourse was had to one of the Bethlehem houses with the lower section provided for the animals, with mangers "hollowed in stone," the dais being reserved for the family. Such a manger being immovable filled with crushed straw, would do duty for a cradle.[13]

For more than a hundred years scholars resident in the Middle East have understood Luke 2:7 as referring to a family room with mangers cut into the floor at one end. If this interpretation is pursued, there remains the question of the identity of "the inn." What precisely was it that was full?

If Joseph and Mary were taken into a private home and at birth Jesus was placed in a manger in that home, how is the word *inn* in Luke 2:7 to be under-

[11]Vatican Arabic MSS 95, Folio 71, italics added.
[12]William Thompson, *The Land and the Book* (New York: Harper & Brothers, 1871): 2:503.
[13]E. F. F. Bishop, *Jesus of Palestine* (London: Lutterworth, 1955), p. 42.

stood? Most English translations state that after the child was born, he was laid in a manger "because there was no room for them in the *inn*." This sounds as if they were rejected by the people of Bethlehem. Was that really the case?

There is a trap in traditional language. "No room in the inn" has taken on the meaning of "the inn had a number of rooms and all were occupied." The "no vacancy sign" was already "switched on" when Joseph and Mary arrived in Bethlehem. But the Greek word does not refer to "a room in an inn" but rather to "space" *(topos)* as in "There is no *space* on my desk for my new computer." It is important to keep this correction in mind as we turn to the word we have been told was an "inn."

The Greek word in Luke 2:7 that is commonly translated "inn" is *katalyma*. This is not the ordinary word for a commercial inn. In the parable of the good Samaritan (Lk 10:25-37) the Samaritan takes the wounded man to an inn. The Greek word in that text is *pandocheion*. The first part of this word means "all." The second part, as a verb, means "to receive." The *pandocheion* is the place that receives all, namely a commercial inn. This common Greek term for an inn was so widely known across the Middle East that over the centuries it was absorbed as a Greek loan word into Armenian, Coptic, Arabic and Turkish with the same meaning—a commercial inn.

If Luke expected his readers to think Joseph was turned away from an "inn" he would have used the word *pandocheion*, which clearly meant a commercial inn. But in Luke 2:7 it is a *katalyma* that is crowded. What then does this word mean?

Literally, a *katalyma* is simply "a place to stay" and can refer to many types of shelters. The three that are options for this story are *inn* (the English translation tradition), *house* (the Arabic biblical tradition of more than one thousand years), and *guest room* (Luke's choice). Indeed, Luke used this key term on one other occasion in his Gospel, where it is defined in the text itself. In Luke 22 Jesus tells his disciples:

> Behold, when you have entered the city, a man carrying a jar of water will meet you; follow him into the house which he enters, and tell the householder, 'The Teacher says to you, Where is the guest room *[katalyma]* where I am to eat the passover with my disciples?' And he will show you a large upper room furnished; there make ready. (Lk 22:10-12)

Here, the key word, *katalyma*, is defined; it is "an upper room," which is clearly a *guest room in a private home*. This precise meaning makes perfect sense when applied to the birth story. In Luke 2:7 Luke tells his readers that Jesus was placed in a *manger* (in the family room) because in that home *the guest room* was already full.

If at the end of Luke's Gospel, the word *katalyma* means a guest room attached to a private home (22:11), why would it not have the same meaning near the beginning of his Gospel? The family room, with an attached guest room, would have looked something like the diagram below:

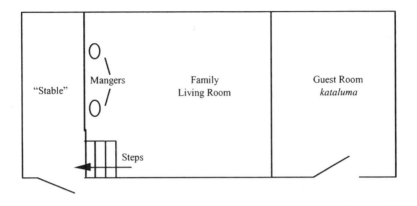

Figure 1.3. Typical village home in Palestine with attached guest room

This option for *katalyma* was chosen by Alfred Plummer in his influential commentary published in the late nineteenth century. Plummer writes, "It is a little doubtful whether the familiar translation 'in the inn' is correct. . . . It is possible that Joseph had relied upon the hospitality of some friend in Bethlehem, whose 'guest-chamber,' however, was already full when he and Mary arrived."[14]

I. Howard Marshall makes the same observation but does not expand on its significance.[15] Fitzmyer calls the *katalyma* a "lodge," which for him is a "public caravansary or khan."[16] I am convinced that Plummer was right. If so, why was this understanding not adopted by the church, either in the East or the West?

In the West the church has not noticed the problems I have already listed. When the traditional understanding of the story, therefore, is "not broken," it would seem that the best course to follow is "don't fix it." But once the problems with the traditional view of the text are clarified, they cry out for solutions. On the other side, in the East, the dominant Christian presence is the venerated Orthodox Church in its various branches. What of its traditions?

---

[14]Alfred Plummer, *Gospel According to S. Luke*, 5th ed., International Critical Commentary (1922; reprint, Edinburgh: T & T Clark, 1960), p. 54.

[15]Marshall, *Gospel of Luke*, p. 107.

[16]Fitzmyer, *Gospel According to Luke (I-IX)*, p. 408.

Christianity in the Middle East has traditionally focused on the birth having taken place in a cave. Many simple homes in traditional villages in the Holy Land begin in caves and are then expanded. The tradition of the cave can be traced to Justin Martyr, writing in the middle of the second century. What I have already suggested is in harmony with this tradition. The Eastern tradition has always maintained that Mary was alone when the child was born. In worship even the altar is hidden from the eyes of the faithful, and the event of the elements becoming the body and blood of Jesus (in the Eucharist) takes place out of sight. How much more should the "Word that became flesh" take place without witnesses? Father Matta al-Miskin, a twentieth-century Coptic Orthodox scholar and monk who wrote six weighty commentaries in Arabic on the four Gospels, reflects with wonder on Saint Mary alone in the cave. He writes:

> My heart goes out to this solitary mother.
> How did she endure labor pains alone?
> How did she receive her child with her own hands?
> How did she wrap him while her strength was totally exhausted?
> What did she have to eat or drink?
> O women of the world, witness this mother of the Savior.
> How much did she suffer and how much does she deserve honor,
> ... along with our tenderness and love?[17]

This genuine and touching piety is naturally not interested in considering birth in a private home with all the care and support that other women would have given. Therefore, among Christians, East and West, there have been understandable reasons why a new understanding of this text has been neglected.

To summarize, a part of what Luke tells us about the birth of Jesus is that the holy family traveled to Bethlehem, where they were received into a private home. The child was born, wrapped and (literally) "put to bed" *(anaklinō)* in the living room in the manger that was either built into the floor or made of wood and moved into the family living space. Why weren't they invited into the family guest room, the reader might naturally ask? The answer is that the guest room was already occupied by other guests. The host family graciously accepted Mary and Joseph into the family room of their house.

The family room would, naturally, be cleared of men for the birth of the child, and the village midwife and other women would have assisted at the birth. After the child was born and wrapped, Mary put her newborn to bed in a manger filled

---

[17]Matta al-Miskin, *al-Injil, bi-Hasab Bisharat al-Qiddis Luqa* (Cairo: Dayr al-Qiddis Anba Maqar, 1998), p. 128 (my translation).

with fresh straw and covered him with a blanket. When Jesus engaged in ministry as an adult "The common people heard him gladly" (Mk 12:37 KJV). That same acceptance was evident at his birth. What then of the shepherds?

The story of the shepherds reinforces the picture I have presented. Shepherds in first century Palestine were poor, and rabbinic traditions label them as unclean.[18] This may seem peculiar because Psalm 23 opens with "The LORD is my shepherd." It is not clear how such a lofty metaphor evolved into an unclean profession. The main point seems to be that flocks ate private property.[19] Five lists of "proscribed trades" are recorded in rabbinic literature and shepherds appear in three out of the five.[20] These lists hail from post-New Testament times but could reflect developing ideas alive at the time of Jesus. In any case, they were lowly, uneducated types.

In Luke 2:8-14 the first people to hear the message of the birth of Jesus were a group of shepherds who were close to the bottom of the social scale in their society. The shepherds heard and were afraid. Initially, they were probably frightened by the sight of the angels, but later they were asked to *visit* the child! From their point of view, if the child was truly the Messiah, the parents would reject the shepherds if they tried to visit him! How could shepherds be convinced to expect a welcome?

The angels anticipated this anxiety and told the shepherds they would find the baby wrapped (which was what peasants, like shepherds, did with their newly born children). Furthermore, they were told that he was lying in a *manger!* That is, they would find the Christ child in an ordinary peasant home such as theirs. He was not in a governor's mansion or a wealthy merchant's guest room but in a simple two-room home like theirs. This was *really* good news. Perhaps they would not be told, "Unclean shepherds—be gone!" This was *their sign*, a sign for lowly shepherds.

With this special sign of encouragement, the shepherds proceeded to Bethlehem in spite of their "low degree" (Lk 1:52). On arrival they reported their story and everyone was amazed. Then they left "praising God for all that they had heard and seen." The word *all* obviously included *the quality of the hospitality* that they witnessed on arrival. Clearly, they found the holy family in perfectly adequate accommodations, not in a dirty stable. If, on arrival, they had found a smelly stable, a frightened young mother and a desperate Joseph, they would have said, "This is outrageous! Come home with us! Our women will take care of you!" Within five

---

[18]Joachim Jeremias, "Despised Trades and Jewish Slaves," in *Jerusalem in the Time of Jesus* (Philadelphia: Fortress, 1969), pp. 303-4.

[19]J. D. M. Derrett, "Law in the New Testament: The Parable of the Prodigal Son," *New Testament Studies* 14 (1967): 66, n. 1.

[20]Jeremias, *Jerusalem in the Time of Jesus*, pp. 303-12.

minutes the shepherds would have moved the little family to their own homes. The honor of the entire village would rest on their shoulders and they would have sensed their responsibility to do their duty. The fact that they walked out, without moving the young family, means that the shepherds felt they could not offer better hospitality than what had already been extended to them.

Middle Eastern people have a tremendous capacity for showing honor to guests. This appears as early as the story of Abraham and his guests (Gen 18:1-8) and continues to the present. The shepherds left the holy family while praising God for the birth of the Messiah and for the quality of the hospitality in the home in which he was born. This is the capstone to the story of the shepherds. The child was born for the likes of the shepherds—the poor, the lowly, the rejected. He also came for the rich and the wise who later appear with gold, frankincense and myrrh.

Matthew informs his readers that the wise men entered *the house* where they saw Mary and the child (Mt 2:1-12). The story in Matthew confirms the suggestion that Luke's account describes a birth in a private home.

With this understanding in mind, all the cultural problems I have noted are solved. Joseph was not obliged to seek a commercial inn. He does not appear as an inept and inadequate husband who cannot arrange for Mary's needs. Likewise, Joseph did not anger his wife's relatives by failing to turn to them in a crisis. The child was born in the normal surroundings of a peasant home sometime after they arrived in Bethlehem, and there was no heartless innkeeper with whom to deal. A member of the house of David was not humiliated by rejection as he returned to the village of his family's origins. The people of Bethlehem offered the best they had and preserved their honor as a community. The shepherds were not hardhearted oafs without the presence of mind to help a needy family of strangers.

Our Christmas crèche sets remain as they are because "ox and ass before him bow, / for he is in the manger now." But that manger was in a warm and friendly home, not in a cold and lonely stable. Looking at the story in this light strips away layers of interpretive mythology that have built up around it. Jesus was born in a simple two-room village home such as the Middle East has known for at least three thousand years. Yes, we must rewrite our Christmas plays, but in rewriting them, the story is enriched, not cheapened.[21]

---

[21]Cf. Kenneth E. Bailey, *Open Hearts in Bethlehem* (Louisville: Westminster/John Knox, 2005). This is a Christmas musical constructed around the ideas presented here.

SUMMARY: THE STORY OF JESUS' BIRTH

1. Jesus' incarnation was complete. At his birth the holy family was welcomed into a peasant home. These people did their best and it was enough. At his birth the common people sheltered him. The wise men came to the *house*. When Jesus was an adult, the common people heard him gladly.

2. The shepherds were welcome at the manger. The unclean were judged to be clean. The outcasts became honored guests. The song of angels was sung to the simplest of all.

I know that in an increasingly secular world "Merry Christmas" competes with "Happy Holidays." I long to turn the traditional "Merry Christmas" the other direction and introduce a new greeting for Christmas morning.

Greeting: The Savior is born.
Response: He is born in a manger.

O that we might greet each other in this manner.

2

The Genealogy and Joseph the Just

MATTHEW 1:1-21

THIS CHAPTER WILL FOCUS ON THE STORIES of the four women who appear in the genealogy of Jesus recorded in Matthew's Gospel, and ask why they are included. I will then examine one of Joseph's most important acts. Reflections on the Christmas story often ignore both.

Matthew 1 contains a genealogy of Jesus that few bother to read. But a second glance reveals some meaningful surprises. Amazingly, along with the men, Matthew includes the names of four women. Middle Eastern genealogies are expected to be lists of men. Sirach began his list by saying, "Let us now praise famous men" (Sirach 44—50) and Luke 3:23-38 is a list of seventy-six men without the inclusion of a single female. Along with a list of forty men, why does Matthew include four women?

To answer this question it is helpful to review what is known about the women.

1. The first on the list is Tamar, who is seen in pre-Christian literature as an Aramean (Jubilees 41:1). According to Genesis 38:1-30, Tamar was married to the eldest of three brothers, but her husband died childless. The custom at the time was that when a woman's husband died without leaving an heir, and the deceased had a brother, the family was expected to marry the widow to that brother. The practice was called "Levirate marriage" and is described in Deuteronomy 25:5-10. Any children born to the widow would be raised to inherit the estate of the deceased first husband. This form of marriage was also concerned "with the support and protection of the widow."[1] Tamar was duly married to the second brother, who also died (in unfortunate circumstances). As the third brother was too young to get married, the father-in-law, Judah, promised Tamar that the fam-

---

[1] V. P. Hamilton, "Marriage (OT and ANE)," in *The Anchor Bible Dictionary*, ed. D. N. Freedman et al. (New York: Doubleday, 1992), 4:565-67.

ily would marry her to the third brother as soon as he became a man. Tamar waited and waited. The third brother grew up, but the promise was not kept.

Tamar then devised a daring plan. Having heard that her father-in-law would be traveling along a certain road at a certain time of day, she dressed like a prostitute, but covered her face, and sat beside the road which Judah, her father-in-law, was expected to pass. He duly appeared, approached her and said, "Come, let me come in to you" (v. 16). She then asked what he was willing to pay, and he offered her a goat. Indicating acceptance, she asked for his staff and signet ring as a guarantee that he would not default on his promise. He agreed, slept with her, left the designated pledges and went on his way, never guessing who she was. On returning home he sent the goat but no one could find the "prostitute" on the road. In time, Tamar became pregnant and word of her condition reached the ear of her guilty father-in-law. Judah was furious and demanded that she be burned. As Tamar was being dragged to her death, she sent a message to her father-in-law along with the signet ring and the staff. The message was, "By the man to whom these belong, I am with child" (v. 25). Judah immediately recognized his signet ring and staff, and declared, "She is more righteous than I, inasmuch as I did not give her to my son Shelah" (v. 26). Tamar's rights were upheld by a bold and daring plan. Sadly, it appears that no other method of securing those rights was available to her. By the Leviticus laws both Judah and Tamar were engaged in incest and should have been stoned (Lev 20:12). The story presents a bold Gentile (?) woman determined to acquire her rights, even if she is obliged to use an irregular method. Amazingly she is listed as an ancestor of Jesus.

2. The second woman on the list is Rahab, known throughout the Bible as a harlot. She was a citizen of the city of Jericho when the Israelites, under Joshua's leadership, conquered the city. Joshua sent two spies prior to the siege of the city (Josh 2). Rahab had the courage to save the spies when their lives were threatened by her countrymen. In return, they promised that she would be spared when the city fell. She was a Gentile and known to be a prostitute. Yet she somehow discovered that the God of the Israelites was the one true God and decided to serve him alone. That discovery led her to make an incredible decision of faith that required the risk of her life. On the basis of her new faith, she acted against her community, its gods and its leaders. She too appears in Jesus' genealogy. In this case the story presents a reformed immoral Gentile woman with a courageous faith.

3. The third female was a Moabite named Ruth. A Hebrew family from Bethlehem, with two sons, moved to Moab where the two sons married Moabite women. After some time the father died, as did the two sons. The family was re-

duced to Naomi, the mother, and her two daughters-in-law, who were both Moabites. Naomi wisely perceived that the only way she could survive was to return to Bethlehem, where she still had some distant relatives. As Naomi prepared to leave, one of the Moabite women decided to remain in her home country. But the other, Ruth, declared that she would go with Naomi, come what may. Ruth then spoke the famous words, "your people shall be my people, and your God my God; where you die I will die, and there will I be buried" (Ruth 1:16-17). The two of them returned to Bethlehem, where Ruth met and married a wealthy distant relative of Naomi's family. Some have suggested that Ruth engaged in seduction and fornication, which is described euphemistically as "uncovering the feet" (Ruth 3:6-9, 14). The case for this is very thin. The text says that after a day of harvesting grain, Boaz lay down and fell asleep. Ruth approached him during the night, "uncovered his feet" and slept at his feet. At some point he woke up, found a woman at his feet, asked her who she was and was told, "I am Ruth, your maid-servant; spread your skirt over your maidservant, for you are next of kin." She is asking for a Levirate marriage. He replied honorably that he would do his duty and commended her for not going "after young men." In the end he married her, and they lived happily ever afterward.

The simple reading of the text is surely the best. Ruth figured out that if she uncovered the feet of the sleeping Boaz, he would wake up naturally when his feet got cold, and she could have an interview with him in total privacy—a brilliant plan. In a brief footnote Raymond Brown dismisses the suggestion that immorality is involved.[2] In the process Ruth became the grandmother of King David. This third female in Jesus' lineage was a Gentile, who from the beginning to the end of her story was a saint. She exhibits faith, love, commitment, intelligence and courage. Without her, David would not have been born.

4. The fourth woman in Matthew's genealogy of Jesus is Bathsheba, whom Matthew did not like. How else to explain the fact that she is included in the list but Matthew refused to record her name? It is impossible to imagine that he did not know it. He simply called her, "the wife of Uriah." Why the circumlocution? She too has a story.

In the Middle East, men and women are exceptionally modest about exposing their bodies. But in this particular story (2 Sam 11:1—12:25), Bathsheba waited until her (Hittite) soldier husband was away fighting for Israel. Then she decided to take a bath in front of an open window *facing the palace*. Why should she spend

---

[2]Raymond E. Brown, *The Birth of the Messiah* (London: Geoffrey Chapman, 1977), p. 72, n. 24.

her life with a lowly paid foreigner if she could manage to move in next door with King David? If taking a bath in front of a window was all she had to do—why not give it a try?

No self-respecting woman, in any culture, would do such a thing. In a traditional Middle Eastern village, only powerful people have second and third floors to their homes. Such people can look down on and see into their neighbor's homes, walled courtyards and windows. The rest of the town cannot observe their private spaces. David's Jerusalem was small (twelve to fifteen acres), and all of it crowded. Archaeologists in Jerusalem have found a "large stone structure" from the time of David that may be his palace. Regardless of whether the building discovered was the actual residence, the space between the palace and Bathsheba's house could hardly have been more than twenty feet.

Bathsheba knew what she was doing and she was no fool. Her plan succeeded, the king noticed her, and within a short time David arranged to have her taken to the palace. She went, slept with him and got pregnant. David then went into "damage control mode" and arranged to have her husband killed in battle at the front. After committing that despicable act, he added her to his collection of wives. The prophet Nathan called the king to account for this profound violation of the law of God; David repented and the tradition says that he wrote Psalm 51 in response. The child died, but a second was born, who they named Solomon.

Matthew was quick to include Solomon but apparently he didn't like Solomon's mother, so he dismissively referred to her as "the wife of Uriah the Hittite," emphasizing her foreign connection. He does not call her "the wife of David." She is, nonetheless, the fourth woman in Jesus' genealogy. She may have been a Hebrew but was married to a Gentile. And unlike Ruth, she was unfaithful to her husband. On the positive side, she demonstrated intelligence, daring, initiative and courage in the advancement of her interests as she understood them. David, therefore, had a Gentile grandmother and Solomon's mother, first married to a Hittite, could have been a Gentile. Both women are in the genealogy.

The list concludes with Mary, a bright, but lowly peasant girl. She was a saint from beginning to end and was willing to accept the costly discipleship of being the mother of Jesus. She accepted her pregnancy as a miracle of God, but it is hard to imagine that many people in her community believed her story. Most of them probably saw her as an immoral woman who should be stoned. When she received the message from the angel, she responded quietly, "Let it be to me according to your word" (Lk 1:38). She humbly accepted a discipleship that she knew would bring shame on her in the eyes of the community and could be the cause of her death.

Why then does Matthew list the above four women in Jesus' ancestry? We cannot be sure.[3] But a number of reasons can be suggested.

1. He includes men and women. This is major. Jesus included women into his band of disciples (Lk 8:1-3) and women have a prominent place in his ministry. His teachings are often geared for both men and women listeners. Matthew may have included women in his genealogy as a sign of the new kingdom of God, where there is "neither Jew nor Greek, there is neither slave nor free, there is no 'male and female' " (Gal 3:28, my translation).

2. He includes Jews and Gentiles. If Matthew wanted to include Jews and Gentiles in his genealogy, how could he do so? All the males in the family tree were Jews. The only way he could include Gentiles at the beginning of his Gospel, looking forward to "The Great Commission" at its end (Mt 28:18-20), was to include these women. Ruth and Rahab were Gentiles, Tamar was probably a Gentile, and Bathsheba was originally married to a Gentile. The startling fact of the presence of women in "a men's club" (a genealogy) would catch the attention of any first-century Jewish reader/listener. After some reflection that same reader/listener might catch the Gentile connection between the beginning and the end of the Gospel.

3. Among the women selected Matthew included saints and sinners. Tamar struggled for justice and was called "righteous." Yet she slept with her father-in-law. Rahab appears on stage as a prostitute. Bathsheba commits adultery and is certainly not innocent. Ruth, by contrast, is a saint throughout the book that carries her name. Mary's saintliness concludes the account.

4. All four women demonstrate intelligence, boldness and courage. As Raymond Brown writes, "The women showed initiative or played an important role in God's plan and so came to be considered the instrument of God's providence or of His Holy Spirit."[4]

With such a list, Matthew gives us clues about the kinds of people that the Messiah came to save. He was to be a Savior for women and men who were both saints and sinners, Jews and Gentiles. This genealogy is truly comprehensive. Many can look at the stories of these women and men and find some reflection of themselves. What then of Joseph?

---

[3]For a review of three major options, see ibid., pp. 71-74.
[4]Ibid., p. 73.

JOSEPH THE JUST

A second surprise in the birth narratives appears immediately after the genealogy and is found in Matthew 1:18-19, which reads:

> Now the birth of Jesus took place in this way. When his mother Mary had been betrothed to Joseph, before they came together she was found to be with child of the Holy Spirit; and her husband Joseph, being a just man and unwilling to put her to shame, resolved to divorce her quietly.

The question is: What does it mean to call Joseph a "just man"? Such a phrase usually refers to a person who obeys the law and applies rules fairly to all. The headmaster who is *just* with his students does not bend the rules for his favorites. The book of Deuteronomy states that if a betrothed virgin meets a man in the city and lies with him, the two of them are to be stoned (Deut 22:23). But Matthew 1:18-19 affirms that because Joseph was "just" he decided to break the law of Moses and divorce Mary quietly rather than publicly exposing her. Such a bold act invites serious reflection.

Joseph clearly applied an extraordinary and unexpected definition of justice to this crisis with Mary. Justice for him was more than "the equal application of law." Was there a broader understanding of justice available to him?

In 1843 Søren Kierkegaard, the famous Danish theologian, wrote a book titled *Fear and Trembling*. In it he argues that authentic faith requires "an absolute relationship to the absolute."[5] The believer stands naked before God without the law standing between the two. Kierkegaard's primary biblical example of this nakedness before God was the story of Abraham, who was willing to sacrifice Isaac (Gen 22) in order to obey God. All laws, ancient and modern, say that a father should not kill his son. Abraham's obedience to God required him to do something that was against any law. Kierkegaard also mentions Mary, who acted in an "absolute relationship to the absolute" in her acceptance of God's will and in that acceptance experienced "distress, dread and paradox."[6] As a third example Kierkegaard could have cited Joseph going beyond the ethical expectations of the law in his obedience to a higher definition of justice. That nobler view of justice was available to him in the book of Isaiah.

In the prophesy of Isaiah there is a picture of a special "suffering servant" through whom God would one day act in history to save. There are four unique

[5]Søren Kierkegaard, *Fear and Trembling*, trans. Walter Lowrie (New York: Doubleday Anchor Books, 1954), p. 66.
[6]Ibid., pp. 75-76.

songs in Isaiah describing that servant. The first of them is found in Isaiah 42:1-
6, verse three of which reads:

> A bruised reed he will not break,
> and a dimly burning wick he will not quench;
> he will faithfully bring forth justice.

Justice, as understood by this special servant of God, is neither "retributive justice" (you harm me and I will see that you are harmed) nor is it "equal application
of law" (I pay my taxes and so must you), but here justice means compassion for
the weak and exhausted. The metaphorical language in this text is striking and
powerful. Reeds were used in the ancient world as pens. In southern Iraq until very
recently they were also used for houses and boats—that is, if the reeds were not
damaged. But what can be done with a crushed reed? The only option is to break
it and use it for cooking or heating.

Every home needed some form of illumination. Small clay lamps were used and
fueled with olive oil. The wicks of such lamps hung from a spout at the side of the
lamp. As the oil ran out, there was danger that the wick might sever through burning and the flaming end fall out of the spout and cause a fire. A bowl of water was
often placed on the floor under the lamp to prevent such an accident. But the servant of God, described in Isaiah 42, will not *break* the first, nor will he *quench* the
second. He will *faithfully bring forth justice.*

Joseph looked beyond the penalties of the law in order to reach out with ten-
derness to a young woman who was no doubt bruised and exhausted. Perhaps he
saw Mary as a "dimly burning wick." This prophetic definition of justice required
a compassionate concern for the weak, the downtrodden and the outcasts in their
need. In his dealings with Mary, Joseph acted out of this prophetic definition of
justice. Without that prophetic understanding of justice embedded in Joseph's
mind, Jesus would not have been born. Joseph is, therefore, not a passive, mute figure. Rather, he acts as a strong, thoughtful person whose bold decision at a point
of crisis saves the life of the mother and her unborn child.

JOSEPH'S FUMING

Matthew not only tells his readers what Joseph *does*, but also describes his *feelings*.
As noted, Joseph was told by the community that his fiancée was pregnant (Mt
1:20). Initially, he did not have a vision from the angel informing him that her
pregnancy was an act of God. How might he have felt on hearing such devastating
news? The common English translation of one critical Greek word is legitimate
but misleading. English texts read, "as he *considered* this . . ." The Greek word, here

translated "he considered" *(enthymēomai)* has two meanings. To be sure, one of them is "he considered/pondered." But a second meaning is "he became angry."[7] That is, he became *very upset.* Isn't anger the natural emotion for him to have felt?

Perhaps long centuries of veneration for "Saint Joseph," have led to an assumption that he could not have become angry—particularly not with Mary! But this is to overlook the pure humanness of the man. On hearing that his fiancée was pregnant, is he expected to sit quietly and "consider" this matter? Or would he naturally feel deeply disappointed and indeed angry? As observed, his understanding of justice led him to "do the right thing" and treat Mary in a humane fashion. But did that prevent him from feeling the anger of betrayal? The root of the Greek verb used here is *thymos,* which occurs once in the Gospels where it is used to describe the "wrath" of the congregation in the synagogue when it rose up to stone Jesus (Lk 4:28). The only verbal use of this same term in the entire New Testament is found in the story of the wise men, where Herod is in a "rage" on discovering that the wise men left Bethlehem without reporting back to him regarding the whereabouts of the young child (Mt 2:16).

A variation of this word appears in Acts 10:19, where Peter received a vision commanding him to visit a Gentile family. Jews considered Gentiles unclean, and Peter was naturally upset by the vision. Again, translations commonly say he "pondered" the vision, but the roots of the Greek terms employed here specify that he was angry because the vision overthrew his long-held opinions. It pressed Peter to change his entire perspective on how God works in the world. All his life Peter had believed that his duty as a Jew was to have nothing to do with Gentiles. Was he now suddenly expected to overthrow the understandings of centuries? One would expect him to be upset. "How can God do this to me?" he might well ask.

In the text the preposition *en* is added to the word to make it *en-thymēomai.* This particular form of the word only occurs one other place in the New Testament (also in Matthew) where the word *evil* is attached to it. The text reads, "But Jesus, knowing their thoughts, said, 'Why do you think evil in your hearts?' " (Mt 9:4). Anger is again assumed. A literal meaning of the Greek word has to do with anger *within (en) the person* involved. This profoundly fits the feelings of Joseph on first hearing the shocking news. This understanding of the text has not been left without a witness.

The oldest Arabic translation of this text, which dates from the eighth century

---

[7]Henry G. Liddell and R. Scott, *A Greek-English Lexicon,* rev. H. S. Jones and R. McKenzie (Oxford: Oxford University Press, 1966), p. 567.

or earlier, translates this phrase, "While he was *disturbed* over this matter . . ."[8] The unknown translator of this early, important Arabic version knew that Joseph was upset. Putting all of this together, perhaps "while he *fumed* over this matter" is a more accurate translation of the original Greek and better captures the authenticity of the human scene.

In his cameo appearance, Matthew presents Joseph as a human being of remarkable spiritual stature. He possessed the boldness, daring, courage and strength of character to stand up against his entire community and take Mary as his wife. He did so in spite of forces that no doubt wanted her stoned. His vision of justice stayed his hand. In short he was able to reprocess his anger into grace.

Two of the parables of Jesus turn on this same remarkable ability. In the parable of the great banquet, a man is insulted publicly. He chooses "in anger" to extend grace to the unworthy outside the community (Lk 14:16-24). In the second parable a farmer builds and rents a vineyard to tenants. When he tries to collect the rent, the tenants mistreat, insult, beat and finally kill the owner's servants who were sent to collect the rent. The master opts to turn his anger into grace by sending his son, alone and unnamed, in the hope that they will be shamed before the total vulnerability exhibited in such an action (Mk 12:1-12). Did Jesus grow up with a living model for these two major characters in his parables?

Finally, in the Middle East, men usually represent their families in any official or legal matters. Why did Joseph take Mary with him to Bethlehem for the registration? The easiest explanation is that he was unsure what might happen to her if he left her in Nazareth without his presence to protect her. It behooves us to see Joseph as a hero of the story without whose courage and understanding of the prophets there would have been no Christmas story to tell.

SUMMARY: THE GENEALOGY AND JOSEPH THE JUST

Some of the theological and ethical themes that appear in these two accounts are as follows:

The Genealogy

1. Women and men are listed in the genealogy. The reader expects to see men alone. This Messiah comes to save all of humankind, not half of it.

2. Gentiles are affirmed as a part of Joseph's bloodline (and by implication Mary's). The Gospel of Matthew begins and ends with a focus on Gentiles.

---

[8]Vatican Arabic 13, folio 1 r. (Arabic: *lemma hamm bithalik*).

3. Saints and sinners appear in this list of women, and the new Messiah came for all.

4. These particular women exhibited courage, intelligence and initiative—characteristics that were not lacking in Jesus.

Joseph

1. Joseph was a theologian whose concept of justice grew out of the Servant Songs of Isaiah. That theology saved the life of Mary and her unborn child.

2. Joseph had the courage to withstand the culture of his day as he lived out his life in the light of the word he received from the angel.

3. He was able to reprocess his anger into grace.

The Savior, the Wise Men and the Vision of Isaiah

MATTHEW 2:1-12; ISAIAH 60:1-7

THE TEXTS RELATED TO THE CHRISTMAS STORY are familiar to Christians, but to the diligent student they yield fresh understanding. This chapter will examine three additional Christmas-related passages that can be summarized in three questions:

1. Who did Jesus come to save?

2. From where did the wise men hail?

3. What do Jerusalem and Isaiah 60 have to do with Christmas?

WHO DID JESUS COME TO SAVE?

In Matthew 1:20-21 Joseph is told, "Joseph, son of David, do not fear to take Mary your wife, for that which is conceived in her is of the Holy Spirit; she will bear a son, and you shall call his name Jesus, for he will save his people from their sins."

In Hebrew or Aramaic these words provide a word play that is lost in Greek and English. "Jesus" in Hebrew is *Yĕšûâ* and the verb "to save" is *yāšaʿ*. If Hebrew and English are combined in a single sentence, it can be translated, "His name will be called *Yĕšûâ* for he will *yāšaʿ* his people."

The first-century Jewish community in the Holy Land was occupied and oppressed by the Romans. Before the Romans, the country had been ruled by the Greeks, and before that by the Persians. At the time of Jesus much of the land was owned by foreigners who controlled huge estates. Local farmers were obliged to rent land and were often treated unfairly. The Jewish revolt in the 60s of the first century was partially sparked by the economic and political oppression of the people.

In a situation of political and economic oppression people naturally want salvation, but from what? The salvation they seek is deliverance from their oppressors. A vivid case of this is the prophetic rejoicing over the fall of Babylon expressed in Isaiah 47, part of which reads:

> Come down and sit in the dust,
>   O virgin daughter of Babylon;
> sit on the ground without a throne,
>   O daughter of the Chaldeans! . . .
> Take the millstones and grind meal,
>   put off your veil,
> strip off your robe, uncover your legs,
>   pass through the rivers.
> Your nakedness shall be uncovered,
>   and your shame shall be seen.
> I will take vengeance,
>   and I will spare no man. (Is 47:1-3)

This text expresses an understandable undisguised glee at the fall of the hated enemy. Any prophet who wants to talk about sin and salvation with a community under occupation already has these words defined for him or her. The concept of *sin* is shaped by what people are enduring from their oppressors, and the word *salvation* is used to express their longing to be free from that oppression. For such a community there is little space in the mind to tolerate anyone talking about its sins and its need for salvation from those sins. An oppressed community perceives its own faults as dwarfed by the enormity of what it is suffering from others. Any discussion of *its sins* will be heard as belittling the harsh world in which they live. It takes a brave man or woman to tell the community that it needs salvation from *its sins*.

During the days of apartheid, Archbishop Desmond Tutu of South Africa published a collection of his sermons and lectures. I read this sincere and moving book with gratitude and appreciation. Naturally, Tutu talks about the sins of the oppressors and argues that outsiders should not be "objective" vis-à-vis apartheid South Africa. To take such a stance, he writes, is like watching an elephant standing on the tail of a mouse. Tutu says, "It is small comfort to a mouse, if an elephant is standing on its tail, to say, 'I am impartial.' In this instance, you are really supporting the elephant in its cruelty."[1]

The outsider must first tell the elephant to get off the mouse before the two

---

[1]Desmond M. Tutu, *Hope and Suffering* (Grand Rapids: Eerdmans, 1984), p. 115.

points of view can be discussed. I agree completely. But what if the mouse is op-
pressing other mice? The observer must not forget the elephant, but must the
mouse's oppressive actions be ignored? What light does this shed on the ministry
of Jesus?

In the birth story the child's name is *Yĕšûâ*, Jesus (Savior), and the text affirms
that he will *yāšaʿ*, he will save his people from *their sins*. This message is surely an
important part of why Jesus faced opposition and ended his earthly life on a cross.
Along with John the Baptizer, he insisted on saying critical things about his own
people, who were indeed oppressed.

This appears clearly and powerfully in Luke 13, where people went to Jesus reporting the story that Pilate had killed some worshipers while they were offering
sacrifices at the great high altar. What could be worse than a group of people being
murdered by foreign troops at the most sacred moment and in the most sacred
place of their religious pilgrimage?

If translated in Christian terms, we would have to imagine terrorists entering
a church and gunning down a pastor and his people in the middle of a communion service! Jesus was confronted with just such a story about Pilate. He was told
an "atrocity story," and his opponents were there to monitor his response. Naturally, he was expected to tear his robe, beat his chest and cry out, "How long, O
Lord! When will you come to save your people and set us free from this brutal
occupation?"

Jesus, however, gave the amazing answer, "unless you repent you will all likewise perish" (Lk 13:5). In a situation of oppression, it takes enormous courage to
tell the oppressed community that all are sinners and that all must repent, for everyone is in need of grace for salvation. The angel affirms this theology to Joseph
before Jesus is born by announcing, "and you shall call his name Jesus, for he will
save his people *from their sins*" (their primary problem is their sin—the Roman occupation is an important concern, but it is secondary).

This same theme appears in a different form in the Song of Zechariah. Luke
1:68-69 reads:

> Blessed be the Lord God of Israel,
>> for he has visited and redeemed his people,
> and has raised up a horn of salvation for us
>> in the house of his servant David.

This is clearly good news for everyone. Zechariah continues with verses 70-71
which read:

as he spoke by the mouth of his holy prophets from of old,
>   that we should be saved from our enemies,
and *from the hand of all who hate us.* (italics added)

Zechariah is still "politically correct." This message is exactly what the people want to hear. The Messiah will drive out the Roman oppressors and ceremonially defiled Gentiles from their midst. God, through the Messiah, will save them from their enemies, and from the hand of all who hate them.

But then Zechariah continues in Luke 1:76-77 with a few words about his son, John, and says:

For you will go before the Lord to prepare his ways,
>   to give knowledge of salvation to his people
in the forgiveness of their sins. (italics added)

Suddenly the tables are turned. Now the community's problem is not merely "those who hate us" but that they are declared to be in need of deliverance from *their own sins.* The oppressed are also sinners! A Savior for sinners is a Savior for all, because all are sinners.

This perspective is present as early as Ecclesiastes 4:1 which reads:

Again I saw all the oppressions that are practiced under the sun.
And behold, the tears of the oppressed,
>   and they had no one to comfort them!
On the side of their oppressors there was power,
>   and there was no one to comfort them.

In such a text both the oppressors and the oppressed are trapped in prisons from which they cannot escape. Each needs grace from outside the prison. The text in Luke speaks of salvation from "our enemies" and of the internal problem of "our sins."

FROM WHERE DID THE WISE MEN HAIL?

Matthew 2:1-2 tells of the wise men:

Now when Jesus was born in Bethlehem of Judea in the days of Herod the king, behold, wise men from the East came to Jerusalem, saying, "Where is he who has been born king of the Jews? For we have seen his star in the East, and have come to worship him."

This section of the story begs a number of questions. If the magi were east of Israel and they saw his star in the east, they should have gone to India! Obviously, they traveled west. The key to this verse is the fact that in Hebrew, the word for

"East" also means "the rising." The Greek text (with the NRSV) can be better translated, "We saw his star at its rising."

What then was the wise men's country of origin? Were they Gentiles? And were
they from Arabia? The answer to the first question is that they were indeed Gentiles.
The shepherds were from the Bethlehem area and were most certainly Jews, yet the
wise men were Gentiles.[2] The new "king of the Jews" was adored at his birth by both
Jews and Gentiles. Furthermore, the wise men were quite likely from Arabia.

When the text describes them as "wise men from the East," the question inevitably emerges: Where in the East? The answer to that question depends on where
the writer lives. If an American is visiting friends in New Jersey and tells them that
he or she came from "the West," the hosts might infer that the guest is from Pittsburgh. If someone in the United States Navy is sent to serve in the "Western Pacific" he or she may be stationed in Pacific waters but a British ship one hundred
yards away is in the "Eastern Pacific." It is the same ocean, but the British look
East to see it and the Americans look West.

Any Christian living in Rome in the early centuries of the church would naturally think of "the East" as Persia, and indeed the word *Magi* in Greek literature
does refer to people from Babylonia or Parthia.[3] But for a Christian dwelling in
the Holy Land, "the East" would refer to the other side of the Jordan River. Indeed, such a designation persists to this day. Living on the West Bank in Israel/
Palestine I observed that visitors arriving from Jordan were always referred to as
having come "from the East" which of course meant "the east side of the Jordan
River." It is only natural to assume that Jewish Christians, living in the Holy Land
in the first century thought and talked the same way. "The East" for them would
naturally refer to the Jordanian deserts that connect with the deserts of Arabia.

According to Matthew 2, the wise men arrived with gifts of gold, frankincense
and myrrh. Rich people usually possess gold, and gold was mined in Arabia.[4] But
more specifically, frankincense and myrrh are harvested from trees that only grow
in southern Arabia. Wealthy dwellers of those desert regions would naturally have
gold, frankincense and myrrh. The early church was aware of this.

The earliest extant commentary about the stories surrounding the birth of Jesus
were written about A.D. 160 by Justin Martyr, a Palestinian Christian who lived
in the city of Caesarea, down the hill from Samaria. Justin recorded a conversation

---

[2]W. D. Davies and Dale C. Allison Jr., *The Gospel According to Saint Matthew* (New York: T & T Clark,
1988), 1:227-31.
[3]Davies and Allison present the evidence for Arabia, Babylon and Persia and find themselves "inclined
to opt for Arabia." Ibid., 1:228-31.
[4]Biblical writers note that gold came from Arabia, Sheba and Ophir (1 Kings 9:28; 10:2; Job 28:16).

with a Jew named Trypho. The book is called *Dialogue with Trypho, the Jew* and has survived. In the book Justin writes, "The wise men from Arabia came to Bethlehem and worshiped the child and offered to him gifts, gold and frankincense and myrrh."[5] Justin does not argue his case, he simply states in five different places that the wise men hailed from Arabia.[6] This location for the wise men is also affirmed by Tertullian and Clement of Rome.[7]

In the 1920s a British scholar, E. F. F. Bishop, visited a Bedouin tribe in Jordan. This Muslim tribe bore the Arabic name *al-Kokabani*. The word *kokab* means "planet" and *al-Kaokabani* means "Those who study/follow the planets." Bishop asked the elders of the tribe why they called themselves by such a name. They replied that it was because their ancestors followed the planets and traveled west to Palestine to show honor to the great prophet Jesus when he was born.[8] This supports Justin's second-century claim that the wise men were Arabs from Arabia. But, other than an historical curiosity, does this fact make any difference? To answer this question it is necessary to turn to the relationship between Isaiah 60 and the Christmas story.

WHAT DO JERUSALEM AND ISAIAH 60 HAVE TO DO WITH CHRISTMAS?

Isaiah 60 opens with words made familiar in Handel's great oratorio *Messiah*. The text reads:

> Arise, shine; for your light has come,
>   and the glory of the LORD has risen upon you.
> For behold, darkness shall cover the earth,
>   and thick darkness the peoples;
> but the LORD will arise upon you,
>   and his glory will be seen upon you.
> And nations shall come to your light,
>   and kings to the brightness of your rising. (Is 60:1-3)

Who is the "you" around whom the glory shines and unto whose light the nations will come? Isaiah continues by affirming that "your sons shall come from far, and your daughters shall be carried in the arms." Verses 5 and 6 proclaim:

---

[5]Justin Martyr, *Selections from Justin Martyr's Dialogue with Trypho, a Jew*, trans. and ed. R. P. C. Hanson (London: Lutterworth, 1963), p. 78.
[6]Ibid., pp. 78-88.
[7]See Raymond E. Brown, *Birth of the Messiah* (London: Geoffrey Chapman, 1977), pp. 169-70.
[8]This conversation between Bishop and the sheikhs was reported to me orally the summer of 1957 in Jerusalem by E. F. F. Bishop.

> The wealth of the nations shall come to you.
> A multitude of camels shall cover you,
>> the young camels of Midian and Ephah;
>> all those from Sheba shall come.
> They shall bring gold and frankincense,
>> and shall proclaim the praise of the LORD.

Midian and Ephah are tribal lands in northern Arabia, and Sheba was the name for the part of southern Arabia from which the Queen of Sheba came with "much gold" (1 Kings 10:2). As noted, frankincense is a unique product of southern Arabia. In verse 7 Isaiah continues as he reports "all the flocks of Kedar shall be gathered to you." Shepherds are also involved. But why are these visitors coming from far and near? What or who is to receive all this lavish attention?

Verses 10 and 11 mention "your walls" and "gates." Isaiah was clearly dreaming about *Jerusalem* and the wonderful things that would happen to the city in the days ahead. But this glorious vision was not realized. The community never saw any great light shining around the city. Nor did wealthy Arab chiefs come from Midian, Ephah and Sheba with gifts of gold and frankincense. Because of the violent and insecure political climate in the centuries before Jesus' birth, the gates were not open during the day or at night (v. 11). It behooves the reader to ask: Do the birth stories have anything to say about Isaiah's great promises?

Matthew and Luke were surely familiar with this text. The Gospel writers had far more information about Jesus' life than they could record on a single scroll. John states specifically that he made a selection and that if all were recorded "the world itself could not contain the books that would be written" (Jn 21:25). On what basis then, did Matthew and Luke *select* the stories of the birth of Jesus that they recorded?

Although the glorious events projected for honoring the city of Jerusalem never happened, the Gospel authors perceived them to be taking place in the birth of Jesus. Around the *child* there was a great light and the glory of the Lord appeared. To the *child* came Arab wise men from the desert on camels bringing gold and frankincense. Shepherds visited the *child*, not the city. The great hopes for the city were transferred to the child in a manger. Indeed, "the glory of the Lord shone round about" the *child*. This shift from the city to the child is significant.

The birth stories "de-Zionize" the tradition. Hopes and expectations for the city are seen as fulfilled in the birth of the child. The earthly Jerusalem is de-absolutized. The new community that would form around the child would be able to empathize with Joseph Plunkett who wrote:

I see his blood upon the rose—
And in the stars the glory of his eyes.
His body gleams amid eternal snows,
His tears fall from the skies.

I see his face in every flower;
The thunder and the singing of the birds
Are but his voice;
And carven by his power,
Rocks are his written words.

All pathways by his feet are worn;
His strong heart stirs the ever-beating seas.
His crown of thorns is twined with every thorn.
His cross is every tree.[9]

There is no particular place where Jesus is to be found uniquely. Sacred history is more important than sacred space. The earthly Jerusalem is, appropriately, a place of pilgrimage, worship and reflection for all three Abrahamic faiths and should be shared equally by them. But the followers of the Christ child know that the Jerusalem that matters is the heavenly Jerusalem that comes down as a gift of God at the end of history (Rev 21:9-27). No wars should be fought and no blood spilled over the earthly city, for Luke tells his readers that the glory of the Lord shone, not around the city, but around the child.

SUMMARY: THE SAVIOR, THE WISE MEN AND THE VISION OF ISAIAH

From this study, the following may be noted:

1. Oppressors and oppressed are sinners and both need the grace of the new Savior.

2. Suffering does not produce people without sin.

3. The prophet needs courage to tell oppressed people of their sins and their need for grace.

4. Isaiah promised special blessings for the city of Jerusalem. Arabs would arrive with gifts and shepherds would appear. A great light, along with the glory of God, would shine upon Jerusalem. The Gospel authors saw these promises fulfilled in the birth of a child. "The hopes and dreams of all the years" are shifted from Jerusalem to a child born in Bethlehem.

5. At his birth Jewish shepherds and Gentile Arabs came together in adoration of a child in a manger.

---

[9]Joseph Mary Plunkett, "I See His Blood Upon the Rose," *The Circle and the Sword* (1911).

4

Herod's Atrocities, Simeon and Anna

MATTHEW 2:13-18; LUKE 2:22-36

SOME STORIES SHOULD NOT BE presented on television. For me, the murder of the children in Bethlehem is such a story (Mt 2:16-18). The scene is simply too brutal for viewers, even in modern times. Two questions arise: Why did such an event happen, and why did Matthew include such an unspeakably repulsive story in his Gospel?

WHY DID THE EVENT TAKE PLACE?

Herod was an exceedingly complex person. Racially, he was an Arab. His father was from an Arab tribe in the southern part of the Holy Land called Idumea. His mother was from Petra, which was the capital of the Nabatean kingdom, an Arab kingdom that inhabited the northern part of Arabia in the first century. One of Herod's brothers was named Faisal, and a second Yusef. His sister was called Salama. The only child in the family with a Greek name was Herod himself.[1]

Religiously, Herod was Jewish. In about 135 B.C. the Jewish ruler Hyrcanus conquered the Idumaeans and on pain of death forced them to become Jews. Hyrcanus then appointed Herod's grandfather, Antipater the elder, governor of the province. That made Herod a "Jew." Culturally, Herod was Greek. Greek culture had spread widely throughout Palestine by that time, and Greek was the lingua franca of the international community. Indeed, Greek was Herod's first language, and Herod was noted for various attempts to turn Jerusalem into a Greek city.[2]

Politically, Herod was Roman. In all the major conflicts during his tenure in power, he sided with Rome. Being racially Arab, religiously Jewish, culturally

---

[1]For a life of Herod see Stewart Perowne, *The Life and Times of Herod the Great* (London: Hodder & Stoughton, 1957).
[2]Ibid., pp. 17-23.

Greek and politically Roman, Herod was a complex man. In his early days he was described as good-looking and powerfully built. He personally led his army in the field of battle in ten different wars. One of the high points of his nobility was when he sided with Antony and Cleopatra against Octavian in the struggle for control of the Roman Empire. After winning decisively against Antony, Octavian (who became Caesar Augustus) traveled to Rhodes to plan his next move. Herod quickly made his way there to meet the new Roman victor and was granted an audience.

For most of his life Herod had been a personal friend of Antony and had supported him against Octavian. How would he manage with the new Caesar? Herod appeared without a crown and boldly confessed to all the support he had given Caesar's enemy. He also admitted that he had remained loyal to Anthony even in his defeat. Herod climaxed his presentation by saying, "What I ask of you is to consider not whose friend, but what a good friend, I was."[3] Caesar decided that Herod was a man he could trust and told him to put his crown back on his head. Herod returned to Palestine with a more secure throne than he had previously enjoyed.

But with the years Herod gradually disintegrated. In all he married ten women. Sons for him were often seen as potential political rivals, and two of his favorites were strangled by his order in a fort in Samaria. Later he became suspicious of the political loyalty of his favorite wife, Mariamne, and had her killed. After that he was known to wander through the palace calling her name and sending the servants to fetch her. When they failed to do so he would have them beaten.

Herod was brilliant and brutal. Toward the end of his life he grew seriously ill with a number of painful diseases. In his very last days he arrested the crown prince and imprisoned him in the dungeon of his palace. When, in pain, the old man tried to take his own life and was prevented by a guard, confusion broke out for a brief time. Word passed through the palace that the king was dead. On hearing the news, the crown prince cried out to be released so that he could assume power. Herod survived his suicide attempt and ordered the death of said crown prince. Five days later Herod himself died. His last order was to command his troops to arrest thousands of notables from across the country and sequester them in the stadium in Jericho. Upon Herod's death the notables were to be executed so that there would be mourning in the land when the king died. Herod knew only too well that no one would weep for *him*. Fortunately, the order was not carried out. With such a record it is understandable that as an old man Herod could have or-

---

[3]Ibid., p. 80.

dered the slaughter of the babies of Bethlehem. It was a brutal world into which Jesus was born, and Herod was nothing if not a man of his times.[4]

WHY IS THIS VIOLENT ACCOUNT INCLUDED IN THE STORY OF THE BIRTH OF JESUS?

The birth of Jesus is always remembered and retold in soft colors with beautiful music playing in the background. The slaughter of the innocents is never a part of any church's "Christmas pageant." I cannot recall ever hearing the story read in any Christmas Eve service. The faithful expect and are generally offered a story limited to joyful angels, excited shepherds and generous wise men. The texts that are read are full of promises of peace mixed with visions of a beautiful child, a holy mother, a courageous father and some humble animals. There appears to be a conspiracy of silence which refuses to notice the massacre. Why then does Matthew include it?

The oft-observed reason is that Matthew is presenting Jesus as the new Moses. Moses was born in the midst of an occasion of the "slaughter of the innocents" as Pharaoh ordered the killing of all male Hebrew babies (Ex 1:8-22). In turn, Matthew relates a parallel story about Jesus.[5] But there may have been another important reason for its inclusion.

Those who lived in the Middle East across the second half of the twentieth century (including this author) experienced frequent warfare. In Lebanon, particularly, there were seven wars in a thirty-five-year period. One lasted for seventeen years. Others were quick yet brutal. People saw friends and family killed by bullets and explosives and all the other horrors of modern war.

How do people retain their faith under such conditions? One answer is that they remember both the Christmas story and the cross. A mindless, bloody atrocity took place at the birth of Jesus. After reading that story, the reader is not caught unawares by the human potential for terror that shows its ugly face again on the cross. At the beginning of the Gospel and at its conclusion, Matthew presents pictures of the depth of evil that Jesus came to redeem. This story heightens the reader's awareness of the willingness on the part of God to expose himself to the total vulnerability which is at the heart of the incarnation. If the Gospel can flourish in a world that produces the slaughter of the innocents and the cross, the Gos-

[4]Ibid., p. 172.
[5]W. D. Davies and Dale C. Allison Jr., *The Gospel According to Saint Matthew* (New York: T & T Clark, 1988), 1:254; Raymond E. Brown, *Birth of the Messiah* (London: Geoffrey Chapman, 1977), pp. 228-29.

pel can flourish anywhere. From this awareness the readers of the Gospels in any age can take heart.

SIMEON AND ANNA—MALE AND FEMALE

There is another element of the story that is often ignored. Jesus as a baby was presented in the temple to Simeon (Lk 2:25-32). The venerable Simeon made some sweeping claims as he addressed God and spoke of the child: the child who had come to redeem both Israel and the Gentiles. Suddenly and unexpectedly an old woman by the name of Anna appears on the scene, who "Gave thanks to God, and spoke of him [Jesus] to all who were looking for the redemption of Jerusalem" (Lk 2:38). Apparently Luke could find no witness to inform him of what Anna said on that occasion. One hint regarding the hopes of her audience is all we have. It is clear that Luke chose not to fabricate a speech. So why is she mentioned at all?

Throughout his Gospel, Luke emphasizes a remarkable aspect of Jesus' life. In the stories Luke chooses to tell he makes it clear that this Savior came for both women and men. A careful examination of the book of Luke unearths at least twenty-seven sets of stories that focus in one case on a man and in the other on a woman.[6]

Among these is the parable of the good shepherd with a lost sheep and the parable of a good woman with a lost coin (Lk 15:3-10). The first story emerges from the world of men and the second from the life experience of women. Then there are the two stories of the farmer who plants a mustard seed in his garden and the woman who kneads some yeast into her bread dough (Lk 13:18-21). Again, the text presents one story from the life experiences of men and a second from the daily life of women. Even so the birth stories of Jesus, recorded in Luke, contain three such pairs. These are:

1. Gabriel visits two people: Zechariah and Mary.

2. Two songs are sung: one by Zechariah and the other by Mary.

3. There are two witnesses in the temple: Simeon and Anna testify to the redemptive plan of God that will be fulfilled through Jesus.

Granted, Simeon is given more attention than Anna. But if Zechariah and Mary are compared, Mary is more prominent. Her response to Gabriel's good news is of a higher quality than Zechariah's. The promise of a son for Zechariah was a gift that fulfilled his dreams while costing him nothing. Yet he failed to believe this good news because his wife was beyond childbearing age. As a result

---

[6]Kenneth E. Bailey, *Finding the Lost* (St. Louis: Concordia Press, 1992), pp. 97-99.

he was confronted with a second miracle: He was struck dumb until the child was born.

By contrast, Mary was told that through an act of God she would give birth to a son. Unlike the promise to Zechariah, the gift offered her could have caused her death. But, unlike Zechariah, she quietly accepted this costly discipleship and said humbly, "Let it be to me according to thy word." Then she too was exposed to a second act of God. But her second miracle was the good news that her cousin was to have a baby. Instead of a miracle of judgment, she witnessed a miracle of blessing.

SIMEON'S PROPHECY

Simeon's *Nunc Dimittis* offers a beautiful promise to Mary, with a warning. Simeon says to her:

> Behold, this child is set for the fall and rising of many in Israel,
> and for a sign that is spoken against
> (and a sword will pierce through your own soul also),
> that thoughts out of many hearts may be revealed. (Lk 2:34-35)

What can this fearsome saying mean? How can the phrase "that thoughts out of many hearts may be revealed" be understood? The text seems to affirm that a sword will pass through the soul of both Jesus and his mother. This text tells the reader that Mary will participate in the event of the cross and her suffering will contribute to exposing "the thoughts out of many hearts." Will Mary's faithful presence at the cross oblige evil forces around her to look at themselves and contrast their brutality with her courageous love?

Around the cross there flows a river of compromise. Everyone involved is strangely exposed. The disciples believe, but in their fear they run away. Peter makes bold promises but falls into denial. The high priest wants to preserve the sanctity of the temple and keep the Romans from intervention in his sacred space. In the process he participates in the death of an innocent man. The soldiers only obeyed orders, and those orders violated Roman justice. Pilate wanted to keep his job and stay out of trouble. He was presumably scared lest the temple authorities send a negative report to Caesar (about him) that would damage his career. Pilate had previously engaged in a number of confrontations with the Jewish populace, all of which he lost. With a checkered past, could his career sustain one more defeat? His personal strategic interests were clearly more important than the innocence of one village carpenter. Pilate's true nature was exposed by the cross. The thoughts of the hearts of many were revealed by the suffering of the cross, and Mary participated in that suffering.

On Golgotha Mary chose to remain to the end and witness the suffering of her son until his death. She was not under arrest and could have walked away. She knew she could not change what was happening before her by arguing with the soldiers or pleading with the high priests. The only decision she was free to make was to choose to remain and enter into Jesus' suffering. Indeed a sword passed through her heart, and in the process, once again, she became a model for Christian discipleship.

These great events are foreshadowed in the Christmas story. As D. T. Niles, the famous Sri Lankan, writes in a Christmas hymn:

On a day when men were counted,
　　God became the son of man;
That his name in every census
　　Would be entered, was his plan.
God, the Lord of all Creation,
　　Humble takes a creature's place;
He whose form no man has witnessed,
　　Has today a human face.

When there shone the star of David
　　In the spangled eastern sky,
Kings arrived to pay their homage
　　To the Christ, the Lord most high.
Yet not all, for lo there soundeth
　　Through the streets a fearful cry,
For a king who will not worship
　　Has decreed that Christ must die.

Yet it's Christmas, and we greet Him,
　　Coming even now to save;
For the Lord of our salvation
　　Was not captive to the grave.
Out of Egypt came the Saviour
　　Man's Emmanuel to be,
Christmas shines with Easter glory,
　　Glory of eternity.[7]

---

[7]Daniel T. Niles, "On a Day When Men Were Counted," *C.C.A. Hymnal* (Kyoto, Japan: Kawakita, 1974), p. 117.

SUMMARY: HEROD'S ATROCITIES, SIMEON AND ANNA

Four points can be made about these texts:

1. Unspeakable brutality characterizes the beginning and the end of Jesus' life. His ministry was within and to a violent world.

2. Matthew wants his readers to see Jesus as the new Moses come to set his people free. He creates, therefore, a parallel between the birth of Moses and the birth of Jesus by including the account of the murder of the innocents.

3. Women and men are prominent throughout the ministry of Jesus. This concern for all humankind surfaces three times in the birth stories.

4. Mary is presented as a model for discipleship. Through her suffering she participates in exposing the evil that needs to be redeemed. This participation is foreshadowed in the words of Simeon.

PART TWO

The Beatitudes

5

The Beatitudes 1

MATTHEW 5:1-5

IN THE BEATITUDES THE READER IS PRESENTED with brief statements phrased in simple words that carry profound meanings. The goal of this chapter is to uncover some of those meanings.

Matthew's Gospel contains a collection of the sayings of Jesus called "The Sermon on the Mount" (Mt 5—7). A similar but shorter collection appears in the Gospel according to Luke named "The Sermon on the Plain" (Lk 6:20-49). A careful comparison between the two collections is beyond the scope of this chapter, but in passing we can note that the two groups of sayings exhibit one primary difference. Luke records four positive Beatitudes ("Blessed are those . . . for . . .") that are balanced with matching negatives ("Woe to those . . . for . . ."). The rhetorical balances exhibited in formatting appear in figure 5.1 (see following page).[1]

The last four couplets (5-8) are the reverse of the first four (1-4). Step parallelism is used to link them. That is, a Beatitude on the poor (1) is balanced with a Beatitude on the rich (5) and so on. The fourth couplet contains extra material placed in its center, creating a "sandwich." The material comprising the sandwich in 4 is carefully arranged. There are seven phrases, with three negatives at the beginning matched by the three positives at the end. The climax in the middle is the only christological reference in the entire passage.

Matthew presents a list of nine Beatitudes, but records no balancing negatives. He includes the same four that appear in Luke and gives his readers five others not found in Luke. The entire set of Beatitudes in Matthew is shown in figure 5.2 (see page 67).

---

[1]The words on the right attempt to summarize the couplet and highlight the parallels that appear in the eight Beatitudes.

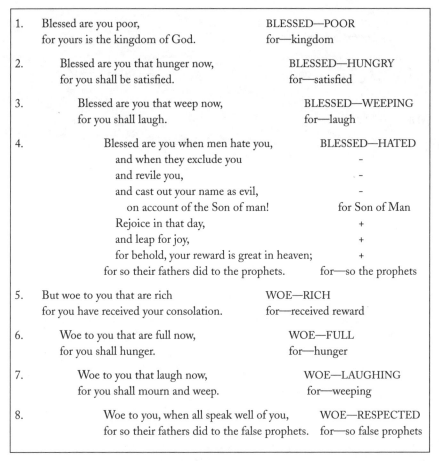

1.	Blessed are you poor,	BLESSED—POOR
	for yours is the kingdom of God.	for—kingdom
2.	Blessed are you that hunger now,	BLESSED—HUNGRY
	for you shall be satisfied.	for—satisfied
3.	Blessed are you that weep now,	BLESSED—WEEPING
	for you shall laugh.	for—laugh
4.	Blessed are you when men hate you,	BLESSED—HATED
	and when they exclude you	-
	and revile you,	. -
	and cast out your name as evil,	-
	on account of the Son of man!	for Son of Man
	Rejoice in that day,	+
	and leap for joy,	+
	for behold, your reward is great in heaven;	+
	for so their fathers did to the prophets.	for—so the prophets
5.	But woe to you that are rich	WOE—RICH
	for you have received your consolation.	for—received reward
6.	Woe to you that are full now,	WOE—FULL
	for you shall hunger.	for—hunger
7.	Woe to you that laugh now,	WOE—LAUGHING
	for you shall mourn and weep.	for—weeping
8.	Woe to you, when all speak well of you,	WOE—RESPECTED
	for so their fathers did to the false prophets.	for—so false prophets

Figure 5.1. The Beatitudes in Luke 6:20-26

Each of the nine couplets opens with a person to whom Jesus gives the title "blessed," and in each case the matching condition follows in the second line. Couplet 9 has extra material placed in the center. It is striking to note that in both Matthew and Luke the couplet that focuses on persecution contains extra material in the center. This additional material, in both texts, begins with negatives which are then balanced by positives. In both passages a christological affirmation appears in the center of the "sandwich." One difference is that in Luke there are seven words/phrases in the center while in Matthew the entire Beatitude forms a "sandwich" of seven phrases. These sandwiches give the topic of persecution a singular and significant emphasis. Before turning to reflect on the first Beatitude the key word *blessed* needs clarification.

1. Blessed are the poor in spirit,
   for theirs is the kingdom of heaven.

2. Blessed are those who mourn,
   for they shall be comforted.

3. Blessed are the meek,
   for they shall inherit the land.

4. Blessed are those who hunger and thirst for righteousness,
   for they shall be satisfied.

5. Blessed are the merciful,
   for they shall obtain mercy.

6. Blessed are the pure in heart,
   for they shall see God.

7. Blessed are the peacemakers,
   for they shall be called sons of God.

8. Blessed are those who are persecuted for righteousness' sake,
   for theirs is the kingdom of heaven.

9. Blessed are you when people insult you
   and persecute you   –
   and utter all kinds of evil against you falsely   –
       on my account.   Jesus
   Rejoice and be glad,   +
   for your reward is great in heaven,   +
   for in the same way they persecuted the prophets who were before you.

Figure 5.2. The Beatitudes in Matthew 5:3-12

BLESSED: TWO WORDS INTO ONE

In Hebrew (as in Greek) there are two words that are translated into English as "blessed." The two Greek words parallel the Hebrew words, and it is important to understand the differences between them. One of these Greek words, *eulogeō,* has the Hebrew word *bĕrākâ* behind it in the Old Testament. *Eulogeō* does not appear in the Beatitudes. This word is used in prayer when the worship leader asks God for some blessing that the individual or community is eager to receive from God. *Eulogeō* is the right word for "O Lord, bless the sick" or "O Lord, bless the children."

The other word in Hebrew, *ʿašîr,* and *makarios* in Greek are word clusters which with their cognates are described by Raymond Brown as "not part of a wish and to not invoke a blessing. Rather they recognize an existing state of happiness or good fortune."[2]

That is they affirm a *quality of spirituality that is already present*. In English we communicate this sense of the word with a hyphen or an accent. When saying, "Ms. So-and-so is a bless-ed person in our church," one is not asking for something but rather affirming a quality in Ms. So-and-so that already exists. In the Beatitudes the term for "blessed" is *makarios*, the second of these two words. The presence of *makarios* in the Beatitudes makes a great difference. The third Beatitude should not be understood to mean, "If you are meek, you will inherit the earth." As a group, the Beatitudes do *not* mean "Blessed are the people who do X because they will receive Y." The point is not exhortation for a certain type of behavior. Instead they should be read with the sense, "Look at the authentic spirituality and joy of these people who have or will be given X." Put in concrete terms we could say, "Bless-ed is the happy daughter of Mr. Jones because she will inherit the Jones's farm." The woman in question is *already* the happy daughter of Mr. Jones. She is not working to earn the farm. Everyone knows that a key element in her happy and secure life is that she and the community around her know that the farm will one day be hers. The first statement affirms a happy state that already exists. The second statement affirms a future that allows her even now to live a happy life. Hauck writes, "The special feature of . . . makarios . . . in the NT is that it refers overwhelmingly to the distinctive religious joy which accrues to man from his share in the salvation of the kingdom of God."[3]

With this definition clearly in mind we turn to the Beatitudes themselves.

FIRST BEATITUDE

> Blessed are the poor in spirit,
> for theirs is the kingdom of heaven.

What does Jesus mean by "the poor in spirit"? Luke merely says, "Blessed are the poor." A debate over these two phrases has continued in Western Christianity for some years. One side of the debate insists that the authentic voice of Jesus is found in the statement in Luke. The poor are blessed by God. Matthew, we are told, spiritualized this simple and powerful statement. A second way to under-

---

[2]Raymond Brown, *The Gospel According to John*, Anchor Bible (Garden City, N.Y.: Doubleday, 1970), p. 553. Also Joseph A. Fitzmyer, *The Gospel According to Luke (I-IX)* (New York: Doubleday, 1981), 2:632-33.
[3]Friedrich Hauck, "μακάριος," *Theological Dictionary of the New Testament*, ed. Gerhard Kittel and Gerhard Friedrich, trans. Geoffrey W. Bromiley (Grand Rapids: Eerdmans, 1967), 4:367.

stand the difference between the two phrases is to see Jesus as part of the prophetic tradition, and that for him, like Isaiah, "the poor" are the humble and pious who seek God. Matthew's phrase serves to bring out the original meaning already present in Luke. Isaiah 66:2, from which Jesus borrows this language, reads:

> But this is the man to whom I will look
> he that is poor [*ʿānî*] and contrite in spirit,
> and trembles at my word. (my translation)

If the reader is already influenced by this text, and others like it from Isaiah and the Psalms, then he or she does not need the additional phrase *in spirit*. If that background in Isaiah is not known, then the phrase *poor in spirit* is critical for comprehension. On rare occasions the word *poor* in Isaiah does refer to people who do not have enough to eat (Is 58:7). But in the majority of cases it describes the humble and pious who know that they need God's grace and "tremble" at his word.[4]

Jesus goes on to affirm that these bless-ed ones make up the membership of the kingdom of heaven, which is already theirs. But what precisely is the kingdom of God? There is no simple answer to this question. Everything Jesus said and did is in some way related to the kingdom of God. It has to do with the rule of God in the lives of individuals and societies. The Lord's Prayer includes the words "Thy kingdom come," which obviously looks to a future that is unfolding. Yet the kingdom has already come in Jesus Christ who said, "But if it is by the finger of God that I cast out demons, then the kingdom of God has come upon you" (Lk 11:20).

We live in the interim between the inauguration of the rule (kingdom) of God in the coming of Jesus Christ and its completion at the end of history. Our struggle for peace and justice is part of our discipleship as we work for and await the coming of that kingdom on earth as a gift of God.

In this Beatitude Jesus declares that the poor in spirit already possess the kingdom. Many people at the time of Jesus used the phrase *the kingdom of God* to describe a Jewish state where God alone was King.[5] In contrast, Jesus declared that the kingdom was already present in the poor in spirit (not among the Zealots).

The Old Syriac translation of this text reads, "Happy it is for the poor in spirit, that theirs is the kingdom of heaven."[6] As mentioned, the second line is not a reward for the first line. Rather, the poor in spirit *already possess the kingdom.*

---

[4]See chapter 12, pp. 158-63.
[5]Martin Hengel, *The Zealots* (Edinburgh: T & T Clark, 1989), pp. 91-94.
[6]See F. Crawford Burkitt, *Evangelion Da-Mepharreshe*, 2 vols. (Cambridge: Cambridge University Press, 1904), 1:19.

SECOND BEATITUDE

> Blessed are those that mourn,
> for they shall be comforted.

This is a clear case of a "divine passive." God will comfort the bless-ed who mourn. The Good News Bible turns the passive into an active and translates, "Happy are those who mourn; God will comfort them!"

About what should we mourn? Why are "those who mourn" called bless-ed? There is a horrible side of the human spirit that enjoys watching others suffer. The film industry has discovered this darkness and makes billions of dollars every year exploiting it. This twisted fascination in the heart of humankind is a despicable form of evil. At the other extreme, forces in society make billions of dollars cushioning the public and protecting them from any form of suffering or even unpleasantness. There is no need for self-discipline in eating, no need to exercise, no need to endure pain. Eat all you like, buy our pills and you will lose weight without discomfort. This Beatitude has nothing to do with either of these attitudes. If there is mourning, some form of suffering lies behind it. How are we to understand these things?

Christians are never urged to seek suffering; they are, however, encouraged to recognize that suffering is an extraordinary teacher. We know little about the great depths of the human spirit until we have endured suffering. Pain rearranges our priorities. To become a refugee is horrible, and the forces that drive people from their homes must be opposed. Yet anyone who is obliged to flee his or her home, as I was on three occasions in Lebanon, quickly learns that what really matters is life itself, and that all possessions are—at the end of the day—worthless. Mourners endure suffering and the bless-ed ones among them experience the comfort of God.

Great natural disasters, such as hurricanes or tidal waves, strike our world. When there is warning, a few brave souls usually choose to remain in their homes. The vast majority of the inhabitants flee the coming devastation. After the storm abates, those who are able to do so return home. And at times there is a pattern that emerges between the lines of the news reports that are written for the world to read. Often there is a striking contrast between those who stay and those who leave. The hearts of the survivors are often full of gratitude that they are still alive. The returnees at times see only devastation and feel only anguish. The one who is lashed by the storm is often the one who is grateful. It does not follow that we seek to stand in the path of destructive storms in order to learn gratitude. But the bless-ed who suffer and mourn deep loss can be blessed by God in that suffering and mourning. Ecclesiastes 7:2-4 reads:

> It is better to go to the house of mourning
>   than to go to the house of feasting; . . .
> Sorrow is better than laughter,
>   for by sadness of countenance the heart is made glad.
> The heart of the wise is in the house of mourning;
>   but the heart of fools is in the house of mirth.

For decades I have pondered these words, wondering what they meant. I still ponder them. Recently I attended the funeral of a dear friend and companion along the pilgrim way. A number of people who knew the departed saint told stories of how he had encouraged and influenced them. As they spoke, and as we remembered his life, the atmosphere among the mourners began to soar in a majestic way. There was an open mike where friends could give their unscheduled witnesses to remembered courage, faith, loyalty, love and vision. Yes, there were tears and some laughter, but all of us heard the great bells of the faith ringing in our minds and hearts, and in a strange, indescribable way, there "the heart was made glad . . . in the house of mourning, " as the Beatitude took on fresh meaning.

The righteous also mourn when they see people treated unjustly. It is easy to develop armor to protect ourselves from feeling the pain of others; and as that happens we cease to mourn for or with them. The bless-ed continue to mourn in the face of injustice. I once read a book of recollections of Anne Frank compiled by her friends. One witness who was with her in the death camp noted "her tears never ran dry." Her body gave out, but her spirit never surrendered to compassion fatigue. To the end she was able to mourn, and she was a bless-ed presence for all who knew her.

This Beatitude also calls on the faithful to mourn over evil in their own lives as they realize their inability to conquer it unaided. Failure to love God and our neighbors should produce grief. The bless-ed are those who experience this mourning.

What happens then to people who mourn because of their own pain and are at the same time insensitive to the pain of others? There is no hint that such people are among the bless-ed. Rather those who are aware of their failures to meet God's royal law to love God and neighbor will experience the comfort of God. From the depths of their souls will come the quiet peace of God in the midst of their mourning. Such people are a bless-ed presence among God's people.

THIRD BEATITUDE

> Blessed are the meek,
> for they shall inherit the land.

Jesus identified himself as a prophet and was identified as such by many. Any prophet of Israel who discusses "the land" has one primary meaning in mind. He is referring to the Holy Land of Israel/Palestine. The Greek word for "land" in this text is *gē* which in the Old Testament translates the Hebrew word *'arez* over two thousand times. In biblical literature *gē* is used to refer to

a. land in general

b. the land of promise

c. the inhabited earth

d. the earth as the theater of history[7]

In the mouth of Jesus the word *'ereṣ* (land) in this text no doubt refers to "the land of promise." Jesus is here quoting and slightly revising three verses from Psalm 37, which reads:

> But those *who wait for the LORD*
>   shall inherit the land. . . .
> But the *meek* shall inherit the land,
>   and delight themselves in abundant prosperity. . . .
> The *righteous* shall inherit the land,
>   and live in it forever. (Ps 37:9, 11, 29 NRSV)

The above psalm is set in Israel, and the "land" and the "inheritance" are the Promised Land. This background is significant for the text before us.

The sequence of the three Beatitudes observed thus far is important. First Jesus told the disciples that the *kingdom* was composed of the *poor in spirit*, not the arrogant and aggressive. Then he declared that the *blessed* are those who *mourn*. In the first century the area that encompassed Galilee, Samaria and Judea was torn with wars and rumors of wars, and such an affirmation would have resonated deeply with the powerless in Jesus' audience. Here Jesus is promising that *the meek* will *inherit the land* (of Israel) rather than the *powerful*. Rome and the Zealots would soon be engaged in all-out war to win political and military control over that same land. Jesus had a different idea about who had rights to it. Being the racial descendants of a particular patriarch was not the point. Joining the Herodi-

---

[7]Hermann Sasse, "γῆ," in *Theological Dictionary of the New Testament*, ed. Gerhard Kittel and Gerhard Friedrich, trans. Geoffrey W. Bromiley (Grand Rapids: Eerdmans, 1964-76), 1:677-78.

ans, who were willing to compromise anything to stay in power was not part of the equation. Joining the Zealots was not recommended. What a strange claim—*the meek* were declared to have already won the jackpot of the inheritance of the land promised to Abraham.

Naturally, these profound sayings of Jesus were repeated beyond the confines of the original audience, and as that occurred they took on wider meanings. By the time Jews and Gentiles read the Gospel of Matthew in Greek, some decades later, they no doubt saw "the land" as "the earth" and thought of the entire created world. Paul's mind turns in the same direction when he discusses the promise of the land to Abraham and universalizes that promise to include the entire earth. He talks of "the promise to Abraham and his descendants, that they should inherit the world" (Rom 4:13). Later in the same letter, Paul affirms that "The whole creation has been groaning in travail together until now;" waiting for humankind to be adopted as children of God (Rom 8:22). In both texts all nature is involved and has become the inheritance of God's family.

Jesus' original audience no doubt heard Jesus talking about "the land" and who could claim it as an inheritance. The answer was "the meek" rather than the racial descendants of anyone or the men of violence. We can assume that Matthew's readers heard this same text identifying the whole earth as a precious inheritance for the children of God who will care for it and live in harmony with it. But in both cases, it is important to ask: Who are the meek?

The Hebrew/Aramaic word probably used by Jesus, and the Greek word that appears in our New Testament, have different emphases. Each offers nuances that enrich the text.

The Hebrew word, *ʿānî*, (poor/humble) has to do with obedience in accepting God's guidance. The Greek term, *praÿs* ("meek"), refers not to a person in the presence of God but rather describes relations between people. Aristotle, in his fifth-century B.C. *Nicomachean Ethics*, defines *praÿs* as the virtue of acting halfway between recklessness on one side and cowardice on the other. For Aristotle, the path of virtue was always the "golden mean" between two extremes. The one who is truly *praÿs* (meek) is the one who becomes angry on the right grounds against the right person in the right manner at the right moment and for the right length of time.[8] The Hebrew meaning of the word behind the text tells us to accept the guidance of God and to obediently follow God's will. The Greek word in this text advises an ethical median way that will assist in working out problems, disputes

---

[8] Aristotle *Nicomachean Ethics* 4.5.3.

and disagreements. Both shades of meaning can surely be affirmed as part of the treasures in the text.

In the Babylonian Talmud, early Palestinian rabbis discuss the reasons for the destruction of the two temples. Rabbi Johanan said: "What was the cause of the first destruction of Jerusalem? Idolatry. And of the second destruction? Causeless hatred." He continues by explaining that causeless hatred "is more grievous than idolatry."[9] That same causeless anger is the exact opposite of the meekness discussed in our text. But what about righteous anger?

The prophecy of Habakkuk describes the terrible power of the Chaldeans. In the middle of this description the prophet writes, "Their justice and dignity proceed from themselves" (Hab 1:7). The Chaldeans created their own definitions of justice. For the prophet, this was horrible. God defines justice and gives it objective authenticity. When the faithful use the measuring stick of the justice of God and with that standard identify injustice, it is surely right to be angry. Those who use that divine standard of justice are the meek (before God) who struggle for God's justice and thereby inherit the land/earth.

Pondering such things, one begins to feel like Paul, who tried to penetrate the wisdom of God and finally burst out with, "O the depth of the riches and wisdom and knowledge of God! How unsearchable are his judgments and how inscrutable his ways!" (Rom 11:33). A cautious beginning of a summary is as follows.

SUMMARY: THE BEATITUDES 1

1. Luke presents four pairs of blessings and woes. Matthew has nine blessings. Persecution is prominent in each collection.

2. *Bless-ed* refers to a spiritual condition of divinely gifted joy already present, not a requirement to be fulfilled in order to receive a reward.

3. In the light of Isaiah's usage, the "poor in spirit" are the humble and pious who seek God. The kingdom of God is theirs.

4. God will comfort the bless-ed who mourn.

5. To deny suffering or to find it darkly entertaining are both wrong.

6. Suffering can become a doorway to profound wisdom.

7. The house of mourning can make the heart glad.

8. The righteous mourn over injustice and do not succumb to compassion fatigue.

---

[9]The Babylonian Talmud, Tractate *Kallah Rabbati* 54b(1).

9. The righteous mourn over their own sin and are comforted.

10. For Jesus, "the land" meant the land of Israel, and only the meek had rights of inheritance, not the violent or the members of a particular clan. The text expanded in the later church to include the whole earth.

11. The meek are those who humbly seek God. They are neither too bold nor too timid.

12. Being meek is in harmony with being angry over injustice inflicted on others.

6

The Beatitudes 2

MATTHEW 5:6-12

IN THIS CHAPTER WE INTEND to reflect on Beatitudes four through eight.

FOURTH BEATITUDE

> Blessed are those who hunger and thirst after righteousness,
> for they shall be filled.

As a good Middle Easterner, Jesus here makes astute use of metaphorical language. To talk about those who "hunger and thirst for righteousness" is to use words rooted in physical needs to describe spiritual realities. The vast majority in the developed world have more than enough food and water to satisfy their bodies. Among the poor, hunger sadly remains and food security is an even greater problem. But across the developed world, serious sustained thirst is almost nonexistent. This has been true for so long that complacency has set in, and both of these precious gifts of God are wasted. By contrast, many in Jesus' world would have personally known both unrelenting hunger and life-threatening thirst.

Once in my life I nearly died of thirst. While living in the south of Egypt, a group of friends and I traveled deep into the Sahara Desert by camel. As our trek began, the temperature soared to above 110 degrees Fahrenheit in the shade, and there was no shade. On our way, one goat-skin water bag leaked all of its precious contents.

With consumption high due to the heat, we ran out of water, and for a day and a half we pressed on while enduring intense thirst. The goal of the excursion was a famous well named Bir Shaytoun, deep in the desert. Our guide promised us that it was never dry—ah, but could we survive to reach its life-giving liquid silver? My mouth became completely dry, and eating was impossible because swallowing felt like the rubbing of two pieces of sandpaper together. My vision became blurred and the struggle to keep moving became harder with each step. We knew that if the well was dry, our armed guards would probably have forcibly seized our three baggage camels and ridden them back to the valley, leaving the rest of us to die. As I staggered on, my mind turned to this verse and I knew that I had never sought righteousness with the same single-minded passion that I now gave to the quest for water.

Yes, we managed to stagger to the well, and it was full of "the wine of God," as water is named by desert tribesmen in the Middle East. In the process I learned something of the power of Jesus' language. In a world where water was scarce and travel arduous, his listeners would have known what it meant to "hunger and thirst" after food and water, and thus could understand what Jesus was saying about an all-consuming passion for righteousness.

But Jesus does not say, "Blessed are those who live righteously and maintain a righteous lifestyle." Rather he affirms, "Blessed are those who *hunger and thirst* after righteousness." The statement presupposes that righteousness is something the faithful continuously strive after. The blessed are not those who arrive but those who continue, at whatever cost, in their pilgrimage toward a more perfect righteousness. The constant, relentless drive toward righteousness characterizes the blessed.

Matthew 13:44-46 includes a pair of parables that illuminate this Beatitude. The first one likens the kingdom of heaven to a man who finds a *treasure in a field* and sells everything and buys that field. The second parable compares that same kingdom to *a merchant searching* for a pearl of great price. Contrary to popular perceptions, in this latter case the kingdom is not compared to the pearl but to the merchant, *who is searching for it.* The Beatitude we are now examining is like the second of these two parables. The believers who *hunger and thirst* after righteousness are called blessed in that striving. But what exactly is righteousness?

The Nature of Righteousness

The great words *ṣĕdāqâ* (Hebrew) and *dikaiousynē* (Greek) are both theologically freighted throughout the Bible. The *Theological Dictionary of the New Testament* article on this family of words extends for fifty-one densely packed pages.[1] The key to it all is that *ṣĕdāqâ* does not refer to an "absolute ideal ethical norm" but is "out and out a term denoting a relationship."[2] Every relationship makes claims on con-

---

[1]G. Schrenk, "δίκη, δίκαιος, δικαιοσύνη," *Theological Dictionary of the New Testament* (Grand Rapids: Eerdmans, 1964), 2:174-225.
[2]Gerhard von Rad, *Old Testament Theology* (New York: Harper & Row, 1962), 1:371.

duct and "the satisfaction of these claims, which issue from the relationship and in which alone the relationship can persist, is described by our term *tsadaq*."[3]

With this fundamental concept in mind it is clear that righteousness is like a diamond with many facets. We will briefly examine four of them.

1. In biblical literature *righteousness* often refers to mighty acts of God in history to save. Again von Rad is helpful where he writes, "from the earliest times onwards Israel celebrated Jahweh as the one who bestowed on his people the all-embracing gift of his righteousness. And this *tsdqh* bestowed on Israel is always a saving gift."[4] One of the places where this is clearly set forth is in Micah 6:3-5 which reads:

> O my people, what have I done to you?
>> In what have I wearied you? Answer me!
> For I brought you up from the land of Egypt,
>> and redeemed you from the house of bondage;
> And I sent before you Moses,
>> Aaron, and Miriam,
> O my people, remember what Balak king of Moab devised,
>> and what Balaam the son of Beor answered him,
> and what happened from Shittim to Gilgal,
>> that you may know the [righteousnesses] of the LORD.

In this text God reviews his past mighty acts in history to save Israel and calls on them to remember all that he has done for them. The declared purpose of this recollection is "that you may know the *ṣĕdāqôt* ("righteousnesses") of the Lord." The RSV correctly here translates *ṣĕdāqôt* as "saving acts," which is exactly what *ṣĕdāqôt* means in this text. But those great saving acts not only deliver Israel, they also grant to her a new status.

2. Righteousness has to do with being "declared righteous." Rudolf Bultmann writes:

> It (righteousness) does not mean the ethical quality of a person. It does not mean any quality at all, but a relationship. That is, dikaiosyne is not something a person has as his own; rather it is something he has in the verdict of the "forum" to which he is accountable.

He continues:

> Mt. 5:6 obviously does not mean those who "ever striving, endeavor" to attain ethical

---

[3]H. Cremer, *Biblisch-theologisches Wörterbuch*, 7th ed. (Gothain: n.p., 1893), pp. 273-75, quoted in ibid.
[4]Von Rad, *Old Testament Theology*, 2:337.

perfection, but those who long to have God pronounce the verdict "righteous" as His decision over them in the judgment.[5]

This understanding of righteous as "affirmed to be righteous" (i.e., vindicated) appears in selected lines from Isaiah 54:10-17, which in part read:

But my steadfast love shall not depart from you,
and my covenant of peace shall not be removed . . .
In righteousness [ṣĕdāqâ] you shall be established. . . .
This is the heritage of the servants of the LORD
and their vindication [ṣĕdāqâ] from me, says the LORD. (vv. 10, 14, 17)

Regarding the above text Schrenk says, "God's righteousness as His judicial reign means that in covenant faithfulness to His people He vindicates and saves them."[6]

If then God acts in righteousness to grant his people a new status, how must they respond? As already noted, every relationship has claims upon conduct. If God's righteousness is God's saving acts, what is the nature of the claims upon conduct that are required from God's people?

3. Righteousness is also a human response to the verdict of "innocent/righteous," which is received as a gift of God. The unspeakable gracious gift of acceptance in the presence of God requires the faithful to respond. Remembering the overlap in meaning between justice and righteousness, it is clear that the righteous person is the one who acts justly. Furthermore that justice/righteousness is not simply "giving every man his due" but includes showing mercy and compassion to the outcast, the oppressed, the weak, the orphan and the widow.

Job is a classical example of a righteous man. When under attack Job defends himself by saying:

I put on righteousness, and it clothed me;
my justice was like a robe and turban.
I was eyes to the blind,
and feet to the lame.
I was a father to the poor,
and I searched out the cause of him whom I did not know. (Job 29:14-16)

Here, as elsewhere, righteousness and justice overlap, and at times are synonyms. And the righteousness that Job claims for himself is compassionate acts for the weak and vulnerable, not objective application of law. Isaiah describes the suffering servant by saying:

---

[5]Rudolf Bultmann, *Theology of the New Testament* (New York: Scribner, 1955), pp. 272-73.
[6]Schrenk, "δίκη, δίκαιος, δικαιοσύνη," p. 195.

A bruised reed he will not break,
and a dimly burning wick he will not quench;
he will faithfully bring forth justice. (Is 42:3)

The nature of the justice that this unique servant of God will demonstrate is
compassionate acts on behalf of the broken and exhausted. Micah continues to
clarify this definition of righteousness by recalling God's "righteousnesses" in deliverance of his people during the exodus. How then should the people respond?
the prophet asks:

With what shall I come before the LORD,
and bow myself before God on high? (Mic 6:6)

Israel personified muses as to whether God wants burned offerings, thousands
of rams, ten thousands of rivers of oil or even the offering of his firstborn. The implied answer is no! The prophet then addresses Israel and says, "He has showed
you, O man, what is good" (Mic 6:8).

Where did God demonstrate the pattern of response that he expects from Israel? Where did he show them "what is good"? The answer is obvious—Israel was
given the expected pattern of response in the saving acts of God toward the nation
(which had just been reviewed in the previous verses). God's great mercy to them
in the exodus and its aftermath was the pattern of the kinds of compassionate acts
that he expected from them toward others. A distillation of these expectations
then appears in the final lines of this passage which read:

And what does the LORD require of you
but to do justice, and to love kindness
and to walk humbly with your God? (v. 8)

How *God treated them* in their need is the model for how *they are to treat others.*

4. Finally righteousness is also connected to peace. This appears in Isaiah 32,
which reads in part:

And the effect of righteousness will be peace,
and the result of righteousness, quietness and trust for ever.
My people will live in a peaceful habitation,
in secure dwellings, and in quiet resting places. . . .
Happy ['*aśrêkem*/blessed] are you who sow beside all waters,
who let the feet of the ox and the ass range free. (vv. 17-18, 20)

Where righteousness and peace are maintained, even the *domestic* animals are
free.

To summarize, blessed are those who strive for righteousness with the same earnestness with which the hungry and thirsty seek food and drink. God's right-eousness is his acts in history to save. That salvation grants to his people the gift of acceptance before him. They in turn tirelessly seek a lifestyle appropriate to the relationship granted to them as a gift. They will model their response after how God has dealt with them in his mighty acts on their behalf. That response will in-clude justice and compassion for the weak.

This Beatitude concludes, "For they shall be satisfied." This is another case of the "divine passive." God is the one who will satisfy them. For many this is a strange idea. Popularly understood righteousness is no more than adherence to an ethical norm. The person who keeps the law, follows the accepted standards of the community and has an admirable personal life will be respected and thereby satis-fied *by the community*. But if righteousness describes a relationship granted as a gift of God that brings peace, then only God can satisfy the longing for that righteous-ness and the approval or disapproval of the community is irrelevant. We are not righteous to please our peers but to show gratitude to God and maintain our rela-tionship with him.

Each day, prompted by hunger and thirst, all people seek food and water, hop-ing to be satisfied. But for how long? A few hours later the cravings return. This Beatitude makes clear that the bless-ed are those whose drive for righteousness is as pervasive, all-consuming and recurring as the daily yearning to satisfy hunger and thirst. Hungering and thirsting for that righteousness can only be satisfied by God.

Everyone who wants to lose weight struggles to curb urges for food and drink. Pills, mind games, exercise, self-control, group peer pressure and the like are all enlisted in the battle against those urges. Among the bless-ed, urges for righteous-ness are equally as powerful but need not be restricted, rather they can be in-dulged—and they are satisfied by a gracious God. You can pig-out on righteous-ness with no negative side effects.

Von Rad summarizes the topic by saying, "Tsdqh can be described without more ado as the highest value in life, that upon which all life rests when it is prop-erly ordered."[7]

FIFTH BEATITUDE

Blessed are the merciful,
for they shall obtain mercy.

---

[7]Von Rad, *Old Testament Theology*, 2:370.

"Showing mercy" has two basic meanings. The first has to do with compassion that is composed of feelings and actions. The father in the story of the prodigal son "had compassion" and "ran." His merciful feelings translated into dramatic actions. Again and again Jesus is described as having compassion for the needy around him (Mt 9:36; 14:14; 18:27; Mk 1:41; 6:34; Lk 7:13; 10:33). At times the feelings are not mentioned and only the compassionate action is recorded. The blind beggar beside the road cried out to Jesus "Son of David, have mercy on me" (Lk 18:38). Jesus responds with healing. To respond to human need with compassion and action is at the core of what being merciful is all about. But there is more.

To be merciful and to obtain mercy are profoundly related to forgiving and being forgiven. But here again we face a paradox that is like a diamond. Any attempt to force a diamond to shed all its light in one direction would destroy it. In like manner the paradox of giving and receiving mercy/forgiveness has to do with three questions: (1) Do we forgive others *as God forgives us?* (2) Or do we forgive others first *so that God will then forgive us?* Or finally, (3) does *God forgive us* and *then we are able to forgive others?* All three of these ideas are available in the New Testament in the following texts.

1. The Lord's Prayer in Matthew 6:9-13 asks that God "forgive us" our sins (our trespasses and debts) "*as* we forgive" the sins of others against us. It sounds as if the two forms of forgiveness happen in parallel.

2. But the Lord's Prayer in Luke 11:4 reads, "Forgive us our sins, *for we ourselves forgive every one who is indebted to us*" (italics added). This reading of the Lord's Prayer affirms that we must forgive others before we can approach God seeking forgiveness for ourselves.

3. Finally there is the story of the unforgiving servant (Mt 18:23-35) who was first forgiven by his master but then refused to forgive another servant. For his failure he was condemned; as 1 John 4:19 affirms, "We love, because he first loved us."

Which of these three patterns of forgiveness best explain this Beatitude? Or should we choose all three? In the ever-changing challenges of striving to be faithful, all three mysteriously make sense. They do not fit together logically, but whoever claimed that mercy and forgiveness are logical? All three are important for Christian faith and life.

To show mercy or to forgive is extremely difficult for those who have been deeply wronged. But the alternative is self-destruction through nursing grudges or seeking revenge. Such grievances are often passed on from generation to generation and become a destructive force in the lives of individuals and societies. The bless-ed escape these self-crippling cycles, for they are merciful. But there is more.

This Beatitude claims that the merciful "shall obtain mercy." From whom will they obtain mercy? Here again Jesus uses a "divine passive." That is, the merciful will obtain the mercy of God. The mercy of their fellow human beings may be in short supply but the mercy of God will never fail them.

SIXTH BEATITUDE

> Blessed are the pure in heart
> for they shall see God.

In the context of Jesus' world, the emphasis here affirmed is striking. The psalms do indeed affirm the need for an interior purity—a purity of heart. Psalm 24:3-4 says:

> Who shall ascend the hill of the LORD?
> And who shall stand in his holy place?
> He who has clean hands and a pure heart.

External purity (clean hands) is not enough, it must be accompanied by an internal purity (pure heart). As seen here, both of these aspects of purity were in the tradition available to Jesus. However the developing rabbinic tradition placed a clear emphasis on the first. The Mishnah includes an entire division on the subject titled "Tohoroth" (cleannesses) that continues for nearly two hundred pages and includes eleven tractates.[8] Among the rabbis quoted in these tractates is the great Hillel, who lived one generation before Jesus. Clearly this extended discussion on cleanliness was in process of development in the first century. It includes tractates on vessels, tents, immersion pools and hands, but not hearts. There are three levels of uncleanness discussed, and hands are always on the second and third level. In this case Jesus is not critical of the developing laws on ceremonial purity, but he makes the courageous decision to place his entire emphasis on purity of heart. What then is meant by the heart?

Søren Kierkegaard, the Danish philosopher-theologian of the nineteenth century, is well known for his argument that the pure in heart are those who will one thing. He recognized the reality that often behind human behavior lies a multiplicity of motives. With the pure in heart, "what you see is what you get," as the

---

[8]*The Mishnah*, ed. and trans. Herbert Danby (1933; reprint, Oxford: Oxford University Press, 1980), pp. 601-789. Hereafter, a Mishnah text from this volume will be presented in shortened form.

colloquial phrase has it. They have one motive for what they do, and they harbor no hidden agendas.

But what exactly is the "heart" in biblical literature? Modern Western culture limits the word *heart* to the feelings. But the heart in the Hebrew mind included the entire interior life of the person. The feelings, the mind and the will were all part of "the heart."[9] The bless-ed exhibit purity in all three of these aspects of the interior world. That purity opens the road to a transparency that can be described as purity of heart.

But how is it that "they shall see God?" This phrase has to do with knowledge or vision of God, and not with physical sight. John 1:18 says, "No one has ever seen God." But knowledge of God and a vision of him are the privileges granted to the angels—and the pure in heart.

SEVENTH BEATITUDE

> Blessed are the peacemakers,
> for they shall be called sons of God.

Peace is often limited to absence of war or the cessation of violence. Ceasefires and surrenders are important as preambles to peace. But peace in the Bible includes the finest of loving relationships between individuals, within families, communities and nations. Peace also includes good health. The peace here discussed is primarily the peace of God, which includes all of the above and "passes all understanding" (Phil 4:7). The word *peacemaker* appears only here in the entire Bible. Semitic languages are obliged to break this unique word into two. It is neither the "peaceful" nor the "pacifists" but the peacemakers.

Given this broad scope of peacemaking, it is easy to see why Jesus called such people "sons/children of God."

EIGHTH BEATITUDE

> Blessed are those who are persecuted for righteousness' sake,
> for theirs is the kingdom of heaven.

People can be opposed or rejected because they are lazy or untrustworthy. Some are fired from their jobs because they cannot get along with others or because they show attitudes that are counterproductive to what their organization is trying to do. At times such folk try to see themselves as "persecuted for righteousness' sake."

We have already defined righteousness to include God's saving acts in history,

---

[9]W. D. Davies and Dale C. Allison Jr., *The Gospel According to Saint Matthew* (New York: T & T Clark, 1988), 1:456.

acceptance in the presence of God and a lifestyle that maintains that relationship. Those who find themselves despised because they promote such things can legitimately claim that they are "persecuted for righteousness' sake" and that the kingdom is theirs.

NINTH BEATITUDE

The ninth Beatitude has the following classical rhetorical style, illustrated in figure 6.1.

Blessed are you when people revile you	
and persecute you	–
and utter all kinds of evil against you falsely	–
on my account.	Jesus
Rejoice and be glad,	+
for your reward is great in heaven,	+
for in the same way they persecuted the prophets who were before you.	

Figure 6.1. The rhetorical style of the ninth Beatitude

The Beatitude style is here expanded into a "theological sandwich." If the five phrases in the middle are removed, this Beatitude would read:

Blessed are you when men revile you
For so men persecuted the prophets who were before you.

All together the text exhibits seven phrases, which is the classical perfect number. What do these phrases mean?

First, we observe that the Beatitude can be reduced to the following:

1. opening line
  2. two negative statements
    3. a *reference to Jesus,*
  4. two positive statements
5. closing line

The opening and closing lines are like the bun of the sandwich. The two negative and two positive statements are like two slices of pickle. The climax comes in the center. This has been called "ring composition" or "inverted parallelism." Other scholars refer to it as "chiasm."

This ancient Jewish pattern of writing was known both to Jesus' listeners and Matthew's readers. It is possible to read the opening and the closing lines as the original Beatitude that was spoken by Jesus. The extra material in the center that turns the Beatitude into a "sandwich" can be seen as an addition to the original saying of Jesus that was created by the church as it began to suffer persecution. That is, Jesus taught the disciples the two-line Beatitude. The disciples added the new material in its center. A second option would be to understand that, late in his ministry, after hostility intensified, Jesus could have expanded his own Beatitude. In either case, the meaning of the "sandwich" is clear. The prophets were faithful and were persecuted. When Jesus' followers are faithful and oppressed for that faithfulness they can rejoice that they have joined the company of the classical prophets and live in the confidence of a great reward. The person of Jesus is the center climax of the seven phrases.

A critical shift has now taken place in the Beatitudes. Up to this point, all of them can be explained out of the Hebrew Scriptures. Yet something has been creeping up on the reader. These eight lofty standards have their finest expression in the life of Jesus. The reader gradually comes to this conclusion as the list lengthens. In the ninth Beatitude loyalty to the person of Jesus is openly introduced. That same loyalty is inevitable if the reader turns to Jesus as a model for the fulfillment of the pattern of righteousness here portrayed.

Jesus may have given his disciples explanatory comments on other Beatitudes, which Matthew did not have the space to record. This last Beatitude, with its interior expansions may have been recorded by Matthew because of the persecutions through which Matthew's readers were passing.

With the conversion of Emperor Constantine to the Christian faith, "the age of martyrs" officially ended. But the twentieth century saw far more Christians die for their faith than was known in the early centuries. In Armenia, Russia, China and the southern Sudan, millions in the modern age have died for their loyalty to Jesus Christ. This final Beatitude, with its expansions, still speaks powerfully to the global church.

SUMMARY: THE BEATITUDES 2

Ideas noted in this theologically rich passage are as follows:

1. Hunger and thirst are powerful images used to describe the strong urge lodged in the hearts of the bless-ed for righteousness. They are bless-ed in that they continue to search like the merchant who searches for a pearl of great price.

2. Righteousness does not refer to an abstract ethical ideal but to the claims of a relationship.

3. The righteousness of God refers to his saving acts in history.

4. Israel's righteousness is the free gift of a verdict about Israel given by God. Israel is declared righteous by God.

5. Israel's response to this gift is to act justly, which includes compassion for the needy, such as was exhibited by Job and the suffering servant of Isaiah.

6. Israel's model for their response is shown in God's dealings with them in the exodus. They are to treat others with the same compassion they received from God.

7. Righteousness creates peace.

8. God, not the community, satisfies the yearning for righteousness.

9. To be merciful is to respond to the needs of others with compassion and action.

10. Showing mercy is related to forgiveness. God's forgiveness of us is related to our forgiveness of others in three ways in the New Testament. God grants mercy to the bless-ed; the community may fail to do so.

11. The *heart* refers to the entire internal life of the person and includes feelings, mind and will. Jesus focuses on the heart, not the hands.

12. Purity of heart has to do with transparency and singleness of motive that can will one thing.

13. Peacemakers are different from peacekeepers and pacifists. Peacemakers work for healed relationships on all levels and will be called "children of God."

14. Jesus is the model for all the Beatitudes, and he "walks on stage" for the first time in the final Beatitude—on persecution for his sake. Those so persecuted can rejoice in having joined the prophetic fellowship of suffering.

PART THREE

The Lord's Prayer

7

The Lord's Prayer: *God Our Father*

MATTHEW 6:5-9

AFTER THE FALL OF THE SOVIET UNION I was privileged to lecture in Riga for the Latvian Lutheran Church. Most of the participants in the seminar were between the ages of 25-35. This meant that all of their education had been in the communist state system, which was determined to indoctrinate them in atheism. I asked one of the young women about how she came to faith.

> "Was there a church in your village?" I asked.
> "No, the communists closed all of them," she replied.
> "Did some saintly grandmother instruct you in the ways of God?"
> "No. All the members of my family were atheists."
> "Did you have secret home Bible studies, or was there an underground church in your area?"
> "No, none of that" came the answer.
> "So, what happened?"

She told me the following story:

> At funerals we were allowed to recite the Lord's Prayer. As a young child I heard those strange words and had no idea who we were talking to, what the words meant, where they came from or why we were reciting them. When freedom came at last, I had the opportunity to search for their meaning. When you are in total darkness, the tiniest point of light is very bright. For me the Lord's Prayer was that point of light. By the time I found its meaning I was a Christian.

The next four chapters will try to uncover some of the meaning of this very bright point of light.

The Lord's Prayer in Matthew is our focus and its important introduction deserves reflection.

EMPTY PHRASES

Before teaching the prayer, Jesus offers his disciples some advice about how to pray:

> When you are praying,
> do not heap up empty phrases as the Gentiles do;
> for they think that they will be heard
> because of their many words. (Mt 6:7 NRSV)

This is puzzling. On the one hand the prayers of Jesus, recorded in the Gospels, are quite short. On the other hand those same Gospels relate that occasionally Jesus prayed all night. This raises the question of the nature of prayer. Did prayer for Jesus include long periods of Spirit-filled silent communion with God that was beyond the need for words?

The Fathers of the Eastern Churches certainly thought so. In the seventh century, Isaac the Syrian wrote about "stillness," which in his writings has been summarized as "a deliberate denial of the gift of words for the sake of achieving inner silence, in the midst of which a person can hear the presence of God. It is standing unceasingly, silent, and prayerfully before God."[1]

It is easy to assume that a long prayer equals a good prayer and a short prayer is an immature prayer. The Gospel account contradicts this. In Matthew 6:7-8 Jesus criticizes the Gentiles for long prayers. When they addressed their gods (which usually included the reigning emperor), the Gentiles used long salutations. They wanted to be sure to use all the correct titles lest the god (Caesar?) take offense. How ponderous this could become appears in the titular names for Galerius Caesar. In the early fourth century a Christian historian named Eusebius quoted a decree issued by Galerius easing the persecution of Christians just before the age of Constantine. It opens:

> The emperor Caesar, Galerius, Valerius, Maximanus, Invictus, Augustus, Pontifex Maximus, Germanicus Maximus, Egypticus Maximus, Phoebicus Maximus, Sarmenticus Maximus [five times], Persecus Maximus [twice], Carpicus Maximus [six times], Armenicus Maximus, Medicus Maximus, Abendicus Maximus, Holder of tribunical authority for the 20th time, emperor for the 19th, consul for the 8th, Pater Patriae Pro-Consul . . ."[2]

---

[1]Helarion Alfeyev, *The Spiritual World of Isaac the Syrian* (Kalamazoo, Mich.: Cisercian Publications, 2000), p. 77.
[2]Eusebius *The History of the Church* 17.5, trans. G. A. Williamson (Baltimore: Penguin Books, 1965), pp. 353-54.

This is how Caesar understood himself and is no doubt the way he expected to be addressed. Such a manner was deemed appropriate and continued in the Middle East through the nineteenth century.

In 1891 a Persian scholar wrote to an American Christian missionary scholar, Dr. Cornelius VanDyke, who at that time was a distinguished professor of medicine in Beirut, Lebanon. The Persian gentleman sent a gift to VanDyke to commemorate his visit to the good doctor. With the gift, he included a covering note:

> A souvenir to the esteemed spiritual physician and religious philosopher, his Excellency, the only and most learned who has no second in his age, Dr. Cornelius VanDyke, the American. As a souvenir presented to his loftiness and goodness and to him that is above titles, who is a propagator of knowledge and the founder of perfections, and a possessor of high qualities and owner of praiseworthy character, the pole of the firmament of virtues and the pivot of the circle of sciences, the author of splendid works and firm foundations, who is well versed in the understanding of the inner realities of soul and horizons, who deserves that his name be written with light upon the eyes of the people rather with gold on paper, at Beirut, in the month of Rabia, in the year 1891, by the most humble.[3]

I trust that Dr. VanDyke was appropriately impressed! Jesus declares that God neither needs nor wants any of this. The one who prays, taught Jesus, must talk to God in a simple, direct fashion. "Do not heap up empty phrases as the Gentiles" was the standard.

In Ecclesiastes the preacher touches on the same topic as he offers advice on how to pray when entering the house of God. He writes, "Be not rash with your mouth, nor let your heart be hasty to utter a word before God, for God is in heaven, and you upon earth; therefore let your words be few" (Eccles 5:2).

In the modern world we are drowning in words. Each day we are bombarded with thousands of billboards, ads, letters, magazines, newspapers, television commercials, radio broadcasts, spam, catalogs, junk mail, phone calls, text messages, faxes and endless email. One can no longer sit in a doctor's office without having thousands of words poured uninvited into the ears. Recently I sat in the departure lounge of an international airport inundated with words. At one time, I could clearly hear seven cell phone conversations, two televisions, a public announcement and three departure announcements. It was the first circle of hell.

We are immersed in words and in the process they have become cheap. Rarely

---

[3]Kenneth E. Bailey, private papers. This document was translated from Persian to English and given to me in 1978 by Dr. Jabril Jabbur, professor of Middle Eastern Languages and Literature at the American University of Beirut, Lebanon.

are words heard as pearls, carefully selected and artistically strung on a golden thread called a sentence. Jesus invites the reader to step into a world where words are few and powerful. In such a world each word must be examined with the care it deserves. With this in mind, it is appropriate to reflect briefly on the style and language of prayer as the disciples must have known it.

THE STYLE AND LANGUAGE OF PRAYER

The Jews knew how to pray, and the pious, like Daniel (Dan 6:10), prayed three times a day: at sunrise, at three o'clock in the afternoon and finally at sundown. This practice was most likely widespread long before Jesus' time. Yet nowhere in the Gospels does Jesus suggest special hours for daily prayer. By its absence, this is the first change to appear in the pattern of prayer commended by Jesus.

The form of the Jewish daily prayer began with the recital of Deuteronomy 6:4-5 which opens with, "Hear, O Israel, the LORD our God is one LORD." Then came a series of eighteen prayers called *Amidah* (standing), because they were prayed while standing. These are also commonly referred to simply as *Tefillah* (prayers) and were in use in some form during Jesus' lifetime. They remain in use in synagogue services today.[4]

There are important points of similarity and difference between these eighteen prayers and the Lord's Prayer. For example, a request for daily bread occurs at about the same place in the middle of both the *Tefillah* and the Lord's Prayer. Some introductory phrases are similar. Both prayers talk about the needs of the present, and both mention the coming kingdom of God. Some of the same rhymes and rhythms appear in each. The doxologies of the two overlap. Finally, both are intended for individual as well as community use. Differences will be noted as we proceed.

THE OPENING PHRASE OF THE LORD'S PRAYER

The first request of the Lord's Prayer flashes across the sky like the opening burst of thunder in a summer storm.

> Our Father who is in heaven,
> let it be hallowed your name. (my translation)

The above word order preserves the flow of the Semitic sentence as it appears in the original Greek and as it is faithfully translated in the three Syriac versions of the Gospels.

---

[4]Joseph Hertz, *The Authorised Daily Prayer Book* (1948; reprint, New York: Bloch, 1979), pp. 130-51.

The *Tefillah* are in Hebrew. The modern consensus among scholars is that the Lord's Prayer begins with the Aramaic word *abba* and therefore we can assume that Jesus taught his disciples to pray in the Aramaic of daily communication rather than in the classical Hebrew of written texts.[5] The Aramaic-speaking Jew in the first century was accustomed to recite his prayers in Hebrew, not Aramaic. Similarly, Muslim worshipers always recite their traditional prayers in the classical Arabic of seventh-century Arabia. Both Judaism and Islam have a sacred language. Christianity does not. This fact is of enormous significance.

The use of Aramaic in worship was a major upheaval in the assumptions of Jesus' day. It meant that for Jesus no sacred language was "the language of God." Across the Christian world jokes circulate about people who assume a particular language to be *the* divine language. My Armenian friends tell me that God has a very learned Armenian monk as his private secretary. This monk knows all the languages of the world, and when prayers from around the world arise to the throne of grace, this clever monk immediately translates them into classical Armenian so that God will be able to understand! A generation ago there were many English speakers who were *very sure* God spoke the King James English. My saintly British mother once confessed to me her shock as a teenager when she discovered that the apostle Paul did not speak English!

Jesus lived in a world where the public reading of the Bible was only in Hebrew, and prayers had to be offered in that language. When Jesus took the giant step of endorsing Aramaic as an acceptable language for prayer and worship, he opened the door for the New Testament to be written in Greek (not Hebrew) and then translated into other languages.

It follows that if there is no sacred language, there is no sacred culture. All of this is a natural outgrowth of the incarnation. If the Word is translated from the divine to the human and becomes flesh, then the door is opened for that Word to again be translated into other cultures and languages. This thesis has been brilliantly explored by Lamin Sanneh in his influential book *Translating the Message.*[6] The long term result is a global church of more than two billion people, almost all of whom have the Bible available in their own language. Believers are thereby able to break into God's presence using the language of the heart. We are so accustomed to this heritage that we scarcely notice its beginning, which was Jesus' choice of Aramaic as the language of the Lord's Prayer. Jesus affirmed the

---

[5]W. D. Davies and Dale C. Allison Jr., *The Gospel According to Saint Matthew* (New York: T & T Clark, 1988), 1:600.
[6]Lamin Sanneh, *Translating the Message* (Maryknoll, N.Y.: Orbis, 1989).

translatability of the message when he began this prayer with the great word *abba*. We turn now to an examination of its meaning.

ABBA'S MEANING AND SIGNIFICANCE

The traditional synagogue prayers of the *Tefillah* begin in different ways. Some of the eighteen open with "God of Abraham, God of Isaac and God of Jacob." "God of our Fathers" also appears. Elsewhere in the *Tefillah* God is addressed as "blessed one," "holy one," "builder of Jerusalem," "mighty one," "redeemer of Israel," "our father" and "gracious one." From this list Jesus chose "Our Father," which appears twice in the *Tefillah* as *Abinu* (Hebrew).[7] To address God as "the God of Abraham, Isaac and of Jacob" is to pray the prayer of a particular people with a particular history. To be sure, Christians are adopted into that great family and thereby these names have rich meanings for all Christians. At the same time, when Jesus taught his disciples to pray *"abba,"* he affirmed a vision of a family of faith that went beyond the community of those who claimed a racial tie to Abraham. By contrast, every human being, of any tribe or nation has a father. Thereby if God is "Our Father," all people are able to address him equally. There is no racial or historical "insider" and "outsider" with the word *abba*.

In addition to noting the inclusive power of this word, it is necessary to inquire into the word itself. What did Jesus mean when he called God *abba*, and how was this word used in his day?

The Aramaic word *abba* (father) was used by an Aramaic-speaking person in talking to his or her earthly father. It was also used to address a respected person of rank. A student could use this word to address a teacher or a child his father.

"Abba" appears three times in the New Testament: on the lips of Jesus in Mark 14:36, in Romans 8:15 and in Galatians 4:6. In each case the Greek expression *ho patēr* (the Father) immediately follows. The writer records the Aramaic word *abba* and then translates it for his Greek readers who may not know Aramaic. Thus the original Greek in each case reads *Abba, ho patēr* (with both Aramaic and Greek side by side in a single phrase). Why this dual language phrase?

It would have been much simpler to be content with *ho patēr* (father). Evidently the word *abba* was so important to the apostolic community that it was retained, even when they were writing in Greek and knew some readers would not understand the Aramaic. All three occurrences of this word in the New Testament are fervent prayers. In Mark 14:36 Jesus is praying in the Garden of Gethsemane.

---

[7]*Abinu* appears in prayers 5 (titled *Teshuba*) and 6 (titled *Selhah*).

The best understanding as to why this Aramaic word was preserved in Greek is to realize that Jesus himself used *abba* as a name for his heavenly father, and taught his disciples to follow his example. He was not the first in the Jewish tradition to do so.

In the Old Testament, the word *father* is used a dozen times in connection with God. Sometimes it is a simile (i.e., "this is *like* that"; see Ps 103:13) and occasionally as a metaphor (i.e., "this *is* that"; see Is 63:16; 64:8), but never as a direct address. In the Jewish writings between the Old and New Testaments (known as the Apocrypha), the word *Father* does occur (in Greek) as a direct address to God (Wisdom of Solomon 14:3) although it is rare. The difference can be seen in any language. To say, "You care for us *like* a father" (simile) or even "You *are* our Father" (metaphor) is one thing, but to say "Good morning, Father" is quite different. The first and second are descriptions, the third is a title. In the Old Testament, *father* is used to describe what God is like. Jesus used it, in Aramaic, as a title. Jesus' use of this word is not unique but has been called "distinctive." Davies and Allison explain:

> Thus, despite legitimate reservations about uniqueness, it appears that when Jesus addressed his prayers to 'abba, he was to some extent differentiating himself from common practice; and perhaps many if not most Jews would have found it awkward and even perhaps verging on the impious to address God simply as *'abba.'*[8]

At the end of the day Jesus could have chosen any one of many words with which to address God; he selected the Aramaic word *abba*.

In at least four countries in the Middle East today, *abba* is still the first word that a young child learns. Several years ago I was privileged to teach the Lord's Prayer in Arabic to a group of village women in the Lebanese mountains. In class I was describing *abba* as a first-century Aramaic word, and as I spoke I noted a certain embarrassed restlessness in the class. I finally stopped and asked the women if they had any comments. One woman at the back shyly put up her hand and very gently told this poor foreigner, "Dr. Bailey, *abba* is the first word we teach our children." On investigating I found this to be true across Lebanon, Syria, Palestine and Jordan. These countries were once all Aramaic speaking, and this precious word has survived even though the language of the people is now Arabic.[9]

The long "a" at the end of the word is the definite article in Aramaic. *Abba* literally means "The Father." But in context it can also mean "My Father" or "Our

---

[8]Davies, *Gospel According to Matthew,* 2:602.
[9]The colloquial Arabic word is *Baba* and the classical is *Abi*. Before a child learns to say *Baba,* he or she is taught to say *Abba*.

Father."[10] Luke's version of the Lord's Prayer opens with "Father" while Matthew begins with "Our Father." Both are legitimate translations of *abba*.

This great Aramaic word affirms both respect in addressing a superior and a profound personal relationship between the one who uses it and the one addressed. It is easy to understand why the early Christian church continued to use it even while praying in Greek. It invoked the quality of relationship the believer had with God through Christ. The early Christian use of the Lord's Prayer substantiates this meaning.

Some of the earliest church buildings that have survived were built with two sections, one for believers and one for the people called catechumens. The latter were people who had not yet professed belief in Jesus and were thereby not baptized. The catechumens sat in a special section at the back. They were welcomed into worship even though they were not yet fully committed to the Christian faith. They would attend, sing the hymns, listen to the sermon and then be politely ushered out. Those who had accepted faith in Christ and had been baptized would remain and participate in the celebration of Holy Communion. It was deemed inappropriate for those not yet baptized to take part in this sacred meal. In their services these Christians always prayed the Lord's Prayer just before Holy Communion.[11] Apparently the church felt that this title for God should only be used by those who had believed and been baptized.

The German biblical scholar Joachim Jeremias was mistaken when he argued that this address in Aramaic on Jesus' lips was unique.[12] It did however affirm a special relationship with the one addressed. Strangers to the Christian faith were not, it seems, encouraged to address God as *Abba*. But there is more.

The title "father" for God has been widely debated over the last fifty years in the Western church. Two aspects of this subject are worthy of note. First there is the Islamic warning. To call God "Father," "My Father" or "Our Father" involves the worshiper in using a human model for God. Islam insists that such a practice will inevitably lead the worshiper down a slippery slope to idolatry. God is God and should not be described in human terms. God can be addressed using adjectives, but not metaphors. God is *rahman* (merciful) and *raheem* (compassionate), *akbar* (all powerful), *'alim* (all knowing) but never "Father." Of Islam's famous ninety-nine names for God, three can marginally be considered metaphors. The

---

[10]Gerhard Kittel, "αββα," *Theological Dictionary of the New Testament,* ed. Gerhard Kittel and Gerhard Friedrich, trans. Geoffrey W. Bromiley (Grand Rapids: Eerdmans, 1964-76), 1:5-6.

[11]Modern Anglican and Roman Catholic liturgies continue this practice.

[12]Joachim Jeremias, *The Lord's Prayer* (Philadelphia: Fortress, 1969), pp. 17-20.

remaining ninety-six are clearly adjectives. What can be said in response?

The warning Islam offers the Christian faith is important for Christians to hear. The danger Islam speaks of is always present when metaphors are used as titles for God. Christians have often used the word *father* and given that word meanings based on experiences with human fathers. This is a form of idolatry. However, God is personal, and there are two kinds of persons, male and female. To address God with both male and female titles opens a path back to the ancient Middle East with its male and female gods and goddesses.[13] The way forward is to ask, Did Jesus define the term *father* in any of his teachings?

In the famous parable of the prodigal son, Jesus is best understood to be defining the word *father* for the use he intends to make of it. In that story Jesus breaks all bounds of human patriarchy and presents an image of a father that goes beyond anything his culture expected from any human father, as we will see. He was not describing fathers as he knew them but rather creating a new image that he intended to use as a model for God. Jesus' probable starting point was Hosea 11:1-9, where the prophet describes God as a compassionate father to Israel who cries out in agony:

I am God and not man,
the Holy One in your midst,
and I will not come to destroy. (Hos 11:9)

In the verses prior to this text Hosea presents God as a tender, loving father with a much-loved rebellious child. The father (God) has the right to respond with anger and punishment, but instead chooses to respond with love. Jesus inherited this understanding of the nature of his divine father from Hosea, and it is easy to assume that he began with Hosea 11, expanded its image of God as Father and created the well known parable. Jesus did not describe God as an emperor exercising absolute sway over his possessions (some fathers and mothers act in this fashion). Rather, Jesus called God "Father" and defined this term in the parable of the prodigal son. This is the only legitimate understanding of "our Father," and any other definition is a rejection of the teaching of Jesus and a betrayal of his person. The warning of Islam stands, and when Jesus is allowed to define his own term, the believing community avoids the idolatry that can follow the use of metaphors as titles for God.

From a second angle the word *abba* (father) is criticized as reflecting "Orien-

---

[13]Female similes are not a problem. In Isaiah God is "like a mighty man" (Is 42:13) and also "like a woman in travail" (Is 42:14). But the Bible never addresses God using both male and female titles.

tal patriarchy" with its subjugation of women. This is not the place to describe and debate the pros or cons of the various patterns of social and family structure in the Middle East. Whatever those patterns were and are, Jesus, in the parable of the prodigal son, does not reflect them. Assumptions in the Western church are often:

1. Oriental patriarchy treats women badly.

2. Jesus called God "Father" and thus affirmed the validity of oriental patriarchy with its harsh treatment of women.

3. Therefore, we can no longer accept to call God "Father."

Ibrahim Sa'id, a twentieth-century Egyptian Protestant scholar, wrote a thoughtful commentary on the Gospel of Luke. In his reflections on the parable of the prodigal son, Sa'id writes:

> The shepherd in his search for the sheep, and the woman in her search for the coin, do not do anything out of the ordinary beyond what anyone in their place would do. But the actions the father takes in the third story are unique, marvelous, divine actions which have not been done by any father in the past.[14]

Henri Nouwen wrote regarding the father in the parable:

> all boundaries of patriarchal behavior are broken through. This is not the picture of a remarkable father. This is the portrait of God, whose goodness, love, forgiveness, care, and compassion have no limits at all. Jesus presents God's generosity by using all the imagery that his culture provides, while constantly transforming it.[15]

Jesus chooses to use the metaphor of father in the parable and in the prayer he gave to his disciples. It is not a patriarchal image. As far as human language has been able to penetrate the mysteries of the nature of a loving God, this parable outstrips all other efforts known to me as it presents the only picture that legitimately defines the word *abba* in the opening phrase of the Lord's Prayer.

In conclusion the phrase in the prayer is "Our Father" not "My Father." The Psalms have frequent reference to "my God," and the personal relationship between the God of the Bible and the individual believer must not be ignored. Yet, as we will see, the Lord's Prayer affirms a family of God that has one Father, and this prayer includes all followers of Jesus in that family. What then can be said about the so called male bias of the title Father?

---

[14]Ibraham Sa'id, *Sharh Bisharat Luqa* (Commentary on the Gospel of Luke) (Beirut: Middle East Council of Churches, 1970), p. 395.

[15]Henri J. M. Nouwen, *The Return of the Prodigal* (New York: Doubleday, 1992), p. 131.

GOD: MALE AND FEMALE METAPHORS

The Bible describes God using both male and female images. On the one hand, he is given the title Father, a male image. At the same time, believers are told that we are "born of God" (1 Jn 3:9). If God gives birth, then God acts like a female. These two are brought together in Deuteronomy 32:18: "You were unmindful of the Rock that begot you, / and you forgot the God who gave you birth."

If we reject the biblical images of God as Father (because it is an exclusively male image), then we also need to reject female images such as "the new birth" (because they are exclusively female). I stand on "Mother Earth" and eat the fruits of "Mother Nature" and serve "the church, the mother of us all" who is "the bride of Christ." As a man, I do not want any of these changed. Jesus describes himself as a "mother hen" and as a woman who finds her lost coin. Paul uses the language of human birth by longing that "Christ might be formed in you." Furthermore the devil is always male in the New Testament, and we will create a hornet's nest of new problems if we try to develop "inclusive language" for our demonology. We can all rejoice that the Scriptures use both male and female metaphors to enrich the readers' understanding of God who is Spirit and thereby neither male nor female. Yet God's image contains both male and female in that both are created from that image (Gen 1:27). To substitute neutral terms for one or the other will inevitably impoverish the richness of the biblical similes and metaphors, or lead us to abandon them.

The Lord's Prayer affirms the critical role of the community in which this title, Father, is used. When using the phrase "Our Father" the worshiper is obliged to look down the pew and across the world and see brothers and sisters in every land. Only in the unity of the family of God is the title "Our Father" legitimately invoked. This brings us to the second part of the phrase.

ABBA WHO IS IN THE HEAVENS

Amazingly, coupled with the rich word *abba* there is a sharp contrast. This "loving father" is *in the heavens*. Modern life creates great distances between members of a family. But in traditional communities in the Middle East this is not the norm. There mother and father live in close proximity to their children for the duration of their lives. In short, the father is near and usually lives in the same house. In contrast, the *Abba* of Christian prayer is indeed near and yet far away; he is in the heavens. The worshiping community is part of the created world. *Abba* is the Creator. The faithful are servants and *Abba* is the Master. Mortals are born and they die, while *Abba* is the eternal One. *Abba*, the loving Father, is approachable and yet dwells in awesome majesty in the heavens in all his glory.

The Hebrew word *Amidah (Tefillah)* means "standing," and worshipers stood to pray the eighteen prayers out of respect for God. The earliest collection of the sayings of the rabbis reports that "The pious men of old used to wait an hour before they said the *Tefillah* that they might direct their heart toward God" (Mishnah *Berakot* 5.1). Entrance into his awesome presence was not a casual or flippant act.

Twice in the recent past it was my extraordinary privilege to personally greet Her Majesty Queen Elizabeth II, once at the Anglican Cathedral in Cyprus and once in her private residence at Windsor Castle, London. As one would expect, all of us who were involved in each occasion dressed immaculately, were properly attentive, focused and coached regarding what to say and how to say it. How much more should we sense the awesome nature of our approach to "Our Father who is in the heavens" and be appropriately prepared to address him?

SUMMARY: THE LORD'S PRAYER: *GOD OUR FATHER*

1. Jesus inaugurated a new age by praying in Aramaic. He thereby set aside the precious heritage of a sacred language and a sacred culture, and made every language into an adequate manger into which the Word of God could be placed.

2. His title for God was *Abba*, which means "Father" as well as "Our Father." This extraordinary title affirmed both a personal relationship and the deference that would be offered to a superior.

3. The accumulating of titles and phrases is discouraged. Words offered to God are precious, must be sincere and can be few.

4. Jesus taught his disciples to pray to God who is near and yet far away. He is "our Father" and at the same time is "in the heavens."

5. Set times for prayer are neither affirmed nor rejected. Jesus apparently wanted his followers to go beyond the pattern of three daily prayers, which was the practice of his day.

6. The title "God of Abraham, Isaac and Jacob" was set aside for the simple phrase *Our Father (abba)*. The new phrase placed all believers on the same level regardless of their racial ancestry or their community history.

7. The address *Abba* was preserved by the Greek-speaking church. It was a precious word that affirmed a special relationship between the worshiper and God. The title was rare and daring, although not unique.

8. "Our Father" is defined by Jesus in the parable of the prodigal son. No other

definition is legitimate. Human fathers and mothers (East or West) are never adequate to give this word its appropriate meaning. Metaphors for God carry with them the risk of idolatry. That idolatry can be avoided when we allow Jesus to define his terms.

9. God is "Our Father." The personal finds its deepest meaning in the communal. God is "my Father" because he is "Our Father."

8

The Lord's Prayer: *God's Holiness*

MATTHEW 6:9

IN CHAPTER SEVEN WE NOTED that the opening of the Lord's Prayer, "Our Father," invokes a loving God who is both near and "in the heavens." He is the Creator God who comes near to us in the incarnation. With the same phrase, Jesus also affirms that God exists apart from our awareness of him. The Bible assumes the existence of God and never argues for it. Prayer rests on the premise that the Creator God can hear us when we speak to him.

Having identified the One to whom we pray, namely "Our Father, who is in the heavens," the prayer presents six requests to God. These are:

1. Hallowed be thy name,
2. Thy kingdom come.
3. Thy will be done,
      On earth as it is in heaven.
4. Give us this day our daily bread;
5. And forgive us our debts,
      As we also have forgiven our debtors;
6. And lead us not into temptation,
      But deliver us from evil.

The first three are often called "Thou petitions" in that they focus on the eagle's-eye view, the metanarrative and remind the worshiper that he or she is a part of the great sweep of history. These are the great lofty themes of:

• making holy the name of God
• the coming of the kingdom of God
• the fulfilling of the will of God

The prayer then focuses on the contemporary world of the worshiper with his or her specific needs. These have been called the "we petitions" and they focus on

- daily bread
- forgiveness in community
- freedom from evil

Each of these six petitions involves an act of God, and each specifies or implies participation on the part of the believer. That is, each involves the sovereignty of God and the freedom and responsibility of the human person. This is as follows:

1. God makes his own name holy,
    and I am expected to live a holy life.

2. God brings in the kingdom,
    and I am to work toward the goal of its coming.

3. God fulfills his will,
    and I am to discover that will and obey it in daily life.

4. He gives the gift of daily bread,
    and I must work to earn it.

5. He forgives,
    and I must forgive.

6. He guides me away from evil,
    and I must live a life of righteousness.

The comprehensive nature of the six petitions, together with the address, is noted by Jeremias who wrote, "the Lord's Prayer is the clearest and, in spite of its terseness, the richest summary of Jesus' proclamation which we possess."[1]

Clearly this was a community-forming as well as a personal-identity-forming prayer.

Each of the three monotheistic religions has such a prayer. The central prayer of Islam is called the *Fatiha* (the opening), and it contains a single request which is, "Guide us in the straight path." That path is then defined in the prayer as

the path of those whom Thou hast blessed,
not of those against whom Thou are wrathful,
nor of those who are astray.[2]

For Islam, the straight path is the path laid out by Islamic law. This single pe-

---

[1]Joachim Jeremias, *The Lord's Prayer* (Philadelphia: Fortress, 1969), p. 16.
[2]Arthur J. Arberry, *The Koran Interpreted* (New York: Macmillan, 1955), 1:29.

tition in the *Fatiha* is in harmony with the overall importance of Islamic law in the religion of Islam.

The eighteen (finally nineteen) benedictions together are the central prayers of Judaism. The composition of these prayers began in the fourth century B.C. and achieved their "final editing" under Gamaliel II, around A.D. 100.[3] They are used in every synagogue service and are a critical component in the forming of Jewish identity. Fifteen out of the eighteen benedictions include petitions. Summarized these include:

4. Vouchsafe unto us—knowledge, understanding and intelligence.

5. Lead us back to Thy Torah, bring us near to Thy service; cause us to return.

6. Forgive us.

7. Look on our affliction; fight our fight; redeem us speedily.

8. Heal us from all our wounds.

9. Bless this year and all of its yield.

10. Blow the trumpet for our liberation; gather our exiles.

11. Restore our judges; establish our innocence.

12. May no hope be left to the slanderers; may all thine enemies be cut off.

13. Grant mercy for the elders, scribes, house of Israel and righteous proselytes.

14. Return to Jerusalem; build her speedily.

15. Cause the horn of David to sprout and bring victorious salvation.

16. Hear our prayer.

17. Return thy sacrificial service to the altar of thy house.

18. Grant peace, happiness, and blessing, grace, loving-kindness, and mercy upon us and upon all Israel Thy people; bless us, our Father, even all of us.

It is generally assumed that most of these prayers were in use at the time of Jesus and thus they are helpful in understanding the theological world of which he was a part. A full comparison between the Lord's Prayer and this collection is beyond the scope of this chapter, but a few observations may be helpful. The petitions include:

- A strong emphasis on Jerusalem and the temple (10, 11, 14, 17).

- A sacred book is identified and loyalty to it affirmed along with a request for knowledge and understanding (4, 5).

---

[3]J. H. Hertz, *Daily Prayer Book* (1948; reprint, New York: Bloch, 1979), p. 131.

- An emphasis on the suffering of the community and its need for relief and restoration (7, 8, 11, 13, 15, 17).

- Forgiveness is requested, but not connected to forgiveness of others (5, 6).

- A prayer for the blessing of the agricultural year (9).

- A call for an attack on the enemies *[ha-Minim]* (12).

- Request for mercy, the answering of prayer, along with peace and happiness. (16, 19).

With all of its honored and admirable aspects, the collection is clearly a prayer for a particular ethnic community centered in Jerusalem. Jesus de-Zionizes the tradition.[4] The Lord's Prayer contains no reference to Jerusalem or the temple, and the disciples are taught to pray for the kingdom of God to come "on earth," which reflects a global concern for all people. Forgiveness is tied to forgiving others. No attack on outsiders is voiced, and there is no request for God to look on the suffering of his people or for God to fight for them.

Any innovator in any age must deal with the tradition of the past. Some things are omitted while others are endorsed unchanged. Still others are accepted and revised through the introduction of new elements. Jesus is no exception. Noting in turn what he omits, what he endorses and what he revises by adding new elements is helpful in understanding his carefully crafted intent. This brings us to the first of the "Thou petitions."

HALLOWED BE THY NAME

After praying "Our Father, who is in heaven," Jesus continues with "May it be made holy, your name." This phrase presents a paradox. To pray to God that his name be made holy is a bit like saying, "May the wood become solid." Or "May the fire become hot." The wood is already solid and the fire already hot. God's name is the most holy reality there is. Everything else may be unclean, but the name of God is holy. It can however become defiled.

In Ezekiel 36:16-23 Israel is told that it had defiled the land by shedding blood and worshiping idols. God then drove the people out, and in the process God's own holy name was defiled in the eyes of the Gentiles/nations because God seemed to be too weak to save them. As illustrated in figure 8.1, God then announces:

---

[4]The entire series has been summarized as "general human needs (both spiritual and material) and national aspirations of Israel" (R. J. Zwi Werblowsky and G. Wigoder, eds., *The Encyclopedia of the Jewish Religion* [New York: Adama Books, 1987], p. 27).

But I had concern for my holy name	MY HOLY NAME
which the house of Israel caused to be profaned	Profaned
among the nations to which they came.	Among Gentiles
"Therefore say to the house of Israel, Thus says the Lord GOD	
It is not for your sake, O house of Israel	NOT FOR YOU
that I am about to act,	FOR MY
but for the sake of my holy name,	HOLY NAME
which you have profaned	Profaned
among the nations to which you came.	Among Gentiles
And I will make holy my great name."	I SANCTIFY MY NAME

Figure 8.1. Ezekiel 36:21-23

The above concept is that God makes his own name holy. This idea is clearly summarized in Ezekiel 20:41-42 which reads, "I will manifest my holiness among you in the sight of the nations. And you shall know that I am the LORD, when I bring you into the land of Israel." Karl Kuhn writes, "it is God himself who demonstrates His name to be holy."[5] Initially, therefore, the phrase "Sanctify/make holy Thy Name" is a work accomplished by God who makes his own name holy, by acting in history to save.

In a more focused sense this is *always true* when the word *to make holy* occurs in the passive. In the Hebrew Old Testament, when the verb *to make holy* is used in the passive, God is always the actor. It follows that the phrase in the Lord's Prayer "May your name be made holy" means "O God, we beseech you to make your own name holy." After all, no human could possibly carry out such an awesome divine act! But even with these ideas clearly in mind, the phrase is still mysterious, partly because the name of God is involved.

What is the significance of God's *name*, which is to be made holy? In its simplest expression the name of God is that point of approach to God where it is possible for humans to communicate with him. This idea comes from the ancient Middle East and is reflected in the speeches of Moses at the burning bush (Ex 3:1-22). There God speaks to Moses, who insists that he be told God's name. The assumption behind the story is that if Moses does not know God's name, he cannot communicate with God. The name is also a summary of the essence of God. To know the name of God is to affirm that God is personal, that he can be known

[5]Karl G. Kuhn, "ἅγιος," in *Theological Dictionary of the New Testament*, 10 vols., ed. Gerhard Kittel and Gerhard Friedrich, trans. Geoffrey W. Bromiley (Grand Rapids: Eerdmans, 1964-76), 1:90.

(Mt 28:19) and that revelation is always an act of God.

A brief diversion is warranted here. When a verb in the passive is connected to God, it is called "a divine passive." Jews of the first century were very careful not to use God's name unless it was absolutely necessary. They sensed that any casual use of God's holy name might inadvertently break the Ten Commandments by taking God's name "in vain" (Ex 20:7). To avoid this possibility they developed ways of referring to God without pronouncing his name. As a binding rule they substituted the words *Adoni* (my Lord) or *Elohim* for the divine name of God *(Yahweh)* when reading Scripture. Sometimes the circumlocution "angels" or even "the name" served the same purpose. In addition, they often simply put the phrase into the passive.

More than two hundred cases of the divine passive are found in the words of Jesus in the Gospels. This is one of the distinctive characteristics of Jesus' speech as a first century Jew. The sentence in the Lord's Prayer that we are examining is one of these divine passives. God is the actor in the process of making his name holy.[6]

This leads to the question of the connection between the holiness of God and the holiness of his people. God acts to reveal himself, that is his holiness, through great acts in history to save, and this involves his name. The community is watching. What effect does or should this have for them?

Because God is holy, his people must be holy (Deut 7:6; 26:18), and as they witness demonstrations of his holiness they are challenged to achieve and maintain that holiness. One of the clearest places where this great act of God demonstrating his holiness and calling forth holiness from his people is on display is the great vision of Isaiah in the temple (Is 6:1-10).

God makes his name holy by demonstrating his holiness. In Isaiah 6:1-5 the prophet describes his great vision of the holiness of God in the temple. In that sacred place he sees "the Lord sitting upon a throne, high and lifted up." Above him are seraphim, each with six wings. These heavenly beings cover their faces and their feet and cry out:

Holy, holy, holy is the LORD of hosts;
the whole earth is full of his glory.

Isaiah senses immediately that he is a man of unclean lips dwelling in the midst of a people of unclean lips. His nearness to the holiness of God brings about this awareness. The contrast between what he knows of his own life and the life of his

---

[6]Ibid., 1:91.

people, and this vision of the holiness of God reveals to him his uncleanness. The prophet then responds by saying:

> Woe is me! For I am lost;
> for I am a man of unclean lips,
> and I dwell in the midst of a people of unclean lips;
> for my eyes have seen the King,
> the LORD of hosts! (Is 6:5)

Isaiah does not then make a sacrifice through which he can purify himself and open a path to the holy God. Rather, when Isaiah cries out that he is unclean, God sends an angel to take a burning coal from the altar of sacrifice to purify his lips. Then God says, "Whom shall I send, and who will go for us?" And Isaiah replies, "Here am I! Send me." This text presents an important sequence which is:

1. Isaiah sees God demonstrating his holiness.
2. Suddenly aware of a lack of holiness, Isaiah cries out confessing his uncleanness.
3. God sends an angel to purify him with fire from the altar of sacrifice.
4. After Isaiah is purified, God challenges Isaiah with "Whom shall I send?"
5. The purified prophet responds, "Here am I, send me."

In the Lord's Prayer the believer, with the phrase "May thy name be made holy," calls for a demonstration of the holiness of God. That is, the worshiper is saying, "May God again demonstrate his holiness." This in turn expresses a willingness to participate in Isaiah's dramatic experience.

Yet, as seen in Ezekiel, we also see the broad sweep of God's mighty, saving acts in history, which are demonstrations of his holiness. At the same time Isaiah, alone in the temple, was given a vision of that very holiness. Both the individual experience of Isaiah and the sweeping narrative of Ezekiel stand behind the Lord's Prayer.

This brings us to reflect on an apparent sharp contrast that appears in the two opening phrases of the Lord's Prayer. In the first phrase, Jesus teaches that God is like a father who *loves us*. On the other hand, God is *holy*, and that holiness *demands purity*, which translates into *righteousness*. As that holiness is demonstrated we sense that we are unclean. Indeed, Israel's sin caused the very holiness of God to be defiled.

How can love and holiness be brought together? The first draws us to God, while the second, as with Isaiah, causes us to withdraw.

CAN LOVE AND HOLINESS COME TOGETHER?

How can God, in dealing with sinners, be both love, which seeks to forgive, and holiness, which requires standards of righteousness without which there must be judgment? The story of the prophet Hosea helps clarify the tension between these two aspects of God's nature.

God tells Hosea to marry a woman named Gomer, who appears to have immoral tendencies (Hos 1:2). Hosea marries her, and three children are born. But Hosea discovers that he is not the father of the last two. Soon afterward Gomer leaves him and becomes a prostitute, presumably in the temple of Baal. In time her usefulness to the cult comes to an end, and Hosea finds her for sale. Strangely, he buys her back and takes her home.

To renew his covenant with her, Hosea realizes that the great principles of *righteousness* and *justice* must prevail in their relationship. Her past behavior cannot and must not be repeated. But justice demands that she be stoned to death for sexual misbehavior. On the other hand, Hosea wants to live with her in a relationship filled with *love* and *mercy*, where the past is forgotten and a new life is begun. Hosea states their current needs as he says to her:

> I will betroth you to me for ever;
> I will betroth you to me in *righteousness* and in *justice*,
> in *steadfast love*, and in *mercy*. (Hos 2:19, italics added)

How can both sides of this equation be implemented given what Gomer has done? Is Hosea to affirm righteousness and justice or love and mercy? Hosea tells his personal story because in it he finds a metaphor for the divine relationship between God and his people. Hosea suffers the agony of rejected love and in the process discovers something of God's divine agony as he deals with his wayward people. Kuhn writes:

> In Hosea, therefore, the concept of holiness takes up into itself as the fullness of deity the thought of love—an insight never again attained in the OT. As Hosea himself in his shattered happiness learned to know love as the indestructible force which could save even his lost wife, so Yahweh's holiness as the sum of His being must contain the creative love which slays but also makes alive again (cf. Hos 6:1).[7]

God is *holy love*, and he faces *unholy nature*. Yet, in his holiness, God is able to reach out to love that unholy nature. Again Kuhn writes, "therefore the antithesis between God and man consists in the very love which overcomes it."[8]

---

[7]Ibid., 1:93.
[8]Ibid.

In the story of Jesus, the cross offers a more perfect resolution to this agony, where justice is served and ultimate, unqualified love is demonstrated.

SUMMARY: THE LORD'S PRAYER: *GOD'S HOLINESS*

What then can be distilled from this first petition in the Lord's Prayer?

1. Many petitions are omitted. There is no invocation of Abraham, Isaac and Jacob, and no prayers for land, temple or imprecations against enemies. The suffering Savior does not want his disciples to dwell on their suffering. Yet the reality of evil is not overlooked.

2. God's holiness is the essence of who he is and his name tells us that he is personal and yearns to be known.

3. That holy name can be defiled by the disobedience of his people.

4. Only God can act to make his name holy, and he does so through mighty acts in history to save (Ezek 36).

5. Because God is holy, his people are to be holy.

6. To "make his name holy" means for God "to demonstrate his holiness." Ezekiel anticipated this drama on an international scale. Isaiah was a witness to a demonstration of the holiness of God that affected his personal life (Is 6). Worshipers who pray the Lord's Prayer yearn for both.

7. The demonstration of the holiness of God, witnessed by Isaiah, invoked a process that included confession, cleansing, a challenge to mission and his response. All who pray "Hallowed be thy name" are affirming the hope of Ezekiel and asking for the experience of Isaiah.

8. The holiness of God requires purity and righteousness. When such lifestyles are not exhibited God cannot ignore their absence. But God is also love, and the love of God is affirmed by his title of "Abba" (Father). These two aspects of the known nature of God are conflicted in the heart of God by the reality of the lives of his people. Hosea understood the problem. The cross of Jesus is the ultimate solution to that problem.

As noted, the ancient rabbis are reported to have stood in silence for a full hour before they prayed the *Tefillah* (the eighteen prayers). With them, some quietness before God could well prepare us to pray these profound words.

The Lord's Prayer:
God's Kingdom and Our Bread

MATTHEW 6:10-11

HAVING BRIEFLY EXAMINED THE OPENING address to God and the request for God to demonstrate the holiness of his name, this chapter will focus on the second and third requests, which are:

> Let it come—thy kingdom,
> let it be done—thy will.

The above rough translation preserves the literal Semitic word order preserved in the Greek text.[1] Inherent within this petition is a philosophy of history. Consciously or unconsciously, every historian examines history with a particular philosophy of history in mind. Three are worth noting, and two of them were widespread at the time of Jesus.

THREE VIEWS OF HISTORY

1. One view declares that history is meaningless. If there is a God, that God is like a watchmaker who creates a watch, winds it up and leaves it on the table to run down gradually. Yes, there may be a God who has created the world, but that God has nothing to do with nature or history. The sun is gradually becoming colder, and life will finally end on earth. The struggles through which human history passes have no meaning, because there is no metanarrative to give it direction and purpose. Shakespeare's *Macbeth* expresses this view when he says,

> All our yesterdays have lighted fools the way to dusty death. Out, out, brief candle! Life's but a walking shadow, a poor player that struts and frets his hour upon the stage, and then is heard no more; it is a tale told by an idiot, full of sound and fury, signifying nothing. (*Macbeth*, Act 5, Scene 5)

---

[1]The Syriac and Arabic versions of this text use this word order.

2. A second view was promoted at the time of Jesus by Greek philosophy, which understood history as a series of events moving in circles. What happened before will happen again. It may require thousands of years, but history repeats itself. As we live out our lives we are simply reenacting an old drama that has already appeared on the world stage and which will one day reappear. Our lives may be full of "sound and fury" but yet they signify nothing.

3. Sections of both the Old and New Testaments, known as apocalyptical writings, offer a third view of history. This perspective views history to be like an arrow that moves toward a target called "the day of the LORD" (Amos 5:18) or "the kingdom of God" (Mk 1:15). In this view, history has direction and meaning. Caught up in the struggles of the present age, the faithful may not always be able to "see the big picture," but there is one. Furthermore, it is inappropriate for the individual to try too hard to discover that purpose in any particular event. No foot soldier can understand the wider scope of a great battle in which he or she is involved. With this third view of history, people can live out their lives with the quiet confidence that the One who holds the rudder of history has not fallen asleep. Building on this view of history, Jesus teaches his disciples to pray, "Thy kingdom come" and within that hope a series of paradoxes can be found.

THREE KINGDOM PARADOXES

The teaching of Jesus on the subject of the kingdom of God has been debated widely for centuries.[2] The subject is complicated by three paradoxes in Jesus' teachings that dominate the discussion. These three paradoxes can be likened to three trains moving side by side on three separate tracks. Each track has two rails. If anyone removes one rail or tries to separate the two or tries to bring them together, the train will wreck. Each train can move on its track only if the two rails are carefully balanced.

1. The first paradox regarding the kingdom of God is that the *kingdom has already come* in the person of Christ but that same kingdom *is still in the future.* Jesus tells his opponents, "If it is by the finger of God I cast out demons, then the kingdom of God has come upon you" (Lk 11:20). This text affirms that the kingdom *is already here.* At the same time in the Lord's Prayer, we are told to pray "Thy kingdom come," which looks to a future that has not yet taken place. So the kingdom is both "now" and "not yet."

2. The second paradox affirms that the kingdom of God is *near* and yet *far*

---

[2]Werner G. Kümmel, *Promise and Fulfillment,* Studies in Biblical Theology 23 (Naperville: Alec R. Allenson, 1957); George E. Ladd, *Jesus and the Kingdom* (Waco, Tex.: Word, 1970).

away. Occasionally, one of the authors of the New Testament expresses the confidence that the end of all things is *near* (1 Pet 4:7; 1 Cor 7:29; 10:11; Rom 13:12). At the same time, on his last journey to Jerusalem Jesus entered the house of Zacchaeus and during a banquet told Zacchaeus, "Today salvation has come to this house, since he also is a son of Abraham" (Lk 19:9). The phrase *Today salvation has come* stimulated the disciples to imagine that the end of history was about to take place, because the text continues,

"As they heard these things, he proceeded to tell a parable, because he was near to Jerusalem, and because they supposed that the kingdom of God was to appear immediately" (Lk 19:11).

Jesus then tells a parable about a man who calls his servants together, gives each of them a sum of money and tells them to get to work. Clearly Jesus told this story to make clear that the coming of the kingdom was still in the unspecified future and that they had responsibilities to fulfill in the meantime. The kingdom is *near,* yet *far off.*

3. The third paradox is that in Luke 21:5-36 Jesus describes signs of the coming of the kingdom and then tells his disciples that they can never determine the time of the coming of the kingdom because "only the Father" knows such mysteries (Mt 24:36). Jesus and the angels are not given these secrets (Mk 13:32). The signs are given to the disciples who are told that they cannot figure them out! The time of the coming of the kingdom is unknown and unknowable, yet here are the signs!

Some believers in every century have held the firm conviction that they were living in the last days. This attitude appears as early as 2 Peter 3:3-10. Christians in every age are encouraged to live expectantly and at the same time never to presume to read the mind of the Father as regards the timing of the end of all things.

By definition, a paradox affirms the truth of two opposing ideas that cannot logically be reconciled. Such truth is greater than either of the two sides of the paradox. To summarize, the kingdom of God gives purpose and direction to history. In the New Testament the kingdom is affirmed to *have come* and yet it lies in the *future.* It is *just about to happen* and is still *far off.* There are *signs,* but the timing of the fulfillment of the kingdom is to us *unknown* and unknowable.

We can affirm in quiet confidence that the ship of history moves in the direction God intends even when we live in the midst of destruction, horror and tragedy. We can pray "Thy kingdom come" in faith and confidence as we labor to prepare for that coming. But what is the nature of this kingdom?

FOUR CLASSICAL UNDERSTANDINGS OF THE KINGDOM OF GOD

There are at least four classical ways to understand the nature of the kingdom of God. The first is *eschatological*. This view focuses on the gift of the kingdom of God at the end of history. The second is *mystical*. Here the kingdom of God is within the hearts of the believers. To enter the kingdom is synonymous with becoming a disciple of Jesus and trying to discern his will and follow it. This view usually locates the kingdom of God in heaven and sees the Christian life primarily (or exclusively) as preparation for the entering of that heavenly kingdom. The third view is *political*. This option discovers the kingdom of God in a particular empire (Byzantium in the East or the Holy Roman Empire in the West). The fourth and final is the identification of the kingdom of God with the *institutional church*. Benedict Viviano affirms that this view was the dominant understanding of the kingdom of God in the Latin Catholic Church from Augustine in the fourth century up through the middle of the twentieth century.[3] Each of these four views contains part of the truth.

Those who affirm the kingdom of God in its fullness as a gift of God at the end of history are faithfully reflecting aspects of New Testament teaching on the subject. Those who have located the kingdom in the hearts of believers on their way to heaven are faithful to other strands of the biblical witness on the subject. The kingdom of God is more than the organized church, yet a healthy church is a key player in preparing hearts to receive the gift of the kingdom of God. Constantine identified the kingdom of God with his empire, and he was wrong, but the kingdom of God has to do with this world and thus peace, justice, ecology and many other things are central to its agenda.

In the last analysis the kingdom of God includes all that Jesus said and did. Each of his parables presents some aspect of it. The kingdom established ethical patterns. It must be approached like a child and it is hard for the rich to enter into it. Its great commandment is to love God and the neighbor. The eucharistic meal is related to it, and it is the central focus of Jesus' preaching. We labor to receive its blessings in our hearts and in our societies as we look to the future with hope.

Viviano writes:

> The Kingdom of God . . . is a new, future divine breaking into history already present in sign, anticipation and momentary ecstasy, especially in the ministry of Jesus him-

---

[3]Benedict Viviano, *The Kingdom of God in History* (Wilmington, Del.: Michael Glazier, 1988), pp. 30-31.

self, yet in its fullness still to come. This divine act will be of a social rather than an individual character and will have as its immediate political manifestations justice and peace. As well it will involve a new and greater outpouring of God's Holy Spirit upon those who enter this kingdom.[4]

Like the request for God to demonstrate his holiness, this request for the coming of the kingdom has to do with a metanarrative that involves the entire world. The faithful who pray this prayer are not an inward-looking circle praying merely for their own needs. This section of the prayer widens the vision of the worshiper to see beyond individual and community needs and catch a vision for the world throughout human history.

THE PETITION FOR THE FULFILLING OF GOD'S WILL

Turning to the third petition, Jesus tells his disciples to pray, "Let it be done—thy will." But what is the will of God? On the simplest level the will of God is God's desire for the good of all his people. God desires that good because he is holy love. This is where the deep mystery of this petition surfaces.

If God is God and if his nature is holy love, then what he wants is surely what is going to happen. The Middle East still has three traditional kings. They rule in Jordan, Arabia and Morocco. The resident of Arabia does not need to wistfully state, "I hope the King's servants will obey the king today." The king's desires will be carried out because he is the king.

If this is true for an earthly king, what of a heavenly king? Isn't God's will that which happens? God's rule is an exercise of his will. If God is not sovereign over history, then no one holds the rudder of the ship of human destiny, and Macbeth is right.

And yet we pray, "Let it be done—thy will"; in so doing we appear to be longing that God's will might come about. In this yearning for God's will, we overhear the assumption that we humans are free to direct our lives and must accept responsibility for what we do. But at the same time, we seek to live in conformity to the divine will of God. With this yearning we discover yet another paradox in the Lord's Prayer. On the one hand, we acknowledge that God directs history. On the other hand, we assume that humans are free and responsible. We can make peace with this paradox, but can never solve it. We must affirm the sovereignty of God along with human freedom and responsibility. To ignore or reject either side of this paradox runs counter to the basic theology of the Lord's Prayer and all of

---

[4]Ibid., p. 149.

Scripture. We are back to the image of the train. Move or remove either rail, and the train will wreck. In this prayer we affirm God's sovereignty (God has a will) and our freedom (we are able to oppose that will and thus we pray, yearning that it might be done). We live our daily lives in the creative tension between these two life-affirming realities.

This creative tension is clarified with the phrase *on earth, as it is in heaven*. In heaven, the will of God flows like a great river that has no barriers to halt its progress. On earth, however, sin interrupts the flow of God's desire for good for all people. Such a desire is his perfect will. We pray, asking that here on earth we might enjoy the perfect will of God as it is enjoyed in heaven.

The defining phrase *on earth as it is in heaven* is critically important and often forgotten. This phrase obliges the disciple of Jesus to care about the earth and what happens to it and to the people who live on it. The Christian faith is not just a methodology for preparing disembodied souls for the next world. The well-known Christmas carol "Away in a Manger" includes:

Be near me, Lord Jesus; I ask Thee to stay
    Close by me forever, and love me, I pray;
Bless all the dear children in Thy tender care,
    And fit us for heaven to live with Thee there.[5]

The unspoken assumption of this language is that the (sole?) purpose of the Christian faith is to "fit us for heaven." Ecology, peace among peoples and nations, economic justice, racial equality, and refugees and land rights are all political issues that have to do with *this world* and are thus beyond the scope of the concerns of the Christian faith. But such is not the case if we pray "thy kingdom come, thy will be done *on earth*." The oft quoted saying of Jesus "My kingdom is not of this world" (KJV) is better translated "My kingdom is not *from* this world. If my kingdom were *from* this world, my followers would be fighting" (Jn 18:36 NRSV, italics added). The origins and inner dynamics of the kingdom of God do not evolve out of the culture and politics of this world. But the kingdom is *on earth* and thereby is deeply concerned for the earth and all that happens to the people who live on it—even though we never absolutize place and nation because we have no abiding city here (Heb 13:14).

This brings us to the conclusion of our brief study of the three "Thou petitions." We now turn to the fourth petition which is the first of the three "we petitions."

---

[5]"Away in a Manger." Verses 1-2, anonymous. Verse three, John McFarland (1851-1913).

FOURTH PETITION

In the fourth petition, we pray:

> Give us this day our daily bread.

This petition occurs at the center of the prayer. In the middle of the eighteen Jewish daily prayers there is a petition for God's blessing on the agricultural year.[6] Bread is the staple food for Middle Easterners, and in the Bible it symbolizes all that we eat.

But the word *daily* presents a problem. In English it is traditionally translated, "Give us *this day* our *daily* bread." The phrase *this day* is clear. We are not asking for bread for next year or for our retirement, but rather for "this day." The problem lies in the Greek word *epiousios*, which for centuries English versions have translated as "daily." The trouble is that this particular word appears nowhere else in the Greek language.[7] Origen, a famous Greek scholar of the early third century, wrote that he did not find this word in use among the Greeks, nor was it used by private individuals. He concluded that it must have been created by the Evangelists.[8]

The only way to discover the meaning of a word in any language is to see how it is used. But if a particular word appears only once in the entire history of that language, the translator has a special problem. Children often create words whose meanings are known only to them. When very young, one of our children created the word, *tonkleach.* If I choose to use *tonkleach* in a sentence, how can any reader possibly understand its meaning? This is the problem with the word *epiousios* in the Lord's Prayer.

If in the third century Origen did not know what this word meant, what hope is there for us in the twenty-first century? Keep in mind that Origen lived in Alexandria, Egypt, which was one of the two great centers of Greek learning in the ancient world. Is the problem unsolvable?

The only open door is to examine how commentators, preachers and translators in the various early Christian communities understood this word. Perhaps some of them caught the meaning of *epiousios* before the word and its meaning evaporated out of the Greek language. The early fathers of the church had two basic solutions to the mystery of this word's meaning, and each solution contained two alternatives.

---

[6]No. 9, Birkat ha-Shanim. (The petition that the year may be fruitful.)
[7]W. D. Davies and D. C. Allison Jr., *The Gospel According to Saint Matthew* (New York: T & T Clark, 1988), 1:607.
[8]Origen *De Oratione* 27.7.

Solution 1—On the one side, some early Christian writers thought that this word *referred to time*. But what kind of time? Option 1a: Some interpreted *epiousios* as referring to *today*. English translations follow this understanding with the well-known reading: "Give us this day our *daily* bread." In the fourth century, Cyril of Jerusalem and many others championed this view.

Option 1b: Other early fathers said, "Yes, *epiousios* has to do with *time*, but it refers to *tomorrow* not *today*." Their translation is, "Give us today our bread for *tomorrow*." In the early fifth century the Latin scholar Jerome claimed he had a "Gospel of the Hebrews" in Hebrew which read, "Give us our bread of tomorrow."

The bread of tomorrow reflects the manna in the wilderness and came to mean the bread that we will eat with the Messiah in a promised great banquet of all believers at the end of history.[9] This is commonly called "the Messianic banquet of the end times." With this line of interpretation, the bread of tomorrow became the bread of the Holy Communion.

Solution 2—Other early church fathers argued that *epiousios* had nothing to do with *time*. Why should this prayer have two time references in one phrase? They understood this word to refer to an *amount of bread*. The discussion then focused on *how much* bread are we to pray for? Again, two points of view were expressed. Some claimed that the faithful should ask for *just enough to stay alive*, the bread of *subsistence*. This is the way most Arabic speaking Christians in the Middle East pray the Lord's Prayer today. Origen, having admitted that he really didn't know the meaning of *epiousios*, opted for this understanding. Chrysostom, the great fourth-century Greek preacher of Antioch, agreed with him.

The Syriac Church of the Middle East agreed that *epiousios* had to do with an *amount* of bread but that "just enough to keep us alive" was too harsh. They softened their translation of this word and opted for "the bread we need," which is gentler in tone. For my sense of well-being perhaps I need to have a full loaf of bread in the cupboard and not just one slice on the table. This alternative is found in the fourth-century translation of the Gospels into Syriac, called the Peshitta.

Now we have moved from no solution to four solutions. These can be summarized as follows:

Epiousios means:

1. the bread of today (time)

2. the bread of tomorrow (time)

---

[9]Davies, *Gospel According to Saint Matthew*, 1:608.

3. just enough bread to keep us alive, and no more (amount)

4. the bread we need (amount)

Each of these options is found in the early centuries of the Christian church. On what basis can we choose between them?

One possible way out of this dilemma is to ask, Is there some concept or interpretation that could have given birth to all four of these possibilities? Did the church in those early centuries provide a theological starting point from which these four options could have developed? If so, what is it and where is it found?

I am convinced that there is such a starting point and that it appears in the Old Syriac translation, which dates to the second century.[10] This translation ceased to be used because the Syriac community at a later date produced a new popular translation called the Peshitta. The Old Syriac (as it is called) faded away and disappeared until the nineteenth century, when two copies were discovered. One remains in the Monastery of St. Catherine on Mount Sinai and the other made its way to the British Museum. This Old Syriac translation of the Gospels is probably the oldest and earliest translation of the Greek New Testament into any language.

Jesus, of course, spoke Aramaic, and Syriac is closely related to Aramaic. Syriac Christians, as they translated the Gospels into Syriac, were therefore taking the words of Jesus out of Greek and returning them to a language very close to his native Aramaic. Most words are the same in these two languages and the Old Syriac translation of the Lord's prayer reads: *Lahmo ameno diyomo hab lan* (lit. "Amen bread today give to us").

Lahmo means "bread." *Ameno* has the same root as the word *amen*, and in Syriac *ameno* is an adjective that means "lasting, never-ceasing, never-ending, or perpetual."[11] This Old Syriac second-century translation means, therefore, "Give us today the bread that doesn't run out." Does this provide the clue to the mysterious Greek word *epiousios?* I think it does.

One of the most basic human fears is the dread of economic privation. Will we have enough? We are managing now, but what about the future? What if I lose my job? What if the kids get sick? What if I am unable to work? How will we survive? One of the deepest and most crippling fears of the human spirit is the fear of not having enough to eat.

Perhaps in the Lord's Prayer Jesus teaches his disciples to pray for release from

---

[10]F. C. Burkitt, *Evangelion Da-Mepharreshe (The Curetonian Version of the Four Gospels, with the readings of the Sinai Palimpsest and the Early Syriac Patristic Evidence Edited, Collected and Arranged by F. Crawford Burkitt),* 2 vols. (Cambridge: Cambridge University Press, 1904), 1:30-31.

[11]J. Payne Smith, ed., *A Compendious Syriac Dictionary* (Oxford: Clarendon, 1990), p. 19.

that fear. To pray for bread without ceasing is to pray for deliverance from the existential angst that there will not be enough. This fear can destroy the human spirit. If Jesus is teaching his followers to pray "Give us today the bread that does not run out," does this include bread for today? It does. Does it also include bread for tomorrow? By all means. Will it be enough to keep us alive? It will. How about a little more than just enough to keep us alive? Does "bread without ceasing" include "the bread we need"? That meaning is also included. The idea that we ask God to give us bread without ceasing covers all four options found in the early church.

Fear of not having enough to eat can destroy a sense of well-being in the present and erode hope for the future. I am convinced that the Old Syriac is correct and that at the heart of the Lord's Prayer Jesus teaches his disciples a prayer that means, "Deliver us, O Lord, from the fear of not having enough to eat. Give us bread for today and with it give us confidence that tomorrow we will have enough."

The language of this petition holds further treasures. Among them are

1. In this petition we ask for *bread, not cake.* Consumerism and the kingdom of *mammon* have no place among those who pray this prayer. We ask for that which sustains life, not all its extras.

2. We ask for *ours, not mine.* Mother Teresa of Calcutta records an occasion from her life in Calcutta. She writes,

> I will never forget the night an old gentleman came to our house and said that there was a family with eight children and they had not eaten, and could we do something for them. So I took some rice and went there. The mother took the rice from my hands, then she divided it into two and went out. I could see the faces of the children shining with hunger. When she came back I asked her where she had gone. She gave me a very simple answer: "They are hungry also." And "they" were the family next door and she knew that they were hungry. I was not surprised that she gave, but I was surprised that she knew. . . . I had not the courage to ask her how long her family hadn't eaten, but I am sure it must have been a long time, and yet she knew—in her suffering. . . . In her terrible bodily suffering she knew that next door they were hungry also.[12]

This woman with eight children may not have known the Lord's Prayer, but there was only "our rice" not "my rice," even when her children were hungry. The prayer for "our bread" includes the neighbors. It is "our Father" and "our bread."

---

[12]Mother Teresa, *The Joy of Living,* comp. J. Chaliha and E. Le Joly (New York: Viking/Penguin, 1997), pp. 337-38.

3. Bread is a *gift*. The one who prays this prayer affirms that *all bread comes as a gift*. It is not a right and we have not created it. Such gifts are in trust for the one who gives them. All material possessions are on loan from their owner; the God who created matter itself. This perspective on the material world is critical for the joyful life commended in the Gospels.

SUMMARY: THE LORD'S PRAYER: *GOD'S KINGDOM AND OUR BREAD*

The Lord's Prayer contains many secrets. What have we learned about petitions 3 and 4?

1. The kingdom of God gives meaning to history by affirming purpose and direction in it. Regardless of rapid change spiraling out of control, and in spite of human suffering and tragedy, the faithful remain confident in God who is bringing in his kingdom.

2. The kingdom is now and not yet. It is near and far away. Its coming has signs, but those signs can never be attached to events around us. What Jesus does not know, I do not know.

3. The kingdom has at least four components. It is a gift of God at the end of history and is also a part of the daily life of the faithful. The church is important to it, and great human issues like peace, justice, ecology and racial equality are central to its purposes.

4. God's perfect will is the good for all people. He is sovereign over all, and at the same time all people are free and responsible for their actions. "Thy will be done" holds these two great realities in appropriate tension.

5. The central goal of the Christian faith is not preparing people for heaven when they die, although it accomplishes that noble purpose. Rather, the worshiper prays, "Thy kingdom come . . . *on earth*."

6. Western churches have traditionally translated the fourth petition as, "Give us this day our *daily* bread." But this request can legitimately be translated, "Give us today the bread that does not run out." This focuses on amount, time and the fear that we will not have enough. It requests deliverance from that fear.

7. The bread requested is bread, not cake, and it is "*our* bread" not "*my* bread." It comes as a gift from the one who owns all things.

10

The Lord's Prayer: *Our Sins and Evil*

MATTHEW 6:12-13

CHAPTER NINE CONSIDERED THE THIRD PETITION, regarding the will of God, and the fourth, which focuses on God's assurance of the gift of bread. The two remaining petitions deal with forgiveness and trials/evil.

THE FORGIVENESS OF DEBTS AND SINS

The Lord's Prayer continues:

> Forgive us our debts,
> as we also have forgiven our debtors.

Once more, our relationships with God and with our neighbors are closely tied. This connection is a departure from the tradition in which Jesus was raised. The *Tefillah* (the eighteen prayers) include a prayer for forgiveness from God (no. 6), but that forgiveness is not connected to forgiveness for others. Jesus makes such a connection in this prayer and elsewhere.

In this petition the believer comes before God asking for forgiveness while affirming that forgiveness of others has been accomplished. One of Jesus' parables expands on this theme. Matthew 18:23-34 recounts the story of a servant whose master forgives an enormous debt. Afterward, the servant turns to his fellow servant and refuses to forgive a very small debt. The master, in anger, consigns the unforgiving servant to prison. In like manner, at the end of this prayer (vv. 14-15), the interconnectedness between our forgiveness of others and God's forgiveness of us is reaffirmed as Jesus says:

> For if you forgive others their trespasses,
> your heavenly Father also will forgive you;
> but if you do not forgive others their trespasses,
> neither will your Father forgive your trespasses.

There is a special slant to what Jesus commands here. The parable of the unforgiving servant is not a precise fit for the Lord's Prayer. In the parable the master has not been wronged by the servant, except in the failure to pay the debt. The servant *borrowed* the money, he did not *steal it*. But in the Lord's Prayer, sin is a more significant part of the equation. More than just the remission of debts is implied. This raises the critical question of injustice and what is to be done about it.

It is a common human assumption that the violator of the rights of others must ask for forgiveness before the wronged party can be expected to accept the apology and grant forgiveness. When the wrong is huge, this is often thought to be impossible. The cry "Never forget and never forgive" has echoed many times down the corridors of history. But here Jesus asks *the person wronged* to forgive the one responsible for the wrongdoing *even when there is no confession of guilt*. Is this really possible? Can the Christians of southern Sudan forgive the Sudanese Muslim government for forty years of murder and mayhem, which the northern Sudanese do not admit ever happened? What of the African Muslims and Christians of Darfur province in Sudan who, as we write, are enduring brutalities that are beginning to be called a genocide? Can the Armenians forgive the Turks for the Armenian genocide, which the Turks to this day deny ever took place? These are hard questions to which those of us who have never endured such suffering cannot presume to give easy answers. Yet there is a voice from the cross that echoes across history to all saying: "Father forgive them for they know not what they do." Neither Pilate nor the high priest nor the centurion offered any apology to Jesus, yet he prayed for divine forgiveness for them *in the midst of their brutality to him*. On the cross Jesus, in total innocence of wrongdoing, acted out the second half of this petition. This is not the cry of the weak but the awesome voice of the strong.

The question remains: What is the nature of the sin that needs forgiveness? This raises the question of debts and sins.

Matthew uses only the word *debts*. Luke's text tells of both *sins* and *debts*. He records, "Forgive us our *sins*, for we ourselves forgive every one who is *indebted* to us" (Lk 11:4). Presbyterians pray "Forgive us our debts" while in the same prayer Episcopalians use the phrase "Forgive us our trespasses." Some wit has offered reasons for this divergence. *Calvinists*, goes the story, are more interested in their *debts* than they are in their *sins*, while *Episcopalians* are *land owners*, so naturally *trespassing* is important to them. Be that as it may, there are important theological meanings in these two words. Matthew's word, *debts*, refers to unfulfilled obligations toward God and our fellow human beings, that is, those things we have left undone. We should have reached out in compassion to our neighbor but have failed to do so, and our love for God is incomplete. On the other side, disciples are faced with "those things we ought not to have done," as is found in the Episcopal Prayer Book.[1] Believers are caught between unfulfilled responsibilities and acts committed that are not in harmony with the will of God.

In Aramaic, Jesus had available to him the word *khoba* which means both *debts and sins*.[2] Greek, like English, expresses these two ideas with separate words. When the Lord's Prayer was translated into Greek, there was a problem. Matthew chose *debts* and Luke managed to use both words. Whichever word is chosen for worship in English, the faithful need to remember that they are asking for forgiveness for failing to fulfill what God requires of them (debts) and for their failure to do the right thing when they did act (trespasses).

Furthermore, this need for two types of forgiveness is a recurring need. The request for forgiveness is side by side with the petition for bread. Daily life requires both bread and forgiveness. In addition, Christians must not think of forgiveness merely as a great dramatic act that occurs at the beginning of the pilgrimage of faith, but as a daily need. Each day the faithful need to ask God to pick up the broken pieces of their lives and restore to them the joy of their salvation. The one who prays this prayer asks for release from the guilt of unfulfilled responsibilities and for a lifting of the burden of wrongdoing.

Provision for community underlies *this* petition as well. Unless people are able to forgive one another and to seek God's forgiveness, they are unable to live together. The healing that comes from forgiveness makes it possible for the faithful to continue their pilgrimage as a community. It is not by accident that Archbishop Tutu of South Africa was chosen to lead the commission on Truth and Reconciliation after the apartheid era in that country. Instead of criminal trials, the truth was told, forgiveness offered and reconciliation achieved.

Furthermore, biblical forgiveness does not mean "Never mind." Offering forgiveness does not dictate that injustice must be tolerated. Various forms of injustice occur in every culture, and people everywhere struggle for justice as they understand it and fight for causes that to them are more sacred than life. Today across the Middle East, from Iran to Sudan various communities seek justice in difficult and critical situations of injustice. Naturally, for them, the word *justice* looms large. Christians must struggle for "justice for all," wherever they live and in whatever circumstances they find themselves. Those who pray this prayer are not affirming,

---

[1]The Book of Common Prayer, pp. 41-42.

[2]The word *khoba* appears in this verse in all three Syriac versions: the Old Syriac, the Peshitta and the Harclean.

"Injustice can continue, it doesn't really matter. We are willing to ignore injustice to ourselves and others." This prayer does not signal to the perpetrator of injustice, "You can do anything you choose with us because to be a Christian means to be a doormat."

How then can forgiveness be understood as it relates to injustice? Let us assume that the person who struggles for justice is not on an ego trip, and that the injustice suffered is genuine. This prayer asks the one who struggles for justice to forgive the person or persons against whom he or she struggles. Through forgiveness the bitterness, anger, hatred and desire for revenge are drained out of the struggle and the person contends with those for whom he or she may now be able to feel genuine compassion. This will influence enormously *the style of the struggle.* After the offered forgiveness, the struggle for justice continues, but now there are things the person will not do. The day of victory or defeat will not become a day of vengeance. In his second inaugural address, delivered as the American Civil War was winding down, Abraham Lincoln said, "With malice towards none; with charity for all; . . . let us . . . do all which may achieve and cherish a just, and lasting peace."[3] Only after forgiving the enemy is it possible to commend such a path of action.

The world despises this theology because it thinks anger is necessary to fuel the struggle for justice, and that forgiveness will dissipate that anger. The Christian disagrees and replies, "No. I will forgive *and* I will struggle for justice. I may still be angry, but my struggle for justice will be purified by forgiveness and thereby become more effective." What then of "historic injustices"?

The South African writer Laurens van der Post was interned by the Japanese during World War II and almost died as a result. In his book *Venture to the Interior,* he describes how after the war he discovered that the War Crimes officers, who had not suffered in the conflict, were "more revengeful and bitter about our treatment and our suffering in prison than we were ourselves." Van der Post goes on to say:

> I have so often noticed that the suffering which is most difficult, if not impossible, to forgive is unreal, imagined suffering. There is no power on earth like imagination, and the worst, most obstinate grievances are imagined ones. Let us recognize that there are people and nations who create, with a submerged deliberation, a sense of suffering and of grievance, which enable them to evade those aspects of reality that do not minister to their self-importance, personal pride, or convenience. These imagined ills enable them to avoid the proper burden that life lays on all of us.

---

[3]Abraham Lincoln, quoted in Ronald C. White, *Lincoln's Greatest Speech: The Second Inaugural* (New York: Simon & Schuster, 2002), p. 19.

Persons who have really suffered at the hands of others do not find it difficult to forgive, nor even to understand the people who caused their suffering. They do not find it difficult to forgive because out of suffering and sorrow truly endured comes an instinctive sense of privilege. Recognition of the creative truth comes in a flash: forgiveness for others, as for ourselves, for we too know not what we do.[4]

Light streams from the Lord's Prayer in many directions.

TEMPTATION AND EVIL

This sixth petition says:

And do not bring us to the time of trial,
but rescue us from the evil one. (NRSV)

This petition is fraught with difficulty. The word traditionally translated "temptation" can also be read, with the NRSV, as "trial." The Arabic word for a scientific experiment is *tajriba*, which also means "temptation." The Greek word and the Semitic words behind it unite "trial" and "temptation." The difference is subtle yet important. God *tried/tested* Abraham but he did not *tempt* him (Gen 22:1-19), for God never leads his followers into temptation (Jas 1:13). This clarification is helpful, but the petition remains mysterious. How can it be understood?

There are at least three solutions to this question. One comes from Jeremias, whose scholarship focused on recovering the Aramaic and Jewish background to the New Testament. The second solution is my own. The third is the word of Father Mattah al-Miskin of Egypt. Each may be of some help in understanding this petition.

First, I offer my own thoughts on the matter. When travelers take long camel trips into the deserts of the Middle East, they must have a guide. The guide knows how to reach the destination. Without that information the traveling party will die. From experience I know that selecting the right guide must be done with great care. The party must trust the guide and have full confidence that he knows exactly where he is going and will not play Russian roulette with their lives. They must feel that the guide is capable of coping with any emergency that might arise on the journey.

Some years ago, in Egypt, my friends and I made a number of extended trips into the Sahara to visit a famous well, named Bir Shaytoun, east of the Nile. For that particular journey we always selected "Uncle Zaki" as our guide. He was a self-confident, humble man with enormous personal dignity. He never *walked* in

---

[4]Laurens van der Post, *Venture to the Interior* (Middlesex: Penguin Books, 1957), p. 26.

the desert but *flowed* over sand and rock like a ship moving gently through calm seas. His gait was akin to a slow run and was beautiful to observe. As we would leave the village on the edge of the Nile and head out into the almost trackless Sahara, each of us in turn felt the inner pressure to say, "Uncle Zaki, don't get us lost!" What we meant by that statement was, "We don't know the way to where we are going, and if you get us lost we will all die. We have placed our total trust in your leadership."

We were not saying to Uncle Zaki, "We don't think we can trust you, and are nervous lest you get us lost. Please don't do so." If that had been our view we would never have followed him out of the village. The phrase in the Lord's Prayer expresses the confidence of an earthly pilgrim traveling with a divine guide. The journey requires the pilgrims to affirm daily, "Lord, we trust you to guide us, because you alone know the way that we must go." This affirmation of the trusting traveler reflects the confidence of the community that prays this prayer.

Jeremias's solution has to do with language rather than culture. At times it is helpful to try to catch the fine tuning of the Aramaic that lies behind the Greek of the New Testament. Jeremias thinks that this is one of those occasions. His argument is that the Greek word for "lead us" that appears in this petition is *eisphero*. The Aramaic equivalent to this Greek word is *nisyon*, which has two shades of meaning. One is causative and the other is permissive. The *causative* means "Do not *cause* us to go into temptation" (that is: do not lead us). By endorsing the *permissive* the text would mean, "Do not *permit* us to go into temptations/trials."[5] On our faith journey, the tendency is to turn aside into trials/temptations, and thus we are instructed to pray, as it were, "Oh, Lord, hold us back and do not let us take that path." We catch overtones of this view in Mark's account of the Garden of Gethsemane when Jesus says to the sleepy Peter, "Watch and pray that you may not enter into temptation" (Mk 14:38). Perhaps this petition of the Lord's Prayer is a request to God for help in avoiding this self-destructive tendency. Regarding this text John Calvin writes, "In brief, being conscious of our own weakness, we ask to be defended by God's protection, that we may have an impregnable position against all devices of Satan."[6]

In an extended discussion of this prayer Father Matta al-Miskin offers a third view.[7] He begins by reflecting on the story of Job, a righteous man who was se-

[5]Joachim Jeremias, *The Lord's Prayer* (Philadelphia: Fortress, 1969), p. 29.

[6]John Calvin, *A Harmony of the Gospels, Matthew, Mark and Luke*, trans. A. W. Morrison (Grand Rapids: Eerdmans, 1972), 1:212.

[7]Matta al-Miskin, *al-Injil beHasab al-Qiddis Matta* (Cairo: Dayr al-Qiddis Anba Maqar, 1998), pp. 273-74.

verely tested by Satan *with God's permission*. Satan's name means "the accuser," and in the book of Job the reader sees him at work. Then turning to Holy Week, Father Matta notes that Jesus warns Peter, saying, "Satan wants to sift you like wheat, but I have prayed for you that your faith might not fail" (Lk 22:31-32). Jesus does not promise Peter that there will be no time of trial. Peter pledges loyalty even unto death, but falls asleep in the garden. Jesus then awakens Peter and tells him to watch and pray lest he enter into temptation, but Peter does not pray and soon thereafter fails in his time of trial by denying Jesus three times. When we pray, argues Father Matta, we are protected by Jesus and his cross from Satan and his attacks. Satan the accuser is not prevented from his work as "the accuser," but the disciples are instructed not only to pray in general but to pray for deliverance from the times of trial that evil brings. Perhaps the larger truth lies in some combination of these three possibilities.

The final phrase is the other side of the coin, which combines, "Keep us out of Satan's courtroom" and "We are not ready for what Abraham had to face."

DELIVER US FROM THE EVIL ONE/EVIL

The above can be translated "deliver us from *the evil one*" or "deliver us from *evil*." The Greek text can be understood either way.[8] Syriac and Arabic translations have unanimously translated it as "the evil one." The King James Version and Revised Standard Version chose "evil" while the New Revised Standard Version opted for "the evil one."

Whatever one's views of the personal or impersonal nature of Satan, it can be said that the way evil functions in society is most appropriately described using personal language. There is a demonic energy that breaks out in people, societies and nations that acts with the force of a guiding evil mind. This brings us to the final affirmation that appears in some early texts.

THINE IS THE KINGDOM

Some ancient texts add the following final affirmation of praise to the Lord's Prayer: "For thine is the kingdom and the power and the glory forever, Amen." This statement of faith is an abridgement of 1 Chronicles 29:11-13. In Jesus' day many Jews would conclude the classic prayers of their tradition and then add personal petitions or acclamations of praise. Many early manuscripts of the Gospels do not have this concluding phrase, although some do. Perhaps the early church

---

[8]*Tou ponērou* can be read as a neuter and mean "evil" or as a masculine and be understood as "the evil one."

followed Jewish practice and added these final words to the prayer.

SUMMARY: THE LORD'S PRAYER: *OUR SINS AND EVIL*

The Lord's Prayer, in very few words, weaves together some of the weightiest themes of Jesus' theology. In petitions five and six we have noted the following:

1. Jesus connects God's forgiveness of his people with their willingness to forgive others.

2. Forgiveness must be offered even when it is not requested. The model is Jesus on the cross.

3. Jesus most certainly used the Aramaic word *khoba* when he taught the Lord's Prayer. That word means both debts and sins. We need forgiveness for both.

4. Forgiveness is a recurring need, like daily bread.

5. Forgiveness is in harmony with a continuing struggle for justice. They are not opposites. Forgiveness purifies the struggle for justice.

6. Historic injustices are a special problem. Those who truly suffer can forgive because they know their own weaknesses.

7. "Lead us not into temptation" is better translated, "Do not bring us to the time of trial." Also "do not bring us" can be understood to mean "Do not permit us to go." This language may be a reflection of the classic request of a trusting pilgrim to a respected guide.

8. The petition for protection from evil, or the evil one, is a cry from the heart in every age.

9. The final ascription of praise is most likely an early prayer of the church and as such is worthy of use.

PART FOUR

Dramatic Actions of Jesus

11

The Call of Peter

LUKE 5:1-11

THE TOPIC OF CHRISTIANS AND MONEY is not primarily about fundraising but concerns the whole of Christian life. William Temple, the great theologian and archbishop of Canterbury, wrote, "The spiritually minded person does not differ from the materially minded person chiefly in thinking about different things, but in thinking about the same things differently. It is possible to think materially about God, and spiritually about food."[1]

The Greek world neatly divided matter and spirit. The first was evil and the second, alone, was considered good. The prophets of the Old Testament and the authors of the New Testament emphasized that the spirit can be either good or evil while material things can be a blessing or a curse. Nowhere is this truth clearer than in the teachings of Jesus of Nazareth.

Jesus had more to say about money than he did about prayer. That is to be expected from a development officer of a church-related college. But from Jesus? Why is such a surprising focus found in the teachings of Jesus?

The biblical understanding of matter begins with the story of creation. God created matter and it was *good* not *evil*. Yes, matter provided the stimulus for disobedience and the expulsion of Adam and Eve from the Garden. Matter, however (in this case, the forbidden fruit) was not at fault; the willfulness of Adam and Eve, who chose to disobey God's command as it related to matter, was. Following that disobedience all of life began to fall apart. But the most important event affirming matter as good rather than evil was the coming of Christ.

When "the Word became flesh and dwelt among us" (Jn 1:14), matter itself was affirmed as an adequate vehicle for the ultimate revelation of God. Yes, the mind of God can be partially understood through creation, through the "things that were made." Beyond creation, the word of God, spoken to the prophets, brought

---

[1]William Temple, *Nature, Man and God* (London: Macmillan, 1953), p. 468.

a higher level of revelation. When, however, the Word of God entered our world in the birth of a child, matter was demonstrated to be worthy of receiving and communicating the fullness of God. Theology calls this "the incarnation," and from that point on matter and spirit were uniquely bonded.

The bonding of matter and spirit is also seen in the way Jesus created meaning and communicated it to those around him. Jesus did not say, "The dialogical nature of ultimate reality requires that all human thought be divided into two spheres, the abstract and the concrete." Rather, he said, "What is the kingdom of God like? . . . It is like a grain of mustard seed which a man took and sowed in his garden. . . . It is like leaven which a woman took and hid in three measures of flour" (Lk 13:18-19, 21). The material world became the cradle into which he placed his spiritual-material message. The incarnation of spirit into matter took place repeatedly throughout the life and teachings of Jesus, and it touched the deepest mysteries of our existence as human beings.

We are not disembodied spirits. Nor are we souls temporarily imprisoned in a body that one day will be stripped away as we return to pure spirit. Death itself is conquered by the resurrection of the *body*, affirmed Paul (1 Cor 15:42-50), not through the transmigration of the soul. Furthermore, Paul called this new body a "spiritual body." When Jesus spoke, therefore, of money/matter/mammon more frequently than prayer, he knew that the human person is a mysterious combination of body and spirit. He addressed that whole person rather than mentally decapitating his listeners with a head trip. This inner connectedness of body and spirit is brilliantly exhibited in the call of Peter recorded in Luke 5:1-11. First is the text with its rhetorical structure (figure 11.1).

THE RHETORIC

Peter's call, as depicted in Luke, has seven scenes and an introduction. Four scenes are presented before the series is repeated backward. There is also an "explanatory note" that appears to be added to an older text. Summarized, the original seven scenes are as follows:

1. The boat goes out (Jesus teaches)
2. Jesus speaks to Peter (catch fish!)
3. Peter speaks to Jesus (in arrogance)
4. A dramatic catch of fish (a nature miracle)
5. Peter speaks to Jesus (in repentance)
6. Jesus speaks to Peter (catch people!)
7. The boat returns (they follow Jesus)

0. While the people pressed upon him to *hear* the *word of God*,
   he was standing by the lake of Gennesaret.   SETTING
   And he saw *two boats by the lake*;
   but the *fishermen* had gone out of them and were *washing their nets*.

1. Getting into one of the *boats*, which was *Simon's*,   WORD—TAUGHT
   he asked him to *put out* a little *from the land*.   (boats out from land)
   And he sat down
   and *taught* the people from the boat.

2.   And when he had ceased speaking, he said to Simon,   JESUS COMMANDS:
            "Put out *into the deep*   catch fish
            and let down your [pl.] nets *for a catch*."

3.   And Simon answered,
            "*Teacher*,   PETER: obeys (?)
            we toiled all night and took *nothing*!   Jesus' word
            But at *your word* I will let down the nets."   as *Teacher*

4.   And when they had done this,
            they enclosed a *great shoal* of *fish*;
            and as their nets were breaking,   POWER OF WORD
            they beckoned to their *partners* in the other boat demonstrated
            to come and help them.
            And they came and filled both the boats,
            so that they began to sink.

5.   But when Simon Peter saw it,
            he fell down at Jesus' knees, saying,
            "Depart from me,   PETER: surrenders
            for I am a sinful man,   to Jesus
            O Lord."   as *Lord*

5b.   (For amazement/fear had seized him
            and all who were with him,   (explanatory
            because of the catch of fish which they had taken; note)
            and so also James and John, sons of Zebedee,
            who were *partners* with Simon.)

6.   And Jesus said to Simon,   JESUS COMMANDS:
            "Do not be afraid;   catch people
            henceforth you will be *catching people*."

7. And when they had brought their *boats to land*,   WORD—OBEYED
   they left everything and *followed him*.   (boats to land)

Figure 11.1. The call of Peter (Lk 5:1-11)

In numbers 1 and 7 the boat goes out and comes back. In numbers 2 and 6 Jesus speaks to Peter, while in numbers 3 and 5 Peter addresses Jesus. The climax is found in the center with the dramatic catch of fish. This text, with its overall format of seven inverted stanzas, is another example of what I have named the "prophetic rhetorical template."[2] The extra note (5b) that breaks the rhetorical template adds new information helpful to the reader of Luke's Gospel. Luke himself may have added it. A similar type note occurs in Luke 4:25b-26. Such notes reinforce the view that the seven-stanza template was recorded (not composed) by Luke.

An additional rhetorical feature that has ancient Jewish precedents is the oc-currence of a nature miracle at the climactic center of the inverted stanzas. That climactic center is sometimes a quotation from an earlier sacred tradition. It can also be a parable or a nature miracle. In this account it is an encased nature miracle. That is, the nature miracle appears in the center and is encased with a series of en-velopes composed of other dramatic material.

1.	And you shall rejoice in the *LORD;*	LORD
	in the *Holy One of Israel* you shall glory.	HOLY ONE OF ISRAEL
2.	When the *poor and needy* seek *water,*	
	and there is *none,*	
	and their tongue is parched with *thirst,*	PEOPLE IN NEED
	I the LORD will *answer them,*	(God acts to save)
	I the God of Israel will *not forsake them.*	
3.	I will open *rivers* on the *bare heights,*	
	and *fountains* in the midst of the *valleys;*	WATER IN
	I will make the *wilderness a pool of water,*	The Dry Land
	and the *dry land springs of water.*	
4.	I will put in the *wilderness* the *cedar,*	
	the *acacia,* the *myrtle,* and the *olive;*	TREES IN
	I will set in the desert the *cypress,*	The Dry Land
	the *plane* and the *pine* together;	
5.	that men may *see* and *know,*	PEOPLE SEE
	may *consider* and *understand* together,	(know and understand)
6.	that the hand of the *LORD* has *done this,*	LORD
	the *Holy One of Israel* has *created it.*	Holy One of Israel[a]

[a]Other encased nature miracles appear in Isaiah 42:13-17; 45:1-3.

Figure 11.2. Isaiah 41:16-20

[2]This seven-stanza rhetorical form is common in the prophetic writings and in the New Testament.

An Old Testament example of this rhetorical composition appears in Isaiah 41:16-20 (see figure 11.2).

This passage begins (1) and concludes (6) with "the LORD" and "the Holy One of Israel." References to the people appear in numbers two and five. A collection of miraculous natural events form the climactic center (3-4). Rivers materialize on bare heights, and pools and springs appear in the wilderness, along with the growth of broad-leaved trees that require significant rainfall.

This same rhetorical style is used in Luke 5:1-11. The composer of the story of Peter's call is a learned Jew writing for Jews, using a classical literary pattern employed by Isaiah. Luke most likely received this story in written form. Its sophisticated literary connections to Isaiah were no doubt understood by Luke's Jewish-Christian readers. His Gentile-Christian readers may have missed them but they are there.

COMMENTARY

In this text the person of Jesus, the material world of Peter and renewal in the spirit come together in a revelatory dramatic action. The introduction (0) sets the stage by presenting the story's important elements. These include: Jesus, the crowd, the word of God, the boats, the fishermen and the empty nets. The account is carefully constructed; it exhibits ancient Jewish rhetoric and has an explanatory note attached. The details of its drama deserve careful examination. The introduction informs the reader:

> 0. While the people pressed upon him to *hear the word of God*,
>   he was standing by the lake of Gennesaret.   WORD—SOUGHT
>   And he saw two boats by the lake;
>   but the fishermen had gone out of them and were washing their nets.

This account does not take place in a synagogue with a hushed crowd listening to an eloquent exposition of a favorite psalm. Instead, the crowd presses around Jesus on a smelly landing with tired fishermen nearby cleaning their empty nets after a long, fruitless night. Jesus enters the world of the people rather than expecting them to step out of that world and come to him.

Furthermore, the people have come for "*the word of God*," which they fully expect to hear *from Jesus*. This language places Jesus in the world of the prophets. Scene 1 opens with a bold move by Jesus:

> 1. Getting into one of the *boats*, which was Simon's,   WORD—TAUGHT
>   he asked him to *put out* a little *from the land*.   (boats out from land)
>   And he *sat down*
>   and *taught* the people from the boat.

Without so much as a "by your leave," Jesus climbs into Peter's boat and requests services. Granted, the reader of Luke's Gospel knows that Peter "owes one"
to Jesus, who had just healed Peter's mother-in-law (Lk 4:38-39). Returning fa-
vors is an integral part of many societies in general and Middle Eastern culture in
particular. Peter *cannot* refuse. But Jesus is not merely collecting on social obligations. He has a more important agenda.

Jesus does not tell Peter how much he, Jesus, has to offer Peter, nor does he
explain the unimagined ways in which Peter's life will change for the better if he
will but pledge loyalty to Jesus. Instead, he approaches Peter by saying, "Peter, I
need your help! Will you help me?" The request for assistance is from within the
earthy reality of Peter's work-a-day world, his boat and his rowing skills. Jesus
chooses to use the boat as a platform and needs Peter to move and control that
boat while he addresses the crowd. In a large lake, rowboats do not remain in
place in the water, they drift. Jesus genuinely needs Peter to control that drift if
the boat is to be effective as a pulpit. Considerable rowing skill is necessary. The
request is not artificially manufactured. Jesus began his conversation with the
woman at the well with the request, "Give me a drink." The same creative dynamic is at work in this story.

At the same time, Jesus is "fishing" from a fisherman's boat. That is, he is engaged in catching people and as he does so he bestows new life. Peter uses that
boat to catch fish and in the process they die. These two kinds of fishing will come
together in the form of a challenge to Peter before the story is finished.

Confident and secure within his own professional world, Peter was able to listen to Jesus speak the Word of God to those assembled on the shore. Indeed, he
had no choice but to listen as he remained on the edge of the interaction between
Jesus and his audience. In the process Jesus changed Peter's familiar surroundings
into a life-transforming meeting between them.

Jesus sat down to teach, assuming a posture of authority.[3] When the teaching
session concludes, the reader/listener expects Jesus to thank Peter, ask to be taken
back to shore and proceed on his way. Amazingly, Jesus (the inland carpenter)
gives orders to the professional fisherman on how and where to catch fish!

The tensions created by this demand appear in scene 2.

2. And when he had ceased speaking, he said to Simon,   JESUS COMMANDS:
   "Put out *into the deep*   (catch fish)
   and let down your [pl.] nets *for a catch*."

---

[3]The rabbis sat down to teach, and there was a teaching chair in the synagogue called Moses' seat.

What a preposterous suggestion. Peter was exhausted. He and his partners had fished all night and caught nothing. They worked at night for one simple reason—the fish in the Sea of Galilee (and elsewhere) feed at night. In the daytime they hide under rocks. Furthermore, they congregate around the streams and springs at the edge of the sea where oxygen-rich fresh water flows into the lake. William M. Christie records:

> We have seen shoals at ʿAin barideh and ʿAin et-Tabigha so great as to cover an acre of the surface, and so compact together that one could scarcely throw a stone without striking several. In such cases the hand-net is thrown out with a whirl. It sinks down in a circle, enclosing a multitude, and these are then gathered in by the hand, while the net lies at the bottom.[4]

The Sea of Galilee drops off into deep water close to the shore, and in most areas is too dangerous for swimming.[5] Casting can be done standing in the water or from a boat. Drag fishing, with a long net and two boats, was also practiced, as evidenced in the parable of the dragnet (Mt 13:47-50). These two types of fishing can be done during the day. But all fishermen working Gennesaret know that most successful fishing takes place at night and primarily near the shore where fresh water feeds into the lake. (I have watched them.) The very idea that a landlubber from the highlands of Nazareth, who has never wet a line should presume to tell a seasoned fishing captain what to do is preposterous. The fish can see and avoid the nets during the day, but they feed at night.[6] The order to launch into the deeps in broad daylight is ridiculous! Joel Green writes, "Jesus' instructions to Peter seem absurd. Not only has a night's work by people who fish by profession produced nothing, but the nets used are for night fishing only."[7]

Peter cannot enter the rabbinic debates. He knows little about the law, and the fine points of sabbath observance are a mystery to him, but he does know a great deal about fishing! He replies in scene 3 with self-confidence and sarcasm:

3.	And Simon answered,	PETER
	"*Teacher!*	obeys (?)
	We *toiled all night* and took *nothing!*	Jesus' word
	But at *your word* I will let down the nets!"	as Teacher

[4]William M. Christie, "Sea of Galilee," in *A Dictionary of Christ and the Gospels,* 2 vols., ed. James Hastings (Edinburgh: T & T Clark, 1908), 2:592.
[5]See E. F. F. Bishop, "Jesus and the Lake," *Catholic Biblical Quarterly* 13 (1951): 398-414.
[6]Joel B. Green, *The Gospel of Luke* (Grand Rapids: Eerdmans, 1997), p. 232.
[7]Ibid., p. 232.

A paraphrase of the above might be:

Listen Teacher! My boys and I are professionals. We know where the fish feed—it's along the shore, and the best time to catch them is at night. That's why we were out on the lake all last night. We're not stupid! We have just worked the fishing areas and caught nothing. We are now dead tired, and I have stayed awake a few more hours—to serve *you*. You rabbis think you know everything and now you order me to fish during the day in deep water. Very well! Let's go out and we'll see who knows what about fishing!

Peter calls Jesus *epistatēs*, which can mean "teacher" but can also be translated "boss" or "chief." Tired and disgruntled, Peter orders his team to push out from the shore once again. The astounding result appears in scene 4.

4. And when they had done this,
   they enclosed a *great shoal* of *fish*;
   and as their nets were breaking,   POWER OF WORD
   they beckoned to their *partners* in the other boat   demonstrated
   to come and help them.
   And they came and filled both the boats,
   so that they began to sink.

This great catch of fish is the climax of the story. The fine points of the manner in which it unfolds demonstrate its authenticity as a Middle Eastern account. Peter does not call his partners in the other boat. He beckons. Sound carries seven times further over water than it does over land. If Peter calls his mates, his voice will most likely be heard on the shore. Has a new spring suddenly opened on the lake floor? Has a new fishing bank formed under water where fish are currently feeding? If so, there is no need for the entire community to have such information. A sudden flood of competing fishermen converging on that spot is the last thing Peter wants. Financial secrets need to be kept. It is best not to raise one's voice but simply to wave to the other boat!

Returning to the story, once again, Jesus approaches Peter at the point of Peter's greatest strength: his ability as a fisherman. What shocks Peter most deeply perhaps is not the "miraculous catch" (as it is often called) but the fact that he, Peter, is suddenly faced with a man who had made a real choice between God and mammon. All night, every night, Peter and his team plied their trade in the hope of netting a great catch. Their sleep was punctuated with vivid dreams of that faint possibility. It's akin to winning the lottery, or like a day trader who buys shares every morning hoping against hope for the lucky day when those stocks will jump dramatically in price before nightfall and he will make a windfall. Peter is a fisherman! This net-tearing, boat-swamping catch can greatly enrich him and his team. At last he has hit the jackpot!

The first thought that likely came to Peter's mind was that Jesus somehow discovered a new spring that had opened in the floor of the lake where fish were gathering. Peter knew full well that any person with such knowledge could become very rich in a matter of weeks. So why was Jesus, a penniless rabbi without a "real job," wandering around teaching people for nothing? How could God possibly be more important than two boatloads of fresh fish? Evidently Jesus cared more about God and people than he did about acquiring wealth. Who was this man who had made such an amazing decision? Peter found himself face to face with a person who challenged his priorities on the deepest level. His response unfolds in scene 5.

> 5. But when Simon Peter saw it,
> he fell down at Jesus' knees, saying,
> "Depart from me,   PETER surrenders
> for I am a sinful man,   to Jesus
> O Lord."   as *Lord*

There was no crowd surrounding Peter in the boat. Jesus saw to it that community peer pressure was left behind on the shore. Only Peter's intimate fishing associates witnessed the rearranging of the furniture in the back of his mind. Like Isaiah in the temple, Peter sensed that he was in the presence of holiness and that he was unclean and should be avoided lest he defile that holiness (Is 6:1-6). Filled with awe, he was afraid. As noted, Peter's first title for Jesus was *epistatēs* (boss/chief/teacher). Now Jesus is his *kyrios* (Lord). These two titles dramatically frame Peter's two speeches. "Teacher" opens the first speech while "Lord" closes the second.

As an aside, it can be noted that this text is the first use of the word *sinner* in Luke's Gospel. Jesus as the Savior who "seeks and saves sinners" appears here for the first time. Telling comparisons can be made between this scene and Jesus' approach to Zacchaeus in Luke 19:1-10, along with the parables of Luke 15. All of these texts focus on finding the lost.

At this point in the story there seem to be two footnotes, recorded together, that interrupt the stanza's careful construction. These are:

> 5b. (For amazement/fear had seized him
> and all who were with him,
> because of the catch of fish which they had taken;
> and so also James and John, sons of Zebedee,
> who were *partners* with Simon.)

The first explanatory addition is the initial three lines which expose the feelings of Peter and his companions in the boat. Amazement and fear fuse in the Greek word used. The second note clarifies the fact that the word *all* in line two includes James and John, sons of Zebedee. Perhaps the apostolic community (or Luke) wanted to emphasize the inner circle of Peter, James and John, and thus added these last two lines. Luke is allowed to add such notes to the fixed tradition that is given to him. If Luke was composing in the 50s in the first century, when he was in Jerusalem with Paul on his last journey, then the original story with its seven scenes could have been committed to writing in the 40s of the first century, or earlier.[8]

Jesus replies with:

6. And Jesus said to Simon,   JESUS COMMANDS:
   "Do not be afraid;   catch people
   henceforth you will be *catching people*."

Dismissing Peter's fears, Jesus assures him that his fishing skills will still be needed but for a different kind of catch. Now he will be catching people. The word *catching* in this scene means "to catch alive." As fish are caught, they die. But Peter will now be catching people, *alive*. From that same boat Jesus had just "caught people alive." Peter can do the same.

A pattern evolves. Jesus started with Peter and his material world (catching fish) and moved him to another "fishing world" where he will catch people. When the Pharisees complained about Jesus' custom of welcoming and eating with sinners, he replied with stories about a shepherd with his lost sheep and a woman with her lost coin (Lk 15:1-10). Only then did Jesus discuss the lost sons (Lk 15:11-32). And again, when attacked for healing a man from dropsy he in effect countered with, "What if a donkey fell down a well and it were yours? How much more this man" (Lk 14:1-6). In all these cases Jesus began with the earthy world of animals, coins and fish and then turned to a discussion of people.

As the story concludes, the reader is told:

7. And when they had brought their *boats to land*,   WORD—OBEYED
   they left everything and *followed him*.   (boats to land)

The story is highly condensed. Naturally, they would not have left the fish to rot and their families to starve. The exaggeration in the text marks it as a genuine Middle Eastern story where dramatic effect is achieved and sincerity demonstrated by exaggeration.

---

[8]Luke was with Paul on his last journey to Jerusalem. Note the use of "we" in Acts 21:17-18.

Jesus demonstrated his ability to "make a lot of money" in a hurry. At the same time he is seen here as a person with a higher commitment. Peter clearly stood in awe of such a person, but could he endorse these new goals as his own? He could and did and the "big fisherman" was born.

SUMMARY: THE CALL OF PETER

What theology and ethics are created by this remarkable scene? I suggest the following:

1. The fusion between the "the Word of God" and the teachings of Jesus places Jesus in the company of the prophets.

2. Nature, humans and God are woven together in ways that affirm the essential connectedness of all three.

3. Jesus reaches out to Peter by asking for help, not by offering it. He deliberately places himself in a position where he genuinely needs the help of the one he seeks to win to discipleship.

4. The help requested is authentic, not fabricated. Jesus needs Peter's boat and rowing skills, and Peter's worth is thereby affirmed on his own terms. Jesus' ministry becomes a partnership with Peter.

5. Jesus isolates Peter from the peer pressure of his community before trying to reach him. In this way it is possible for Peter to expose himself on a deep level rather than responding to Jesus in the light of his perceptions of the community's expectations.

6. Peter is confronted with a value system and a set of commitments radically different from his own. He is attracted, awed and challenged to make a choice.

7. Faced with authentic holiness, Peter senses that he is "unclean/sinful."

8. Peter told Jesus to "Depart from me." Peter's attitude was clear: The unclean will defile the clean on contact. Jesus had another view. For Jesus the clean (Jesus) can purify the unclean (Peter). All that was needed was contact.

9. Jesus the "teacher" *(epistatēs)* evolves into the "Lord" *(kyrios).*

10. Peter is granted continuity between his past and his future. His acquired skills will be put to use to serve a greater purpose. Catching and killing fish will be transformed into catching people and bringing them to new life.

11. Jesus was not only calling Peter to become a "fisher of people" but was acting out the very ministry he was commending. In the boat Peter was catching fish from the lake. At the same time Jesus was "a fisher of people" as he "landed"

Peter and his fishing associates. It was a large miraculous catch. Jesus, the friend of sinners, who came to seek and to save, surfaces for the first time.

In this story matter/mammon/money are woven together with the things of the spirit. Peter faces a man who wins the "fishing lottery" but doesn't want it. Stunned, Peter realizes the inadequacy of his own values and priorities. The impact on him, by the gentle man who radically de-absolutizes mammon, is enormous. Taking his former skills with him, he moves forward into a new venture of faith.

12

The Inauguration of Jesus' Ministry

LUKE 4:16-31

THE MOST DETAILED ACCOUNT of the inauguration of Jesus' public ministry is recorded in Luke 4:16-31. This rich and densely packed passage merits an attempt to unlock at least a few of its secrets. But first, the setting in Luke must be noted.

After the delightful story of Jesus as a boy in the temple, Luke provides no further information about what Jesus was doing from ages twelve to thirty. In all likelihood he was at home in Nazareth, employed as a carpenter/builder and joining nightly in discussion of the law with the local *ḥāberîm*. This Hebrew word means "the friends" and was the name of a lay movement that sprang up in the villages of the Holy Land around the time of Jesus. In any given village, serious-minded Jews would gather and devote themselves to studying the Torah and applying its laws to their day. Everybody "kept their jobs" but spent their spare time discussing the law. We can be confident that Jesus was a part of this group because in the Gospels he demonstrates skills in the rabbinic style of debate such as were nurtured in these fellowships. After those eighteen years of "theological education" Jesus was ready to begin his public ministry.

After his baptism and a period of temptation in the wilderness, Jesus returned to Galilee to begin a popular public ministry (Lk 4:14-15). Apparently part of that ministry was a number of unrecorded works of healing in Capernaum. Then, abruptly, Jesus returned to his home village of Nazareth and attended sabbath worship in the local synagogue. It was customary for worship leaders to invite a worthy person in the congregation to read from the Scriptures and comment on the reading. In Antioch of Pisidia, Paul and Barnabas were invited to offer a "word of exhortation for the people" (Acts 13:15) in just such a setting. Luke states simply that Jesus "stood up to read," yet it appears that some things had been arranged. The book of Isaiah was given to him. Jesus may have quietly requested to have a scroll of Isaiah ready for him to use, or perhaps the synagogue was following a lectionary that necessitated readings from Isaiah. At any rate, Jesus took the scroll, selected an obviously prepared text and read it to the congregation. This led to an interchange with the congregation after which Jesus invoked two heroes of faith from the Old Testament tradition to support his views. The scene closes with a foiled attempt to kill him. Each part of the story requires scrutiny. The first is the reading and editing of Scripture. The text is shown in figure 12.1.

And he came to Nazareth, where he had been brought up;

1a. and he entered (as his custom was) on the sabbath *into the synagogue,*
  b. and he *stood up* to read;
  c. and there *was given to him the book* of the prophet Isaiah,
  d. and *he unrolled the scroll,* and found the place where it was written,

2. "The *Spirit* of the Lord is upon me
   for he has *anointed me*
     a. to *preach good news* to the *poor.**   PREACH
      b. He has *sent me* to proclaim to the *prisoners—freedom,*   SENT
       c. and to the *blind*—recovery of *sight,*   SIGHT
      b. 'to *send forth* the *oppressed—in freedom,*' *   SEND
     a. to *proclaim** the acceptable year of the Lord." *   PROCLAIM

3d. And *he rolled up the scroll,*
  c. and *gave it back* to the attendant *[hypēretēs],*
  b. and *sat down*;
  a. and the *eyes* of all *in the synagogue* were fixed on him.

Figure 12.1. Jesus' reading of the scroll (Lk 4:16-20)

THE RHETORIC

Clearly, the dramatic framework around the reading of Scripture is carefully worded. The ideas of "in the synagogue," "stood up," "given the scroll" and "unrolled the scroll" in stanza one are repeated in reverse order in stanza three. The climax in the center is the text from Isaiah. That text is also rhetorically structured.

In the Old Testament ideas are often presented and then reversed, with a parable/metaphor in the center. Such rhetorical structures appear in both Testaments and can be called "encased parables."[1] The call of Peter places a "nature miracle" in the center of the account. Here, as elsewhere in the New Testament, the center is

---

[1]Cf. Is 53:7-8; 55:8-9; Lk 7:36-50; 1 Cor 2:10-11; 3:1-2; 12:1-30. Cf. also Kenneth E. Bailey, *Finding the Lost* (St. Louis: Concordia Press, 1992), p. 17f.

filled with an Old Testament quotation.[2] Paul also employs this rhetorical device (e.g., 1 Cor 6:13-20).

This encasing of an Old Testament text within a series of ideas or actions is a distinctively Jewish rhetorical device, and its appearance is evidence that the recorder of this scene was a Jew who had accepted Jesus as the Messiah. He or she wrote for Jewish readers who would appreciate the biblical artistry involved. Luke did not compose this for Theophilus and other Gentile readers (Lk 1:1-4).

COMMENTARY

Jesus unrolled the scroll to Isaiah 61 and proceeded to read the text, which in Luke's Gospel shows careful editing. We have indicated the points in the text where this editing takes place by inserting four asterisks in the above rhetorical presentation of the text. Each of these asterisks represents a point at which the text of Isaiah is changed or interrupted. In the first of them the phrase "to bind up the broken hearted" is left out. The second appears after an entire phrase that has been brought in from Isaiah 58:6. The third asterisk marks where the word "to call" has been upgraded into a word that means "to proclaim a message." The final asterisk indicates where a verse has been cut in half with the second half omitted. Both the selection of the text and its editing are important. Why this particular text, and why these editorial changes?

It is often assumed that Luke (or his source) did the editing. It is also possible to trace the editing to Jesus. One of the keys to understanding the guiding principle behind the editing is to note an important Dead Sea Scroll fragment. This scrap of pre-Christian papyrus (4Q521) describes the coming Messiah as one who will "preach good news to the poor" and provide "release for the captives." He will also "open the eyes of the blind" and "raise up the downtrodden."[3] A second fragment from the same cave (4Q278) mentions that the "Holy Spirit rests on his Messiah."[4] The text that Jesus chose to read is clearly in tune with what the Jewish counterculture visionaries of his day expected from the Messiah. The comparisons between these two fragments and the text of Luke 4:18-19 can be seen in figure 12.2.

---

[2]There are hints of this rhetorical form in the Old Testament where the center of an inverted rhetorical piece is occasionally a reference to earlier sacred history. Cf. Is 55:1-3 where Abraham and Sarah along with the Garden of Eden are placed in the center with related material appearing before and after them.

[3]Robert H. Eisenman and Michael Wise, *The Dead Sea Scrolls Uncovered* (Rockport, Mass.: Element, 1992), p. 23.

[4]Michael O. Wise and James D. Tabor, "The Messiah at Qumran," *Biblical Archaeology Review* 18, no. 6 (1992): 60-65.

Qumran 4Q278, 521	Luke 4:16-30
1. (4Q278) The *Holy Spirit* rests	1. The *Spirit of the Lord* is upon *me* on his *Messiah*
2. (4Q521) The *Messiah is exalted*	2. For He has *anointed me* [i.e., made me into *Messiah*]
3. (4Q521) *To preach good news to the poor*	3. *To preach good news to the poor*
4. (4Q521) *Release for the captives*	4. *Release for the captives*
5. (4Q521) *Opening the eyes of the blind*	5. *Opening the eyes of the blind*
6. (4Q521) *Raising up the downtrodden*	6. *Set free the oppressed*
7. (4Q521) His mighty works: *heal the sick*	7. *What* we have heard you *did* at Capernaum do also here [i.e., *heal the sick*; cf. Lk 4:38-40]
8. (4Q521) His works: *Raising the dead*	8. Luke 7:22 affirms the *raising of the dead* as one of Jesus' messianic acts.

Figure 12.2. Comparison of Qumran fragment 4Q278 , 521 with Luke 4:16-30

Jesus claims that he is the anointed One (the Messiah) and then sets forth an agenda that is in close harmony with what at least some of the Jewish community of the time anticipated.[5] We would expect the audience to be pleased. And initially they may have been, but as he proceeded the mood changed. What was the problem?

For a long time English language versions have translated Luke 4:22-30 in a manner that presents a pleased audience that quickly turned into a howling murderous mob. Yet it is possible to understand the Greek text as describing a congregation which is upset *from the beginning*.

Luke 4:22 is usually translated:

And all spoke well of him,
and wondered at the gracious words which proceeded out of his mouth;
and they said, "Is not this Joseph's son?"

Put simply, this translation means: they liked it. In this case "Is not this Joseph's

[5]From these comparisons it is evident that the entire scene takes place in a Jewish setting. This gives weight to the assumption that Luke is using early apostolic sources and not creating an imaginative story. Wise writes, "This new Dead Sea Scroll text provides a direct and very significant example of a common messianic hope among the followers of John the Baptist, Jesus and (so it appears) the Dead Sea Scrolls." *Teacher of Righteousness* (ibid., p. 65).

son?" means, "We knew this young man as a child. He is Joseph's son. We had no idea he was so bright and poised. How well he read the Hebrew in the synagogue. We are so proud of him."

But Joachim Jeremias has pointed out that the key words in the Greek text, *emartyroun autō*, can be translated two ways. Literally, these two words read "they witnessed him." But did they witness "for him" or "against him?" The Greek can be read either way. The original Greek sentence does not have "for" or "against" in the text. The key is the fact that the word *him (autō)* is in the dative case. This can be a "dative of advantage" or a "dative of disadvantage." If the translator decides that the audience *liked* what Jesus read, he or she will read the text as a "dative of advantage" and translate "all spoke well of him." But if the translator senses that the audience is *not pleased*, then the dative *autō* will be read as a "dative of disadvantage," and the text will be translated as:

And all *witnessed against him*,
and were amazed at the words of mercy that came out of his mouth;
and they said, "Is not this Joseph's son?"

In this case the question: "Is not this Joseph's son?" means "Didn't this young man grow up here!? Doesn't he know how we feel and how we understand this text?" Jeremias suggests that the congregation was angry because Jesus quotes "to proclaim the acceptable year of the Lord" but leaves out the second half of the verse, which reads "and a day of vengeance of our God."[6] Ibn al-Tayyib argues that the crowd is angry due to envy—he is the son of a carpenter—and thus cannot be taken seriously. He writes, " 'Is not this Joseph's son?' This statement is evidence of extreme envy and a hearty attempt to demean along with lack of faith in Jesus."[7]

When Luke 4:22 is translated as "all witnessed against him," there is no "break of attitude" in the middle of the passage. The people are not initially pleased and then suddenly irritated. Jeremias writes:

Luke 4:22 exhibits no break in the attitude of his audience towards Jesus. On the contrary it records that from the outset unanimous rage was their response to the message of Jesus. The good news was their stumbling block, principally because Jesus had removed vengeance on the Gentiles from the picture of the future.[8]

Granting Jeremias's point, perhaps the hometown crowd had additional rea-

---

[6]Joachim Jeremias, *Jesus' Promise to the Nations*, Studies in Biblical Theology 24 (Naperville, Ill.: Alec R. Allenson, 1958), pp. 44-45.
[7]Ibn al-Tayyib, *Tafsir al-Mashriqi*, ed. Yusif Manqariyos (Egypt: Al-Tawfiq Press, 1907), 2:85.
[8]Jeremias, *Jesus' Promise to the Nations*, p. 45.

sons for hostility. To understand this it is necessary to look back in history to the founding of Nazareth.

There is no mention of the village of Nazareth in the Old Testament. Aside from the presence of a few scattered Middle Bronze age Canaanite dwellings, the settlement of the town is known to have taken place in the second century B.C.[9] During that period Aristobulus the Maccabean "conquered Galilee and Judaized it."[10] Nazareth was known to have remained an all-Jewish town until the fourth century.[11] Furthermore, a stone fragment found in Caesarea records that after the fall of Jerusalem, one of the twenty-four courses of priests from the temple, now refugees, settled in Nazareth.[12] It had to have been a conservative all-Jewish town for this to have happened. Taken together, these facts depict Nazareth as a "settler town." Galilee had become "Galilee of the Gentiles" (Is 9:1; Mt 4:15). In the second century B.C., Maccabean nationalism sought to "create facts on the ground." The plan of action was to conquer the area and move Jewish settlers from Judea onto the land in Galilee. Colonial enclaves, be they Greek, Roman, British, American or Jewish have a strong tendency, in any age, to be politically, culturally and religiously self-conscious and intensely nationalistic. Nazareth, it appears, was such a town. In such a cultural world, how would Isaiah 61 have been understood?

Isaiah 61:1-7 falls into three short connected stanzas with the rhetorical structure formatted for clarity (figure 12.3).

Aspects of each of the three sections must be noted.

A careful look at the verses in the first section (stanzas 1-4) clarifies what Jesus read and what he left out. As noted, he omitted the phrase, "He has sent me to bind up the brokenhearted." Two lines later he borrowed a sentence from Isaiah 58:6 and added it to the reading. Finally, he cut the final verse in half and deleted the phrase "and the day of vengeance of our God." I have added a broad line in the text to highlight where Jesus stopped reading. His omission of the second half of the verse in 4 no doubt deeply angered the crowd in the synagogue. But his total omission of the second and particularly the third stanza in Isaiah was in all likelihood even more infuriating.

The second section (stanzas 5-6) assured comfort and gladness for the mourners. Leaving that material out could have disappointed some but would not have

---

[9]Eric M. Meyers and J. F. Strange, *Archaeology, the Rabbis & Early Christianity* (London: SCM Press, 1981), p. 57.

[10]Clemens Kopp, *The Holy Places of the Gospels* (New York: Herder & Herder, 1963), p. 52.

[11]Ibid., p. 55.

[12]Meyers, *Archaeology, the Rabbis & Early Christianity*, p 57.

Section 1

1. The *Spirit of the Lord* GOD is upon *me*,   THE LORD'S SPIRIT
   because the LORD has *anointed me*   The Lord's anointing

2.   to bring *good tidings* to the *poor*,   POOR
      [he has sent me to *bind up* the *brokenhearted*,]   Brokenhearted

3.   to proclaim *liberty* to the *captives*,   CAPTIVES
      and the *opening* of the prison to those who are *bound*;   The bound

4. to proclaim the year of the *LORD's favor*   THE LORD'S FAVOR
----
   and the day of *vengeance* of our *God*;   The Lord's vengeance

Section 2

5. to comfort all who *mourn*;
   to grant to those who mourn *in Zion*—   TO COMFORT THE MOURNING
   to give them a *garland* instead of *ashes*,   To give them: flowers
   the *oil of gladness* instead of *mourning*,   Gladness/praise
   the *mantle of praise* instead of a *faint spirit*;

6. that they may be called *oaks of righteousness*,
   the *planting of the LORD*,   THEY—OAKS OF THE LORD
   that he may be *glorified*.   God—glorified

Section 3

7. They shall *build up the ancient ruins*,
   they shall *raise up the former devastations*;   RUINS REBUILT
   they shall *repair the ruined cities*,   Cities repaired
   the devastations of *many generations*.   (from the past)

8.   *Aliens* shall stand and *feed your flocks*,   ALIENS YOUR SHEPHERDS
     foreigners shall be *your plowmen* and *vinedressers*;   And farm workers

9.   but *you* shall be called the *priests of the LORD*,   YOU—PRIESTS
        men shall speak of you as the *ministers of our God*;   You—ministers

10. *you shall eat* the *wealth of the nations/Gentiles*   THE GENTILES
     and *in their riches* you shall glory.   Wealth is yours

11. Instead of your shame you shall have a *double portion*,
    instead of dishonor you shall *rejoice in your lot*;   A GOOD LOT
    therefore in *your land* you shall possess a *double portion*; In your land—joy
    yours shall be *everlasting joy*.   (to the future)

Figure 12.3. Isaiah 61:1-7

given offense. But in the third section (7-11) Isaiah uses "inverted parallelism." This means that stanzas 7 and 11 form a pair, stanzas 8 and 10 form a second pair and the climax appears in the middle, stanza 9.

The first pair begins with stanza 7, which speaks of repairing the ruined cities. Its matching section is stanza 11, where the people are promised a double portion of their land. "To build and to plant" was a part of the call of Jeremiah (Jer 1:10), and these two stanzas summarize why the town of Nazareth was founded. As a settler community, their town was established "to build and to plant." Their goal was to "raise up the former devastations" and in *their land* they intended to possess a *double portion*. But the three stanzas in the middle are even more critical.

The text of stanzas 8 and 10 promises that the Gentiles around them will be their servants, and that the wealth of said aliens and foreigners will flow to them. With cheap foreign labor available they will have the leisure to devote themselves to being "priests of the Lord" (9). It is easy to understand the strong attraction such a text would have in a settler community. It is impossible to imagine that the community had overlooked this passage and did not know what these verses contained.

This text was surely at the heart of their history and self-understanding. Here in Isaiah the anticipated golden age of the Messiah promised great things. With the coming of the anointed one of God, all the hard work would be done by foreigners, and they, the settlers, would become wealthy, thanks to the labor of others. Applied to their day this vision of the messianic age would naturally have been very attractive to the people of Nazareth.

A clue to how this text was popularly understood around the time of Jesus can be found in the translations of the books of the Hebrew Bible into Aramaic. This translation as a whole was called the Targum, which stems from the first century.[13] The most important feature of this version is the addition of many words and phrases to the text, illuminating how the Aramaic-speaking Jewish community understood the material. In his English translation of the Targum of the book of Isaiah, Chilton italicizes these extra words and phrases to highlight the expansions. The Aramaic version of Isaiah 61:6-7 reads:

> You shall eat *the possessions* of *the Gentiles*, and in their glory you shall be *indulged*. Instead of your *being ashamed and confounded, two for one the benefits I promise you I will bring to you*, and *the Gentiles will be ashamed who were boasting in* their lot.[14]

---

[13] *The Isaiah Targum, The Aramaic Bible II,* trans. Bruce D. Chilton (Edinburgh: T & T Clark, 1987), p. xxiii.
[14] Ibid., pp. 118-19.

Clearly, the Aramaic expands the glorification of the readers at the expense of their Gentile neighbors. Such language reflects the kinds of ideas that were no doubt popular in the minds of Jesus' audience in the synagogue. Chilton, in commenting on the Targum writes, "The Targum informs us much more than any other sort of rabbinic literature about the understanding of Isaiah which ordinary attendees at synagogues might have shared."[15]

With this in mind, we can reconstruct the following. Jesus, the local boy, came to town as an itinerant rabbi and was given a chance to have his say. His audience of settlers understood the text of Isaiah 61 along the lines just indicated. With everyone listening intently, Jesus chose this familiar and deeply beloved passage, but to their shock and amazement he stopped reading at the very point at which judgment and servitude is pronounced on the Gentiles, whom they, as a settler community, were there to displace. Their goal was to make "Galilee of the Gentiles" into "Galilee of the Jews." So why did Rabbi Jesus omit the verses that the audience thought were critical to the text? Stunned, they awaited his comments on the reading.

It was not, however, simply a case of cutting the reading short. Jesus edited what he read. One phrase is omitted, a second is borrowed from Isaiah 58:6 and the final sentence is cut in half, as noted. Who is responsible for the omission, interpolation and truncation in the text?

It is often assumed that Luke constructed the scene and shaped the reading according to his interests. It is also possible to trace these changes to the documents and eyewitness accounts that Luke lists as his sources (Lk 1:1-4). Jesus lived near the beginning of the rabbinic period of Jewish history. The Mishnah is the earliest collection of the sayings of the Jewish rabbis and was compiled by Judah the prince in about the year A.D. 200. It contains reflections and regulations set down by the rabbis from around 100 B.C. (and before) up to the time of the book's compilation. In it there are rules about the reading of the Scriptures in the synagogue. The reader was obliged to read the Torah as it was written. But if the reading was from the book of the Prophets, one was allowed to "leave out verses in the Prophets."[16] How much could the reader skip? The Mishnah stipulates that the reader could omit "Only so much that he leaves no time for the interpreter to make a pause."[17] The reading was in Hebrew. But most of the people only understood Aramaic. So when Scripture was read, a translator stood beside the reader and translated verse

---

[15]Ibid., p. xxvi.
[16]Mishnah, *Mo᾽ed* 4.4 (Danby, p. 206).
[17]Ibid.

by verse into Aramaic for the benefit of non-Hebrew speaking listeners. As regards skipping back and forth, the idea was that the reader could read a verse for the translator to translate. While the translator was so engaged, the reader could turn to a verse somewhere else in the same book as long as it wasn't too far away. The reader was expected to read the new verse before returning promptly to where he began. The goal was to maintain a steady flow of reading and translating.

Furthermore, some things could be read but not translated.[18] Apparently, the reader and translator would agree on what was to be omitted and then the selected words or phrases would be read in Hebrew but not translated into Aramaic for the congregation. It is not possible to definitively determine that these precise guidelines were in force at the time of Jesus, but they do indicate that at a very early stage in the rabbinic movement there was a certain freedom in the reading of the Prophets that was not allowed in the reading of the Torah. What is clear is that the editing found in Luke 4:17-19 is within the framework of these rules. It is possible, therefore, to see Jesus as the editor and to affirm that it is Jesus' agenda which Luke records.

In any case, the editing was done by a Jew for other Jews, because rabbinic rules are followed. The text, as it appears in Luke, deserves careful scrutiny by looking at the reading from Isaiah with a view to discovering why the text was chosen and why these particular changes were made.

Jesus began with the bold words, "The Spirit of the Lord is upon me!" This is a clear reference to his baptism.[19] In his first comment after the reading, Jesus stated that he was the anointed one promised in the text. The Qumran community fragment 4Q521 claimed this anointing as a future promise. Jesus affirmed it as a present reality fulfilled in his person. This left the audience with two alternatives. Either Jesus was indeed the anointed one of God and should be followed or he was an arrogant, presumptuous and perhaps dangerous young man who must be silenced. There is little ground between the two options. Jesus read from the fixed written Scripture, but in the process he infused that Scripture with new meaning. The great William Temple once wrote, "There are two duties, each relatively easy to fulfill in isolation, not easy to combine; . . . 'quench not the spirit; hold fast to that which is good.'"[20]

In this text Jesus announces, "The Holy Spirit is upon me," even as he "holds fast" to the book of Isaiah, a fixed treasure from the past. Paul tells the Corinthians

---

[18]Ibid., 4.10. (Danby, p. 207).

[19]Ibn al-Tayyib, *Tafsir al-Mashriqi*, 2:83.

[20]William Temple, *The Church Looks Forward* (London: Macmillan, 1944), p. 23.

not to go beyond Scripture (1 Cor 4:6). At the same time he describes great new things that God has done in Christ. Even so, Jesus confirms the past and announces the new that God is doing through the Spirit.

After this startling opening Jesus continues to read. With editing, the text reveals that the anointed one has three tasks. These are set forth and then repeated in figure 12.4 (see p. 163).

> The *Spirit* of the Lord is upon me
> for he has *anointed me*
> A to *preach good news* to the *poor.*   PREACH
>   B He has *sent me* * to proclaim to the *prisoners—freedom,*   SENT
>   C and to the *blind*—recovery of *sight,*   SIGHT
>   B' 'to *send forth* the *oppressed*—in *freedom,'* *   SEND
> A' to *proclaim* * the acceptable year of the Lord. *   PROCLAIM

What is "good news for the poor"? Do the following lines in the text define it? If so, then "good news for the poor" is "release to the captives" and "liberty" for the oppressed. In such a case, Jesus' ministry was to break the power of the economic, social and political chains that kept people in bondage. Or, should the Greek words *euangelizō* (to preach good news) and *kēryssō* (to proclaim) be emphasized and the text be interpreted as referring to the new reality of God breaking into history in Jesus Christ to save us from our sins?

To begin to sort out these questions it should first be noted that the text presents a list of three tasks using an A-B-C-B'-A' format. The outer envelope (A-A') has to do with *proclamation.* The second idea (B-B') speaks of *justice advocacy,* and the climax in the center (C) tells of *compassion* (sight for the blind). I have noted the four major editorial changes that Jesus made in order to shape this carefully constructed list. With editing the text focuses on:

> proclamation
>   justice advocacy
>   compassion
>   justice advocacy
> proclamation

The editorial changes found in the text are necessary, pivotal and deserve attention.

The two lines emphasizing proclamation (the first and the last) are:

> A To *preach good news* to the poor
> A' To *proclaim* the acceptable year of the Lord

In the New Testament the two great words for the proclamation of the message of salvation in Jesus Christ are *euangelizō* and *kēryssō*. The first produced the English word *evangel* and the second created the theological word *kerygma*. As noted, the word *kēryssō* (in Greek and Hebrew) is an upgrade from the word *to call*. With the introduction of the word *kēryssō* the parallel between *the evangel* and *the kerygma* is created. Throughout the New Testament these are the two Greek words which refer to the preaching of the message of the gospel. But in this text what is that message?

Surely the key to this question is found in the definition of "the poor." When Isaiah speaks of good news *for the poor* what does he mean by "the poor"? Is the prophet primarily referring to those who do not have enough to eat, or is he addressing those who sense their spiritual hunger and seek God?

Fortunately, Isaiah provides a fairly straightforward answer. In Hebrew two words are being used; one of them is *ʿānî* (often translated "poor") and the other is *ʿanāw* (usually translated "meek"). The two are virtually synonymous and often used interchangeably. The text in Isaiah 61:1 has *ʿānāwîm*, which tends in the direction of "meek." In Isaiah these two words appear fifteen times. Three of them lean in the direction of "the people with not enough to eat" and the other eleven are clearly oriented to "the humble and pious who seek God." In Isaiah 66:2 the prophet writes:

> But this is the man to whom I will look,
> > he that is poor [*ʾānî*] and contrite in spirit,
> > and trembles at my word.

Isaiah 29:19 reads:

> The meek [*ʿānāwîm]* shall obtain fresh joy in the LORD,
> > and the poor [*ĕbyônê]* among men shall exult in the Holy One of Israel.

This same definition of "the poor" resurfaces in the Qumran community, which used "the poor" as a means of self-identification. It understood itself to be the community of true believers who had the right to claim the promises of God for "the poor." Some of the newly published fragments of the Dead Sea Scrolls have been called "Hymns of the Poor" (4Q434; 436). Eisenman and Wise summarize these hymns by saying, "In the *Hymns of the Poor*, the Poor are 'saved' because of their 'Piety', and God's 'Mercy', and because they 'walked in the Way of His heart.' "[21]

---

[21]Robert H. Eisenman and Michael Wise, *The Dead Sea Scrolls Uncovered* (Rockport, Mass.: Element, 1992), p. 237.

Early Jewish Christians called themselves the *Ebionites* (the poor).[22] In Matthew Jesus says, "Blessed are the poor in spirit" (Mt 5:3). It is possible to read this text as a clarification of the shorter text in Luke 6:20, which reads, "blessed are you poor," rather than a correction of it. In addition, Paul occasionally refers to the church in Jerusalem as "the poor" (Rom 15:26; Gal 2:10).

Finally, post-Christian Jewish texts describe the poor/meek in the same manner. The *Mekilta of Rabbi Ishmael* reads, "Scripture tells that whosoever is meek [ˈānāw] will cause the Shekinah to dwell with man on earth."[23] Here also "the poor" means the humble and pious who seek God. Six hundred years of use (before and after Jesus) confirm the word *poor* as meaning *primarily* "Those who tremble at the word of God" (Is 66:5).

To turn this word in Luke 4:16 into nothing more than politics and economics is to ignore history. Luke's Gospel affirms that in Jesus, God "has visited and redeemed his people" (Lk 1:68). In every age the church has proclaimed that in Jesus there is hope, light and direction for those who earnestly seek to love God and their neighbors.

The matching line of this list of five is "To proclaim the acceptable year of the Lord." This can be read as meaning the coming of the year of Jubilee, in which all slaves are released, debts canceled and prisoners set free. It can also be seen, using the language of Jubilee, to proclaim "The age of the Messiah, which is Jehovah's time for bestowing great blessings on His people."[24]

In summary, the proclamation of good news to the humble and pious who sincerely seek God is affirmed in the opening and closing phrases of this list of goals endorsed by God's anointed one.

The second theme is also presented with two phrases:

B He has *sent* me to proclaim to the prisoners—*freedom*
B' "to *send forth* the oppressed—in *freedom*"

Each of these lines begins with the word *sent* and concludes with the word *freedom*. The parallels are not accidental. Nor is it by chance that the two lines represent slightly different aspects of the same topic. The striking difference is that in the first line the anointed one *is sent* out in freedom. In the second, the anointed

---

[22]Jean Daniélou, "The Ebionites," in *The Theology of Jewish Christianity* (Philadelphia: Westminster Press, 1964), pp. 55-64.

[23]*Mekhilta de-Rabbi Ishmael*, trans. J. Z. Lauterbach (Philadelphia: Jewish Publication of America, 1976), 2:273.

[24]Alfred Plummer, *Gospel According to S. Luke*, 5th ed., International Critical Commentary (1922; reprint, Edinburgh: T & T Clark, 1960), p. 122. For a detailed discussion of this point cf. John Nolland, *Luke*, 3 vols., Word Biblical Commentary (Dallas: Word, 1989), 1:197-98.

one *sends out* someone else in freedom. These two lines affirm two complimentary theologies of mission embodied by Elijah and Elisha. Elijah is *sent* by God out of Israel to the widow of Zarephath of Sidon (1 Kings 17:8-16). Elisha *sends* Naaman the Syrian to the Jordan to receive freedom from his leprosy (2 Kings 5:1-14). The second line of this pair is introduced into the text from the distance of three chapters. What then is its original setting?

The phrase "To send forth the oppressed in freedom" is borrowed from Isaiah 58:6, which discusses fasting and declares that God is not impressed with empty, pious gestures. He asks:

> Is not this the fast that I choose:
> > to loose the bonds of wickedness,
> > to undo the thongs of the yoke
> *to let the oppressed go free?* . . .
> Is it not to share your bread with the hungry
> > and bring the homeless poor into your house? (Is 58:6-7)

The meaning of the selected phrase is unambiguous; it refers to *justice advocacy*. The line in Isaiah 61:2 that matches 58:6 has the same emphasis. When Isaiah wrote, "He has *sent* me to proclaim to the prisoners freedom," he was talking about *refugees going home*. His community was living in exile in what is now southern Iraq. Cyrus the Persian had just conquered the Babylonian rulers of that area and had allowed the various refugee peoples in Babylon to return home. The subject in both phrases (B and B') in this matching pair is *"justice advocacy."* This paring of ideas is created deliberately by the introduction of the phrase borrowed from Isaiah 58:6. The emphasis on *justice advocacy* is thereby powerfully reinforced through editing.

Having worked for decades in the Middle East with Armenians and Palestinians, I know something of the special longing and pain of those who have been driven by violence from their homelands. When such peoples hear the phrase "release to the captives" they instinctively understand it to mean "freedom to return home." Surely this is what Isaiah intended. To limit the word *captive* to some form of bondage to sin is to fall into the same error we labored to avoid in the previous discussion of "the poor"—namely, to forget history. Finally, as regards this composite quote, what should motivate both the *proclamation* and *justice advocacy?* The climax in the center of the edited Isaiah quotation in Luke 4:18-19 provides the answer.

The middle of the text (C) reads, "The opening of the eyes of the blind." The original Hebrew of this phrase is ambiguous. It literally reads, "The opening—to those who are bound." The reader is not told if this refers to "the opening of the eyes of the blind" or the "opening of the prisons for those who are bound." Imagination can take the text either way. At the same time, the Qumran community was clear about including *the opening of the eyes of the blind* as part of the Messiah's task. The following early texts are significant as background to understanding this phrase.

- Original Hebrew: "The opening to those who are bound."

- Aramaic Targum of Isaiah: "To those who are bound, Be revealed to light."

- Greek Old Testament (LXX): "Recovery of sight to the blind."

- Qumran's view of the Messiah (4Q521) included: "Opening the eyes of the blind."

- Psalm 146:7-8: "The LORD sets the prisoners free; / the LORD opens the eyes of the blind."

- The Suffering Servant in Isaiah 42:7 was to: "open the eyes that are blind, / to bring out the prisoners from the dungeon."

It is impossible to discern with precision the source of the text of Luke 4:18 as regards this phrase. Jesus could have changed the wording himself, as permitted to the synagogue reader. Or he could have left the Hebrew before him unchanged and read, "The opening—to those who were bound." Did Luke change this into "recovering of sight to the blind" (following the LXX)? Was this an accommodation to Qumran, the psalmist, the Suffering Servant of Isaiah or the Aramaic Targum? As the popular Targums allowed for interpretive translation, the apostles could have exercised this same freedom. Or did Jesus read the Hebrew and the translator (by agreement) introduced a reference to the blind into the reading? There are no clear-cut answers to any of these questions. What is evident, however, is that a great deal of Jewish thought included the opening of the eyes of the blind as a part of the messianic agenda. Here, in Luke's Gospel, this compassionate act (of opening the eyes of the blind) is at the center of the messianic agenda delineated in this carefully edited Old Testament text.

"Now faith, hope, love abide, these three; but the greatest of these is love" (1 Cor 13:13). An act of compassion/love is placed in the center of the list comprised of *proclamation, justice advocacy* and *compassion*. A critical component of the challenge this text presents to the church in every age is to strive to keep this brilliant holistic package together. Each is meaningful, but only together in their christological setting do they achieve their full healing power.

Every disciple of Jesus Christ has his or her special calling. The *preacher* knows that those marching for justice are an important part of the team. Thoughtful *justice advocates* know that the justice of God must judge the justice for which they strive.[25] Those who show *compassion*, in whatever form, realize that without a message that changes hearts and without a just society, their work is incomplete. The greatest of all is love.

To continue with the story, when Jesus completed the reading he rolled up the scroll, returned it to the synagogue official and sat down to comment on the text. His opening sentence was a lightening bolt. He announced the dawning of the messianic age as an event that was taking place in him before their eyes. As noted above, they "witnessed against him" not "for him" and were offended at how he took a text of judgment and turned it into an affirmation of mercy. Their hostility was evident immediately. They must have been thinking something along the lines of:

> What is the matter with this boy? He has quoted one of our favorite texts, but has omitted some of its most important verses. In the process he has turned a text of judgment into a text of mercy. This is outrageous! The messianic age is a golden age *for us* and a day of God's *vengeance* upon *them*. How could this boy grow up here and not know this? Doesn't he remember why this village was founded?

Jesus replied to the hostility rising before him by saying, "You will probably quote me the proverb, 'Physician, heal thyself; what we heard happened at Capernaum do also in your own country.' And he said, 'Truly, I tell you, no prophet is acceptable in his own country'" (Lk 4:23-24).

In short, they know that Isaiah 61 promises material benefits for the believing community. Jesus shifts the text from "Here is what you will receive" into "Here is what you are expected to give." "I am the anointed one of God," says Jesus, "and to follow me you must engage (with me) in proclamation, justice advocacy and compassion." This shift irritates the congregation who are still focused on what they will receive if he is the Messiah.

To this question Jesus turns his attention by invoking two stories from the Hebrew Bible, one about Elijah and the other concerning Elisha. The text is composed of four tightly constructed Hebrew parallelisms put together in "step parallelism." There is one "footnote." Formatted in figure 12.4 to expose its composition, the text is:

---

[25]Lesslie Newbigin, *The Open Secret* (Grand Rapids: Eerdmans, 1979), pp. 124-27.

> But in truth, I tell you,
>
> a. there were many *widows in Israel*
>   b. in the days of *Elijah*
>   (when the heaven was shut up three years and six months, when there came a great famine over all the land;)
>   c. and *Elijah* was sent to *none of them*
>   d. *except* to Zarephath of Sidon, to a *woman*, a widow.
>
> a. And there were many *lepers in Israel*
>   b. in the time of the prophet *Elisha*,
>   c. and *none* of them *was cleansed*
>   d. except *Naaman, the Syrian*. (Lk 4:25-27)

Figure 12.4. Widows and lepers in Israel (Lk 4:25-27)

Four themes are presented in the first four lines and then repeated in the same order in the last four. These are:

a. many widows/lepers in Israel

b. in the days of Elijah/Elisha

c. none helped

d. except a widow/Naaman

Within this carefully balanced set of four parallels a "footnote" appears. If the reader is a Greek who is unfamiliar with the Hebrew Scriptures he or she will nonetheless be able to figure out the second story in spite of his or her ignorance of the original account. A leper is cleansed, but what about the first story? If the reader is unfamiliar with the original narrative, the four matching lines about the widow are meaningless. Naaman is sick with leprosy. But what is the woman's problem?

Someone, perhaps Luke, added some background information in the form of a type of "footnote." As a result of no rain for three and a half years there was famine. This footnote interrupts the carefully constructed eight lines. The ancients had no system of adding notes to the bottom of the page. The only way the editor of a text could clarify its meaning was to add the extra information to the text itself. The appearance of such a footnote in this text is significant. The Jewish listener/reader could be expected to be familiar with both stories. Jesus would not have needed to tell the synagogue of the drought and ensuing famine. But Luke is composing his Gospel in Greek for Theophilus and other Gentiles. Most likely Luke added the note to help his non-Jewish readers understand the text. By the time Luke received this story it was already part of a fixed tradition.

In summary, the overall story is comprised of three layers:

1. Jesus edits and reads from Isaiah 61. In commentary on the reading he composes eight lines of Hebrew rhetoric as he invokes the stories of the widow and Naaman.

2. The dramatic confrontation is committed to writing by the apostolic community, which remembers this event. The community uses Hebrew stylistics in the composition and places the Isaiah quotation in the center of eight matching lines of narrative framework.

3. Luke received this story in written form and added one historical footnote to help his Gentile readers understand the material.[26]

What of the accounts themselves? First Kings 17:1-16 records the story of Elijah and the woman of Zarephath. In the eighth century B.C. the prophet Elijah denounced King Ahab for worshiping Baal, announced a famine and then fled for his life. As the predicted famine set in, Elijah escaped to a small village called Zarephath near Sidon. There he found a widow gathering sticks to bake a final loaf of bread for her only son. With no extended family to care for them and with their food supply exhausted due to the famine, this was her final act before surrendering to the Grim Reaper.

The prophet told her, "Feed it to me!" What arrogance! How could he ask a desperate woman for her last morsel of food and expect her starving son to stand by watching? But there is more.

According to her worldview, each god's power was limited to his territory. Yahweh, of the land of Israel, could only help those who lived in Israel. Sidon was Baal's country, and only Baal had power there. The widow naturally assumed that the God of Israel was powerless in her district. Jonah thought he could escape Yahweh by escaping the land of Israel on a ship (Jon 1:3). Naaman, the visiting general from Damascus, took soil from Israel with him on his homeward journey so that he could pray to Israel's God while living in Damascus. Obviously, if each god held sway only over a certain territory, Naaman did not expect the God of Israel to hear him unless he stood on at least some soil from the land of Israel! He solved his problem by taking the necessary soil from Israel with him to Damascus (2 Kings 5:17). In a world holding such views, how could Elijah possibly expect this starving widow to trust a prophet of Israel whose god was (in her view) pow-

---

[26]Mark records the same story but does not mention the violent response of the community. This omission may be traceable to Mark's assumed concern to keep the peace between his Jewish and Gentile Christian readers in Rome.

erless to help anyone in the region of Sidon, where she lived?

The woman makes an astounding leap of faith into the unknown. She obeys the prophet and gives him the loaf of bread. As she does, she is rewarded with a cruse of oil that never runs dry. Her radical faith in the God of Israel was sustained by God's gifts of oil and meal. Her story was remembered and she became a model of faith for all Israel.

Jesus' second story is also from the Hebrew Scriptures. As recorded in 2 Kings 5:1-15, Naaman was the commander-in-chief of the Syrian army and a confidant of the King of Damascus. Suddenly struck with leprosy, he followed a tip from his wife's maid and traveled to Israel for a cure. After a disastrous courtesy call on the king, he turned to the prophet Elisha. As the commander of the Syrian army, Naaman was a powerful, dangerous man and could expect extraordinary courtesy anywhere he might choose to go. But to his surprise, on arriving at the house of the prophet, he was not invited in. Instead, Elisha sent a servant out to talk to him! Preposterous! Insulting! Outrageous!

What did Naaman want? Ah, yes, the issue of leprosy. The prophet ordered Naaman, via the servant, to wash in the Jordan. Custom demanded that Elisha prepare a huge banquet for the distinguished guest and at its conclusion deferentially inquire, "What can your humble servant do for you?"

Naaman was accustomed to the melted snows of Mount Hermon that flowed through his hometown. The dwellers of Damascus have always enjoyed the finest source of ever-flowing water in the Middle East. How could he be expected to lower himself and get dirty in one of Israel's muddy streams? Naaman started home in a rage! His servants then skillfully suggested that had he been asked to do some great and noble act he would have obeyed. So why not absorb the insult and take the bath? He agreed, bathed in the Jordan and was healed. By invoking this story Jesus presented a second Gentile whose remarkable faith was rewarded.

To the congregation in the synagogue Jesus was saying:

> If you want to receive the benefits of the new golden age of the Messiah, you must imitate the faith of these Gentiles. I am not asking you merely to tolerate or to accept them. You must see such Gentiles as your spiritual superiors and acknowledge that they can instruct you in the nature of authentic faith. The benefits of the "acceptable year of the Lord," which I have come to inaugurate, are available to such people.

Jesus wanted models of authentic faith. To find them he reached beyond the ethnic community of which he was a part and invoked these two stories of Gentile heroes of faith.

The gospel is not safe in any culture without a witness within that culture, from beyond itself. D. T. Niles the famous Sri Lankan theologian quotes James Matthews and writes, "Because we have come to terms with our own society, the total word of God has to be declared to us by another."[27] In every culture the message of the gospel is in constant danger of being compromised by the value system that supports that culture and its goals. The stranger to that culture can instinctively identify those points of surrender and call the community back to a purer and more authentic faith. But such infusions of new life are usually resented and resisted. This very pattern of hostility emerges in this story. And there is more.

In the synagogue at Nazareth, Jesus presents a two-sided theology of mission. In the text of Isaiah that Jesus edits and reads there is a delicate balance between "go out" and "attract in." The anointed one is "*sent* to proclaim to the captives— freedom." This is illustrated by Elijah, who leaves Israel and goes to the woman of Zarephath in Sidon. The Messiah will also *attract people in*, even as Elisha attracted Naaman to Israel. These two forces can be called the centrifugal and centripetal forces of mission. Loyalty to this text requires commitment to the ministries of Elijah and Elisha.

These stories also instruct the reader regarding the nature of authentic faith. Faith in the New Testament has three major components: *intellectual assent, a daily walk of trust* and *obedience*.

Someone may say, "I believe the bishop is telling the truth." The word *believe*, in this instance, has to do with *intellectual assent*. So it is with faith. The believer grants intellectual assent to a series of affirmations. We believe that God is three in one.

The *daily walk of trust* is also a critical part of faith. All of us have known people of "great faith" who, through the deepest tragedies, have managed to maintain faith in spite of cruel, unanswered questions.

Finally, faith is something we do. I *believe* I should get more exercise, but often fail to do so. Paul clarifies this understanding of faith when he writes: "whatsoever is not of faith is sin" (Rom 14:23 KJV). We expect him to say "whatsoever is not of faith is *unbelief*." But for Paul the opposite of faith is sin because his understanding of faith includes obedience. Clearly, the opposite of obedience is sin. Paul can talk about "the obedience of faith" because for him the two words are almost interchangeable. I *believe* I should write this chapter and am now doing so. My belief is authentic in that I am acting upon it.

---

[27]D. T. Niles, *Upon the Earth* (London: Lutterworth, 1962), p. 166.

Both of the stories in this text bring these elements together. The widow of Zarephath does not say, "This prophet is talking nonsense. His god, Yahweh, cannot help me in Baal's country." Such a statement would be a refusal of the *intellectual assent* component of faith. Nor does she say, "I believe your god can help me, but to give you this last loaf of bread is unthinkable." To say that would be to grant *intellectual assent* but refuse the *daily walk of trust* and *obedience*. Instead, she grants that Yahweh has power in Baal's territory. She also *obeys* the prophet's command and is willing to *trust* the God of Israel for tomorrow. She combines *intellectual assent, obedience* and *trust*.

In like manner, by traveling to Israel Naaman the Syrian *grants validity to the idea* that the God of Israel can help him. He then obeys the prophet's command and washes in the Jordan. Without *trusting* the God of Israel for his future he would not have done so. What might they say in Damascus?

Another significant factor of these two stories has to do with gender. The first story concerns a woman; the second recounts the tale of a man. They are parallel, and the woman is mentioned first. None of this is accidental. Jesus was looking for stories of heroes of faith and could have chosen Abraham, Moses or David. He chose one woman and one man because he was inaugurating a new fellowship in which men and women would share together as equals. What then was the congregation's response to his sermon illustrations?

Jesus knew that the town's agenda was to reclaim land from Gentiles who had moved into Galilee from places such as Zarephath and Damascus. He must have known that these stories would upset the congregation before him. But he told them anyway and the room exploded in anger!

Settler types often see religion and politics as a single package. When Jesus disagreed with their political and economic goals they decided to kill him.

The text says:

> And they rose up and put him out of the city, and led him to the brow of the hill on which their city was built, that they might throw him down headlong. But passing through the midst of them he went away. (Lk 4:29-30)

The story concludes with strong hints of both the cross and the resurrection. Anyone condemned for the sin of blasphemy was stoned, which seems to be what is happening in this story. If religion and politics are a single ideology, then any serious rejection of the community's political goals would have been seen as blasphemy against God. Jesus appears to be so accused.

Jesus rejected the narrow nationalism of his day. A text of judgment was transformed into a message of grace, and his listeners were incensed.

The rabbinical tradition stipulated that blasphemy was to be punished by stoning so Jesus was taken to a hill outside town for execution.[28] This also was regulated. The culprit was to be thrown off a cliff. If the fall did not kill the accused, the community at the top of the hill was to complete the task by raining heavy stones down upon the blasphemer.

History is replete with examples of one ethnic community displacing another. To accomplish such a goal the aggressors usually feel the need to demean those they are brutalizing. Words such as *savages, vermin* and now *terrorists* ring down the centuries. When a land-grabbing venture is in progress, woe to the brave soul who dares select models of faith from among the victims, especially when the aggressors are certain that God is on their side. From this day forward Jesus knows that his message and person will continue to trigger deep and violent hostility. To what end?

At the edge of the cliff, Jesus walks away! With nothing save his gentle presence, John Wesley was able to melt murderous opposition to his preaching. Charles "Chinese" Gordon[29] was cut from the same cloth. Jesus came and proclaimed his message, which triggered interest and then hostility. That hostility turned violent and his audience tried to kill him—but *didn't quite manage!* The thoughtful reader of Luke's Gospel now has a notion as to how it will all end.

It is not easy for a young man to invoke a serious hearing in his hometown. The reader fully expects Jesus to attempt to please. Surely he will support the traditional values of the community. He could offer a word of encouragement for their efforts at reclaiming the countryside from the Gentiles and emphasize the importance of sabbath laws. He can add several guarded comments on the Roman occupation and how the Messiah will bring relief from injustice.

But no attempt is made to shape his message along the lines of their agenda. In bold and uncompromising terms Jesus announces his ministry of proclamation, justice advocacy and compassion to be inaugurated by himself, as the anointed one of God. They can join him by imitating the remarkable faith of a Phoenician widow and a Syrian general. He knows his edited version of the text of Isaiah 61 will trigger deep anger, and it is a risk he is willing to take. Violence hovered in the air, as did a mysterious victory over it.

---

[28]Mishnah, *Sanhedrin* 6:1-6 (Danby, pp. 389-91).
[29]Charles Gordon was a famous nineteenth-century Scottish general who with his commanding presence could electrify a rebellious mob of mutinous troops into obeying him. His exploits in China earned him the title "Chinese Gordon." In 1885 he was killed in Khartoum, Sudan, and became "Gordon of Khartoum." See Lord Elton, *Gordon of Khartoum* (New York: Knopf, 1955), pp. 26-75.

SUMMARY: THE INAUGURATION OF JESUS' MINISTRY

The remarkably rich text of Luke 4:16-30 contains a series of theological themes:

1. *Jesus* is the unique prophet on whom the Spirit *remains*. He is also the anointed one (Messiah) of God.

2. The "anointing of the Messiah," the "gift of the spirit" and the "acceptable year of the Lord" together form the bookends of the Isaiah quote. There can be no kingdom without the king.

3. *Salvation comes from beyond the community.* It is not community generated. The anointed one/Messiah is the bearer of that salvation. The text is fulfilled in him.

4. The *ministry of Jesus* (and thereby the nature of the kingdom) is for the *whole person*. It involves: *proclamation/evangelism*, *justice advocacy* and *compassion*. The climax of the inverted list is *compassion*. This compassion is meant to inform both the *witness* and the *justice advocacy*.

5. Jesus *refuses to endorse the narrow nationalism* of his own community. Instead he stands in prophetic judgment over it.

6. A *theology of mission* is established. Both the centripetal and the centrifugal forces of mission are illustrated. The messenger *goes out* with the message (to the woman), and Naaman is *attracted in*to the community of faith and its prophet.

7. The *universality of the message* is affirmed. Jews (the people of Capernaum) and Gentiles (cf. vv. 25-27) are recipients of grace.

8. Faith is illustrated by two heroes, a woman and a man. The two are parallel, and the woman is listed first. *Equality between women and men* in the kingdom is clearly affirmed.

9. The message of the good news calls for a *radical response of faith*. The faith exhibited here involves intellectual assent, trust and obedience.

10. The topic of *rewards* is opened. Significant *far-reaching blessings* are available to those who, like the woman and Naaman, make radical decisions of faith.

11. The reader senses a foreshadowing of Jesus' coming, his ministry, his rejection, his death and his victory over death (resurrection).

As a result of this stunning scene, the ministry of Jesus was indeed inaugurated.

13

The Blind Man and Zacchaeus

Luke 18:35—19:10

Ecclesiastes 4:1 provides a background for reflection on the blind man and Zacchaeus. That remarkable verse reads:

Again I saw all the oppressions that are practiced under the sun.
And behold, the tears of the oppressed,
and they had no one to comfort them!
On the side of their oppressors there was power,
and there was no one to comfort them.

When Jesus arrives in the town of Jericho, two events occur that need to be examined together. In the first Jesus heals a man, *oppressed*. In the second Jesus extends love to an *oppressor*. The New Testament's chapter divisions, following the fourth-century Greek paragraph divisions, break the two Jericho stories apart and place them in different chapters. But when viewed together they form a pair.

It is common knowledge that for some decades Christians around the world have increasingly been discovering that the God of the Bible sides with the oppressed. In Scripture the poor, the widow, the outcast, the refugee and the marginalized all receive God's special attention and compassion. But what can be said about the *oppressor?* The natural assumption is that he or she must be opposed. The Magnificat states, "He has put down the mighty from their thrones . . . and the rich he has sent empty away" (Lk 1:52-53). All who seek to support the oppressed must surely oppose the oppressor! Is it possible to oppose oppressors and at the same time extend "comfort" to them? The two stories that took place on the edges of Jericho provide an opportunity to reflect on Jesus dealing with the oppressed and then the oppressor.

THE BLIND MAN BESIDE THE ROAD

In the first story (Lk 18:35-43) Jesus "drew near to Jericho" and interacted with a blind beggar in the setting of a crowd (figure 13.1).

---

1. As he drew near to Jericho,
   a blind man was sitting by the roadside begging;

   INTRODUCTION

2. and hearing a multitude going by,
   he inquired what this meant.
   They told him,
   "Jesus of Nazareth is passing by."

   CROWD:
   Jesus of Nazareth

3. And he cried,
   "Jesus, Son of David,
   have mercy on me."

   BEGGAR
   Jesus, Son of David
   Mercy

4. And those who were in front rebuked him,
   telling him to be silent;

   CROWD:
   Be silent

5. but he cried out all the more,
   "Son of David
   have mercy on me."

   BEGGAR
   Son of David
   Mercy
   ----

6. And Jesus stopped,
   and commanded him to be brought to him;
   and when he came near, he asked him,
   "What do you want me to do for you?"

   JESUS
   Beggar summoned
   and examined

7. He said,
   "Lord,
   let me receive my sight."

   BEGGAR
   Lord
   Sight!

8. And Jesus said to him,
   "Receive your sight;
   your faith has saved you."

   JESUS
   Sight given
   Faith and salvation

9. And immediately he received his sight
   and followed him,
   glorifying God;

   BEGGAR
   Sight Received
   Follow/Glorify God

10. and all the people,
    when they saw it,
    gave praise to God.

    CONCLUSION

Figure 13.1. Jesus' healing of the blind man (Lk 18:35-43)

THE RHETORIC

This short story is constructed with great care. Inside an introduction (1) and a conclusion (10) the beggar engages in conversation with the crowd (2-5) and with Jesus (6-9). In each case two interchanges occur. Indifference and hostility on the part of the crowd gives way to praise. A christological progression appears in the story as follows: :

Crowd: (2) Jesus of Nazareth
Beggar: (3) Jesus, Son of David
Beggar: (5) Son of David
Beggar: (7) Lord
Crowd: (10) Praise to God (for healing by Jesus)

Only after the beggar's cries become specific are they answered. A straight-line progression moves through the story from beginning to end.

COMMENTARY

The story begins with a blind beggar, seated beside the road, who hears "a multitude going by." In the Middle East, village people show honor to an important guest by walking some distance out of town to greet the guest and escort him or her into the village. At times, the popularity of a guest can be measured by how far the crowd walks to welcome the visitor. In the early 1960s our family resided in Assiut in the south of Egypt. At that time, the late President Gamal Abdel Nasser was at the height of his power and popularity. While we were there, Nasser visited Assiut. As his entourage approached the city, thousands walked more than ten miles out of town to greet him. The enthusiastic patriots then obliged all the cars in the presidential party to turn off their motors while the crowd tied ropes to the bumpers of the vehicles and pulled them the last ten miles into Assiut as a gesture of honor to the great man. A modern Western equivalent might be the inevitable crowd that fills an airport when a famous, victorious athletic team returns home.

Some of the crowd with Jesus may have followed him from Galilee, but the majority greeting him were most likely from Jericho. This public attention signals to the reader that a banquet was prepared in Jericho, where the famous rabbi would be expected to spend the night.

The beggar heard the crowd and asked what was happening. The guest was identified as "Jesus of Nazareth." The beggar then began crying for attention using the rare title "Son of David." During Jesus' public ministry, as recorded in the Synoptic Gospels, this title is only used by the Syro-Phoenician woman (Mt 15:21-28) and by this blind beggar. Here, at the beginning of his ascent to Jerusalem,

Jesus is identified as "Son of David" (Mt and Lk), and at the end of his earthly life a Roman centurion gives him the title "Son of God" (Mt and Mk).[1] This story can therefore be rightly seen as a prologue to the Passion narrative with its bookends of "Son of David" and "Son of God."

The beggar makes his appeal to the now widely acclaimed son of the house of David, whereupon the crowd rebukes the beggar by telling him to be quiet. Perhaps out of delicacy Luke does not tell his readers that the beggar was called Bartimaeus, which can be translated "Son of filth" (Mk 10:46). Again, Mark records stronger language with the word *siōpaō*, which as an ingressive aorist can be translated "shut your mouth."[2] But in spite of the demands from the crowd to "shut up," he cries ever louder, abbreviating Jesus' name to "Son of David." In sharp contrast to the crowd's attempt to marginalize the beggar, Jesus stops and "commanded him to *be brought*." The very people who are insulting the beggar are ordered to escort him to Jesus for an "audience" (a nice touch). They become the "servants of the king" bringing a guest into his presence.

The beggar approaches Jesus only to face an exam. The question, "What do you want me to do for you?" appears tasteless and heartless. The man is blind and a beggar! Is it not evident to everyone that he needs healing from his devastating darkness?

In traditional Middle Eastern society beggars are a recognized part of the community and are understood to be offering "services" to it. Every pious person is expected to give to the poor. But if the poor are not readily available to receive alms, how can this particular duty be fulfilled? The traditional beggar does not say, "Excuse me, Mister, do you have a few coins for a crust of bread?" Instead, he sits in a public place and challenges the passerby with "Give to God!" He is really saying, "My needs are beside the point. I am offering you a golden opportunity to fulfill one of your obligations to God. Furthermore, this is a public place and if you give to me here, you will gain a reputation as an honorable, compassionate, pious person."

When a beggar receives money (whatever the amount) he usually stands up and in a loud voice proclaims the giver to be the most noble person he has ever met and invokes God's grace and blessing on the giver, his family, his friends and associates, his going out and coming in, and many other good things. Such public praise is surely worth the small sum given the beggar.

The difficulty with this profession is that some visible handicap is necessary. A man with one leg or one arm might manage to support himself by begging on a

---

[1]Rom 1:3 brings these two titles together.
[2]Max Zerwick and Mary Grosvenor, *A Grammatical Analysis of the Greek New Testament,* rev. ed. (Rome: Biblical Institute Press, 1981), p. 143.

street corner, but a blind man is virtually guaranteed success. At the same time, a blind man, such as the beggar in this story, has no education, training, employment record or marketable skills. If healed, self-support will be extremely difficult. Indeed, is it not in his interests to remain blind? The grace of God, mediated through Jesus, is free but not cheap, as Dietrich Bonhoeffer has affirmed.[3] Is this blind man ready to accept the new responsibilities and challenges that will come to him if he is healed? Jesus' exam presses this stark question upon him.

The beggar passes the exam. He is ready and responds to Jesus directly as "Lord" rather than using the more general title "Son of David." At the same time, he moves from requesting some nebulous form of "mercy" (a coin?) to a specific yearning to be healed of his blindness. The Arabic Diatessaron of this verse adds a christological flourish. It says, "Let me receive my sight *that I might see you.*"[4] Although this is an imaginative gloss, it is thoughtful. No doubt the beggar does want to see Jesus.

Jesus grants his request and says, "Receive your sight; your faith has saved you." What faith has he affirmed? On reflection, three aspects of the blind man's faith can be detected.

- He has faith that Jesus has the power of God to heal.
- He believes that Jesus has compassion on the poor, which includes him.
- He is confident that Jesus is the Son of David (a messianic title), and he accepts Jesus as his "Lord."

Granted, the word *kyrios* can also mean "sir," but as used in this story the title carries a deeper resonance, even though its exact content cannot be determined.

The beggar is "saved." The Greek word *sōzō* (to save) means many things. Good health is part of its rich nuance. The healed man follows his Lord, "glorifying God" whom he recognizes as the source of Jesus' power to heal.

The reaction of the crowd is significant. In this story Jesus sides with the oppressed (the blind man) and the community is his oppressor. As noted, the community marginalized the beggar but is then ordered by Jesus to escort him into Jesus' presence. By extending special grace to the very man the crowd has just rejected, Jesus gives the crowd a verbal slap on the wrist! Would they be able to absorb Jesus' public criticism of them? Yes, indeed, for they join the former blind man in his praises to God. As long as Jesus is offering special grace to *the oppressed* it would be churlish to make a fuss. When he offers special grace to *the oppressor* it may be a different story, as the reader soon discovers. To that second story we now turn.

---

[3]Dietrich Bonhoeffer, *The Cost of Discipleship* (New York: Touchstone, 1995).
[4]*Diatessaron de Tataien*, ed. A. S. Marmardji (Beyrouth: Imprimerie Catholique, 1935), p. 298.

JESUS AND THE OPPRESSOR (JERICHO AND ZACCHAEUS)

This account (Lk 19:1-9) is carefully constructed in near-perfect "ring composition" (chiasm/inverted parallelism). The text in full is:

1. He *entered Jericho* and was passing through.	JESUS ENTERS	
2. And there was a man named *Zacchaeus;* he was a *chief tax collector,* and *rich.*	ZACCHAEUS (wealth kept for its owner)	
3. And he sought to *see who Jesus was,* but could not, on account of the *crowd,* because he was small of stature.	THE CROWD (hostile)	
4. So he *ran* on ahead and *climbed up into a sycamore tree* to see him, for he was to pass that way.	UP THE TREE	
5. And when Jesus came to the place, he looked up and said to him, "*Zacchaeus*, make haste and come down; for *I must stay at your house today.*"	UNEXPECTED Love	
6. So he made haste and *came down* and *received him joyfully.*	DOWN THE TREE	
7. And when *they* saw it they *all murmured,* "He has gone in to *spend the night* with a man who *is a sinner.*"	THE CROWD (angry)	
8. And Zacchaeus stood and said to the Lord, "Behold, Lord, the *half of my goods I give to the poor;* and if I have defrauded any one of anything, I restore it *fourfold.*"	ZACCHAEUS (wealth used for many)	
9. And Jesus said to him, "Today *salvation has come* to this house, since he also is a *son of Abraham.*	JESUS' FINAL WORD OF LOVE	

Figure 13.2. Jesus and Zacchaeus (Lk 19:1-10)

Summarized, the themes that repeat are shown as follows:

1. *Jesus* comes
 2. *Zacchaeus*—a rich man
  3. The *crowd* (hostile)
   4. Up the *tree*
    5. *Jesus'* act of costly love
   6. Down the *tree*
  7. The *crowd* (angry)
 8. *Zacchaeus*—money for others
9. *Jesus'* final word of love

THE RHETORIC

The story is composed of nine cameo scenes. A series of five is presented and then repeated backward (with important differences). Jesus appears in the beginning, the middle and the end. The tying of the beginning to the end and the middle is one of the common features of "ring composition." The climax, as usual, is in the center, where Jesus selects Zacchaeus to be the recipient of costly love. The crowd's *rejection of Zacchaeus* (3) turns into *anger against Jesus* (7). The entire story is finely composed with careful, balanced scenes and no excess verbiage.

COMMENTARY

The second story seamlessly follows the first. Jesus (with the crowd) flows into Jericho. The text quickly affirms that Jesus "was passing through." But rather than turning aside to accept the assumed hospitality of the community, Jesus resolutely moves through the town on his way to Jerusalem, thereby signaling that he is *not* intending to stay the night in Jericho. There will be no long discussion with the community regarding his future plans in Jerusalem. No doubt the community is deeply disappointed. As Jesus continues on his way, the anticipated banquet is canceled when suddenly, out of nowhere, Zacchaeus appears.

Scene two identifies Zacchaeus as the town tax collector and notes that he is a rich man. The system of taxation then in place was called "tax farming." The local person who acquired the right to collect taxes for Rome was expected to turn over a set amount to the authorities at the end of the year. How much was to be paid was at times predetermined, but as Otto Michel notes, "in practice the tax-collectors were often the only ones with precise knowledge of the relevant statutes."[5] The tax-collector was despised in rabbinic literature and in the New Testa-

---

[5]Otto Michel, "τελώνης," *Theological Dictionary of the New Testament,* 10 vols., ed. Gerhard Kittel and Gerhard Friedrich, trans. Geoffrey W. Bromiley (Grand Rapids: Eerdmans, 1964-76), 8:100.

ment, and he and his family were considered unclean. Lying to him was condoned.[6] The system naturally produced graft and economic injustice. It was bad enough that Zacchaeus was a tax collector, but he had *become rich* in the process. In the vocabulary of the day "tax collectors" and "sinners" were often paired. The town naturally hated its chief collaborator.

The third scene informs the reader that Zacchaeus wanted to see Jesus but was unable to do so "because of the crowd." Zacchaeus's problem was that he was short *and* hated. Were he respected the crowd would naturally have "made way" for such a rich and powerful person. Middle Eastern culture requires such treatment. But Zacchaeus was a *collaborator* and thereby despised. The collaborator dared not ask the crowd to make way for him and doubtless was afraid even to mix with them.

Living on the West Bank of the Jordan River, in Israel/Palestine, for ten years, I discovered some of the tensions between the local Palestinian population living under military occupation and the Palestinian collaborators who worked for the occupiers. Collaborators *did not* mix in crowds. They were always careful about "their backs." This problem would be greatly intensified for a collaborator who was short. What would happen to him if he dared push his way into the crowd? The quick flash of a knife, a stifled cry, and it would all be over. Only after the crowd moved on would the body be found and by then the perpetrators would have disappeared. Yet, for undisclosed reasons, Zacchaeus wanted to see Jesus. To fulfill that intense desire he carried out two highly unusual acts: he ran and he climbed a tree.

Scene 4 (Lk 19:4) records Zacchaeus's first action with the words "So he ran on ahead." Middle Eastern adults do not run in public if they wish to avoid public shame.[7] Furthermore, powerful, rich men do not climb trees at public parades anywhere in the world. Zacchaeus knew this only too well. So he ran *ahead* of the crowd and, trying to hide, climbed into a tree with dense foliage hoping no one would see him. Why is a sycamore fig mentioned?

Sycamore fig trees have large leaves and low branches. One can climb into them easily and just as easily hide among their thickly clustered broad leaves. Both of these features were important to Zacchaeus. Additionally, such trees were only allowed some distance from town. Zacchaeus chose to climb a tree growing outside Jericho, assuming the crowd would have dispersed by the time Jesus reached the tree.

---

[6]Ibid., 9:99-100.

[7]In Luke 15:20 the father in the parable of the prodigal son exposes himself to public humiliation by running down the road. See Kenneth E. Bailey, *Jacob and the Prodigal* (Downers Grove, Ill.: InterVarsity Press, 2003), pp. 109-10; and idem, *Poet and Peasant and Through Peasant Eyes* (Grand Rapids: Eerdmans, 1980), pp. 181-82.

Sycamore figs, of the variety that grow in the Jordan valley, are mentioned in the Mishnah and in the Babylonian Talmud. They were cultivated for their value as beams for the roofs of houses. One example being, "Abba Saul said; There were sycamore tree trunks in Jericho, and the men of violence seized them by force, [whereupon] the owners arose and consecrated them to Heaven."[8]

The "dedication to heaven" was a way of saying, "These belong to God and you can't take them!" Also important for this subject is the Mishnah reference to sycamore trees that reads, "A tree may not be grown within a distance of twenty-five cubits from the town, or fifty cubits if it is a carob or a sycamore-tree."[9]

Danby explains that a tree was seen as a kind of tent and if any form of ceremonial uncleanness occurred under the tree, that uncleanness was automatically transferred to anyone under any section of the tree. People who had trees on their property were obliged to cut all branches that overhung a property-line wall. Carob or sycamore trees were a special problem because they are large trees with wide-spreading branches.[10] The Babylonian Talmud gives a slightly different slant on this question when it notes that large trees, such as sycamores, had to be some distance from the town "to preserve the amenities of the town." The key Aramaic word translated here "amenities" is *ywn* and has to do with "beauty" and "adornment." Marcus Jastrow understands this *Baba Batra* passage to refer to "the health of the town which suffers from trees." Offering a second view, Jastrow then quotes Rashi, the famous medieval Jewish commentator on the Talmud, who said, regarding this same Talmudic passage, "because of the beauty of the town which requires an open space all around."[11]

Whether the issue was the "beauty of the town" or the "health of its citizens" cannot be determined. What is clear is that this large tree, with its spreading branches, was outside Jericho on the road up to Jerusalem. A cubit being about eighteen inches, a sycamore fig had to be at least seventy-five feet from any town, and naturally it could be a great deal further away. In spite of its brevity, the story tells us Zacchaeus climbed into *a sycamore* tree, and the word occurs solely in this reference in the New Testament. Zacchaeus did not want to be seen by the crowd!

John Badeau, the American Ambassador in Cairo, Egypt, under John Kennedy, records in his memoirs that he once climbed a tree in the back garden of

---

[8]Babylonian Talmud, *Pesahim*, 57a.

[9]Mishnah, *Baba Batra,* 2:7 (Danby, p. 368).

[10]Herbert Danby, *The Mishnah*, p. 368, n. 6; p. 649, n. 3.

[11]Marcus Jastrow, *A Dictionary of the Targumim, the Talmud Babli and Yerushalmi, and the Midrashic Literature* (New York: Padres, 1950), 2:887.

the ambassador's walled residence in order to fix some lights for an embassy garden party. This private act became known and caused such a stir that Badeau was soon asked by a very puzzled President Nasser (during an audience) if the story were true. Nasser had heard the unbelievable tale and was so amazed he felt the need to check its veracity with the ambassador himself. In the Middle East, powerful, prominent men *do not* climb trees, even in the privacy of their own walled gardens. Zacchaeus breaks with his culture both by running and by climbing a tree. He hopes desperately that neither act will be observed and carefully chooses a tree with thick foliage, some distance from town.

As indicated, Jesus is on his way out of Jericho and, therefore, has refused the local hospitality, which naturally would have been pressed upon him.[12] As the crowd moves with him through and out of town, the locals are inevitably disappointed that he is leaving. The scene at the sycamore tree must be examined in light of this discontent.

In spite of Zacchaeus's hope of remaining unseen, he is spotted. The reader knows this indirectly because by the time Jesus stops opposite the tree, he sees Zacchaeus and calls his name. If Jesus can see Zacchaeus, so can the crowd. But how did Jesus learn Zacchaeus's name?

The natural explanation for Jesus' awareness of Zacchaeus's name and history is that all this information is gathered by Jesus from the crowd that is insulting the humiliated collaborator caught up a tree. The "polecat" is at last treed! This encourages the crowd to fling at him all the choice insults they have wanted to use for years in his office, but could not. In Zacchaeus's office they had names and faces, and he was the one with power. Outside, under the tree, they are anonymous and anyone can shout from the crowd using any four-letter word that comes to mind. One insult stimulates others, quickly darkening the atmosphere and likely producing a whiff of anticipated violence. Was it not Passover? Were they not preparing to celebrate their political liberation from Egypt? What happened to Pharaoh's hosts as the Hebrews left Egypt?

Jesus astutely sizes up the tensions of the scene and decides to intervene.

Naturally, Jesus is expected to support the oppressed (as he did with the blind man) and to address Zacchaeus with something like the following:

> Zacchaeus, you are a collaborator! You are an *oppressor* of these good people. You have drained the economic lifeblood of your people and given it to the imperialists.

---

[12]Mark omits the story of Zacchaeus but includes the story of the blind man on the road to Jericho. This may be because of Mark's "bookends" telling of the passion of Jesus. The blind man affirms Jesus as the "Son of David" and the centurion sees him as the "Son of God."

You have betrayed your country and your God. This community's hatred of you is fully justified. You must quit your job, repent, journey to Jerusalem for ceremonial purification, return to Jericho and apply yourself to keeping the law. If you are willing to do these things, on my next trip to Jericho I will enter your newly purified house and offer my congratulations.

Such a speech would have provoked long and enthusiastic applause. Instead, having signaled that he does not intend to spend the night in their town, Jesus changes his mind and invites himself into the house of the town collaborator! This is both unthinkable and unprecedented. For more than forty years I was entertained in countless Middle Eastern towns and homes. As is typical anywhere, the community selects the form of hospitality, not the guest. The former naturally chooses a host who can provide a level of hospitality that will bring honor to the community. The Talmud notes that a king and his servants enter a town by the same gate, but each is given hospitality "as befits his honor."[13] No guest selects his own host, nor does any guest (especially in a situation of oppression) invite himself in public into the house of a despised collaborator!

In the story of the blind beggar the crowd was at first hostile but then expressed approval of Jesus' healing grace. Again, in this second account there are two crowd reactions. The first is another case of rejection and hostility. The community shuts Zacchaeus out when he wants to see Jesus. But at the dramatic climax of the story, Jesus shifts the crowd's hostility against Zacchaeus to himself. Zacchaeus is the recipient of a costly demonstration of unexpected love. Jesus stands with the *oppressed* (the blind man) and at the same time extends costly grace to the *oppressor* (Zacchaeus). He neither endorses the oppression nor ostracizes the oppressor. Instead he loves him. Zacchaeus accepts being found and by so doing exemplifies the redefinition of repentance set forth by Jesus in the parable of the good shepherd.[14]

The next scene occurs in Zacchaeus's house, where Jesus has chosen to spend the night. The crowd murmurs and says, "He has gone in to spend the night *[katalysai]* with a man who is a sinner." The verb *katalyō* literally means "to find lodging,"[15] which gives the reader an important key to why they are so angry. Zacchaeus's house is defiled. If Jesus enters Zacchaeus's house, sits on his chairs and sleeps in his guest bed, he will emerge the following morning defiled and in need

---

[13]Babylonian Talmud, *Šabbat*, 152a.
[14]For Jesus, repentance is not simply confession of sin. Rather it is "acceptance of being found." The lost sheep in Luke 15:4-7 becomes a symbol of repentance, as does the prodigal son. See Bailey, *Jacob and the Prodigal*, pp. 79-83.
[15]Walter Bauer, *A Greek-English Lexicon of the New Testament*, trans. W. F. Arndt, F. W. Gingrich and F. W. Danker (Chicago: University of Chicago Press, 1979), p. 414.

of ceremonial cleansing. Is this the way a messiah should behave on the eve of Passover?

Zacchaeus hosts a banquet that evening. As was the custom at the time, all are reclining and no one tells Zacchaeus what he must do. Inevitably, he senses the pressure to respond to the courageous man who has "crossed the picket line," entered his house as his guest for the night and by so doing has taken upon himself the hostility of an entire town. The moment comes (v. 8) when Zacchaeus, who has been reclining with Jesus and the other guests, stands to give his formal response. In traditional Middle Eastern style, he exaggerates in order to demonstrate his sincerity and pledges to give away 50 percent of his assets. Then he says he will pay back fourfold anyone he has cheated. If all the money he has ever collected unjustly from the community over the years amounts to 13 percent of his remaining assets, he cannot fulfill this pledge. No one expects him to do so. If he were a contemporary Westerner he would say:

> Rabbi Jesus, I have been robbing these people blind for years and I now deeply regret it. The money is spent and I cannot pay it back. But I will do all I can. I hereby pledge myself to start with a large gift to the poor of the community. Furthermore, I will review my accounts, choose those whom I have hurt the most and within my limited remaining assets, will pay back as much as I can. I hope the community will recognize my limitations in these matters.

Such a measured, realistic promise would have been understood to mean "He is not going to give us anything."[16] In good village fashion, however, Zacchaeus affirms his sincerity by exaggeration. If he does not exaggerate, the crowd will think he means the opposite. But there is more.

Not only does Zacchaeus demonstrate his sincerity via exaggeration, but he is the recipient of costly love. Such love is a powerful life-changing force. After receiving such love, Zacchaeus will never be the same. One of the important aspects of this story is that it presents a rare view of a person who has received costly love from Jesus, and it records his response. What does the prodigal do the morning after the banquet? We do not know. Is the older son willing to join the banquet? We are not told. What radical changes can be expected in the lifestyle of the wounded man aided by the good Samaritan? The text does not say. But here the reader is given a rare glimpse of the world of a recipient of costly love, and his response is profoundly instructive. He responds out of the depths of *who he is* and

---

[16]Herod Antipas exaggerated greatly in his promise to the dancing girl at his birthday party. He did not expect to be taken seriously. Unfortunately he was, and the death of John the Baptizer was the result (see Mk 6:21-29).

pledges himself to clean up his financial act with the community. No one tells him, "Your life has now been touched by the costly love of Jesus. Here is a copy of the Ten Commandments. Check them and reform your life accordingly." Any obedience to the person of Jesus will necessarily commence with his life as a model. The costly love that Zacchaeus received will be the standard. Operating from that standard, Zacchaeus starts from where *he is* not from where *others may be*, and publicly commits himself to begin showing costly love to the community he has harmed. The final word is delivered by Jesus.

The ring composition concludes with Jesus' final speech. In that concluding remark, Jesus says three important things. These are:

1. "Today *salvation has come* to this house" (v. 9). This is a "divine passive." If salvation "has come," someone has brought it. The actor is Jesus, who that very day took salvation to the house of Zacchaeus at great cost. With Bonhoeffer, there is no cheap grace—only costly grace. Grace is costly for the one who offers it (Jesus) and the one who receives it (Zacchaeus). The life-changing power that entered Zaccheus's house was not Jesus' decision to stay overnight. Rather, it was Jesus' deliberate act of shifting the town's hostility away from Zacchaeus to himself. "With his stripes we are healed" (Is 53:5).

In this scene it is possible to observe Jesus acting out one of the deepest levels of the power of his own cross. The disciples are watching and participating. If they can observe and understand what Jesus is doing with Zacchaeus, they may be able to comprehend the greater events soon to take place in Jerusalem. A fourfold movement can be observed:

1. Jesus offers costly love to Zacchaeus.

2. Zacchaeus accepts that love and in so doing accepts being found. That acceptance is his *repentance*, which takes place as he descends from the tree to welcome Jesus into his home.

3. Zacchaeus is given the huge gift of acceptance in the eyes of Jesus. Jesus is willing to enter his house, eat his "polluted food" and sleep in his "defiled" guest bed.

4. Zacchaeus responds to Jesus' gift out of the deepest level of who he (Zacchaeus) is, and the model of his response is what Jesus has done for him. Zacchaeus receives costly love and is thereby empowered and motivated to offer costly love to others. His engagement in mission has already begun.

The sequence observed is remarkable in another way. As noted, Jesus declares that "salvation has come." What is he affirming? The rabbis said, "Come and hear:

'For shepherds, tax collectors and revenue farmers it is difficult to make repentance, yet they must make restitution [of the articles in question] to all those whom they know [they have robbed].' "[17] In this text "repentance" is a work accomplished by the sinner that requires "restitution." Michel writes, "The Rabb. demanded in principle that a thief or robber who wanted to 'convert' should restore goods illegally taken or make good any loss; otherwise his conversion could not be recognized as complete."[18]

In the story of Zacchaeus, however, Jesus declares that "salvation has come" when restitution has been promised but not yet enacted. Clearly, salvation in this story has to do with acceptance and is almost a synonym for the person of Jesus. Jesus *accepts* Zacchaeus and enters his house, granting to him a new status. This initiates a process of salvation, and Zacchaeus will spend the remainder of his life living out that process. Salvation is more than a moment of decision. Indeed, Zacchaeus makes the decision to accept Jesus' bold offer to spend the night in his house. Zacchaeus pledges to return what he stole and more! But that is not all. The reader knows that Zacchaeus's entire life will change. Salvation includes a radical transformation and reformation of life as it is lived out day by day in the present. This dynamic is clearly demonstrated in this story. Jesus continues with his second concluding statement.

2. Jesus said to Zacchaeus, "since he also is a son of Abraham" (v. 9). Abraham went forth not knowing where he was going. Zacchaeus is, at last, starting to follow in Abraham's footsteps. His new journey of faith will take Zacchaeus into many unknown places. Furthermore, the community had understandably ostracized Zacchaeus. Jesus is affirming Zacchaeus's acceptance in *the eyes of God*, regardless of how the community reacts. Zacchaeus also "is a son of Abraham," declares Jesus.

3. Finally, Jesus says, "The Son of man came to seek and to save the lost" (v. 10). Jesus identifies himself as the Son of Man and reaffirms his ministry as a good shepherd who seeks the lost and brings them home. The righteous who think they "need no repentance" have no need of him (Lk 15:4-7). He will search for and bring home the lost.

This story is remarkable in yet another regard. As he began his ministry Jesus promised that his task was proclamation, justice advocacy and compassion (Lk 4:16-30). This story is one of the few places where all three of these aspects of

---

[17]Babylonian Talmud, *Baba Qamma* 94b.
[18]Otto Michel, "τελώνης," *Theological Dictionary of the New Testament,* 10 vols., ed. Gerhard Kittel and Gerhard Friedrich, trans. Geoffrey W. Bromiley (Grand Rapids: Eerdmans, 1964-76), 8:103.

Jesus' ministry are on display. Here Jesus offers a costly demonstration of unexpected love, which is the heart of the *proclamation*. Jesus also engages in *justice advocacy* by indirectly lifting oppressive aspects of the tax system from the town of Jericho. In this story Jesus demonstrates *compassion* for the beggar, the town and the collaborator.

SUMMARY: THE BLIND MAN AND ZACCHAEUS

The following aspects of the Gospel are presented in Luke 18:35—19:10:

The Story of the Blind Man

1. Jesus demonstrates compassion both for the oppressed (the blind man) and the oppressor (Zacchaeus).

2. Oppressors who have marginalized the blind man are taught a lesson as they are turned into "courtiers" who are ordered to take the blind man to Jesus.

3. The blind man is given an exam to see if he is willing to accept the responsibilities that come with God's free grace. He passes the test.

4. The blind man demonstrates full confidence in Jesus as the messianic Son of David who has the power of God to heal and who has authentic compassion for outcasts like he is. That faith is justified in his healing. His faith in Jesus grows throughout the story, as seen in the progression of the titles he uses for Jesus. His faith saves him.

5. The crowd praises God for the healing power demonstrated by Jesus. It also accepts his implied criticism of them when the beggar they attempted to marginalize is selected for special grace.

The Story of Zacchaeus

1. Jesus observes intense hostility against Zacchaeus and transfers it to himself.

2. Zacchaeus *accepts being found* and thereby demonstrates the authentic repentance that Jesus set forth in the parable of the good shepherd (Lk 15:4-7).

3. Jesus demonstrates costly love to Zacchaeus and that love becomes a life-changing force in the latter's life. In the process Jesus enacts an important part of the theology of his own cross.

4. By entering Zacchaeus's house for the night, Jesus grants Zacchaeus the gift of a new status, that of acceptance in Jesus' sight.

5. Zacchaeus responds to the costly love offered him by pledging to demonstrate

costly love to the community. The gift of grace he receives creates the energy and will to offer grace to others.

6. Jesus restores Zacchaeus to the family of Abraham, who went out responding to the call of God, not knowing where he was going.

7. Jesus declares that "Salvation has come" to the house of Zacchaeus before Zacchaeus carries out the restitution he promises. Salvation is clearly more than a single decision, it is also a process that affects all of life. Jesus is the agent of that salvation, and he is the one who brings salvation to Zacchaeus's house.

8. In his inauguration Jesus declares his ministry to involve proclamation, justice advocacy and compassion (Lk 4:16-30). All three elements are present in this story. The message of life-changing costly love is demonstrated. Financial oppression on the community is significantly lifted by changing the heart of the oppressor, and Zacchaeus is the recipient of compassion on many levels.

9. Jesus demonstrates compassion to both the oppressed (the blind man) and the oppressor (Zacchaeus).

These two stories offer a preview of dark and glorious days soon to come.

PART FIVE

Jesus and Women

14

Jesus and Women

An Introduction

THE PLACE OF WOMEN IN THE CHURCH has rightly received a great deal of attention in worldwide Christianity in recent years. Critical to that discussion is how Jesus dealt with women. In this section we will reflect on a series of six New Testament "cameos," each of which presents Jesus interacting with individual women. The intent is to present something of the radical new departure that Jesus inaugurated in relation to the equality of men and women.[1] In this brief introduction we will note in passing the place of women in Middle Eastern society as seen in the Hebrew Scriptures and in the writings of Ben Sirach. After highlighting the significance of the Song of Mary I will focus on the women disciples of Jesus and conclude with a glance at how the Gospel authors reacted to Jesus' understanding of women.

The Old Testament offers some high points regarding the place of women. The books of Ruth and Esther along with the story of Deborah the prophetess and Jael, the wife of Heber, are prime examples (Judg 4—5).[2] To this list must be added the remarkable description of a good woman by the Arab sage Lemmuel, king of Massa, recorded in Proverbs 31.[3] However, a deterioration seems to have taken place in the intertestamental period, as seen in the writings of Ben Sirach the aristocratic scholar of Jerusalem who lived and wrote in the early second century B.C. For Ben Sirach women could be good wives and mothers and are to be respected. But if you don't like your wife, don't trust her (Sir 7:26). Be careful to keep records of the supplies you issue to her (Sir 42:6-7). Deed no property to her during your

---

[1]For a discussion of the broader topic of the New Testament and women see Kenneth E. Bailey, "Women in the New Testament: A Middle Eastern Cultural View," *Theology Matters* 6, no. 1 (2000): 1-11.

[2]Leonard Swidler, *Biblical Affirmations of Women* (Philadelphia: Westminster, 1979), pp. 158-59.

[3]Tony Maalouf, *Arabs in the Shadow of Israel* (Grand Rapids: Kregel, 2003), pp. 138-43.

lifetime and do not let her support you (Sir 33:20; 25:22-26). Women are responsible for sin coming into the world and their spite is unbearable (Sir 25:13-26).
Daughters are a disaster.[4]

Indeed, to Ben Sirach a daughter was a total loss and a constant potential
source of shame (Sir 7:24-29; 22:3-5; 26:9-12; 42:9-11). There is no discussion of
women apart from their relationship to men, and Ben Sirach's list of heroes of
faith records only males (Sir 44—50). A low point is reached where Ben Sirach
writes,

> Do not sit down with the women;
> for moth comes out of clothes,
>> and a woman's spite out of a woman.
> A man's spite is preferable to a woman's kindness;
>> Women give rise to shame and reproach. (Sir 42:12-14)

On the positive side, the intertestamental literature includes the book of Judith
that champions a courageous, daring, brave woman who saves her city and people.
Yet, with the passage of time and the rise of the rabbinic movement, the position
of women by New Testament times was, on all levels, inferior to men.[5] The question is, Did Jesus reinforce the attitudes toward women that were widespread in
his time, or did he seek to reform them?

It is impossible to discuss Jesus and women without noting his mother, Mary.
There is neither time nor space to review this topic thoroughly, but parts of the
famous "Song of Mary" need to be noted in passing. The text is shown in figure
14.1.

The song is clearly divided into two sections. The first (1-6) focuses on the person of Mary, and three themes appear: praise, salvation and humiliation/exalta-
tion. Each theme is presented and then repeated in inverse order. The climax is in
the center, where Mary is exalted. The second half of the song (7-12) presents a
vision of the community of faith and focuses on mercy, salvation and humiliation/
exaltation. What happens to Mary is a foreshadowing, a model of what is to happen to the believing community. They, like her, will be exalted out of their lowli-
ness. Furthermore, the "community section" opens with a generalized promise for
"those who fear him" (7) and ends with assurances for "Abraham and his seed forever" (12). The "envelope" of 7 and 12 match: "assurance for those who believe" (a
general reference) with "assurance for Israel" (a specific reference).

---

[4]Kenneth E. Bailey, "Women in Ben Sirach and in the New Testament," *For Me to Live: Essays in
Honor of James Leon Kelso,* ed. R. A. Coughenour (Cleveland: Dinnor/Leiderback, 1972), pp. 56-60.
[5]L. Swidler, *Biblical Affirmations of Women* (Philadelphia: Westminster, 1979), pp. 150-59.

A. Personal Section (Lk 1:46–49)

And Mary said,

1. "My soul magnifies the Lord,   PRAISE

2.   and my spirit rejoices in God my savior,   SALVATION

3.   because he looked upon the low estate of his handmaiden.   LOWLY
4.   For behold, from now on all generations will call me blessed; Exalted

5.   because he made for me great things the Almighty   SALVATION

6. And holy is his name.   PRAISE—HIS NAME

B. Communal Section (Lk 1:50-55)

7. And his mercy is from generation to generation   MERCY
   to those who fear Him.   To all who Fear Him

8.   He made mighty deeds with his arm,   SALVATION
       he scattered the arrogant in the thoughts of their hearts, (judgment)

9.   He put down the mighty from thrones,   HUMILIATION
           and exalted those of low estate;   Exaltation

10.   he filled the hungry with good things,   EXALTATION
           and the rich he sent away empty.   Humiliation

11.   He aided Israel His servant,   SALVATION
           ---------------------------?   (judgment?)

12. to remember mercy as he spoke to our fathers,   MERCY
    to Abraham and to his seed forever."   To Israel

Figure 14.1. The Magnificat (Lk 1:46-55)

Furthermore, the second half is composed of double lines, with one line apparently left out. Lines 8, 9 and 10 each have one line of exaltation and a matching line of humiliation, with the exception of 11. To balance the rest of the double lines and to match line 8, we would expect line 11 to read something like:

He aided Israel His servant
and cut off the hope of the Gentiles

The balance for "aiding Israel" would necessarily be "opposing the Gentiles." But this word of judgment does not appear. This song contains no nationalistic attack on the Gentiles. In like manner, Jesus exhibits no hostility against the Gentiles, as is demonstrated in Luke 4:16-30. Did Jesus absorb these attitudes from his mother?

In short, this song presents a woman with boundless compassion for the oppressed, along with a clear vision for the lifting of that oppression. The Gentiles are not opposed, but the mighty and the arrogant are. Mary is also seen as an intelligent woman who knows that God has grace for her ethnic community and for all who believe. She becomes a model for what will happen to all believers, and she is exalted from her lowly estate.

The verbs used in this great text are in the past tense and can be seen as describing what has already taken place. These same words can be read as "historic past tenses," that is, as a vision for the future.[6] Regardless of one's views on the origins of this hymn of liberation, it links Mary and Jesus. The text of Luke affirms the sentiments in this text to be the views of Mary. Thereby the reader is led to understand that Jesus was raised by an extraordinary mother who must have had enormous influence on his attitudes toward women. How then did this play out in his public ministry?

Initially we observe that Jesus *had women disciples.*

Four texts are significant in this regard. First, although occurring only once, the word *disciple* does appear in the New Testament as a feminine. In Acts 9:36 Tabitha (Dorcas) is called *mathētria* (disciple).

Second, in Matthew's Gospel, Jesus' family appears and asks to speak with him. Jesus replies:

> "Who is my mother, and who are my brothers?" And stretching out his hand *toward his disciples,* he said, "Here are my mother and my brothers! For whoever does the will of my Father in heaven is my brother, and sister, and mother." (Mt 12:48-50, italics added)

In our Middle Eastern cultural context, a speaker who gestures to a crowd of *men* can say, "Here are my brother, and uncle and cousin." He *cannot* say, "Here are my brother and sister and mother." The text specifically affirms that Jesus is gesturing "toward his disciples," whom he addresses with male and female terms. This communicates to the reader that the disciples before Jesus were composed of men *and* women.

Third, in the remarkable report of Luke 8:1-3 the reader is told:

> Soon afterward he went through cities and villages, preaching and bringing the good

---

[6]Kenneth E. Bailey, "The Song of Mary: Vision of a New Exodus (Luke 1:46-55)," *Theological Review* 2, no. 1 (1979): 29-35.

news of the kingdom of God. And the twelve were with him, and also some women . . . who provided for them out of their means.

We note that Jesus is *traveling* through cities and villages with a band of men *and women* who are naturally known to be his disciples. This implies that they were spending night after night in strange villages. Today social customs are more relaxed than they were in the first century (as evidenced from the Mishnah and the Talmuds). Yet in the contemporary Middle East, I know of no place in traditional society where the social scene presented in this text is possible. Women can travel with a group of men but must spend their nights with relatives. Three astonishing points emerge. These are:

- The story itself is very surprising for the reasons already mentioned.
- The women are paying for the movement out of resources under their control.
- Luke (a man) admits all of this in writing. He wants his readers to know who paid for "the Jesus movement" when it was small and vulnerable. Ben Sirach's attitudes and those of his ilk are flatly rejected.

Fourth, in Luke 10:38 Jesus enters the house of Martha. Luke says, "And she had a sister called Mary, who *sat at the Lord's feet* and listened to his teaching" (v. 39). In Acts Paul describes himself as having been "brought up . . . at the feet of Gamaliel" (Acts 22:3). To "sit at the feet" of a rabbi meant that one was a disciple of a rabbi. Mary thus became a disciple of Rabbi Jesus. Martha, we are told, is "distracted" (not burdened) with much serving. To be distracted one must be distracted from something by something.

Clearly Martha is distracted *from* the teachings of Jesus *by her cooking*. In the account, Martha then asks Jesus to send Mary to the kitchen to help her. The point is not Martha's need for someone to peel the potatoes. In our Middle Eastern cultural context, Martha is more naturally understood to be upset over the fact that her "little sister" is seated with the men and has become a disciple of Rabbi Jesus. It is not difficult to imagine what is going through Martha's mind. In all likelihood she is thinking: *This is disgraceful! What will happen to us! My sister has joined this band of men. What will the neighbors say? What will the family think? After this who will marry her? This is too much to expect!*

Jesus does not reply to her words but to their meaning. In context his answer communicates the following:

Martha, Martha, you are anxious and troubled about *many* things. I understand the *entire* list. One thing is needed. What is missing is not one more plate of food but rather for you to understand that I am providing the meal and that your sister has already chosen the good portion. I will not allow you to take it from her. A good student is more important to me than a good meal.

The word *portion* can mean a portion of food at a meal.[7] Jesus is defending Mary's right to become his disciple and continue her "theological studies." The traditional cultural separation between men and women no longer applies.

From these four texts it is evident that in the Gospels women were among the disciples of Jesus.

If then Jesus had women disciples, both among the crowds and also among his band of traveling companions, did this make any discernable difference in the content and style of his teaching? Indeed it did. Jesus selected images and created parables with a deliberate concern to communicate his message to his women listeners on as deep a level as to his male followers. The following are prime examples of this commitment.

1. In his first sermon in his home town of Nazareth, Jesus tells two stories out of the tradition. One story is the account of the woman of Zarephath to which Jesus adds the story of a man, Naaman the Syrian (Lk 4:25-27). Both are Gentiles, and both are heroes of faith. Do we see here the influence of his mother who knew that "his mercy is on those who fear him" (Lk 1:50) and not exclusively on "Abraham and his seed" (Lk 1:55)?

2. Jesus presents (Lk 5:36-39) the twin parables of the mending of the garment (the task of a woman) and the making of wine (the work of men).

3. Jesus had a deep concern for repentant sinners, particularly their rejection by "the righteous." This concern appears and is focused on a rejected *woman* in the house of Simon (Lk 7:36-50), and it also surfaces in the parable of the Pharisee and the (male) publican (Lk 18:9-14).

4. Two parables offer assurance that prayer will be answered. The first is called "The Friend at Midnight" (Lk 11:5-8) and the second is about a woman struggling with an indifferent judge (Lk 18:1-8). The first is a story of a man, and the second focuses on a woman.

5. Divisions in one household over Jesus and his message are projected to include broken relationships between men and between women (Lk 12:51-53).

6. The parable of the mustard seed (men do the farming) is linked to the story of the woman kneading leaven into bread dough (Lk 13:18-21).

---

[7] J. A. Fitzmeyer, *The Gospel According to Luke* (X-XXIV) (New York: Doubleday, 1985), p. 894; cf. LXX Gen 43:34; Deut 18:8.

7. Jesus asks his disciples to demonstrate loyalty to him beyond the loyalty they offer to male and female family members (Lk 14:26-27).

8. The parables of the lost sheep and the lost coin (Lk 15:3-11) are taught together. Men herd the sheep while women's lives are centered more in the home. It is a woman who loses her coin and sweeps the house to find it. In an early rabbinic commentary on the Song of Songs, Rabbi Phinehas has ben Jair (second century A.D.) tell a story of a man who loses a small coin and "lights lamp after lamp, wick after wick, till he finds it."[8] Did Rabbi Phinehas know Jesus' parable and change the central character to a man, or were both storytellers using a traditional theme independently of each other? We cannot tell. What is clear is that Jesus deliberately chose a woman for the hero of his parable of the lost coin when it would not have been culturally offensive to tell the same story (like Rabbi Phinehas) with a male hero. The woman in Jesus' parable is also praised subtly in that she calls in her friends and neighbors for a party and publically admits to them that she was at fault. She tells her friends that *she lost her coin*. In the parable of the lost sheep the shepherd tells his friends that he found the sheep "which was lost." Unlike the woman, he does not admit any fault.

9. In debating with the Pharisees Jesus affirms equality between men and women in the resurrection (Lk 20:27-36).

10. A poor woman (Lk 21:1-4) is praised over rich givers (assumed to be mostly men) for her offering of two pence.

Clearly the teachings of Jesus were carefully crafted by him to speak to both men and women on the deepest level. Furthermore, this deep concern on the part of their Master was not missed by the recorders and editors of the tradition.

In Luke's Gospel I have identified twenty-seven cases in the text of the pairing of men and women. These begin with the angel who appears to the man Zechariah (Lk 1:5-20) and to Mary (Lk 1:26-36).[9] It ends with the presentations of men and women in the passion narratives.

In Mark's Gospel it is instructive to compare the account of the burial of Jesus (Mk 15:40-47) with Mark's account of the resurrection (Mk 16:1-8). Both texts are put together with "ring composition" (see figure 14.2 on pp. 196-97).

---

[8] *Midrash Rabbah, Song of Songs*, trans. M. Simon (New York: Soncino Press, 1983), 11.
[9] This entire list is available in Kenneth E. Bailey, *Finding the Lost* (St. Louis: Concordia, 1992), pp. 97-99.

Comparing these two accounts highlights many things. Significant for this study is the shift in the place of the women from the first story to the second. Initially, a brief comment on the rhetoric of the two passages is in order.

THE RHETORIC

Both accounts are examples of the prophetic rhetorical template that we have often noted. Each has seven sections. The first three stanzas match the last three in an inverted fashion. The climax of each appears in the center. The center of the first has to do with the finality of death and the witness of the centurion to that

---

The Burial of Jesus (Mk 15:40-47)

1. There were also *women looking on* from afar,
   among whom were Mary Magdalene   WOMEN
   and Mary, the mother of James the younger and of Joses, and Salome,
   who, when he was in Galilee, followed him, and ministered to him;
   and also *many other women* who came up with him to Jerusalem.

2.   And when evening had come,
      since it was the day of Preparation,
      that is, the day before the sabbath,   JOSEPH
      Joseph of Arimathea, a respected member of the council,
      who was also himself looking for the kingdom of God,

3.   took courage and went to Pilate,   REQUESTS
         and asked for the body (*sōma*) of Jesus.   BODY

4.   Pilate wondered if he were *already dead;*
            and summoning the centurion,   CENTURION
            he asked him whether he was *already dead*,   Death confirmed
            and when he learned from the centurion that *he was dead*,

5.   he granted the corpse (*ptōma*)   GRANTED
         to Joseph.   CORPSE

6.   And he bought a linen shroud,
      and taking him down,
      wrapped him in the linen shroud,   JOSEPH
      and laid him in a tomb which had been hewn out of the rock,
      and he rolled a stone against the door of the tomb.

7. *Mary Magdalene* and *Mary the mother of Joses*
   saw where he was laid.   WOMEN

Figure 14.2. Women in Mark's account of Jesus' burial and resurrection

fact. The word *dead* appears three times. In the second text, the climactic center witnesses to the resurrection. In passing, note that the seven stanzas in the second story complete the rhetorical form. There is no "lost final page" or any other such theory required. The reader is told in Mark 1:1 that this book is about "The beginning of the good news of Jesus Christ the Son of God." With the completion of the rhetorical template, the reader is at *the end of the beginning* of the good news. The one who reads or hears the story knows that the women overcame their fears and witnessed to the resurrection. All are challenged to follow their example.

With this carefully crafted rhetorical presentation of these two matching sto-

---

The Resurrection (Mk 16:1-8)

0. And when the sabbath was past, *Mary Magdalene* and *Mary* the mother of James, and *Salome* bought spices, so that they might go and anoint him.
SETTING (Saturday night)

1. And very early on the first day of the week they went to the tomb when the sun had risen. And they were saying to one another, "Who will roll away the stone for us from the door of the tomb?" And looking up, they saw that the stone was rolled back; for it was very large.
WOMEN GO (Sunday morning) Talking/Uncertain

2. And entering the tomb, they saw a *young man* sitting on the right side, dressed in a white robe; and they were *afraid*.
ENTER THE TOMB Afraid

3. And he said to them, "Do not be afraid; *you seek Jesus* of Nazareth, who was crucified.
SEEK JESUS

4. He has *risen*, he is *not here*; see the place where they laid him.
RISEN Not Here

5. But *go, tell his disciples* and Peter that he is going before you to Galilee; *there you will see him*, as he told you."
FIND JESUS

6. And they went out and *fled from the tomb*; for *trembling and astonishment* had come upon them;
EXIT THE TOMB Trembling

7. and they *said nothing* to any one, for they were *afraid.*
WOMEN RETURN Silent, Afraid

Figure 14.2. Continued

ries we note the following features in *the account of the burial of Jesus*.

1. The women are peripheral to the story. They follow quietly at a distance and only appear in the beginning and at the end of the narrative.

2. Joseph of Arimathea is the central figure as he seeks the body of Jesus.

3. An outsider (the centurion) is called on as a witness to the death of Jesus.

4. Pilate is the antagonist from whom Joseph must rescue the body.

5. Joseph is afraid and must "take courage" in order to accomplish his task.

In the *account of the resurrection* (Mk 16:1-8) five points match the five in the account of Jesus' burial:

1. The women again appear at the beginning of the account (chatting) and at its conclusion (trembling, silent and afraid).

2. The women are the central figures throughout the story, and they (not Joseph) are seeking the body of Jesus.

3. The initial witness to the resurrection of Jesus is a young man dressed in white.

4. The antagonist is no longer Pilate but death itself. The success of the rescue is not an act of the will of Joseph or the women—it is an act of God.

5. The women, like Joseph, are afraid. They are challenged to overcome their fears and declare the message of resurrection to the men.

When these two accounts are compared, it is clear that the *men* dominate the account of the burial (and before it the cross); the women are present but always in the background. But in the resurrection the only male is the angel, and the *women* are the central figures all through the story as it appears in Mark. They step out of the shadows to the center of the stage and everything hangs on the question, Will the women overcome their fear? The reader knows that the resounding answer is yes! The men failed at the cross and ran away. At the resurrection, the women also failed—but like Joseph they "took courage" and bore witness to all, both men and women.

This movement on the part of the women, out of the shadows of the accounts of the cross and burial and into the bright light of Easter morning, is a fitting climax to the dramatic affirmation of the radical equality of men and women in the fellowship that Jesus created. Indeed, all through the Gospels Jesus treats all women with respect and compassion. The one apparent exception is the story of Jesus and the Syro-Phonecian woman that will be discussed in full later (pp. 218-27).

SUMMARY: JESUS AND WOMEN: AN INTRODUCTION

1. In the classical past, women like Ruth, Esther, Deborah and Judith were heroines. But by the time of Jesus they were clearly inferior (e.g., Ben Sirach).

2. Mary's influence on Jesus' attitude toward women cannot be precisely known, but it must have been positive and beyond measure.

3. Jesus had women in his band of disciples. They traveled with him and some of them funded the movement.

4. Jesus deliberately shaped his teachings in order to communicate his message as powerfully to women as to men.

5. The Gospel authors/editors selected and presented stories from and about Jesus that continued Jesus' elevation of women to a place of equality with men in the community he created.

With these points in mind we turn to the previously mentioned series of cameos in which Jesus' attitudes toward women are on display.

15

The Woman at the Well

JOHN 4:1-42

MANY IMPRESSIVE COMMENTARIES on the Gospel of John are available to the serious student.[1] The twentieth century also witnessed the publication of two important works on John's Gospel in Arabic by Ibrahim Sa'id and Matta al-Miskin.[2] Along with these formal commentaries are the reflections on John's Gospel by William Temple and Lesslie Newbigin.[3] This brief chapter will focus on Jesus and the nature and marvel of his conversation with the unknown woman at the well and follow (at a respectful distance) the interpretive style set by Temple and Newbigin. Ten surprises await us in Samaria.

INTRODUCTION

> Now when the Lord knew that the Pharisees had heard that Jesus was making and
> baptizing more disciples than John (although Jesus himself did not baptize, but only
> his disciples), he left Judea and departed again to Galilee. He had to pass through
> Samaria. So he came to a city of Samaria, called Sychar, near the field that Jacob gave

[1]C. K. Barrett, *The Gospel According to St John* (London: SPCK, 1960); George R. Beasley-Murray, *John*, Word Biblical Commentary 26 (Waco, Tex.: Word, 1987); Raymond E. Brown, *The Gospel According to John*, Anchor Bible, 2 vols. (Garden City, N.Y.: Doubleday, 1966); F. F. Bruce, *The Gospel of John* (Grand Rapids: Eerdmans, 1983); Rudolf Bultmann, *The Gospel of John* (Philadelphia: Westminster, 1971); Gary Burge, *John*, NIV Application Commentary (Grand Rapids: Zondervan, 2000); C. H. Dodd, *The Interpretation of the Fourth Gospel* (Cambridge: Cambridge University Press, 1965); Barnabas Lindars, *The Gospel of John*, in New Century Bible (London: Oliphants, 1972); Alfred Plummer, *The Gospel According to St. John*, Cambridge Greek Testament for Schools and Colleges (Cambridge: Cambridge University Press, 1982); B. F. Westcott, *The Gospel According to St. John* (1908; reprint, Ann Arbor, Mich.: Baker, 1980); Rodney A. Whitacre, *John*, IVP New Testament Commentary (Downers Grove, Ill.: InterVarsity Press, 1999).
[2]Ibrahim Sa'id, *Sharh Bisharat Yuhanna* (Cairo: Dar al-Thaqafa, n.d.); Matta al-Miskin, *al-Injil, bi-Hasab al-Qiddis Yuhanna*, 2 vols. (Cairo: Dayr al-Qiddis Anba Maqar, 1990).
[3]William Temple, *Readings in St. John's Gospel*, 1st and 2nd ser. (London: Macmillan, 1955); Lesslie Newbigin, *The Light Has Come* (Grand Rapids: Eerdmans, 1982).

to his son Joseph. Jacob's well was there, and so Jesus, wearied as he was with his journey, sat down *upon* the well *[epi tē pēgē]* as it was about the sixth hour. (Jn 4:1-6)

In Shakespeare's play *Romeo and Juliet*, the nights are beautiful. At night Romeo first meets his lover. At night he gazes at her on her balcony and summons his courage to talk to her. They enjoy one night of love together after their secret marriage by the monk.

By contrast, the days are evil. In the heat of the day the Capulets and the Montagues wage war. In the daytime Romeo accidentally kills Tybalt and during the day he is banished.

The exact opposite happens in the Gospel of John. The wavering Nicodemus comes at night, and in the night he cannot get his mind around the new reality before him in Jesus. Judas leaves the Upper Room after the foot washing "and it was night." Jesus is betrayed by Judas at night, tried by Annas at night and denied by Peter at night.

But under the bright noonday sun, the Samaritan woman comes, hears, believes and becomes the first woman preacher in Christian history. During the day people are healed and the five thousand fed. "I am the light of the world" affirms Jesus, and "he who follows me will not walk in darkness, but will have the light of life" (Jn 8:12).

The *nighttime* story of Nicodemus, the scholar of Jerusalem who wavers, and the *noontime* account of a simple Samaritan woman who believes are side by side in the text. This is not an accident. Her story is now before us.

To avoid dissension between his disciples and the disciples of John, Jesus decides to return to Galilee. Pious Jews usually traveled around Samaria to avoid defilement, but for Jesus defilement came from within, not from without, and thus he took the shortest route, which was along the top of the ridge that passed by Sychar and Jacob's well.

As a poor man, Jesus walked with his disciples and grew weary. John's Gospel has a high view of the person of Jesus, the divine Word that became flesh and dwelled among us. But in that same Gospel Jesus is very human. He gets tired and thirsty. He weeps and falls asleep. His humanity is as unmistakable as his divinity.

Furthermore, the text says he sat "on the well." From the Old Syriac to the modern times the Syriac and Arabic versions have always translated this minor point literally. Major wells in Roman Palestine had large capstones in the shape of huge donuts over them. I have seen three of these capstones in Israel/Palestine. The capstone over Jacob's well in Samaria is still in place. It is eighteen to twenty inches thick and about five feet across, with a small hole in the center for lowering a bucket. The capstone keeps dirt from blowing into the well and prevents children from falling into its dangerous depths. It also provides a working surface to assist travelers in transferring water into a jar or leather bag. Jesus indeed sat *on* the well. This simple act sets the stage for his interactions with the woman, evidenced in the first of the surprises in the story.

1. THE SURPRISE OF INTENTIONAL SELF-EMPTYING

There came a woman of Samaria to draw water. Jesus said to her,
  "Give me a drink,"
because his disciples had gone away into the city to buy food.
The Samaritan woman said to him,
  "How is it that you, a Jew, ask a drink of me,
  a woman of Samaria?"
For the Jews did not use vessels in common with Samaritans.
(Jn 4:7-9, my translation)

Middle Eastern village women avoid the heat of the day by carrying water from the village well early in the morning and just before sundown. For propriety's sake, they always go to and from the well as a group. Furthermore, the jars are heavy when full and are very difficult for a woman to lift onto her head alone. The woman in this story appears at the well *alone* at noon. Only a "bad woman" would be so blatant. She is either a social outcast or knows that travelers can be found at the well at noon and wants to contact them.

Middle Eastern wells do not have buckets attached to them. Each traveling group must have its own. It is still possible to buy such buckets in the covered market in Aleppo, Syria. Crossed sticks in the top keep the soft leather mouth open to allow the bucket to fill as it is lowered into the well. When not in use the traveler can roll up the bucket for transport. The text assumes that Jesus and the disciples had such a bucket, but the disciples had taken it with them to the city. Jesus could easily have requested that they leave it behind for his use. But he had a plan.

By deliberately sitting on the well without a bucket, Jesus placed himself strategically to be in need of whomever appeared with the necessary equipment. The woman approached. On seeing her, Jesus was expected to courteously withdraw to a distance of at least twenty feet, indicating that it was both safe and culturally appropriate for her to approach the well. Only then could she move to the well, unroll her small leather bucket, lower it into the water, fill her jar and be on her way. Jesus did not move as she approached. She decided to draw near anyway. Then comes the surprise.

Jesus asks for a drink. By making this request Jesus does four things:

1. He breaks the social taboo against talking to a woman, particularly in an un-

inhabited place with no witnesses. Throughout forty years of life in the Middle East I never crossed this social boundary line. In village society, a strange man does not even make eye contact with a woman in a public place. One of the oldest tractates of the Mishnah is *'Abot*, which states:

> and talk not much with womankind. They said this of a man's own wife: how much more of his fellow's wife! Hence, the Sages said: He that talks much with womankind brings evil upon himself and neglects the study of the Law and at the last will inherit Gehenna.[4]

Jesus not only talked to women, he invited women into his band of disciples, was financed by them and some of them traveled with him (Lk 8:1-3). The radical nature of the changes in the attitudes toward women that Jesus introduced are beyond description.

2. Jesus ignored the five-hundred-year-old hostility that had developed between Jews and Samaritans. Three hundred years earlier the Greeks had used Samaria as a base for their control of Jewish territory.[5] The Jews found occasion to retaliate (128 B.C.) by destroying the Samaritan temple on the summit of Mt. Gerizim. The Samaritans responded by penetrating the temple area of Jerusalem a few years before the birth of Jesus and scattering bones of the dead across the area on the eve of Passover in order to defile the complex and make it impossible for the Jews to keep the feast. Jesus set aside all the bitterness of past history as he requested a drink from this Samaritan woman.

3. Contained in this dramatic action is a profound theology of mission. Jesus so totally humbles himself that he needs her services. Jesus does not establish his initial relationship with her by explaining how she needs him and his message. That will come later. Rather his opening line means, "I am weak and need help! Can you help me?"

Daniel T. Niles, the great Sri Lankan theologian, has written of Jesus:

> He was a true servant because He was at the mercy of those whom He came to serve. . . . This weakness of Jesus, we His disciples must share. To serve from a position of power is not true service but beneficence."

Niles continues:

> One of the features of the life of the Christian community in the lands of Asia is the number of institutions of service which belong to this community. We run

---

[4]Mishnah, *'Abot* 1:4 (Danby, p. 446).
[5]Burge, *John*, p. 141.

schools, hospitals, orphanages, agricultural farms, etc. But, what we do not adequately realize is that these institutions are not only avenues of Christian service
but are also sources of secular strength. Because of them, we can offer patronage,
control employment, and sometimes make money. The result is that the rest of
the community learn to look on the Church with jealousy, sometimes with fear,
and sometimes even with suspicion. . . . The only way to build love between two
people or two groups of people is to be so related to each other as to stand in need
of each other. The Christian community must serve. It must also be in a position
where it needs to be served. . . . Let me say it as an aside, that, in my view one of
the biggest problems to be solved in the years that lie ahead is how Inter-Church
Aid can be given and received without destroying that weakness of the churches
in which lies their inherent strength.

Niles concludes with, "The glory of the Lion is the glory of the Lamb."[6]

The first "mission trip" in Christian history was the sending out of the twelve
disciples recorded in Mark 6:7-13. The disciples were commanded to, "take nothing for their journey except a staff; no bread, no bag, no money in their belts; but
to wear sandals and not put on two tunics" (Mk 6:8-9).

They were to go in need of the people to whom they went.

A babe in a manger is an ultimate example of one who comes in need of those
to whom he or she comes. The incarnation affirms this profound theology. Even
so here with the woman; as an adult engaged in ministry, Jesus lives out this same
theology. His request is genuine. He is thirsty and has no leather bucket.

In our day, a style of mission appears to continue to flow from the developed
nations to the developing world that affirms the strength of the giver and the
weakness of the receiver. We in the West go with our technology, which often is
the point of our greatest strength and often reflects the developing world's greatest
weakness. This tends to stimulate pride in the giver and humiliation in the receiver. Again Niles is helpful. Regarding the "technical aid" that developing nations often need he writes, "Essentially the missionary must come as a bearer of
the Gospel. When he does that, he will be both a giver and a receiver . . . and all
his other gifts will find their proper place."[7]

As a bearer of the gospel, the one sent will participate in the life of the church
in that place, receive the sacraments from its leadership, and be enriched by its fellowship in Christ. In this way the cycle of pride in the giver and humiliation on
the part of the receiver is broken.

---

[6]Daniel T. Niles, *This Jesus . . . Whereof We Are Witnesses* (Philadelphia: Westminster, 1965), pp. 23-27.
[7]Daniel T. Niles, *Upon the Earth* (London: Lutterworth, 1962), p. 39.

Jesus understands profoundly the need to be a receiver. His initial contact with Peter (Lk 5:1-3) was to request his help. There was a crowd on the seashore and Jesus needed a boat for a pulpit. Peter's boat and his skills in controlling it were required. Jesus needed Peter and asked for his help—the rest is history. Jesus was ready to serve, and his self-emptying was so total that he needed to be served.

4. Jesus elevates the woman's self worth. Only the strong are able to give to others. The woman's dignity is affirmed by being asked to help Jesus out of her available resources.

In this story the woman was no doubt amazed that a male Jew was talking to her, a female Samaritan. The idea that he really wanted to drink out of her (defiled) leather bucket was a second shock. Yet, as she discovered, both were true. Her response was understandable and slightly provocative.

In an aside, John explains that Jews and Samaritans did not use vessels in common. The late Nagib Khouri of Nabulus (the modern-day West Bank) once described to me the protocol that he and his family used in the 1950s when the Samaritan high priest at Nabulus came to call at the Khouri ancestral home. The expectations of hospitality required that they offer him something to eat or drink. Knowing the rules he lived by, they would bring him a banana or an orange on a plate. The high priest would take his own (pure) knife from his pocket, peel the fruit, drop the (defiled) skin on the (defiled) plate and eat the (undefiled) fruit that had not touched the (defiled) hands of the Gentiles. There was nothing they could offer him to drink, because all their vessels were, in his eyes, unclean.

Like Greek, all Semitic languages are highly inflected. A *Shamari* is a male Samaritan, while a *Shamiriyah* is a female Samaritan. As she addresses Jesus the woman literally asks, "Why are you, a Jewish *male* talking to me a *woman*, a Samaritan *woman?*" The extra verbiage focuses on her gender. Westcott comments, "What further," she seems to ask, "lies behind this request?"[8] Jesus does not respond to her suggestive question but continues to present his agenda now that he has her full attention.

2. The Surprise of Discovering That the Gift of God Is a Person, Not a Book

Jesus answered her,

"If you knew the gift of God,

and who it is that is saying to you,

---

[8]Westcott, *Gospel According to St. John*, p. 68.

> 'Give me a drink,'
> you would have asked him,
> and he would have given you living water."
> The woman said to him,
>> "Sir, you have nothing to draw with, and the well is deep;
>> where do you get that living water?
>> Are you greater than our father Jacob, who gave us the well,
>> and drank from it himself, and his sons, and his cattle?" (Jn 4:10-13)

For this woman "the gift of God" was primarily the Torah of Moses. For the Jew it was the Law and the Prophets, while for the Muslim it is the Qur'an. That is, God's ultimate gift was and is a book. But the Suffering Servant of Isaiah was told by God,

> I have given you as a covenant to the people,
> a light to the nations. (Is 42:6)

Here the covenant is not words in a book but a person. For the woman, as for all Christians, the supreme gift of God to his people is not the New Testament but rather the person of Jesus.

For Jeremiah, God was "living water" that the people had rejected as they dug their own "broken cisterns that can hold no water" (Jer 2:13). In the story before us, language applied to God is reused to describe Jesus.

The woman replies with doubt that Jesus can acquire "living water" (i.e., spring water). Without a bucket he can't even draw well water—how is he going to produce spring water?

She continues with a nationalistic affirmation as she reminds him that "*our* father Jacob . . . gave *us* the well" (v. 12). She could be saying, "You and I are really of the same extended family even if you Jews reject us." More likely her words mean, "This is *our* well, not *yours*. Jacob gave it to *us*, not to *you*." In either case the average Jew of the times would have replied, "You Cuthite, what right have you to claim Jacob as your father? We know that you are the descendants of Gentile tribes brought in to take our places when we were in captivity! You have no right to claim Jacob as your ancestor!"

She has yet to make the connection between Jesus and the "living water."

3. THE SURPRISE OF THE DRINK THAT CONQUERS TIME

> Jesus said to her,
>> "Every one who drinks of this water
>> will thirst again,

but whoever drinks
of the water that I shall give him
will never thirst;
the water that I shall give him
will become in him a spring of water
welling up to eternal life."
The woman said to him,
"Sir, give me this water,
that I may not thirst,
nor come here to draw." (Jn 4:13-15)

Just as Jesus declined her gender-related challenge, here he declines her political challenge. He will not discuss who can claim Jacob as an ancestor or who inherited the well. As William Temple wrote:

> He [Jesus] as usual when confronted with a question which arises from the superficiality and unspiritual quality of men's thoughts, deals with the question by penetrating to the principle governing the sphere of life which it concerns.[9]

Jesus turns at once to the subject of the drink that permanently conquers thirst and becomes a spring for others overflowing "to eternal life." At this point the woman can only "hear" the first.

She will be glad to have a magical drink that will conquer her thirst and lighten her daily grind. Religion that will

- ease my psychic pain—and make me feel good
- deliver me from my fear of dying
- lift my depression
- lower crime in society (and make the streets safer for me)
- curb corruption so I don't have to pay as many taxes
- provide a social community for me and my children—then I will be interested

Religion produces a product. I'll do my "shopping" and pay for what I want. The woman is not interested in becoming a spring for others—not yet. The dialogue continues.

4. THE SURPRISE OF THE SPRING FOR OTHERS

Jesus said to her,
"Go, call your husband and come here."

---

[9]Temple, *Readings in St. John's Gospel*, p. 59.

The woman answered him,
  "I have no husband." (Jn 4:16-17)

The woman is issued three commands. She is to *go*, *call* and *bring*. These commands require that she, a *woman*, become a witness to a *man*. In her world, is that possible?

Jesus assumes it is and challenges her to believe that with him a woman's witness can be judged reliable. In John's Gospel the next time Jesus makes this type of request is in a garden outside a tomb where he says to Mary Magdalene, "Go to my brethren and say to them . . . " (Jn 20:17). You, a *woman*, go and tell the *men*.

If she is to become a spring for others, her family should be the first to benefit from the water of life that he offers her. As he creates a spring in her, Jesus challenges her to allow its waters to flow to those around her.

Put another way, the woman is given a new understanding of herself and of her surroundings. In like manner, Isaiah in the temple experienced a vision of God and with it a new understanding of himself. He confessed, "I saw the Lord sitting upon a throne, high and lifted up. . . . And I said: . . . 'I am a man of unclean lips, and I dwell in the midst of a people of unclean lips'" (Is 6:1, 5). The new vision of God triggered a new self-understanding. Can the woman respond in the same way?

Her initial reaction is to try to hide behind a prevarication. "I have no husband," she answers (v. 17). When caught in sin, try withholding information! She is not the last to choose this option.

5. THE SURPRISE OF AN ESCAPE INTO RELIGION

Jesus said to her,
  "You are right in saying, 'I have no husband';
  for you have had five husbands,
  and he whom you now have is not your husband.
  This you said truly."

The woman said to him,
  "Sir, I perceive that you are a prophet.
  Our fathers worshiped on this mountain;
  and you say that in Jerusalem
  is the place where people ought to worship." (Jn 4:17-20)

The water of life was flowing over her, and, like the water of a stream that exposes the roots of a tree growing on its banks, her roots were exposed. Technically the woman was telling the truth, but actually she was lying. Embarrassed at the unexpected exposure, she became a "theologian" and launched into a discussion of the major ideological divide between the Jews and the Samaritans. Such a diversion would surely derail the conversation about her private life.

She was clearly trying to change the topic. But as Lesslie Newbigin has noted, in the process something very profound is presented to the thoughtful reader of the Gospel. Regarding Jesus, Newbigin writes:

> He has done what true prophets have always done—exposed the sin which sin itself seeks to hide. . . . Where sin has been exposed one must ask about the possibility of atonement, or forgiveness. A prophet can bring no healing if the ministry of the priest is not available, if there is no "mercy seat" where sacrifice can be accepted and sin put away. Where is that mercy seat, that true temple, where true worship may be offered by consciences cleansed from sin? Is it on Mount Zion as Jews believe, or on Mount Gerizim where the Samaritans worship? This is . . . the proper pressing of the question which must be asked when sin has been brought to the light and exposed.[10]

The woman is responsible for continuing to try to hide her sin. But in her attempted escape, she asks a profound and relevant question.

Once again, Jesus does not scold her for changing the subject but uses her polemical question as an occasion to move the five-hundred-year-old debate to a new and profound level.

6. The Surprise of the De-Zionizing of the Tradition

Jesus said to her,
>   "Woman, believe me, the hour is coming
>   when neither on this mountain nor in Jerusalem
>   will you worship the Father.
>   You worship what you do not know;
>   we worship what we know,
>   for salvation is from the Jews.
>   But the hour is coming, and now is,
>   when the true worshipers will worship the Father
>   in spirit and truth,
>   for such the Father seeks to worship him.
>   God is spirit and those who worship him
>   must worship him in spirit and truth."

The woman said to him,
>   "I know that Messiah is coming
>   (he who is called Christ);

---

[10]Newbigin, *Light Has Come*, p. 52.

when he comes,

he will show us all things." (Jn 4:21-25)

Jesus treats the woman as a serious theologian and reveals to her the most important teaching on worship in the entire New Testament. Once again he elevates her
as a person—and in the process all women with her.

Where was the Shekinah, the divine presence of God to be found? Did God
dwell uniquely in Jerusalem or on Mount Gerizim? Both are already obsolete, answers Jesus. Jesus de-Zionizes the tradition and chooses this simple woman as the
appropriate recipient of this stunning news.

The new hour that is coming, writes Newbigin, is

> the cross, the resurrection, and the outpouring of the Spirit. Then both Jews and Sa-
> maritans, and indeed all the world, will be summoned to the true worship. . . . God
> is not essence but action. His being is action, and the action is the seeking of true
> worshippers out of Jewry and out of Samaria and out of every nation.[11]

Salvation does not have many sources—it is of the Jews. God has acted decisively in history to save through his grace to the patriarchs and their people. These
events climax in the life, death and resurrection of Jesus.

This text makes clear that in our day John's Gospel is unjustly attacked as being
anti-Semitic. Later in the Gospel Jesus says, "No one takes it [my life] from me,
but I lay it down of my own accord. I have power to lay it down, and I have power
to take it again" (Jn 10:18). The Jews are not to blame. Jesus lays down his own
life and has power to do so.

James Dunn has described the major issues that caused the division between
the synagogue and the church.[12] These are Christology, the incorporation of the
Gentiles into the people of God, loyalty to the temple and the land, and the precise keeping of the law. This text involves all four as follows:

1. Christology: Jesus is the gift of God, the Messiah, the Savior of the world.

2. Gentiles: A half-breed Samaritan woman and her village are welcomed as
    believers.

3. The temple: Both Jerusalem and Gerizim are declared obsolete.

4. The law: Jesus does not condemn her and demand that she be stoned for
    immorality.

The meaning of true worship, here so simply and profoundly defined, is inexhaustible and has inspired William Temple to write:

---

[11]Ibid., p. 53.
[12]James D. G. Dunn, *The Parting of the Ways* (London: SCM, 1991), pp. 230-59.

Worship is the submission of all our nature to God.
It is the quickening of conscience by His holiness;
the nourishment of mind with His truth;
the purifying of imagination by His beauty;
the opening of the heart to His love;
the surrender of will to His purpose—
and all of this gathered up in adoration, the most selfless
emotion of which our nature is capable.[13]

The woman's response appears to be a huge sigh—along with the hope that one day the Messiah will come and clarify all such complicated questions.

7. THE SURPRISE OF THE FIRST "I AM"

Jesus said to her,
   "I that am talking to you, I AM." (Jn 4:26, my translation)

The phrase "I AM" that appears here in the Greek text of John is the exact phrase that is used in the Greek Old Testament to translate the Hebrew of what God said to Moses at the burning bush. Moses asked who was speaking to him and the voice from the bush said, "I AM."

The Gospel of John records a list of "I AM" sayings, as they are called. The list includes:

- I am the bread of life.
- I am the light of the world.
- I am the door.
- I am the good shepherd.
- I am the resurrection and the life.
- I am the true and living way.
- I am the vine.

Amazingly, this famous series opens with the self-revelation to the Samaritan woman. The psalmist wrote, "Say to my soul, 'I am your salvation' " (Ps 35:3 NRSV). William Temple observes, "That is the assurance that we need: that He with whom we know we have dealings is none other than the eternal God. If my soul can hear that word, then it can rest. . . . I need the divine assurance of the divine love."[14]

---

[13]Temple, *Readings in St. John's Gospel,* p. 68.
[14]Ibid.

8. THE SURPRISE OF THE APPEARANCE OF THE FIRST CHRISTIAN FEMALE PREACHER

> Just then his disciples came. They marveled that he was talking with a woman, but none said, "What do you wish?" or, "Why are you talking with her?"
>   So the woman left her water jar, and went away into the city, and said to the people,
>   "Come, see a man who told me all that I ever did.
>   Can this be the Christ?"
> They went out of the city and were coming to him. (Jn 4:27-30)

The disciples appear on the scene and are amazed. A self-respecting rabbi did not even talk to his wife in a public place. So why is their revered Master engaged in a private conversation with this, this, Samaritan woman? But no one dares ask, "What do you want?" This is an idiom that I have noted for decades across the Middle East. A servant enters his master's presence and asks such a question. In this setting it implies, "Would you like us to get rid of her for you?" The disciples dare not ask this traditional question because, perhaps, he *wants* to talk to her! (What next?) Nor do they presume to scold him by asking, "Why are you talking with her?" They dare not assume the role of a traditional servant or that of a disturbed colleague, so they fall silent.

The air is heavy with rejection, and feeling their hostility in the silence, she withdraws. After all, they are Jews and she has two strikes against her. She is a *woman* of *Samaria*. But she departs not simply to carry out Jesus' command, "Go call your husband and come here"; she expands her mandate and witnesses to the entire community.

In her hurry she leaves her jar behind. This is a simple eyewitness recollection. No allegorization is necessary. She is not leaving behind the law or her former life. But on the theological level John may have had a reason for including this seemingly trivial observation. She came to draw the water that will quench thirst for an hour or two. She returns to the village without that water. Instead, she carries a witness to the water that quenches the thirst of the spirit—forever. [15] She begins to become a spring for others, even as Jesus directed.

Her witness is true to her bold instincts. She announces, "Come and see a man who told me all that I ever did. Can this be the Christ?"

The first statement is calculated to catch their attention, given her reputation in the village (a sensational but effective ad!). The question that forms the second part of her witness offers hints as to what they might find if they choose to return

---

[15]Newbigin, *Light Has Come*, p. 54.

with her to the well. She knows that they may not believe her witness because she is a woman. At the same time she invites them to make their own discoveries.

9. THE SURPRISE OF THE INVISIBLE FOOD

> Meanwhile the disciples besought him, saying, "Rabbi, eat." But he said to them, "I have food to eat of which you do not know." So the disciples said to one another, "Has any one brought him food?" Jesus said to them, "My food is to do the will of him who sent me, and to accomplish his work. Do you not say, 'There are yet four months, then comes the harvest'? I tell you, lift up your eyes, and see how the fields are already white for harvest. He who reaps receives wages, and gathers fruit for eternal life, so that sower and reaper may rejoice together. For here the saying holds true, 'One sows and another reaps.' I sent you to reap that for which you did not labor; others have labored, and you have entered into their labor." (Jn 4: 31-38)

The woman comes seeking well water and carries divine living water with her back to the village. But before she leaves the well, the disciples return bringing human food from the village, only to discover that Jesus has been renewed by divine food that they as yet do not adequately understand. It is the sustaining nourishment received when one is engaged in fulfilling the will of God and accomplishing his task. Two kinds of drink and two kinds of food are woven into the story for the reader to note and ponder.

Jesus has been sowing, and the harvest is already visible on the road from the village. The prophet Amos left his readers with a vision of hope when he wrote:

> "Behold, the days are coming," says the LORD,
> "when the plowman shall overtake the reaper
> and the treader of grapes him who sows the seed; . . .
> I will restore the fortunes of my people Israel." (Amos 9:13-14)

Plowing takes place in September and reaping occurs the following April or May. In this vision of restoration the two actions of plowing and sowing take place at the same time as reaping. The telescoping of time that occurs in the text before us suggests Jesus is claiming Amos's vision for his own ministry.

10. THE SURPRISE OF THE DISCOVERY OF THE TRUE SAVIOR OF THE WORLD

> Many Samaritans from that city believed in him because of the woman's testimony, "He told me all that I ever did." So when the Samaritans came to him, they asked him to stay with them; and he stayed there two days. And many more believed because of his word. They said to the woman, "It is no longer because of your words

that we believe, for we have heard for ourselves, and we know that this is indeed the Savior of the world." (Jn 4:39-42)

The Samaritans were not anticipating a messianic ruler, as were the Jews, but rather a *Taheb* who was modeled after Deuteronomy 18:18, which says, "I will raise up for them a prophet like you from among their brethren; and I will put my words in his mouth, and he shall speak to them all that I command him." This *taheb* was to be a teacher like Moses. After spending some time with Jesus, their vision was stretched to look beyond a teacher to a Savior. To understand this it is necessary to look briefly at the city of Samaria and its relationship to Augustus Caesar.

Augustus Caesar ended the devastating Roman civil war and created an era of unparalleled peace throughout the region. Herod the Great rebuilt the city of Samaria, and on a clear day the western point of the plateau on which the city stood could be seen from as far away as Caesarea, on the coast. Herod was always looking for ways to flatter his Roman overlords. Accordingly, on that western edge of the city, facing the sea, he built a temple in honor of Augustus. With a grand staircase in the front, an altar fourteen feet high and a large statue of Caesar, the temple must have been an impressive sight. Caesar died in A.D. 14 and was deified by the Roman Senate with the title "Divus Augustus." Roman officials landing at the port of Caesarea could look up across the hills and see this gleaming temple to their god. Herod had a feel for politics.

For centuries, both Greek and Roman rulers were given the title of *sōtēr* (savior). Many gods and demi-gods held the title "Savior of the World," as did Roman emperors from Nero to Hadrian.[16] By the time of the ministry of Jesus, Augustus Caesar was already declared "god." His temple was a scant ten miles from Jacob's well. Was the full title "Savior of the World" officially applied to him fifteen years after his death? We do not know.[17] Was he unofficially and locally referred to with that title by the time of Jesus' ministry? Perhaps.[18] The Samaritans must have known of the temple to Augustus and that the Romans venerated him. Naturally the Samaritans did not share the Roman views. After two days of intense discussion with Jesus, the Samaritans can be seen affirming an alternative. Jesus—*not Augustus*—is the *true* Savior of the *world*.

The great Eastern father Ephrem the Syrian wrote concerning this overall passage:

[16]E. C. Hoskyns, *The Fourth Gospel,* ed. F. N. Davey (London: Faber & Faber, 1947), p. 247.
[17]The question is complicated by the fact that Augustus, during his lifetime, did not like lofty titles. See Suetonius, *The Twelve Caesars,* trans. Robert Graves (London: Penguin Books, 1979), p. 84.
[18]E. F. F. Bishop, biblical scholar and professor of Arabic at Glasgow University, in a public lecture in Jerusalem in 1957 affirmed this identification.

At the beginning of the conversation he [Jesus] did not make himself known to her, but first she caught sight of a thirsty man, then a Jew, then a Rabbi, afterwards a prophet, last of all the Messiah. She tried to get the better of the thirsty man, she showed dislike of the Jew, she heckled the Rabbi, she was swept off her feet by the prophet, and she adored the Christ.[19]

As a Middle Easterner, Ephrem understood many of the nuances I have tried to expose.

SUMMARY: THE WOMAN AT THE WELL

It is not possible to summarize adequately the inexhaustible richness of this scene but the following ideas are at least available to the reader:

1. *Christology.* Jesus appears as a thirsty man, a rabbi, a prophet, the Messiah, the "I AM" and the Savior of the world.

2. *Women.* The new movement, centered on Jesus, elevates the position of all women. Jesus talks directly to the Samaritan woman and chooses her as an appropriate audience for profound expositions of the nature of God and the nature of true worship. She becomes an evangelist to her own community and foreshadows the women who witness to the men regarding the resurrection.

3. *Incarnation and mission.* Jesus "empties himself" to the extent that he needs the help of an immoral foreign woman. In requesting her assistance he models incarnational mission for all his followers.

4. *Revelation.* As in the case of the Suffering Servant of Isaiah, the focus of revelation is a person, not a book.

5. *The gender barrier.* The social "separation wall" between men and women is destroyed.

6. *Worship and the temple.* True worship, "in spirit and in truth," needs no particular geography. Neither Jerusalem nor Mt. Gerizim are relevant to it. Jesus de-Zionizes the tradition and declares the temple in Jerusalem to be obsolete.

7. *Theology.* The nature of God as Spirit is revealed to the community through this woman.

8. *A focus of mission.* Jesus accepts, cares for, takes seriously, challenges, recruits and inspires a simple Samaritan woman with a life-changing message centered in himself. A rich harvest results from this unique "sowing."

---

[19]Ephrem the Syrian, quoted by Beasley-Murray, *John,* p. 66.

9. *The community around Jesus.* A Samaritan woman and her community are sought out and welcomed by Jesus. In the process, ancient racial, theological and historical barriers are breached. His message and his community are for all.

10. *The water of life.* Those who accept this water are called to share it with others.

11. *Religion and escape from God.* The woman tries to use "religion" as a means of escape from Jesus' pressing concern about her self-destructive lifestyle.

12. *Prophet and priest.* The voice of the prophet is incomplete without the complementary priestly ministry of true worship.

13. *Salvation.* God's acts in history to save "through the Jews" are a scandal of particularity that proves to be a blessing for the Samaritan woman.

14. *Christian self-understanding.* Four important aspects of Christian self-understanding appear in this story. These are (1) the confession of Jesus as the Savior of the world, (2) the obsolescence of the temple, (3) the incorporation of non-Jews into the people of God, and (4) the deabsolutizing of the law.

15. *Food and drink.* Two kinds of drink (one passing and the other permanently sustaining) and two types of food (physical sustenance and spiritual fulfillment) are prominently featured in the story.

16

The Syro-Phoenician Woman

MATTHEW 15:21-28

THIS STORY IS OFTEN VIEWED as a troubling embarrassment. A sincere foreign woman seeks help from Jesus. At first he ignores her. He then appears to exhibit racism and insensitivity to her suffering as he insults her in public. Yes, he does finally heal her daughter, but only after the mother demonstrates a willingness to be publicly humiliated. Why, the reader inevitably asks, is this poor woman "put through the wringer" before Jesus accepts to exorcise the demon from her daughter? These serious concerns virtually guarantee the authenticity of the story. How then can the story be best understood?

The rhetorical flow of the account is shown in figure 16.1.

THE RHETORIC

The outer bookends are composed of the woman's request (1) and a final healing word from Jesus (5). In the opening scene Jesus is uncharacteristically silent. A word is requested and denied. At the conclusion of the story the healing word is given. In the middle there are three dialogues involving Jesus, the disciples and the woman. In the first of this trilogy (2) Jesus affirms his task as a good shepherd seeking the lost sheep in the house of Israel. In the very center (3) Jesus breaks into metaphorical language with a miniparable about children, crumbs and little dogs. This rhetorical feature also appears in Luke 7:36-50 where the parable of the creditor and the two debtors is in the center of the story. In scene 4 Jesus observes and affirms great faith in a Canaanite woman. In each of these three scenes a statement is made to Jesus and he responds. The appearance of the disciples in the initial dialogue is unusual. The training of the disciples is a prominent feature in all four Gospels. But characteristically some story about Jesus takes place and at its conclusion the disciples pose a question seeking clarification, and Jesus offers some telling comment. Here the dialogue *opens* with an exchange between Jesus and the

And Jesus went away from there and withdrew to the district of Tyre and Sidon.

1. And behold, a *Canaanite woman* from that region came out and cried,
   "Have mercy on me, O Lord, Son of David;   THE WOMAN'S REQUEST
   my *daughter* is *severely* possessed by a demon."   No Healing Word
   But he did not answer her a *word*.

2. And his *disciples* came and begged him, saying,
   "Send her away, for she is crying after us."   Jesus for
   He answered,   Lost Sheep of Israel
   "I was sent *only* to the *lost sheep* of the *house of Israel*."

3. But she came and knelt before him, saying,
   "Lord, *help me*."
   And he answered,   The Parable of
   "It is not fair to take the *children's bread*   Children, Bread
   and throw it to the *little dogs*."   and Dogs

4. She said,
   "Yes, Lord, yet even the *little dogs* eat the crumbs
   that fall from their *masters'* table."   Jesus for
   Then Jesus answered her,   Woman of Great Faith
   "O woman, great is your faith!"

5. *"Be it done for you* as you desire."   THE WOMAN'S REQUEST
   And her *daughter* was *healed* instantly.   A Healing Word

Figure 16.1. The Syro-Phoenician woman (Mt 15:21-28)

disciples. This initial conversation sets the tone for what follows, as we will see.

COMMENTARY

A critical component in both the parables of Jesus and the dramatic stories about him is the ever-present community. In much current reflection on many of these texts, the community is ignored. Contemporary Western society is highly individualistic. Most of the societies in the majority world still function as tightly knit communities. Descartes, the seventeenth-century French philosopher, concluded, "Cogito, ergo sum" (I think, therefore I am). African theologians reply, "I am, because we are." The individual lives, moves and has his or her being as part of a community. That community gives identity and profoundly influences both attitude and lifestyle. In the stories from and about Jesus, the surrounding community (on- or offstage) is a critical component in all that takes place and its presence must be factored into any interpretive effort.

Each day Lazarus "was laid" (a passive in the original Greek text) outside the gate of the rich man's house (Lk 16:20). This means that he was too sick to walk but was respected by the community. As a result his neighbors carried him daily and placed him at the gate of the rich man. The Revised Standard Version translates, "And at his [the rich man's] gate lay a poor man." The passive verb disappears along with the caring community behind it. Syriac and Arabic versions of the last 1,850 years have not made this mistake. The translators of those Gospels instinctively understood the presence and importance of the community surrounding Lazarus. In that parable the community is offstage and yet plays an important role in the parable. In like manner the Gentile citizen in the far country who hires the prodigal never appears onstage but is an important figure in the story nonetheless (Lk 15:11-32). He owns pigs and feeds his pig herder, but does not pay him.

But in the story before us the ever-present community is composed of the disciples who are onstage and in dialogue with Jesus near the beginning of the account. Jesus is not simply dealing with the woman, he is also interacting on a profound level with the disciples. This double interaction needs to be monitored throughout the story.

The story opens with:

And Jesus went away from there and withdrew to the district of Tyre and Sidon.
And behold, a *Canaanite woman* from that region came out and cried,
"Have mercy on me, O Lord, Son of David;   THE WOMAN'S REQUEST
my *daughter* is *severely* possessed by a demon."   No Healing Word
But he did not answer her a *word*.

Unlike Mark and Luke, Matthew was one of the disciples. He had to be fluent in Greek to administer a tax office. Perhaps he understood and recalled (or recorded) details that others missed.[1]

The scene takes place in a Gentile province. Clearly, Jesus could speak to the people, just as he was able to talk to Pilate, without need of a translator. More and more evidence from the first century in the Holy Land points to the fact that a great deal of Greek was spoken in Galilee at that time. Sepphorus, the new capital of Galilee, was four miles from Nazareth and a large Greek theater was constructed within it during the first century.[2] The city itself was being built during the early life of Jesus, and Joseph (along with Jesus) may have found work there in the building trade. The natural assumption is that Jesus was able to converse in Greek. Thus

[1]See Richard Bauckham, *Jesus and the Eyewitnesses* (Grand Rapids: Eerdmans, 2006).
[2]Richard A. Batey, *Jesus & the Forgotten City* (Grand Rapids: Baker, 1991), p. 90.

he was able to talk to this non-Jewish woman either in Greek or Aramaic.

The woman begins with the traditional cry of a beggar, "Have mercy on me."[3] She reaches out to Jesus across two barriers. She is a woman, and Jesus is a man. Even today in the Middle East, in conservative areas, men and women do not talk to strangers across the gender barrier. In public rabbis did not talk to female members of their own families. Furthermore, the woman in this story is a Gentile seeking a favor from a Jew. Mark notes that early in his ministry Jesus became known in the region of Tyre and Sidon (Mk 3:7-8). Clearly the woman has some prior knowledge of Jesus and of his compassion for all, be they Jews or Gentiles, male or female.

Her initial request is studied. She opens with the title *Kyrie* (Lord/Sir), to which she adds a relatively rare Jewish messianic title, "Son of David," which implies some contact with Judaism. Without the second title it would be possible to translate *Kyrie* as "Sir." But when she adds "Son of David," she means more than "Sir." For a Gentile woman to use this combination of titles with an itinerant Jewish teacher is quite unexpected.

Ibn al-Tayyib was one of the most distinguished medical doctors of the eleventh century in the Middle East. In his thoughtful thousand-year-old commentary he notes that the woman does not cry out, " 'O Lord, have mercy on *my daughter*,' but rather, 'Have mercy on *me*.' This was because her daughter was not able to feel what the mother was enduring. The mother was in pain!"[4] Ibn al-Tayyib then notes that at the end of the story "Jesus does not say, 'O woman your daughter is healed,' but rather he says, 'let it be to you as you desire.' "[5] It is the theologian/physician who notices that the caregiver is at the end of her rope and that she also needs healing. Jesus empathizes with her deep needs and responds to them on two levels. But this takes us ahead of the story to which we must return.

Jesus responds to the woman's request with silence. Is this indifference and rejection? Before drawing either conclusion it is important to note that Jesus is dealing with the woman *and* at the same time educating the disciples. As regards the woman, Jesus chooses to give her a critical test. Tough exams are not a negative putdown. The student who struggles through such ordeals acquires the honor that accrues to the student who passes a challenging exam. On other occasions Jesus administers similar exams. When dealing with the man who lay for thirty-eight years beside the pool of Bethzatha Jesus asks, "Do you want to be healed?" (Jn 5:6). The reason for the exam is to say to the paralytic, "You have survived as a beg-

---

[3]Lk 18:38.
[4]Ibn al-Tayyib, *Tafsir al-Mashriqi*, ed. Yusif Manqariyos (Egypt: Al-Tawfiq Press, 1907), 2:281-82.
[5]Ibid.

gar for years. If healed, you will have your livelihood stripped from you because no one will give to a healthy man. Are you ready for the new responsibilities that will come with healing?"

The same question/test appears in Luke 18:41, where Jesus is dealing with the beggar outside Jericho. But the more obvious parallel to this text is the story of Elijah's visit to the region of Sidon, which was observed in the above chapter on Luke 4:17-30.

Here Jesus, like Elijah, is in the region of Sidon dealing with a Gentile widow who has a needy child. Like Elijah he begins with an exam. Only in Jesus' case the exam process is carefully observed by his disciples. That is, the rabbinic scholar (Jesus) is reenacting his authoritative source (the story of Elijah) for the benefit of the woman and for the education of his graduate students (the disciples). In the process he not only heals the woman's daughter but he gives the woman the privilege of earning the unfading honor of passing a very tough exam that immortalizes her. The complete exam has three parts, of which this is the first. Here Jesus pretends indifference as he sets the stage for his dialogue with his disciples and with the woman.

As mentioned, self-respecting rabbis did *not* talk to women. About two hundred years before the time of Jesus, a scholar of Jerusalem called Ben Sirach composed proverbs and wisdom sayings. In the book that bears his name he writes:

A man's spite is preferable to a woman's kindness;
women give rise to shame and reproach. (Sir 42:14)[6]

In fairness to Ben Sirach, he has positive things to say about a good wife (Sir 26:1-4) but this quote demonstrates that there were some extremely negative ideas about women available to Jesus in his inherited tradition.

Thus when Jesus did not respond to the woman's plea, he was no doubt seen by the disciples as acting in an entirely appropriate manner. That is, by ignoring the woman's desperate cries he appears to endorse views toward women with which the disciples were comfortable. This is clear from their response:

And his disciples came and begged him, saying,   DISCIPLES
    "Send her away, for she is crying after us."
He answered,   JESUS
    "I was sent only to the lost sheep of the house of Israel."

---

[6]Cf. Kenneth E. Bailey, "Women in Ben Sirach and in The New Testament," in *For Me to Live: Essays in Honor of James Leon Kelso*, ed. R. A. Coughenour (Cleveland: Dinnon/Liederbach, 1972), pp. 56-73.

The disciples note Jesus' initial refusal to talk with this Gentile woman. Taking their clue from his silence, they then petition him with the cry, "Send her away!" In Luke 18:39 the crowd rebukes a blind man and tells him to be quiet. Like the disciples in this text, the throng assumes that Jesus has no time for a shouting beggar. They are mistaken.

In like manner in John 4:27 the disciples return to Jacob's well only to find Jesus talking to a Samaritan woman. The text states, "They marveled that he was talking with a woman, but none said, 'What do you wish?'" Both Matthew's story and the above Johannine text reflect the same tension. Except that in the latter, the disciples feel the urge to ask, "What do you wish?" which is a deeply engrained style of talking. The Western ear may glean its meaning from the paraphrase, "Is there something we can do for you?" (i.e., Would you like us to get rid of her?). They do not ask such a question but they somehow think they should. That same urge surfaces in the scene with the Syro-Phoenician woman but here it is expressed openly in the form of a request to send the woman away.

"Send her away; for she is crying after us," they demand. But this outburst merely begins the three-scene dialogue. The text can be understood as follows: Jesus is irritated by the disciples' attitudes regarding women and Gentiles. The woman's love for her daughter and her confidence in him impress Jesus. He decides to use the occasion to help her and challenge the deeply rooted prejudices in the hearts of his disciples. In the process he gives the woman a chance to expose the depth of her courage and faith.

Jesus' approach to the education of his disciples is subtle and powerful. He does not lecture them about negative stereotypes. On the contrary, he appears to agree with them by seeming to say:

> I will start by shutting her out and hopefully she will leave of her own accord. As a self-respecting rabbi I do not talk to women—particularly Gentile women. If I do talk to her, all of us could be thrown out of the district by an angry mob. If she persists, I will make clear to her that my healing ministry is only for Israel. She will then have no choice but to leave.

In Galilee it was easy to think about Jesus as the exclusive possession of the "House of Israel." In the district of Tyre and Sidon, faced with a needy widow, such ethnocentric views were inevitably uncomfortable. Jesus was voicing, and thereby exposing, deeply held prejudices buried in the minds of his disciples. In the process he was speaking to both audiences. To the disciples he was saying, "Of course I want to get rid of her! We have no time for such female Gentile trash." But to the woman, Jesus was initially communicating, "You are a Canaanite and a woman. I am a son of David. You are not part of my divine mandate. Why should I serve Gentiles like you?"

This first round of the three-part dialogue was no doubt followed by a tense pause. Would the woman "catch the hint" and leave? She did not move because she *believed* Jesus did not mean it. With that implied affirmation she passed the first part of the exam.

The second stage of her exam was quick to follow. Was her concern for her child *so deep* and her confidence in the universal compassion and healing power of Jesus *so profound* that she would proceed with her request in spite of this apparent slamming of the door in her face? Her reaction to apparent rejection was:

But she came and knelt before him, saying,
"Lord, help me."   WOMAN
And he answered,   and Jesus
"It is not fair to take the children's bread
and throw it to the [little] dogs."

Her response is both moving and magnificent. She omits the messianic title and the beggar's traditional petition. With the sobbing screams of her child ringing in her ears, she kneels in stark simplicity before Jesus and reduces her request to an elemental cry of an anguished human soul, "Lord, help me!" She may not be aware of the story of Elijah and the woman of Zarephath, but the disciples know it well. They are also familiar with the classical prophetic concern for the widow and the orphan. Thus far in his ministry Jesus' compassion for all was constantly on display and the disciples could not have missed it. Only the hardest of hearts would be unmoved by the woman's dramatic action and her simple yet desperate words. Will Jesus venture beyond his mandate to serve Israel and help this Gentile?

Not quite yet. Jesus chooses to take the theological attitudes of the disciples and press them to their ultimate conclusion with a *reductio ad absurdum*. In effect, Jesus tells the disciples, "You will be happy if I get rid of this woman, and limit my ministry to Israel. Very well, I will verbalize where your theology leads us. This will give you a chance to observe the response of this 'unclean' Gentile woman."

Jesus here gives concrete expression to the theology of his narrow-minded disciples, who want the Canaanite women dismissed. The verbalization is authentic to their attitudes and feelings, but shocking when put into words and thrown in the face of a desperate, kneeling women pleading for the sanity of her daughter. It is acutely embarrassing to hear and see one's deepest prejudices verbalized and demonstrated. As that happens one is obliged to face those biases, often for the first time. Contemporary history is punctuated with many examples of this dynamic from Gandhi to Martin Luther King and beyond.

The language Jesus uses is very strong. Dogs in Middle Eastern traditional culture, Jewish and non-Jewish, are almost as despised as pigs. Pigs are worse, but only slightly so. Dogs are never pets. They are kept as half-wild guard dogs or left to wander unattended as dangerous street scavengers who subsist on garbage. Neglecting a beggar is one thing. But to insult her with such language is something else.

Yet the harsh language carries a touch of gentleness. Jesus speaks of the *kynarion* (diminutive of the noun *kyōn*). These are "little dogs," not sixty pound guard dogs that no one, aside from their handlers, dares approach. In spite of this, the language is still insulting. The reference to *dogs* is primarily for the disciples' education. Jesus is saying to them, "I know you think Gentiles are dogs and you want me to treat them as such! But—pay attention—this is where your biases lead. Are you comfortable with this scene?"

How will she respond? Her exam has reached its most demanding section. Will she reply with a corresponding insult against the haughty Jews who despise and verbally attack Gentiles, even those in pain? Or is her love for her daughter, her faith that Jesus has the power of God to heal, her confidence that he has compassion for Gentiles and her commitment to him as Master/Lord so strong that she will absorb the insult and press on, yet again, with her request?

> She said,
>   "Yes, *Lord,* yet even the *[little] dogs* eat the *[little] crumbs*
>   that fall from their masters' table."
> Then Jesus answered her,
>   "O woman, great is your faith!"

Superb! The woman passes the entire exam with flying colors! She accepts the insult and deftly turns it, with a touch of light humor, into a renewed request. She says,

> Yes, I know that in your eyes we may appear as little dogs, and as little dogs we deserve nothing. But the little dogs are thrown the little pieces of bread (diminutive) at the end of the meal. You are still my Lord/Master. I know that you can heal and that you have compassion for all. Do you not have a crumb for my daughter?

The disciples are watching and listening. Indeed, in all Israel they have seen neither such total confidence in the person of Jesus in spite of his hard words nor such compassionate love for a sick child. Her response is a deadly blow to their carefully nurtured prejudices against women and Gentiles. A new paradigm of

who God is and to whom he extends his love (through Jesus) will inevitably struggle to be born as a result of this dramatic scene. In the process the woman's faith
is rendered unforgettable and is, like the faith of the woman who anointed Jesus
in the house of Simon the leper (Mk 14:3-9), proclaimed wherever the gospel is
preached.

Jesus pronounces the woman to be great in faith. But what is the meaning of
the word *faith* in this context? Her faith is expressed in her unfailing confidence
in the person of Jesus as the agent of God's salvation for all, both Jew and Gentile.
She confesses him as Lord and Master. A final, almost indefinable, element in that
faith is her willingness to pay any price, even public humiliation, in order to receive
the grace mediated by Jesus, who concludes by saying:

"Be it done for you as you desire."	THE WOMAN'S REQUEST
And her daughter was healed instantly.	A Healing Word

The silence with which Jesus began is now broken with a word of healing
power. The verb "was healed" is in the passive. God restores the daughter through
the agency of Jesus. The powerful word spoken by Jesus is a divine act. The woman
is elevated as a gold medal Olympian in a great test of faith. Ibn al-Tayyib summarizes her sterling qualities by noting three virtues:

> First is her humility as she lowers herself to the place of a dog. Second, her deep faith
> that a small amount of His food, like the small pieces of bread that fall from the table,
> is enough. This faith is praised by Christ for it is the primary virtue and the founda-
> tion of all other virtues. Third is her wisdom in that she was willing to act the part
> of a dog until she achieved her goal.

In a marginal note Ibn al-Tayyib continues to praise her by adding: "a. Her
motherly love and her display of that love in the best way, which is to request assistance from the Christ for her daughter. b. Her persistence in her request
(prayer), and the relentlessness of that persistence."[7]

Concurrently, an enormous amount of sophisticated spiritual formation is taking place in the hearts of the disciples and indeed potentially in the hearts of any
readers of Matthew's Gospel.

SUMMARY: THE SYRO-PHOENICIAN WOMAN

The theological and ethical content of the story of the Syro-Phoenician woman
includes:

---

[7]Ibn al Tayyib al-Mashriqi, *Tafsir al-Mashriqi*, 1:282-83.

1. Jesus is declared by a Gentile to be Lord and Son of David. In his inaugural sermon in Nazareth he held up the faith of two Gentiles as models for Israel. Here, in real life he does the same.

2. Jesus breaks (1) the gender barrier by talking to a woman and (2) a racial barrier by healing a Gentile.

3. Jesus compliments the woman by giving her a tough exam. A good coach honors a good runner by placing her in the toughest race.

4. Evil cannot be redeemed until it is exposed. In his dialogue with the woman Jesus exposes deep prejudices in the hearts of his disciples. They remembered the story. Was it a critical event in their journey to a vision for the world?

5. Jesus cares about the woman, her daughter and the disciples. The story demonstrates that caring.

6. The woman is praised by Jesus for her faith. She believes he has the power of God to heal and that he cares for all people, particularly those who suffer. That faith is sustained.

17

The Lady Is Not for Stoning

JOHN 7:53—8:11

WHY IS THE DEATH OF JESUS DIFFERENT from the death of Socrates or the death of John the Baptizer? It is not enough to simply confess "Christ died for our sins" (1 Cor 15:3). There must be some understanding of the connection between the death of Jesus and our sins. This subject is called the doctrine of the atonement.

The famous English theologian Lesslie Newbigin, who served for many years as a bishop in India, wrote a book for the Indian church titled *Sin and Salvation*. In that book he creates a parable to clarify the problem. Newbigin writes:

> If I am drowning in a well and another man jumps into the well and rescues me, while he himself is drowned in the effort, then there can be no doubt about that man's love. He has given his life for me. But if I am attacked by a tiger I need a different kind of help. My friend may jump into the well and drown himself, but that will not rescue me from the tiger. In that case, even though my friend gave up his life, I cannot say that he loved me or saved me. Christ gave up His life on the cross, but how does that save me? How does it rescue me from my sin? Unless we can show that there is some connection between Christ's death and my sin I cannot believe that Christ's death is proof of love for me, or that it has saved me from sin. Clearly it is not enough simply to say that the cross is a revelation of God's love, unless we can answer these questions.[1]

ATONEMENT

Already in the New Testament there is serious reflection on this question. By the time Paul wrote his first letter to the Corinthians, the church had already decided that the death of Jesus was different from the death of John the Baptist. To see the death of these two cousins as having the same meaning would have been easy. The

[1]Lesslie Newbigin, *Sin and Salvation* (Philadelphia: Westminster, 1956), p. 72.

death of John (Mk 6:14-29), contains the following significant features:

1. A proclaimer of the Gospel made powerful enemies because of his proclamation.

2. That proclaimer was unjustly imprisoned.

3. A ruler admired the prisoner but was too weak to act on his scruples.

4. That ruler acted to protect his own interests and ignored the demands of justice.

5. Intrigue and power politics were involved.

6. The wife of the ruler was also involved.

7. The keeping of the Jewish law was at issue.

8. An innocent man was brutally murdered (justice was violated).

9. The ruler ordered the murder to please someone else.

10. Soldiers were given the gruesome task.

11. Disciples of the victim took the body and buried it.

12. Resurrection was supposed by some, but nothing came of it.

As young men, Jesus and John both labored to renew Israel and both were murdered for their efforts. Clearly the realities of both men's deaths tie these two men together. But the reality of the resurrection led the followers of Jesus at an early stage to conclude, "Christ died for our sins" (1 Cor 15:3). Yet Newbigin's question remains: On what basis did they reach this conclusion?

A partial answer to this question can be found in the metaphors of the New Testament that describe this great mystery.

The first metaphor is the picture of a *law court* where the prisoner is condemned because of sin. The judge, in effect, says, "I will take the prisoner's place." Accordingly the judge steps down from the judicial bench and stands beside the prisoner saying, "I will die for the prisoner." This picture is found behind the text in Romans 3:26 where God is both *just* and the *justifier*. He is himself just (on the cross a penalty is paid for sin) and the sinner is thereby declared "righteous," that is, "justified" before the judge who himself paid the price for that justification.

The second metaphor is the *sacrificial altar*. Jesus is the lamb without blemish, which was an important part of the sacrificial system of the Old Testament. Paul uses this picture in 1 Corinthians 5:7, where he affirms, "Christ, our paschal lamb, has been sacrificed."

Third is the picture of a *battlefield*. Jesus is described as the victor over sin and death. There has been a great confrontation between good and evil that Jesus won and wins. Paul thinks in these terms when he writes, "Thanks be to God, who gives us the victory through our Lord Jesus Christ" (1 Cor 15:57).

Fourth is the language of *a prisoner exchange*. On occasion the Romans would lose a famous general to their enemies and would then negotiate the return of that general. The word they used for this was *redemption*. They would redeem the general. This language is used to describe our "redemption through his blood" (Eph 1:7).

Fifth is the *slave manumission*, where Paul writes to the Corinthians "You are not your own; you were bought with a price" (1 Cor 6:19-20). The language is taken from the process of paying a price to set a slave free from bondage.

Sixth is an idea that comes from *wisdom literature*. Turning once again to 1 Corinthians, Paul writes eloquently about the cross as the wisdom and power of God (1 Cor 1:17—2:2).

The seventh metaphor is the *canceling of a bond*. Jesus, through his death has stamped "paid" on the bond of our sins (Col 2:14).

Finally is the picture of *a triumphal procession*. Jesus leads a triumphal procession over the powers of evil (Col 2:15).

Almost unconsciously, Christians connect sin and the death of Jesus using one or more of these pictures. But what about Jesus? Does he ever explain the meaning of his own suffering? It is my conviction that he does. One of the occasions in which his thinking is demonstrated is the dramatic account of the woman taken in adultery (Jn 7:53—8:11). To this text we now turn, only to discover a textual problem.

A TEXTUAL DILEMMA

For centuries John 7:53—8:11 has been a challenge for biblical scholars. Many of the early manuscripts of the New Testament do not record it. Others do, and a few copies include it in Luke. Some modern translations place it in the margins of the text. What can be said about this confusion?

One way to deal with this problem is to see this story as an *agrapha*, an unwritten story known to the church and passed on in oral form and finally recorded in some copies of the Gospel of John. Bruce Metzger writes, "[this] account has all the earmarks of historical veracity. It is obviously a piece of oral tradition which circulated in certain parts of the Western church."[2] This view affirms that John did not include this account in his Gospel but that the church remembered it and

---

[2]Bruce M. Metzger, *A Textual Commentary on the Greek New Testament* (London: United Bible Societies, 1971), p. 220.

loved it. At some point in the early centuries scribes began to add it to the text. Others read it as fiction.

There is a third possible solution to this problem. For centuries traditional Middle Eastern culture has understood the honor of the family to be attached to the sexual behavior of its women. Thereby in conservative traditional village life, women who violate the sexual code are sometimes killed by their families.

Added to this is the fact that in the days of hand-copied manuscripts, the person who wanted a copy of anything usually acquired it by hiring a copyist. This was a private business arrangement. Since printing began, official committees of churches have determined the text of any Bible selected for publication. But in the early centuries of the life of the church it would have been very easy for the head of a household to take a copy of the Gospel of John to a professional copyist and say

> I want a copy of this document. Please leave out the story of this adulterous woman.
> I don't want my daughters committing adultery and telling me, "Jesus forgave this woman and therefore you should forgive me!"

The copyist would naturally oblige his customer. Other Christians were brave enough to preserve the story even though it violated deeply rooted cultural attitudes.[3] The end result is that this story appears in some ancient texts and is missing from others. If this view is accepted, or if one considers it an *agrapha*, the story is authentic to Jesus. Raymond Brown writes, "There is nothing in the story itself or its language that would forbid us to think of it as an early story concerning Jesus."[4] Brown also notes, "Its succinct expression of the mercy of Jesus is as delicate as anything in Luke; its portrayal of Jesus as the serene judge has all the majesty that we would expect of John."[5] With Metzger and Brown, I am convinced that it is a historical account. Furthermore, its current position in the Gospel can be seen to fit the context, as we will see.[6]

Properly understood the story opens at John 7:37-38, which reads:

---

[3]I am fully aware of the fact that this particular story contains rare Greek words that the Gospel of John does not ordinarily use. Thus the history of the transmission of this story is probably more complicated than what I have suggested. Yet the above explanation is for me a serious starting point for an understanding of this particular textual problem.

[4]Raymond E. Brown, *The Gospel According to John*, Anchor Bible (Garden City, N.Y.: Doubleday, 1966), 1:335.

[5]Ibid., 1:336.

[6]Many commentaries include extensive discussions of this textual problem. See Gary Burge, *John*, NIV Application Commentary (Grand Rapids: Zondervan, 2000), pp. 238-41; Frédéric Louis Godet, *Commentary on the Gospel of John* (1893; reprint, Grand Rapids: Zondervan, 1969), pp. 83-86.

On the last day of the feast, the great day, Jesus stood up and proclaimed, "If any one thirst, let him come to me and drink. He who believes in me, as the scripture has said, 'Out of his heart shall flow rivers of living water.'"

The feast mentioned was and is a seven day celebration called Succoth, known commonly as "the Feast of Booths." Jesus was in attendance in Jerusalem, and on the last climactic day he stood up and made the claim (Jn 7:37-38) that is suspiciously close to what God says about himself in Isaiah 55:1-3. This naturally caused a huge stir.

Jesus was not, however, the first Jew of the time to take language about God and apply it to himself. One generation before Jesus, the famous rabbi Hillel made the same kind of claims.[7] The late Israeli scholar David Flusser has noted these claims and has pointed out that the Jewish tradition decided that Hillel did not mean what he said. The Gospels and the birth of the church are clear witness to the fact that the disciples of Jesus believed him when he made such claims, but not immediately.

John recorded two instantaneous reactions to Jesus' Jerusalem speech. The crowd was confused and divided. The chief priests and the Pharisees were sufficiently angered that they ordered his arrest. But the officers sent to apprehend him were unable to carry out their orders because Jesus was too popular. As they reported, "No man ever spoke like this man" (Jn 7:46). The Pharisees then opened the subject of the law and said, "this crowd, who do not know the law, are accursed" (Jn 7:49). Jesus was barely thirty years old. How dare he make such incredible claims about himself? Nicodemus tried feebly to defend Jesus but was quickly silenced. Everybody then went home (vv. 50-53). Round one was over.

THE TRAP

Overnight Jesus' opponents were able to plan "round two." The issues were clear. Jesus had claimed to be the living water promised by God to his people. "The Law" in popular usage often meant all the books that were considered authoritative, and by the time of Jesus this included the Prophets and the Psalms (Lk 24:44). In all likelihood, therefore, the Pharisees were upset over the Isaiah 55 passage. This challenge to them and their authority had been made on their turf. They had to respond, and their initial reaction was to craft an astute "game plan."

If they could humiliate Jesus in public by posing a question of interpretation of

---

[7]David Flusser, "Hillel's Self-Awareness and Jesus," *Judaism and the Origins of Christianity* (Jerusalem: Magnes Press, 1988), pp. 509-14.

the law that Jesus could not answer without destroying himself, his popularity would fade quickly and their problem with him would be solved. Presumably overnight they arrested a woman whom they claimed was "caught in the act of adultery" and held her for the showdown with Jesus.

The following morning Jesus could have avoided the temple. The previous day he had made a stunning public statement. He knew that there was considerable confusion among his listeners over his claims and he must have known that the temple guards had appeared to arrest him. The next morning, the temple police might well be waiting for him at the gates of the temple to apprehend him before a crowd could gather.

It has often been said that Robert E. Lee, the famous general of the Confederate Army during the American Civil War, had an uncanny ability to read the minds of his opposing generals in battle. The same can be said for Jesus. He may well have surmised that if the temple authorities arrested him they would only make him more popular. Knowing this, his opponents would somehow try to discredit him in public. In any case he bravely and resolutely returned to the temple the following morning.

According to Jewish law the day after any major feast had to be observed as a sabbath. On such a day, no work was allowed. On this "eighth day of the feast" Jesus returned to the temple area. A crowd quickly gathered. In good rabbinic style Jesus sat down (affirming his authority as a teacher) and began to teach them. Only then did the Pharisees make their move. They wanted witnesses, lots of them!

The scribes and Pharisees suddenly appeared and interrupted Jesus in front of his listeners. They brought with them the woman they had arrested the previous night, and publicly declared that she had been caught in the act of adultery.

The inevitable question immediately arises: How do religious professionals catch a woman in the act of adultery? Furthermore, adultery is rather difficult to do alone, and if she was caught "in the act" her partner was seen and thereby identified. The law dictated that both should be stoned (Lev 20:10). Where was the man? And why did they not arrest both of them if they were so zealous for the law? The previous day these same leaders had invoked a curse on the crowds that did not know the law. Now they were violating the law in the name of enforcing it! What therefore was the real agenda?

The fact that they brought the woman but not her male partner clearly indicates that their concern was not preservation of the law but rather the public humiliation of Jesus. The woman was merely a prop in their plan. But the story has a second important component. The temple area is about thirty-five acres. At that time, around three sides of that large enclosure there was a long, covered walkway. The best English word we have for this is *cloister*. Connected to this walkway on the north end of the temple area, Herod the Great had constructed a large military fort. He knew that civil unrest often began in the temple enclosure, so he insured that there was access from the fort both to the temple area and to the roof of this covered walkway. Josephus, a Jewish historian of the first century, records that during feast days Roman soldiers would patrol along that walkway and through the crowds, keeping a sharp eye out for any unrest. He wrote, "a Roman legion went several ways among the cloisters, with their arms, on the Jewish festivals, in order to watch the people, that they might not there attempt to make any innovations."[8] The entire scene unfolding around Jesus was under Roman observation, and everyone was conscious of this armed military presence.

JESUS RESPONDS

The Pharisees did not ask a hypothetical question—"What if we caught a woman . . . ?" Instead they brought the accused, presented her and then asked:

> Teacher, this woman has been caught in the act of adultery.
> Now in the law Moses commanded us to stone such.
> What do you say about her? (Jn 8:4-5)

The scene could hardly be more dramatic. They quoted Moses and then directly challenged Jesus, in public, to agree or disagree with the great lawgiver. The crowd was listening intently, and the Roman soldiers were watching.

The Pharisees assumed that Jesus had two options. On the one hand, he could say, "Yes, let's stone her." Such a ruling would have caused an outcry and triggered enough commotion that Jesus would surely have been arrested even if the violence against the girl had not begun. John records that the Romans had denied the Jews the right to put anyone to death (Jn 18:31).[9]

Jesus' other option was to say something like:

> Gentlemen, we know what the law of Moses requires, but the realities of the political world in which we live cannot be avoided. Just look around you. Yes, we long for the day of liberation from Rome, after which we will be able to obey the law of Moses in a strict fashion. But in the interim we are obliged to be patient and make allowances.

---

[8]Josephus, *The Wars of the Jews* 5.5.244, *The Works of Josephus*, trans. William Whiston, rev. ed. (Peabody, Mass.: Hendrickson, 1987), p. 709.
[9]Sometimes they did it anyway, but not in public with the Romans watching. In Acts 7:57-60 Stephen is stoned.

If he had given such a speech, his opponents would have accused him of cowardice. Was he against the law of Moses? Or was he simply unwilling to pay a price to pursue the national cause? In short, if he decides to carry out the law of Moses, he will be arrested. If he opts to set it aside he will be discredited. What is it going to be: Moses or Rome? Either way he loses and his opponents win.

Because of their total confidence in victory, the Pharisees planned this confrontation in public on their own turf. How did Jesus respond?

All through the rest of the story, Jesus is subtly debating the nature of justice. Is justice primarily a strict application of law, important though that may be? Or must the prophetic definition of justice found in the Servant Songs of Isaiah be considered? Concerning that Suffering Servant, Isaiah wrote:

> A bruised reed he will not break,
>   and a dimly burning wick he will not quench;
>   he will faithfully bring forth justice. (Is 42:3)

The Pharisees want strict application of the law. Jesus fights for compassion for the bruised reed and the dimly burning wick that he sees in the woman before him. Each seeks "justice." In this case, which should prevail? Jesus makes his choice and acts on it.

That "eighth day of the feast" was treated as a sabbath with all the sabbath laws in force. The primary requirement for keeping the law on the sabbath was to refrain from work, and the rabbis defined writing as work. They then determined that "writing" was making some kind of permanent mark like putting ink on paper. Writing with one's finger in the dust was permissible because it "leaves no lasting mark."[10] The wind would soon blow it away and it was thereby an acceptable activity on the sabbath. The Mishnah was recorded as a book in about A.D. 200, and its legislation may not have been in force at the time of Jesus, but it is the best source available for Jewish life in the first century. Jesus' actions in the story seem to be informed by these sabbath rules.

Jesus' first response was to bend down and write with his finger in the dust. By doing this he made it clear to his accusers that he was not only familiar with the written law but also well versed in the developing oral interpretation of that law. He was saying, "I am not a country bumpkin. I know the law very well, and I also know current interpretation of it. This is a day that must be kept as a *shabbot* (sabbath) and you can see that I am strictly observing the appropriate rulings. I am writing in the dust and such writing is permissible."

---

[10]Mishnah, *Šabbat* 12:5 (Danby, pp. 111-12); Babylonian Talmud, *Šabbat* 104b.

What does he write? Scholars have argued this question for centuries. I am convinced that he wrote, "death" or "kill her" or "stone her with stones." His following words presuppose that he decreed the death penalty. He opted for a strict observance of the law of Moses.

Having made that judgment, Jesus then announced the method of execution: "Let him who is without sin among you be the first to throw a stone at her" (Jn 8:7). Mobs will do anything! In the aftermath of war, or when civil authority breaks down, or when a crowd overwhelms the police force, mobs will loot, destroy, kill, burn—anything![11] With so many people involved, there is no one to arrest. In a mob, individuals can escape accountability for their behavior. If therefore everyone in the crowd stones the woman, no individual will bear responsibility for her death.

But when Jesus says, "Let the one among you who is without sin cast the first stone," he puts a name and a face on everyone in the crowd. He asks each individual to acknowledge responsibility for participation in the act. When the Roman guards step forward to "break up the crowd," their first question will be "Who started this?" The second question "Who ordered it?" would likely come later.

With this challenge Jesus says to his opponents, "Gentlemen, you clearly want *me* to go to jail for the law of Moses. I am willing to do so. I have ordered that she be killed. But I want to know which one of *you* is willing to volunteer to accompany me into that cell?" Furthermore, the Middle East is a "shame-pride culture." The child is not told, "That's wrong!" but "Shame on you!" Certain acts bring shame and others bring honor on the family. He or she is to avoid shame and defend honor. In this story, if a person steps out of the crowd claiming to be *sinless*, such an act will be remembered to his shame because Isaiah wrote, "All we like sheep have gone astray" (Is 53:6). Ecclesiastes 7:20 says, "Surely there is not a righteous man on earth who does good and never sins." With such texts in the tradition, would any religious teacher dare claim to be sinless?

Suddenly and dramatically the entire scene is changed. Jesus' opponents are now under pressure, and each of them must make a decision. In the Middle East, in such circumstances, people naturally turn to the eldest person present. The crowd turns to see if that elder has the courage to respond to Jesus' challenge. From the oldest to the youngest his opponents withdraw, humiliated. As this is happening Jesus bends down and writes a second time in the dust. The story leaves no clue as to what he wrote, but by looking at the ground, he chooses not to watch

---

[11]I was able to observe such tragic behavior personally in Beirut, Lebanon, during the first nine years of the Lebanese civil war (1975-1984).

the public humiliation of his opponents. He does no crowing and refrains from "twisting the knife." It is a nice touch that fits perfectly with the larger Gospel picture of Jesus. He takes no pleasure in humiliating them—he simply wants to save the woman.

The stage empties and Jesus is alone with the accused. In any culture, one of the quickest ways to get into trouble is to humiliate powerful people in public on their own turf. Yet this is precisely what Jesus does. The Pharisees planned to humiliate Jesus but were themselves put to shame before a crowd. A few minutes earlier the terrified woman had expected brutal violence and a painful death. Suddenly the Pharisees are angry at *Jesus* rather than at her. At great cost he has shifted their hostility from her to himself, and he doesn't even know her name! The famous Servant Song of Isaiah affirms, "with his stripes we are healed" (Is 53:5 KJV). She knows that Jesus' opponents will be back with a bigger stick and that Jesus is in process of getting hurt because of what he is doing for her. She is the recipient of a *costly demonstration* of unexpected love that saves her life. Jesus demonstrates the life-changing power of costly love. This scene provides an insight into Jesus' understanding of the significance of his own suffering. A core aspect of his "doctrine of the atonement" is here displayed.

In his final words to the woman Jesus neither condemns her nor overlooks her self-destructive lifestyle. He walks a razor's edge between the two with the words, "Neither do I condemn you; go, and do not sin again."

Looking at the larger picture, Jesus accepts the sexual code of the Old Testament tradition, but *removes its penalty.* The lady is not for stoning!

Great theological and ethical bells ring in this story and the greatest among them is Jesus interpreting his own cross.

SUMMARY: THE LADY IS NOT FOR STONING

The meaning of the story can be organized under the categories of the various players on the stage.

The Scribes and Pharisees

1. These men demonstrate corrupting influences that are always potential in organized religion. The law matters, people do not. The woman is used as a pawn in a power play to discredit Jesus and reaffirm their authority. For the accusers in the story turf is more important than truth, justice or people.

2. They worked with the all-too-familiar combination of sex, a woman, sin, public humiliation and a double standard. They did not bring in a murderer or a

thief, but a woman caught in adultery. The man was allowed to disappear. There was no evident effort to help her—only to use her and then kill her. Her public humiliation was irrelevant. At whatever cost, Jesus stands in firm opposition to all of this.

The Woman

1. Some form of this woman's story has been played out for centuries by countless thousands of women. All those around her, except Jesus, are indifferent to her suffering.

2. She has no opportunity to tell her story or explain what happened. Her name is legion.

3. As with many of the stories from and about Jesus, the ending is missing. How did this woman respond? She knows Jesus will suffer for what he has done for her. Will the knowledge of the price paid for her salvation become a life-changing force in her life? The potential is there and the imagination of the reader is powerfully stimulated to "finish the play." The reader is also challenged to internalize the story.

The Crowd

On the previous day, the crowd protected Jesus. The guards sent to arrest him could not carry out their orders because of the crowd. A solid mass of supporters around him made that impossible. But it appears that on the "eighth day" of the feast, when this incident took place, the accusers and the crowd disappeared. It seems that when the temple authorities themselves appeared and a showdown between them and Jesus evolved, the crowd evaporated like dew on a hot summer morning. If you can smell trouble in the air, the best thing to do is go home—never mind who might get hurt. It's better not to get involved!

Jesus

1. The story displays the compassion of Jesus in a telling fashion. The woman's sin in no way diminished his willingness to get hurt to save her. For Jesus a woman who had violated the sexual code was not a person to reject instinctively. As Gary Burge has aptly stated, "Jesus had different reflexes."[12]

2. Jesus demonstrates brilliance and astuteness in dealing with conflict. From a position of total political and institutional weakness he manages to turn the ta-

---

[12]Burge, *John,* p. 250.

bles on the woman's accusers and save her life.

3. The story exposes the courage of Jesus. After a day in which he was almost arrested, he bravely reenters the arena and is in no way intimidated by the powerful opponents awaiting him there.

4. Jesus is not against the law. He demonstrates that he knows the written law and is also well-informed regarding fine points of its interpretation. He also recognizes that the woman is destroying herself by her unfaithfulness to her husband (or her fiancé). He upholds the sexual ethics of the biblical tradition but removes its penalty.

5. Jesus walks the razor's edge between trivializing the woman's sin and condemning her as a person. As William Temple has written regarding Jesus' final words to the woman, "It is not a formal acquittal; it is a refusal to judge. He who so refuses is the only one who ever was *without sin*; He alone was entitled to condemn; and He did not condemn. But neither did He condone."[13]

6. Jesus presents a call for reformation of life to both sides. He delivers a challenge to the consciences of the accusers. Yet he does not romanticize the woman. Rather he leaves her with a charge to reform her lifestyle. In short, he tells the woman and the men, "You are both wrong. Both of you have sinned and both of you need to change your ways." This same utter honesty with the "righteous" and the "sinners" appears in the story of Jesus and the woman in the house of Simon (Lk 7:46-50) and in many other Gospel texts.

7. Jesus' struggles for justice are defined by the Servant Songs of Isaiah, where we are told, "a bruised reed he will not break, / and a dimly burning wick he will not quench" (Is 42:3).

8. Jesus lives out a core meaning of the cross. He offers the woman a costly demonstration of unexpected love. The reader is obliged to reflect on how the woman in the story may have responded, and in the process think deep thoughts regarding his or her response to the costly love of God offered on the cross to the world (Jn 3:16).

---

[13]William Temple, *Readings in St. John's Gospel*, 1st and 2nd ser. (London: Macmillan, 1955), p. 152.

18

The Woman in the House of
Simon the Pharisee

LUKE 7:36-50

ONE OF THE TRULY WONDROUS STORIES in the Gospel of Luke is the account of Jesus with the woman in the house of Simon the Pharisee recorded in Luke 7:36-50. Dramatic turns reflect deep aspects of serious theology as this scene unfolds.[1]

The drama is recorded in the seven-scene "ring composition" style traceable to the writing prophets. Summarized these scenes are as follows:

Introduction (the Pharisee, Jesus, and woman)
> The outpouring of the woman's love (in action)
>> A dialogue (Simon judges wrongly)
>>> A parable
>> A dialogue (Simon judges rightly)
> The outpouring of the woman's love (in retrospect)
Conclusion (the Pharisee, Jesus and the woman)

The full text of Luke 7:36-50 formatted to show this outline is shown in figure 18.1.

THE RHETORIC

The parable at the center of these seven scenes is the climax of the story. In Luke 4:16-20 we observed an encased Old Testament Scripture. Then in Luke 5:1-11 there appeared an encased miracle story. Here we have the third common type of climax for such inverted parallelism. This is an encased parable. The account of Jesus and the

---

[1]For an earlier and shorter version of this essay, see Kenneth E. Bailey, "The Parable of the Two Debtors," in *Through Peasant Eyes*, in *Poet and Peasant and Through Peasant Eyes* (Grand Rapids: Eerdmans, 1980), pp. 1-21.

1. One of the *Pharisees* asked him to eat with him,
   and he went into the Pharisee's house and *reclined*.   INTRODUCTION
   And behold, there was a *woman* who was a sinner in the city.

2.   And having learned, "He is dining in the Pharisee's house,"
       bringing an alabaster flask of *perfume*,
       and *standing* behind him at his *feet*,   THE WOMAN'S ACTS
       weeping, she began to wet his feet with her *tears*.
       And she *wiped* them with the *hair* of her head,
       and *kissed* his *feet*,
       and *anointed* them with the *perfume*.

3.   Now when the Pharisee who had invited him saw it, he said to himself,
          "*If this were a prophet*, he would have known who and
          what sort of woman this is who is *touching* him, for she *is a sinner*."
          And Jesus answered and said to him,   DIALOGUE 1
          "Simon, I have something to say to *you*."
          And he answered, "Teacher, speak up!"

4.   And Jesus said,
             "Two debtors there were to a certain money lender.   A PARABLE
             The one owed fifty denarii and the other five hundred.
             They, not being able to pay, he freely forgave them both.

5.   Which of them will love him the more?"   DIALOGUE 2
          Simon answered,
          "The one, I suppose, to whom he freely forgave the more."
          And he said to him, "You have judged rightly."

6a.   Then turning to the woman he said to Simon,   THE WOMAN'S ACTS
       "Do you see this woman?
       I entered your house!

 b.   You gave me *no water* for my *feet*,
       but she has wet my feet with her tears, and wiped them with her hair.

 c.   You gave me *no kiss*,
       but from the time I came in she has not ceased to kiss my feet.

 d.   You did *not anoint* my *head* with *oil*,
       but she has anointed my feet with perfume.

 e.   In consequence I say to you,
       It is evident that her many sins have already been forgiven,
       for she loved much.

 f.   But he who is forgiven little,
       loves little."

 g.   And he said to her, "Your sins have been forgiven."

7. Then *those* who were *reclining with him* began to say to themselves,
   "*Who is this* who *also* forgives sins?"   CONCLUSION
   And he said to the woman, "Your *faith* has *saved* you, go in peace."

Figure 18.1. The woman in the house of Simon the Pharisee (Lk 7:36-50)

Canaanite woman also had a brief parable in its center. Here the parable is also fairly short. But for the Hebrew reader a *māšāl* (a parable) could be many things, and among them are a metaphor, a simile, a proverb, a parable or a dramatic action.

In Luke 7, the writer uses a full bag of tricks. Four features are prominent.

1. The passage uses the prophetic rhetorical template of seven inverted stanzas with a climax in the center. The parallels between the various sections are bold and clear.

2. There is an encased parable at the center.

3. The six lines in number 2 exhibit an additional case of ring composition. The outer envelope focuses on the perfume. Then come (top and bottom) two references to feet, and in the center the stanza climaxes on the woman's tears and her hair. In its briefest outline this is:

> *Perfume* brought
> > *Stand at feet* (of Jesus)
> > > *let down the hair*
> > > *use the hair*
> > *Kiss the feet* (of Jesus)
> *Perfume* poured out

Thus the passage exemplifies ring composition within ring composition.

4. There is a straight-line progression of six sets of Hebrew parallelisms in number 6. Most of the lines in 6 are in pairs. Three of those pairs present "You did this; she did that." Two of them focus on "forgiven much—love much" and "forgiven little—love little."

COMMENTARY

As a whole the passage is a literary gem. This homily has been composed by a messianic Jew for Jewish readers. Aside from probably changing "rabbi" to "teacher," there are no explanatory footnotes added to the text such as we observed in Luke 4:25 and Luke 5:9-10. It is best understood to have been written before the composition of the Gospels. Most likely it was given to Luke in written form during his sojourn with the apostolic community in Jerusalem A.D. 56-58[2] and thereby it records eyewitnesses' testimony (Lk 1:2).

---

[2]In Acts 21:1-18 Luke uses the pronoun *we* in reference to himself and Paul. From that point onward the word *we* disappears. But Luke is still in the holy land in that in Acts 27:1 "we" sailed to Italy. Thus Luke indirectly affirms that for two years he was near Paul but not with him. It is reasonable to assert that during that time Luke was gathering material for his Gospel. Some of his sources were in written form (cf. Lk 1:1-2).

The story assumes that before the drama opens, the woman had heard Jesus proclaiming his message of grace for sinners. The entire account makes no sense without this assumption. Ibn al-Tayyib, writing in the eleventh century from Baghdad, affirms that she had both heard and believed. He says:

> There is no doubt that the woman previously heard the preaching of the Christ and was deeply moved by it and believed, and repented and was anticipating a chance to make visible her thanks to the Christ and to confirm forgiveness for her sins and the salvation of herself.[3]

Ibn al-Tayyib affirms that the woman was coming to express thanks for forgiveness received.

Clearly, Jesus had been proclaiming his message that God loves sinners. The Pharisees did not agree, because in their view God cared for the righteous who kept the law. Jesus, a young rabbi, was just getting started, and they could yet correct and mold him, or so they apparently assumed. As a group, his elders could come together and offer the badly needed advice. Also Jesus had already declared himself to be a prophet (Lk 4:24). This possibility needed to be investigated, so a meal was planned and Jesus invited. The first scene in the drama is as follows:

1. One of the *Pharisees* asked him to eat with him,
   and he went into the Pharisee's house and *reclined*.   INTRODUCTION
   And behold, there was a *woman* who was a sinner in the city.

This scene is filled with tension introduced by what *did not happen*. As Jesus entered the house, all the traditional courtesies were omitted. Custom required a kiss of greeting, usually on the face. After the guests were seated on stools around the broad U-shaped dining couch, called a *triclinium*, water and olive oil would be brought for the washing of hands and feet.[4] Only then could the grace be offered. Finally the guests would recline on the couch (or couches) and the meal would begin. The Babylonian Talmud says, "Our Rabbis taught: The absence of oil is a bar to the saying of grace. . . . R. Zuhamai said: Just as a dirty person is unfit for the Temple service, so dirty hands unfit one for saying grace."[5]

But what is happening in the house of Simon? Every culture has rituals for welcoming guests. These usually function unconsciously but are important, and their omission communicates many things. Traditional courtesies for welcoming a

---

[3]Ibn al-Tayyib, *Tafsir al-Mashriqi*, ed. Yusif Manqariyos (Egypt: Al-Tawfiq Press, 1907), 2:129.
[4]Olive oil was the soap of the first century. Olive oil soap is today widely used across the Middle East.
[5]Babylonian Talmud, *Berakot* 42-43; 53b.

guest in many modern countries are composed of some variation of the following:

1. Hello John, it's nice to see you.
2. Wouldn't you like to come in?
3. May I take your coat?
4. Wouldn't you like to sit down?
5. May I bring you a cup of coffee?
6. (The host then turns off the television—a sure sign that the guest is welcome and that the host has plenty of time to see him or her!)

To omit the entire list would be a calculated and pointed insult. Abraham had three famous visitors and acted in the appropriate traditional manner with water for the feet and a generous meal (Gen 18:1-8). Rabbinic literature affirms that hosting a rabbi was a great honor. The text reads, "If one partakes of a meal at which a scholar is present, it is as if he feasted on the effulgence of the Divine Presence."[6] When Simon addressed Jesus as "Teacher," he was acknowledging that his guest was a scholar.[7] Special courtesies were therefore expected, not pointed insults.

Abraham "bowed himself to the earth" before his guests and stood by (like a servant) while they ate (Gen 18:2, 8). The minimum Jesus could expect would have been a kiss of greeting, a little water for his feet and some olive oil with which to wash and anoint himself. Olive oil was and is available in every home.[8] In the story the omission of these three courtesies is mentioned specifically by Jesus. No one in the room could have failed to observe their omission. When these common acts of welcome were omitted, Jesus had the full right to say, "I see that I am not welcome here!" and leave, flushed with anger. This is not the way he responded.

The text says, "he entered *and reclined*." By reclining, Jesus takes the part of the eldest, because the eldest was expected to recline first. Traditional British high society makes a point of the order in which the guests are invited to enter the dining room for a formal banquet. The guest with the highest rank is called to dinner first. In similar fashion, after the washing of the feet and hands, and the anointing with oil, the rabbis reclined on the broad couches, in order of age. The Babylonian Talmud records, "R. Shesheth then said: I only know a Baraitha, in which it is taught: 'What is the order of reclining? When there are

---

[6]Ibid., 64a.
[7]*Teacher* is Luke's word for rabbi.
[8]Such oil was (and is) used for cooking, lighting, anointing and washing. Every home has it.

two couches in a set, the senior one reclines first, and then the junior takes his place below him.' "[9]

It is impossible to imagine that Jesus, at the age of thirty, was the oldest man in the room. Certainly most if not all of those around him were chronologically his seniors. Yet his response to the omission of the traditional courtesies was to recline on the couch immediately after entering, as if he were the eldest person in the room. This was a stunning and highly dramatic reaction. What will happen next?

The story relates that a woman was present in the room, "who was a sinner in the city."[10] Later in the story Jesus tells Simon, "From the time I came in she has not ceased to kiss my feet." This detail is revealing. Jesus clearly affirms her presence in the room when he enters and thus she was a witness to his public humiliation. Later in the story he deliberately reminds the assembled guests that the woman observed their rudeness to him. Why and how was she there?

Jesus was known to "receive sinners" and eat with them (Lk 15:2). In Luke's Gospel he had just attended a banquet with Levi the tax collector, and the Pharisees complained with the question, "Why do you eat and drink with tax collectors and sinners?" (Lk 5:30). Clearly, in their view, no law-abiding Jew should do so. As they saw it, a sinner should first confess his or her sins, make compensation for them and then demonstrate sincerity by keeping the law. All of this was spelled out by the rabbis.

George Foot Moore writes:

> Repentance, in the rabbinical definition of it, includes both the *contrititio cordis* and the *confessio oris* of the Christian analysis. Nor is the element of *satisfactio operis* lacking. . . . [I]n the case of a wrong done to a fellow man . . . reparation is the indispensable condition of the divine forgiveness.[11]

As affirmed and documented by Moore, contrition of heart, confession of the lips and compensation were all essential for divine forgiveness. To this must be added the determination not to sin again. Again, Moore says, "Repentance, as a turning from sin unto God, involves not only desisting from the sinful act, but the resolve not to commit it again."[12]

---

[9]Babylonian Talmud, *Berakot* 46b. Also see Babylonian Talmud, *Derek Ereṣ Zuṭa* 58b(3).

[10]The natural and nearly universal assumption is that she was a prostitute. The translation "she was a sinner in the city" is my own. The text highlights her lifestyle, not her address.

[11]George Foot Moore, *Judaism in the First Centuries of the Christian Era* (New York: Schocken, 1971), 1:514.

[12]Ibid., 1:510.

With such standards in place, it does not take much imagination to understand the kind of trap such a world set for a prostitute. If she asks about "compensation for her sins," she will likely be told, "In your case it is impossible!" Along with the community at large, she no doubt observed that Jesus was willing to "receive sinners and eat with them." More likely she heard him teach his message of the good news that God loves sinners (like her). This meant that the grace of God was available to her even though she could not make full compensation for her sins.[13] Overwhelmed with joy she was eager to show her gratitude (as Ibn al-Tayyib affirms) to this good man who had set her free. Her response to his public humiliation is as follows:

2. And having learned, "He is dining in the Pharisee's house,"
> *bringing* an alabaster flask of *perfume*,
>> and *standing* behind him at his *feet*,   THE WOMAN'S ACTS
>>> *weeping*, she began to wet his feet with her *tears*.
>> And she *wiped* them with the *hair* of her head,
>> and *kissed* his *feet*,
> and *anointed* them with the *perfume*.

In the original Greek, the first line of the above (Lk 7:37) has no verb "to be." I have added a present tense verb "to be" and translated, "And when she learned, 'He *is* dining in the Pharisee's house.'" Hebrew/Aramaic has no verb "to be" in the *present tense*. The omission of such a verb in a Greek text (that has a Hebrew background) most naturally assumes the present tense. Also the sentence, "He [is] dining at the Pharisee's house" can best be translated as a quotation.[14] This assumes the following: (1) Jesus taught in the community about the love of God for sinners. (2) The woman heard him and believed his liberating message. (3) Anxious to show her gratitude, she asked, "Who is entertaining the guest?" (4) She was told, "He is dining in the Pharisee's house." This does not mean that the meal had been served and the people had started to eat. Rather it was a way of describing the arrangements that had been made. We use the same idiom in English: "Who is entertaining the preacher?" someone asks, and is told, "He is eating at so-and-so's house." This does not mean that the meal has begun. To understand the story in this fashion allows the text

---

[13]Quite likely her "customers" were the greater sinners. But this is not what she would have been told.
[14]The Greek word *hoti* that opens this sentence can be indirect speech and thereby translated as "that," or it can mean direct speech and translated by using quotation marks. The latter is grammatically possible, and direct speech harmonizes with the rest of the story.

to harmonize with itself. As noted, later in the story Jesus affirms that she was in the room when he arrived (v. 45), and thus she witnessed the hostility that confronted him as he entered.[15]

Her acts are not random, nor are they entirely premeditated. We are told that she "brought" the perfume with her, probably planning to anoint his hands and head. She did not plan to wash his hands or his feet (she brought neither water nor a towel). She must have assumed that the host would extend the traditional courtesies to all his guests. He didn't, and her game plan fell apart as a result. What could she now do?

After reclining, Jesus' hands and head were no longer available to her. Suddenly she made a decision. The host refused the traditional courtesies, very well, she will compensate for his rudeness and offer them herself! But if she asks for water they will not give it to her because they want Jesus humiliated. Angry over the rudeness Jesus had just endured and frustrated at her powerlessness to do anything about it, she begins to weep. Suddenly the light dawns. That's it—*her tears!* She will wash his feet with her tears.

The text is very precise. First she begins to weep and then approaches his feet to wash them. To climb up on the couch and try to wash his hands and anoint his head would be highly improper, and would trigger criticism for engaging in "sexual misconduct." But his unclean feet are another matter.[16] Furthermore, her gesture is financially and socially costly. She pours expensive perfume on his feet. Olive oil would have been enough. No doubt she only intended to anoint his hands, and perhaps his head after he or someone else had washed them. After reclining, only his feet are available to her for washing. Surely no one could criticize her (or him) if she washed his feet! They do. But the prior question is, Why did she come in the first place?

She did not enter Simon's house in order to "make a fuss over him," hoping to earn forgiveness. Some of the early Greek and Latin fathers taught that she was weeping because of her sins and that by her actions she hoped to earn her salva-

---

[15]At traditional Middle Eastern village meals, the outcasts of the community are not shut out. They sit quietly on the floor against the wall, and at the end of the meal are fed. Their presence is a compliment to the host who is thereby seen as so noble that he even feeds the outcasts of the community. The rabbis insisted that the door be open when a meal was in progress lest you "lack of food" (i.e., lest you shut out the blessing of God). Cf. Babylonian Talmud, *The Minor Tractates, Derek Ereṣ Zuṭa* 59a(l) [chap. 9.4].

[16]The feet in Middle Eastern culture have always been considered defiled. The enemy in the Old Testament is humiliated by being made into a foot stool (Ps 110:1). Edom is insulted with the taunt, "On Edom I cast my shoe" (Ps 60:8). Moses must remove his shoes on sacred ground (Ex 3:5). Cf. Bailey, *Through Peasant Eyes,* p. 5.

tion.[17] Such is not the case, and others among the early fathers were aware of this. Ambrose noted, "Only someone who had been forgiven much and therefore loved much could anoint Jesus' feet as the sinful woman did."[18]

Origen wrote, "she, who owed the great debt and was forgiven, showed great love." John Cassian observed, "She loves more because she has been forgiven more."[19] These three fathers clearly affirmed (with Ibn al-Tayyib) that she entered the room as a forgiven woman. Had Jesus not been publicly humiliated, she might have affirmed an ascription of praise to Jesus or simply fallen on her knees before him vocalizing thanks and joy at her newfound freedom as a forgiven woman. But she begins to weep, and, with Origen and Ambrose, it is clear that her tears are not for her sins but for his public humiliation. She is in anguish because, before her eyes, this beautiful person who set her free with his message of the love of God for sinners, is being publicly humiliated.

Dietrich Bonhoeffer catches the scene correctly when he writes, "Being swept into the messianic suffering of God in Christ happens in the most varied ways in the New Testament; . . . through the actions of the woman who was a sinner."[20]

The woman was deeply dismayed at the insult to Jesus, and said to herself, "*They* will not offer these courtesies! Very well, *I will offer them* instead!" She washed his feet with her tears and dried them with her hair.[21] Once washed, she kissed and anointed them with perfume. With this dramatic act she entered into Jesus' pain of rejection and public humiliation. Simon's "plan" was now frustrated. The person he and his friends were deliberately humiliating was now receiving special honor.

As noted, the woman was a "sinner in the city." Obviously, the room was occupied with two types of sinners: law-keepers and lawbreakers. The entire scene unfolds within the tensions that develop between these two kinds of people. Law-keepers often condemn lawbreakers as "sinners." Lawbreakers generally look at law-keepers and shout "hypocrites." But not in this story. Here the woman's total focus is on Jesus. Her acts not only irritate, but also shock the "righteous" in the room. How so?

---

[17]Augustine wrote, "The woman's humility secures her forgiveness of sins" (*Luke*, ed. Arthur Just, Ancient Christian Commentary on Scripture [Downers Grove, Ill.: InterVarsity Press, 2003], p. 125. Cf. also Clement of Alexandria and Peter Chrysologus, *Luke*, ed. Arthur Just, Ancient Christian Commentary on Scripture [Downers Grove, Ill.: InterVarsity Press, 2003], pp. 126-27).

[18]Ambrose, quoted in *Luke*, ed. Arthur Just, Ancient Christian Commentary on Scripture (Downers Grove, Ill.: InterVarsity Press, 2003), p. 125.

[19]John Cassian, quoted in *Luke*, ed. Arthur Just, Ancient Christian Commentary on Scripture (Downers Grove, Ill.: InterVarsity Press, 2003), p. 125.

[20]Dietrich Bonhoeffer, *Meditations on the Cross*, ed. Manfred Weber (Louisville: Westminster John Knox, 1998), p. 61.

[21]For her, a kiss of greeting on the face would have been unthinkable in that culture.

The woman uncovered her hair and "touched" Jesus! In traditional Middle Eastern society, from the days of the Jewish rabbis to the present, a woman was and is obliged to cover her hair in public. The Mishnah lists the offenses that justify a man divorcing his wife without giving her a *ketubah* (a financial settlement).[22] Among the items mentioned are "If she goes out with her hair unbound, or spins in the street, or speaks with any man."[23]

In any culture, to be divorced with no *ketubah* is an extremely serious matter for a woman. If going out "with her hair unbound" would trigger such a personal and financial disaster, then clearly such an act was considered an intolerable offense with dire consequences. Rabbi Meir's (second century A.D.) teachings on divorce are recorded in the Babylonian Talmud. He talks about "a bad man who sees his wife go out with her hair unfastened and spin cloth in the street with her armpits uncovered and bathe *[sic]* with the men." The text goes on to state, "Such a one it is a religious duty to divorce."[24]

To "go out with her hair unfastened" appears in the same list with "bathe with the men," and in each case the woman is to be divorced as a religious duty. It seems that for such rabbis, when a woman uncovered her hair in public she was offending God, because a woman's hair was considered sexually provocative.

Tractate *Berakot* records a discussion of that which in a woman causes sexual excitement.[25] Each of three rabbis offers an explanation.

> R. Hisda said: A woman's leg is a sexual incitement, as it says, *Uncover the leg, pass through the rivers* (Is 47:2).

> Samuel said: A woman's voice is sexual incitement, as it says, *For sweet is thy voice and thy countenance is comely* (Song 2:14).

> R. Shesheth said: A woman's hair is a sexual incitement, as it says, *Thy hair is as a flock of goats* (Song 4:1).

In modern times, the recent prime minister of Iran, Rafsanjani, was asked by the press why his country insisted on women covering their hair. He replied, "It is the obligation of the female to cover her head because women's hair exudes vibrations that arouse, mislead, and corrupt men."[26] Thus this Middle Eastern

---

[22]The *ketubah* was a sum of money the bridegroom pledged himself to assign to the bride in case of his death or his divorcing her. It can also mean the sum of money itself. Cf. Herbert Danby, ed. and trans., *The Mishnah* (1933; reprint, Oxford: Oxford University Press, 1980), p. 794.

[23]Mishnah, *Ketubbot* 6.6 (Danby, p. 255).

[24]Babylonian Talmud, *Giṭṭin* 90a-b.

[25]Babylonian Talmud, *Berakot* 14a.

[26]Jan Goodwin, *The Price of Honor* (Boston: Little, Brown, 1994), p. 107.

attitude toward women's hair has persisted among the socially conservative for millennia.

Returning to the first century, on the positive side, for a woman to keep her hair covered was a sign of piety. The Babylonian Talmud records an important incident in the religious life of the nation that took place when R. Ishmael B. Kimhith was high priest. This man was appointed by Gratus in the year 17-18 A.D., which makes him a contemporary of Jesus.[27] The tractate *Yoma* describes the one time in Jewish history in which the high priest was defiled during the celebration of the liturgy of the day of Atonement. The text reads:

> Furthermore, it is told of R. Ishmael b. Kimhith that he [the high priest] went out and talked with a certain lord in the street, and spittle from his mouth squirted on his garments, whereupon Joseph his brother entered and ministered in his stead so that their mother saw two high priests on one day. The Sages said to her: What hast thou done to merit such [glory]? She said: Throughout the days of my life the beams of my house have not seen the plaits of my hair.[28]

This very pious woman did not uncover her hair even at home! In her view this act earned her the honor of being the mother of two sons, each of which, on the same day, officiated at the celebration of the liturgy of the Day of Atonement. In such a world the "sinner" woman in the house of Simon was obliged to make an important choice. Both men and women wore long robes. Jesus was reclining, probably on the broad couch of a *triclinium*. The woman was kneeling behind him. After washing his feet with her tears she wanted to dry them but had no towel. The voluminous folds of her dress were gathered before her as she knelt and were available for use as a substitute towel. Why did she let her hair down instead and use it to dry the feet of Jesus, and in the process inevitably "touch him"?[29]

In traditional Middle East society, a bride on her wedding night lets down her hair and allows it to be seen by her husband for the first time. No one around the room could have missed the overtones of this woman's gesture. By unloosing her hair, she is making some form of an ultimate pledge of loyalty to Jesus.[30] The crit-

---

[27]Gratus deposed the high priest almost every year until the year eighteen, at which time he picked Caiaphas.

[28]Babylonian Talmud, *Yoma* 47a. The same story also appears in *'Abot de Rabbi Nathan* 31a(2) and Tosefta, *Yoma* 3.

[29]The verb "to touch" is used in biblical language for the marital relationship (see 1 Cor 7:1).

[30]In Genesis 41:45 Joseph marries Asenath, the daughter of an Egyptian priest of On. Then in the pseudepigrapha, the book *Joseph and Asenath* presents some interesting parallels to aspects of this story. Written in Greek (with a possible Hebrew origin) *Joseph and Asenath* is usually dated from the first century B.C. to the second century A.D. In it Joseph is called "son of God" (6:3; 13:13) and as a part of their wedding banquet Asenath insists on washing Joseph's feet (20:3-5).

ical question is, Will he accept or reject this extraordinary act?

At every turn in the stories about and from Jesus it is important to ask, In the light of the cultural world of his day, what was Jesus expected to say or do? An answer to this question is sometimes hard. In this case it is easy. He was expected to be embarrassed over the "touching" that he was receiving from the woman and shocked that she exposed her hair. Everyone in the room would assume that he would instinctively judge these acts as beyond the range of "acceptable behavior" and reject her. One word to Simon and she would be quickly removed from the room by a servant! But to the amazement of the entire assembled crowd, Jesus allowed the scene to proceed and accepted her gestures. Did he have no sense of shame? Simon's response is recorded in the text:

3. When the Pharisee who had invited him saw it, he said to himself,
   "*If this were a prophet,* he would have known who and
   what sort of woman this is who is *touching* him, for she *is* a *sinner.*"
   And Jesus answered and said to him,   DIALOGUE 1
   "Simon, I have something to say to *you.*"
   And he answered, "Teacher, speak up!"

Simon was clearly surprised and shocked at Jesus' acceptance of these attentions. Up to this point Jesus had not spoken to the woman. Simon and the others would at least have been pleased that Jesus did not cross that boundary. But to let such a woman "touch" him, even on the feet, was simply too intimate. From Simon's response we discover a part of the agenda. Jesus was invited by the Pharisees for an examination! Was he a prophet and worthy of respect or not? Jesus' acceptance of the woman's actions provided Simon with what he thought was the right answer. Surely no man of God would ever personally accept such outrageous behavior! But there is more.

The Pharisaic anxiety over Jesus' acceptance of sinners already appears in Luke 5:30. The woman was not upset by Jesus' acceptance of sinners, she was overjoyed by it. She had come to offer her thanks—to Jesus! From the Pharisaic point of view Jesus should have told her:

> Stop! If you are grateful to God for having received forgiveness, go to the temple and offer a thanksgiving sacrifice. In the court of the women you can draw as close to the divine presence of God in the holy of holies as is allowed. There your thanks is appropriately expressed. But do not do this to me. I am only a prophet speaking God's word!

Jesus' acceptance of her acts is critical to the story in a number of ways. Among them are:

1. He empathizes with the cost and nature of her gesture, and accepts it. Rejection on his part would devastate her and he knows it.

2. Jesus observes that the woman is the only person in the room who feels the pain of his rejection by Simon and the other guests. They snubbed him. She does her best, at considerable risk, to oppose them in public, demonstrating solidarity with him and trying to compensate for their rudeness. She entered into his suffering, and he felt her compassion.

3. She made a decision. For her the right place to offer her thanks for forgiveness received was to Jesus. She sensed that the Shekinah of God was present in this man. It was to him, therefore, that she offers her thanks. He accepted that gratitude, confirming her understanding of who he was.

Once during the decades I lived in the Middle East, a desperate man fell on his knees before me and began to kiss my feet. Embarrassed, I pulled him up from the ground, seated him on a chair and said, "Muhammad, tell me your troubles and I will do my best to help you. But I cannot accept this gesture—it is too much!"

When the city of Richmond, Virginia, fell at the close of the American Civil War on April 4, 1865, Abraham Lincoln insisted that he be taken to visit the still-burning southern capital. On arrival, he was pointed out to a former slave, who rushed to the president, fell on his knees and began to kiss Lincoln's feet. Embarrassed, Lincoln replied, "That's not right. You must kneel to God only, and thank him for liberty."[31]

Jesus accepted the woman's extraordinary demonstration, and in that acceptance confirmed her judgment regarding who he was—the divine presence of God among his people. His body was now the temple, and God's spirit was upon him (Lk 3:21-22). But Simon either could not see or perhaps could not accept any of this. So Jesus turned to him (and through him to the entire assembly) to explain his actions. The phrase "I have something to say to you" is a classical Middle Eastern idiom that introduces blunt speech that the listener may not want to hear.[32] Jesus then told a brief parable about two debtors:

4. And Jesus said,
   "Two debtors there were to a certain money lender.
   The one owed fifty denarii and the other five hundred.
   They, not being able to pay, he freely forgave them both.

This parable is a "sleeper" that is often neglected among the parables of Jesus.

---

[31]Birke Davis, *To Appomattox: Nine April Days, 1865* (New York: Popular Library, 1960), p. 165.
[32]Cf. Bailey, *Through Peasant Eyes*, p. 12.

However on close examination it clearly merits serious attention.

In both the Old and New Testaments the phrases "canceling a debt" and "forgiving a debt/sin" overlap and indeed at times are expressed with the same words. In discussing the use of this verb in the Greek Old Testament, Rudolf Bultmann writes, "The one who forgives is God." Regarding the New Testament, Bultmann notes that the verb "to forgive" means, " 'to remit' or 'to forgive' whether in the profane sense in Mt. 18:27 and 32 or more often in the religious." [33] These two come together in this text. The creditor in the parable freely forgave the debts of each debtor.[34] A few verses later Jesus says to the woman, "Your sins have been forgiven." The verb here is *aphiēmi*, the common word for the forgiveness of sins. A different Greek word is used in the earlier text, but the meanings overlap significantly. This financial and theological use of the verb *forgive* appears numerous times in the New Testament. This is particularly the case where the metaphors of creditor and debtor are used to refer to God and sinners. Coupled with this is the fact that evil acts are of two basic kinds. Simply put, "sins" are those acts that a pious person should not commit, while "debts" are responsibilities that one has failed to fulfill. Thereby sin is made up of evil deeds and failures to do good. These are expressed as "trespasses/sins" and "debts." In summary, the various witnesses in the New Testament to the forgiveness of debts/sins as they relate to God are as follows:

1. The Aramaic word *ḥôbâ* means both *debts* and *sins*. When Jesus talked about "sins" he certainly used the word *ḥôbâ*, and thus "debtors" and "sinners" combined for him into a single term.

2. The Lord's Prayer in Matthew uses the word *debts*. Luke has *debts* and *sins*. Again, Jesus most certainly used the word *ḥôbâ* which had both meanings.

3. In two parallel passages in Luke this same set of words appears. Luke 13:2 uses the word *sinners* and Luke 13:4 reads *debtors* (RSV: offenders). Again the Aramaic word *ḥôbâ* is behind each of these words.

4. In Matthew 18:23-35 a servant is forgiven a large debt by his master and then fails to forgive a fellow servant a small debt. The unforgiving servant is punished. Jesus responds, "So also my heavenly Father will do to every one of you, if you do not forgive your brother from your heart" (v. 35). The remission of a

---

[33]Rudolf Bultmann, "ἀφίημι, ἄφηεσις, παρίημι, πάρεσις," *Theological Dictionary of the New Testament*, ed. Gerhard Kittel (Grand Rapids: Eerdmans, 1965), 1:510-11.

[34]Here the verb is *charizomai*, which has *charis* (grace) as its root. The unearned and undeserved grace of forgiveness is thereby emphasized.

debt is there used in a parable focused on the forgiveness of sin with God as the creditor.

5. The twin parables of the talents (Mt 25:14-30) and the pounds (Lk 19:12-28) are stories of a master who distributes cash and leaves only to return and make an accounting for the money. Again the language of creditor and debtor is used to refer to God in his dealing with frail humans.

6. In Colossians 2:13-14 Paul uses the symbolism of the canceling of a bond to explain the significance of the cross. That is, a certificate of indebtedness, a bond, is used as a metaphor for sins.

Moore nicely summarizes the rabbinic view: "Man owes God obedience, and every sin, whether of commission or of omission, is a defaulted obligation, a debt. A guilty man, who is liable to punishment, is said to be 'owing the penalty.' "[35]

Keeping in mind this New Testament understanding of "debt" as an important part of "sin," and the parabolic use of a creditor as a symbol for God, in figure 18.2 we can observe the following:

The parable	To Be Noted in the Parable
1. A CREDITOR has two DEBTORS:	The creditor is assumed to be God
a. one debtor owes 500 denarii	[like the woman]
b. one owes 50 denarii	[like Simon]
2. The DEBTORS cannot pay	Sinners cannot compensate God for their sins
3. The CREDITOR forgives both:	The creditor begins to look like Jesus
a. the 500 denarii debtor	[He forgives the *woman*]
b. the 50 denarii debtor	[Does he also forgive *Simon?*]
4. The DEBTORS respond with love for the CREDITOR:	The creditor is clearly Jesus
a. The debtor who was forgiven 500 loves much.	[like the woman]
b. The debtor who was forgiven 50 loves little.	[like Simon]

Figure 18.2. The parable of the creditor and the two debtors (Lk 7:41-42)

A gentle, subtle move is observable in the parable. As the parable opens, the

---

[35]George Foot Moore, *Judaism in the First Centuries of the Christian Era* (New York: Schocken, 1971), 2:95.

creditor is naturally assumed to be God and the debtors represent the condition of fallen humankind. As the parable unfolds, the debtors cannot pay, and once again the creditor is clearly God. But then the creditor "freely forgave them both," and the obvious symbol for God begins to look like a symbol for Jesus. Is Jesus actually forgiving Simon for his rudeness? Yes, and there is both a gentleness and a boldness involved in Jesus' construction of the parable. Simon is being reminded that he has just acted in a rude and unjustifiable manner and that Jesus is not going to ignore the insult. Simon is also a sinner. At the same time Simon's faults are affirmed, in some sense, to be less than those of the woman. Indeed, she owes 500 and Simon only 50. Yet they are parallel in the sense that neither can pay, and the creditor (Jesus? God?) is willing to freely forgive both of them. (What has happened to the rabbinic demand for compensation?) By the end of the parable the subtle fusion between the creditor as God and the creditor as Jesus is complete. This can be called "hermeneutical Christology." Jesus takes a recognized symbol for God and subtly transforms it into a symbol for himself. This is of particular significance because it is Jesus himself defining his own identity. In the Gospel of John, Jesus says, "I and the Father are one" (Jn 10:30). Here the same theology is affirmed in action and set forth in a parable.[36]

The parable ends with a shift of focus away from the debts to the debtors' responses to grace (the canceling of those debts). Simon wants to focus on: "Look at the great sins of this woman who 'is a sinner.'" By contrast Jesus shifts attention to "Look at the response of this woman who has accepted to be freely forgiven."

This shift of emphasis is *huge* and it transforms the entire scene. After this quiet, simple, yet stunning parable, the second dialogue between Jesus and Simon occurs.

5. "Which of them will love him the more?"   DIALOGUE 2
   Simon answered,
   "The one, I suppose, to whom he freely forgave the more."
   And he said to him, "You have judged rightly."

Using a modified Socratic method, Jesus starts to corner Simon through the use of Simon's own response to Jesus' question. Obviously, the one who is forgiven more will love more. Jesus compliments Simon by saying, "You have judged rightly."[37] (In the first dialogue with Jesus, Simon had judged the woman

---

[36]This hermeneutical Christology deserves far more attention than it has in the past received.

[37]Every rabbi worked for a living but spent all available free time in debating the law and giving rulings on various legal niceties. "You have judged rightly" is the kind of a compliment every rabbi was happy to receive.

wrongly!) Jesus then proceeds to reflect on the woman's response to grace.

The difficulty is that we already know the "end of the play." To more fully appreciate what is happening at any critical point in a biblical story, it is important to reflect on the various options open to the main characters at that point in the drama. Here Jesus is expected to apologize for the woman's "outrageous" acts that are obviously an attempt to compensate for the host's failures. If Simon wishes to insult his guest, what business is it of hers to interfere and try to blunt his purposes? To intervene by doing the very things the host deliberately chose not to do is an affront to the host and everyone knows it. Jesus can (1) reject her, (2) apologize for her actions or (3) defend her. Jesus did not reject her. He could have apologized by saying:

> Gentlemen, I am embarrassed by all of this. Yes, on occasion I do eat with sinners, but we always keep the numbers down and we try to clean them up a bit before our meals, which are always in private. This is not at all the kind of a scene with which I am comfortable, and so do not be upset. I grant that no easy acceptance of such types is possible. Standards must be maintained! These "people of the land" must learn how to behave!

Instead, Jesus chooses to defend her by attacking the host with a coup de grace.

Imagine a man walking through a darkly wooded area in the dead of night when suddenly a gang of ruffians jumps out of the forest, apprehends him and marches him off deeper into the woods. There they join a circle of men around a fire. Together they decide to "have a little fun" with the captive. After stripping him naked they begin to mock him with rude and profane comments. After a few moments a woman, previously unnoticed, steps quietly from the outer edge of the fire light with a blanket over her arm. Silently she opens the blanket, removes a knife from her pocket and slits the center of the blanket which she then slips over the head of the naked captive. Weeping she drops to her knees, kisses the captive's hand and then withdraws to her place in the darkness.

Naturally the gang of thieves is furious. The captive they chose to humiliate is being honored by the woman, as she compensates for their rudeness. It is they who are now humiliated, and in public.

The same kind of a dynamic takes over in the biblical story before us. Simon and his guests choose to humiliate Jesus. The woman alone feels the pain of Jesus' public humiliation and steps in to join that suffering and, as much as possible, alleviate it. In the process the woman earns the intense anger of the circle of guests. She spoils their carefully laid plans by honoring the one they deliberately humiliate.

In his comments on the woman's actions, Jesus shifts the hostility of the assembled guests from the woman to himself. "With his stripes we are healed" (Is 53:5 KJV). Initially they were angry because she spoiled their self-righteous game plan. In the following attack on Simon, Jesus leaves them angry at him. His comments on the woman's actions are as follows:

6a. Then turning to the woman he said to Simon,   THE WOMAN'S ACTS
"Do you see this woman?
I entered your house!

  b. You gave me *no water* for my *feet,*
but she has wet my feet with her tears, and wiped them with her hair.

  c. You gave me *no kiss,*
but from the time I came in she has not ceased to *kiss my feet.*

  d. You did *not anoint* my *head* with *oil,*
but she has anointed my feet with *perfume.*

  e. In consequence I say to you,
it is evident that her many sins *have already* been *forgiven,*
for she loved much.

  f. But he who is *forgiven little,*
loves little."

  g. And he said to her, "Your sins have been forgiven."

Simon is ignoring her. Jesus calls on Simon to look at her. Then Jesus speaks words of hard steel. The opening phrase is critical. "I entered your house!" says Jesus. How these words were spoken, whether gently or accusingly, is impossible to determine. But their meaning is clear. Jesus is saying:

Simon, I am a Middle Easterner and you are a Middle Easterner. I do not have to explain to you your duty to your guest. You have called me "Teacher (Rabbi)." At your invitation I have entered your house and become your guest. You refuse to notice this woman whom you see as no more than a "sinner" and you expect me to do the same. But, can't you see Simon, that she is making up for your inexcusable failures as a host, and if I am to avoid sinners then I will be obliged to avoid you?

Never in my life, in any culture, anywhere in the world have I participated in a banquet where the guest attacked the quality of the hospitality! I have never heard a guest say to a host, "Mrs. Jones, you could have at least served me a decent meal!" Such words are unthinkable, yet the insult expressed in them appears in this story.

Jesus attacks Simon in public in his own home. He is not a fool and must have a very good reason for launching such a public attack. The reader is not told the reason, and we can only reflect on what it might be.

By aggressively defending the woman Jesus endorses her willingness to get hurt for him. She empathizes with his suffering, and in Bonhoeffer's language is "drawn into the messianic suffering of God in Christ." Jesus responds with a *costly* demonstration of unexpected love. The woman is watching! She sees Jesus defending her, confirming her and in the process carving out space for her in the community of his followers. This scene could not be and was not forgotten.[38] She knows that this is "round one." Simon and his friends are deeply offended and will return with a bigger stick. Jesus' costly love extended to her will inevitably become a life-changing force in her life. Like the woman in John 8, she says to herself, "He is going to get hurt—for me—and he doesn't even know my name!" Jesus is demonstrating a part of the meaning and power of his own suffering.

Peter describes himself as "a witness of the sufferings of Christ" (1 Pet 5:1). But Peter was not present at the cross. The only way to understand his meaning is to hear him remind his readers of the suffering of the messianic agenda that he witnessed all through Jesus' public ministry. Doesn't the reader/listener to this story also become "a witness to the suffering of Christ"? By choosing to offer Jesus her thanks for forgiveness received, rather than presenting a thanksgiving sacrifice in Jerusalem, the woman has already affirmed her sense of the divine presence in his person. That profound awareness is confirmed by his life-changing demonstration of costly love.

For centuries there has been an error in the translation of this text.[39] A correction of that error now appears in many recent versions (JB, NRSV, NIV). The woman is not offering her love hoping to receive forgiveness. Rather she is responding to the fact that she has *already* received much forgiveness and thus has much love to offer, as Ambrose observed.[40] In like manner, Simon, who has been forgiven little, loves little. Forgiveness is first and the offer of love is a response to it.

After this public attack on Simon, Jesus at last speaks to the woman, reconfirming her forgiveness by saying, "Your sins have been forgiven." A rabbi was strictly warned again and again not to talk to women in any public place, not even to his own wife.[41] Jesus violates that dictum as he speaks to the woman with his word of assurance. But he does so as a climax to her identification with his suffering and

---

[38]Indeed, it was remembered and recorded with great care and considerable rhetorical artistry.

[39]Cf. KJV and RSV where it appears the woman offers her footwashing and is rewarded with forgiveness.

[40]The perfect tense of the verb *forgive* in v. 47, with many recent versions, is rightly translated "it is evident that her many sins have already been forgiven for she loved much." Cf. Bailey, *Through Peasant Eyes*, p. 17.

[41]Babylonian Talmud, *Berakot* 34b.

his costly defense of her. The final scene is as follows:

7. Then *those* who were *reclining with him* began to say to themselves,
   "Who is this who *also* forgives sins?"
   And he said to the woman, "Your *faith* has *saved* you, go in peace."

Along with other outrageous acts, Jesus also forgives sins! The accusation is not precise.[42] In this story Jesus confirms her forgiveness. Yet Luke's readers know that Jesus does indeed forgive sin (Lk 5:24). More to the point is the fact that Simon and his friends refuse to follow Jesus' lead and shift their focus from the sin of the woman to her response to grace. Simon focused on the woman's mistakes. Now the invited guests focus on Jesus' "mistakes." Criticizing Jesus is much easier than dealing with their failures to accept forgiveness and respond with love. "Deny the message and attack the messenger" is the order of the day. But Jesus' final word to the woman is again astounding!

The woman does not utter a single word, yet Jesus commends the power of her faith! What is the content of the wordless faith that he perceives and praises? With Paul, faith for Jesus is composed of (1) intellectual assent, (2) a daily walk of trust, and (3) a response in obedience. Biblical faith is never merely something we think; it is also something we do. She says nothing, but acts in confirmation of her confidence that he is the appropriate recipient of her thanks for forgiveness received. For her the Shekinah of God is uniquely present in the person of Jesus. She joins in his messianic suffering through a powerful act of identification with it. Her daily walk of trust had already begun because it was that walk that led her to risk rejection and insult by entering the house of Simon in the first place. (She had no idea as to how she would be treated on arrival.) Her obedience, expressed in her entering into his suffering, was daring and costly. Thus her faith was composed of all three of the above components.

At the end of the day Jesus made clear that both law-keepers and lawbreakers are sinners and equally in need of forgiveness, a forgiveness that he freely offered to all. The woman accepted. Simon's final response is unknown.[43]

Simon and his friends invited Jesus to a meal so that they could cross-examine him, discover if he was or was not a prophet and chastise him for accepting sinners.

---

[42]Again the verb is in the perfect tense. Jesus is saying, "Your sins have been forgiven." That is, he is confirming something that has already happened.

[43]This same open-ended story reappears in the great parable of the prodigal son. At the end of the drama Jesus is on stage in the person of the Father, and the audience (again the Pharisees) on stage in the person of the older son. The younger son accepts to be found and will participate in the banquet. What will the older son do? We are not told. Cf. Kenneth E. Bailey, *Jacob and the Prodigal* (Downers Grove, Ill.: InterVarsity Press, 2003), pp. 111-15.

A true prophet for Simon was someone who avoided sinners—particularly female sinners! For Jesus, true prophethood involved getting hurt for sinners by confronting their attackers. As the story/parable ends, Simon is under the glass and is challenged to accept offered forgiveness, respond with love and revise the default setting of his outlook on the world.

Jesus' final word to the woman was to remind her that her faith in and obedience to him was a saving force in her life that would lead her in the path of peace.

SUMMARY: THE WOMAN IN THE HOUSE OF SIMON THE PHARISEE

The theological meanings set forth in this rich story/parable are:

1. *Forgiveness and love.* The more forgiveness the believer receives *from* Jesus the more costly love he or she offers *to* Jesus.

2. *Sin.* Two overarching types of sinners are clarified. Both law-keepers and law-breakers are sinners in need of forgiveness.

3. *The cross.* Jesus offers a costly demonstration of unexpected love to the woman. In the process he exposes one of the deepest levels of his saving ministry, which climaxes on a cross.

4. *Faith, obedience, forgiveness, salvation and peace.* These five great themes are linked in a single story. The woman is forgiven and saved by a faith in Jesus that is obedience. The result of this process is peace.

5. *Women.* The position of women is elevated. Jesus is willing to get hurt to publicly reach out in costly love to this unknown, immoral woman.

6. *Prophethood.* The nature of prophethood is clarified. Simon thinks a prophet avoids contact with sinners. For Jesus a prophet offers costly love to sinners.

7. *Christology.* Jesus duplicates the actions of the creditor in the parable. He confirms forgiveness to the woman and accepts in his person her grateful response. Such thanks was expected to be offered in the temple by means of a thanksgiving sacrifice. Jesus is at least saying, "I am the unique representative of God to whom such thanks is appropriately expressed." God now dwells among his people in the person of Jesus.

8. *Messianic agenda.* The woman suffers with Jesus as she reaches out to enter his pain. Paul yearns to "share his sufferings, becoming like him in his death" (Phil 3:10). Does the woman provide glimpses of what Paul is talking about?

9. *Inevitable decision.* After such a scene, the participant/reader must believe or be offended. Either Jesus is an outrageous egotist or he is the unique agent of

God who mediates forgiveness and is the appropriate one to whom a forgiven sinner offers thanks.

There is little wonder that this story was remembered, recorded with great care, preserved intact and selected in its entirety by Luke for incorporation into his Gospel. May its richness and power continue to bless all who contemplate its meaning.

19

The Parable of the Widow and the Judge

LUKE 18:1-8

THIS PARABLE IS DEEPLY IMBEDDED in traditional Middle Eastern public chivalry toward women, and needs to be compared to a similar account composed more than two hundred years earlier in a book titled the Wisdom of Ben Sirach (or Ecclesiasticus).[1]

This book is often referred to as deutero-canonical and is read as Scripture by Eastern Orthodox and Catholic Christians. Ben Sirach 35:14-18 appears in figure 19.1.

He will not ignore the *supplication of the fatherless*,	
nor the *widow* when she pours out *her story*.	WIDOW HEARD
Do not the *tears of the widow* run down her cheek	Against Adversaries
as she *cries out* against him who has caused them to fall?	
He whose *service is pleasing* to the *Lord* will be *accepted*,	
and *his prayer* will reach to the clouds.	OBEDIENT/HUMBLE HEARD
The *prayer of the humble* pierces the clouds,	Persistence
and he will not be consoled until it *reaches the Lord;*	Justice for the Righteous
he will not desist until the *Most High visits him*	Judgment (on adversary)
and does *justice* for the *righteous* and *executes judgment*.	
The *Lord will not delay*,	
neither will he be *patient* with them,	LORD NOT PATIENT
till he *crushes the genitals* of the *unmerciful*,	Brutal on Gentiles
and repays *vengeance on the Gentiles*.	

Figure 19.1. Widows and adversaries in Ben Sirach 35:14-18

---

[1]For an extended and more technical discussion of this parable see Kenneth E. Bailey, *Through Peasant Eyes*, in *Poet and Peasant and Through Peasant Eyes* (Grand Rapids: Eerdmans, 1980), pp. 127-56.

Clearly, there are similarities and differences between the words of Sirach and Jesus. As recorded in Luke, the parable of Jesus appears in figure 19.2.

1. And he told them a parable,	
to the effect that they ought always to pray and not lose heart.	
He said,	
2. "In a certain city there was a *judge.*	JUDGE
God he did *not fear*	God
and before people he was never ashamed.	People
3. And a *widow* there was in that city	WIDOW
who was *coming* to him	Coming
saying, *'Vindicate me* from my adversary.'	Vindication
4. *He did not want* to for a time. Then he said to himself,	JUDGE
'Although I do *not fear God*	God
and *do not respect people,*	People
5. yet because *she causes me trouble,* this widow,	WIDOW
I will *vindicate her,*	Vindication
lest in *continual coming* she *wear me out.'* "	Coming
- -	
6. The Lord said, "Hear what the unrighteous judge says.	
And *will not God vindicate his elect*	FUTURE
who cry to him day and night?	Present
Also he is slow to anger with them.	Present
I tell you, *he will vindicate them speedily.*	FUTURE
7. Nevertheless, when the Son of man comes,	SON OF MAN
will he find faith on the earth?"	Future—Faith?

Figure 19.2. The parable of the widow and the judge (Lk 18:1-8)

There are a number of contrasts between the two accounts. First, Sirach begins with a woman and immediately shifts to a man. No such shift appears in Jesus' parable, where the woman maintains her presence throughout the story. Second, in Sirach, God responds "to the one whose service is pleasing to the Lord." Such a person receives rewards. In Jesus' parable there is no mention of any good works done by the woman that earn her the right to a hearing. Third, at the end of Sirach's account the reader is told that God will crush the genitals of the Gentiles.

Jesus' parable ends with a wistful hope that the Son of Man might find faith at the end of all things. No word of judgment appears, but in its place there is a realistic awareness that all may not be well when history comes to its close.

Both stories include a judge, but Sirach assumes the judge to be God. Jesus introduces a very human judge who did not fear God or respect people. Ibrahim Sa'id succinctly explains these two aspects of the judge's character by noting, " 'He does not fear God' means that he does not grant God's authority, 'and does not respect people' means he pays no attention to the opinions of people."[2]

Literally the Gospel text says, "He felt no shame before people." Middle Eastern culture is often called a shame/pride culture, in which social behavior is guided by a community sense of honor and shame more than by means of an individual sense of loyalty to an abstract principle of right and wrong. Such an outlook is common to many cultures. A common American phrase affirms that "You don't kick a man when he's down." To do so would be dishonorable. A community sense of honor dictates a code that should not be violated. It is in light of such things that the judge in the parable must be seen.[3] Luke's introduction to the parable is as follows:

1. And he told them a parable,
   to the effect that they ought always to pray and not lose heart.

The introduction to the parable is clearly supplied by Luke or his source. One strand of interpretation suggests that such Lucan settings should be set aside to let the parable speak for itself. Whenever that happens, the interpreter inevitably adds his or her own frame of reference. A green and brown picture may be mounted with a brown frame. As that happens the brown frame will highlight the browns in the painting. But if the frame is removed and the picture placed on a green wall, the greens of the picture will be reinforced. When the first-century "frame" is removed from this parable, consciously or unconsciously a modern frame is added by the commentator. Surely Luke's understanding of the focus of the parable is superior to the views of any modern commentator (including me).

Furthermore, the Jewish tradition expected that the *māšāl* (the parable) should be accompanied by its *nimšal* (that extra bit of information that the listener/reader

---

[2]Ibrahim Sa'id, *Sharh Bisharat Luqa* (Beirut: Middle East Council of Churches, 1970), p. 435.

[3]Arland Hultgren thoughtfully observes six points of contact between this parable and the parable of the friend at midnight (Lk 11:5-8) (Arland J. Hultgren, *The Parables of Jesus* [Grand Rapids: Eerdmans, 2000], p. 253). The two accounts are also balanced in the composition of the center section of Luke's Gospel. See Kenneth E. Bailey, *Poet and Peasant*, in *Poet and Peasant and Through Peasant Eyes* (Grand Rapids: Eerdmans, 1980), pp. 80-82.

needed to understand the parable). Isaiah's parable *(māšāl)* of the vineyard (Is 5:1-6) is followed by its *nimšal*, which appears in verse 7 and identifies the symbols of the parable. The parable is not a balloon to be carried with the wind of the interpreter's experience or perceptions. Rather, the text itself provides the author/editor's understanding of what the parable is about. This pattern is already clear in the Isaiah passage. In Luke the text makes clear that persistence in prayer and fear are together a major thrust of the parable. By this point in Jesus' ministry there was considerable opposition to his message, and the passage that appears just before this parable is not reassuring. The parable presents two opposing forces, the judge and the widow.

The textual picture of the two of them is as follows:

2.	"In a certain city there was a *judge.*	JUDGE
	God he did *not fear*	God
	and before people he was never ashamed.	People
3.	And a *widow* there was in that city	Widow
	who was *coming* to him	Coming
	saying, '*Vindicate me* from my adversary.'	Vindication

As regards the judge in the parable, people cannot appeal to him saying, "for the sake of God," because he does not fear God. Nor can anyone plead, "for my sake," because he does not care what anyone thinks about him. He possesses no inner sense of honor to which supplicants can appeal. In the Middle East these two approaches are the standard ways to appeal to someone for help. But with this judge neither appeal will be successful, and thereby the widow's situation appears hopeless.

The widow in the Old Testament is the classic symbol of the most vulnerable adult in the culture. In Middle Eastern society, women do not go to the courts; men go for them.[4] When this woman appears, the reader knows that she is alone, with no father, uncle, brother or nephew to speak for her. She must plead her case alone. The parable continues.

4.	*He did not want* to for a time. Then he said to himself,	JUDGE
	'Although I do *not fear God*	God
	and *do not respect people,*	People
5.	yet because *she causes me trouble*, this widow,	WIDOW
	I will *vindicate her,*	Vindication
	lest in *continual coming* she *wear me out.*' "	Coming

---

[4]Hultgren, *Parables of Jesus*, p. 255.

Alone and against impossible odds, the widow plays the only card she has, which is her loud persistent pleading. She refuses to be quiet or to go away until the judge surrenders and says, in effect, "She is giving me a headache. I cannot put up with this racket any longer." Finally he agrees to settle her case favorably in order to be rid of her.

The chivalry that surrounds women in Middle Eastern culture is striking. In situations of extreme danger women can do things that men dare not do. At the height of the Lebanese civil war (1975-1991) radical militias were kidnapping male Westerners. Teaching at a seminary in the center of Beirut, the time came when it was no longer safe for me to walk the four blocks to the seminary building. In order to survive I imposed "house arrest" on myself, and the militia that controlled our quarter granted permission for my students to come to the house for classes in our living room. For four months I did not leave the house and avoided kidnap because my brave wife and daughter could come and go, buy the food, do the banking and make it possible for us to survive. They were not under threat of being kidnapped, because traditional chivalry protected them.

In another incident, before I was obliged to go underground, I vividly remember a particularly violent militia that had its headquarters a few blocks away. Walking by, I chose not to notice the heavily armed men guarding the entrance and certainly did not engage them in any conversation. The community did not "see" them. But there was one old woman, dressed in a traditional long black dress with a black head covering who would regularly go to that building, stand out front, point her finger at the guards and shout invectives at them, telling them to get out of the quarter. The guards would smile, address her politely and tell her not to get upset. Had any man in the quarter engaged in such activity, he would have been shot *at once*. It is not by accident that the women disciples followed Jesus to the cross. Had the men appeared they could have been arrested, but the women were safe. John, being young, was the exception that proves the rule. Furthermore, he was protected by being with Mary. In like manner, in the parable, a man would be thrown out at once if he tried to pester the judge with his shouting.[5] But the widow can manage if she has courage and persistence.

The parable presupposes that the woman is in the right but the judge is dragging his feet. Perhaps someone was bribing him from the other side. The

---

[5]This cultural reality makes untenable Hedrick's attempt to turn the judge into a man of integrity and the widow into a vengeful violent woman (C. W. Hedrick, *Parables as Poetic Fictions* [Peabody, Mass.: Hendrickson, 1994], pp. 193-203).

woman's response is to persist and continue shouting until he settles her case favorably.

Jesus uses the rabbinic principle of interpretation "from the light to the heavy." If in this somewhat humorous scene, such persistence pays off, *how much more* is persistence appropriate in prayer where we kneel before a compassionate God? Jesus makes clear that we are not in the presence of a grim judge who is taking bribes from someone else and wants nothing to do with us. On the contrary, in prayer believers are in the presence of a loving father who cares for his children.

The parable concludes:

6. The Lord said, "Hear what the unrighteous judge says.	
And *will not God vindicate his elect*	FUTURE
who cry to him day and night?	Present
Also he is slow to anger with them.	Present
I tell you, *he will vindicate them speedily.*	FUTURE
7. Nevertheless, when the Son of man comes,	SON OF MAN
will he find faith on the earth?"	Future—Faith?

The critical sentence is, "Also he is slow to anger with them." I read this as a statement rather than as a question. The Greek verb used here literally means, "He pushes anger far away." It is one of the three Greek words in the New Testament for *patience*. Usually, this sentence is seen as a question and is translated, "Will he delay long over them?" But the elect are not sinless and their faith is not always strong. Being the elect does not automatically protect them from failure. Too easily those who suffer injustice assume that the injustice they suffer automatically renders them righteous. Their opponents are evil. Because of the oppression they endure, God will most certainly be angry *at their oppressors*, but never *at them!* Such is not the case. Only if God is able to "put his anger far away" is he able to come and hear them. The very wistfulness of the final question, "Will he find faith on the earth?" makes clear that Jesus is realistic about the frailties of those he has chosen.

SUMMARY: THE PARABLE OF THE WIDOW AND THE JUDGE

What is this parable trying to say? I would suggest the following:

1. A woman is the hero of the story. Sirach began with a woman and he quickly shifted to a male image. Not so Jesus. The woman is presented as a model to emulate in regard to confidence and persistence in prayer.

2. As the saints and martyrs have known for ages, prayer can conquer fear. The suffering church across the centuries has found encouragement in this parable as Ibn al-Tayyib wrote in Baghdad a millennium ago: "It is said that the purpose of this parable is to clarify what is incumbent on the believers during the life of the present church as regards perseverance and persistence in heartfelt, fervent prayer. [The faithful pray] with full confidence that if they accomplish this, there is no doubt that God will come to them with joy, look upon their suffering and torment, and grant them victory at the appropriate time."[6]

3. Persistence in prayer is appropriate for the believer up until there is an answer. If God denies the request or offers a solution other than the one requested, the faithful person is expected to respond with "Thy will be done." But before the answer is clear, persistence in pray is a part of genuine piety.

4. Unlike the woman, the believer faces a loving Father, not a capricious Judge. Within that relationship of love and confidence, prayers are offered to God.

5. History is not random. Rather it moves toward a goal, and the future is secured for the community of faith—God will vindicate his elect.

6. Vindication is assured in spite of our failures. God is able and willing to put his anger far away in order that he might reach out to us in love.

7. Such a promise does not free the believer from self-examination and renewal lest the Son of Man appear and find that faith has evaporated from the earth.

As the cross approached, the role of the women in the band of disciples became more prominent. A woman anointed the Messiah as he approached the triumphal entry. Women were faithful to the end at the cross. They had the courage to follow Joseph of Arimathea as he made his way to Pilate to request the body, and on to the tomb. Thereby the women knew where Jesus was buried. On Saturday evening it was the women who ventured out to buy spices for the anointing of his body. Sunday morning they made their way to the tomb, heard the glorious yet frightening word of the angels, overcame their fears and took the good news to the absent disciples. In like manner the hero of this parable is a woman, a woman with persistence and courage—the very virtues that his female disciples so nobly exhibited all through Holy Week. To them and to him, the church remains forever in debt.

[6]Ibn al-Tayyib, *Tafsir al-Mashriqi,* ed. Yusif Manqariyos (Egypt: Al-Tawfiq Press, 1907), 2:311.

Regarding the parable as a whole, Hultgren aptly concludes:

Soon Jesus and his disciples will be in Jerusalem. That could mean disaster, even death, for Jesus and his followers. But within such perilous times, one should not lose heart. God will not only care for his own, but even vindicate them. Therefore the disciples should persist in prayer and faith.[7]

---

[7]Hultgren, *Parables of Jesus*, p. 259.

20

The Parable of the Wise and Foolish Young Women

MATTHEW 25:1-13

THIS PARABLE TOUCHES ON A VARIETY of ethical and theological topics. The text exhibits a modified prophetic rhetorical template of seven stanzas with a climax in the middle. Its rhetorical structure is shown in figure 20.1.

THE RHETORIC

This parable consists of seven stanzas with the climax in the center. As is usually the case, that center is related to the beginning (1) and the end (7). It is a further case of the prophetic rhetorical template. The center climax around which the story revolves is the cry, "Behold the bridegroom! Come out to meet him!" As is common in this particular rhetorical form, the theme that appears in the center (meeting the bridegroom) is also prominent in the beginning and at the end. The word *bridegroom* appears only in stanzas 1, 4 and 7.

The "wise" and the "foolish" young women are contrasted in 2 and 6. Numbers 3 and 5 focus on sleeping and rising up. I have called this a *modified* prophetic template, in that there is an extra stanza at the end that needs to be examined. The rhetorical style identifies the parable as being deeply rooted in the Hebrew tradition.

COMMENTARY

Before examining the parable, it is important to note the comparisons between it and the parable in Luke 12:35-38, which I prefer to name "The Parable of the Serving Master." The list is as follows:

1. Both stories occur at night.

2. Both are wedding feasts.

1. It shall be compared the kingdom of heaven   MEET THE GROOM
   to ten young women   (expectation)
   who took their lamps and *came out*   Ten Come Out
   to *meet the bridegroom* [and the bride].[a]
   Five were *dimwitted* and five were *thoughtful*.

2.   When the *dimwitted* took their lamps,
       they took *no oil* with them.   DULL—NO OIL
       But the *thoughtful* took *flasks of oil*   Thoughtful—Oil
       with their lamps.

3.   As the bridegroom was delayed,   ALL SLEEP
           they *all dozed* and *fell asleep*.

4.   But at midnight there was a cry,   MEET THE GROOM
               "*Behold the bridegroom!*   (arrival imminent)
               Come out to meet him!"

5.   Then *all* those young women *arose*
           and *serviced their lamps*.   ALL ARISE

6.   And the *dimwitted* said to the *thoughtful*,
       "*Give us some of your oil*,   DULL—NO OIL
       for our lamps are going out."   Thoughtful—Oil
       But the thoughtful replied,
       "Perhaps there will *not be enough for us and you*.
       Go rather to the dealers and buy for yourselves."

7a. And while they went to buy,
    the *bridegroom came*,   MEET THE GROOM
    and *those prepared went in* with him   (realization)
    to the marriage feast,   FIVE GO IN—
    and the *door was shut*.   FIVE SHUT OUT

   b. Afterward the other young women came
      saying, "*Lord, Lord, open to us*."
      But he replied,   TOO LATE!
      "Amen I say to you, I do not know you."
      Watch therefore for you know neither the day nor the hour.

---

[a]"And the bride" appears in some ancient Greek texts and in most early translations into Latin, Syriac, Armenian and Georgian. It is defended as original by F. C. Burkitt in *Journal of Theological Studies* 30 (1929): 267-70, as noted in T. W. Manson, *The Sayings of Jesus* (1937; reprint, London: SCM, 1964), p. 244.

Figure 20.1. The parable of the wise and foolish young women (Mt 25:1-13)

3. In each there are people waiting for something important to happen.

4. The question of being prepared or not prepared is important in both.

5. Having lamps, burning or not, at the moment of the arrival of the master is important in both stories.

6. "Staying awake" versus "falling asleep" is important in each parable.

7. The door of the house is a dramatic prop in both. (Is it open or closed, and who is to open it?)

8. The delay of the "big man" is an issue in each account.

9. The time of his arrival is unknown in both stories.

10. The central figure is called master/bridegroom in Matthew. In Luke he is master/Lord.

The close relationships between the two parables are clear. One way to understand this data is to affirm that the two parables were created in some form by the same mind. W. D. Davies and Dale C. Allison present a detailed discussion of the various options regarding the history of the composition of this parable.[1] I note the above list of comparisons to make the point that both of these parables have similar traditional Middle Eastern culture behind them and to that culture we now turn.[2]

The scene focuses on preparations for a wedding banquet that is to take place in the home of the groom. A great crowd of family and friends fills the house and pours out into the street in front of the dwelling. As the crowd is gathering, the groom and several close friends are making their way to the home of the bride, which is assumed to be across town or in a nearby village. From there the groom collects his bride and escorts her back to his family home, where the crowd awaits and the marriage feast will be held. Several of the ancient Greek, Latin and Syriac texts of this parable specifically mention the groom *and* the bride.[3] This reading of the story fits traditional village life and is probably the original. In any case, the presence of the bride is implied even if not mentioned. When she was ready, she

---

[1]W. D. Davies and Dale C. Allison Jr., *The Gospel According to Saint Matthew* (New York: T &T Clark, 1988), 3:391-401.

[2]Arland J. Hultgren presents full documentation for the Jewish sources on marriage customs of the time, in *The Parables of Jesus* (Grand Rapids: Eerdmans, 2000), pp. 170-73.

[3]This phrase may have been omitted because copyists were influenced by the idea that "the church is the bride of Christ" and so Jesus, the bridegroom, *comes* to his bride; he does *not bring her with him*. But in the village that is precisely what happens. For a further discussion of this question see Bruce M. Metzger, *A Textual Commentary on the Greek New Testament* (London: United Bible Societies, 1971), pp. 62-63.

would be placed on the back of a riding animal, and the groom, with his friends, would form a disorganized, exuberant parade. This happy group would take the longest possible route back to the groom's home deliberately, wandering through as many streets of the village as possible so that most of the populace could see and cheer them as they passed.

In traditional village life in the Middle East, weddings take place during the seven months of the hot and cloudless summer. At the groom's home some of the crowd would therefore wait in the street as they anticipate the arrival of the meandering wedding party. The parable takes place at night, and among the guests are ten young women. Each of them has a lamp, and of course all ten lamps are lit. It is one thing for young men to roam about at night without lamps. Starlight or moonlight is usually bright enough to see by in the dry, clear air of the Middle East. But women, young and old, always carry lamps. Their reputation, and in some cases their personal safety, depends on the lamps. For young unmarried women to move around in the dark without carrying lamps is unthinkable! What might they be doing in the dark and with whom? Also, with a lamp, no one can harass them unseen. I have observed that village women do not carry such lamps conveniently close to the ground (like a flashlight) so that they can see the street. Instead, they carry them directly in front of their faces so that all can witness who they are and where they are going.

The ten young women are very circumspect in their behavior. All have lamps, and each of the lamps is burning. But there are differences among them. Half of them have brought extra olive oil with them in small flasks, while the other half have not taken this precaution.

The parade, winding slowly through the village, takes a bit longer than these ten young women, in their youthful enthusiasm, anticipate. Such things usually do. The wiser young women realize that it could be the middle of the night before the wedding party arrives at the groom's ancestral home. The young women become drowsy, carefully place their burning lamps on a window ledge or some other appropriate sheltered place and doze off inside or outside the house.

Finally, the front of the parade enters the alley and the cry goes out, "Behold the bridegroom. Come out to meet him."

Guests and family still in the house rush into the street. The ten young women arise quickly, recognizing that some time has passed and begin to "service their lamps." The loose unattached wicks must be adjusted, and the oil reservoirs inside the lamps replenished. To their horror, five of the women suddenly realize their mistake. Their lamps are almost out of olive oil and they have no reserves. The other five take out their little clay flasks and calmly replenish their lamps. The five foolish women crowd around them demanding oil. Politely (and no doubt firmly) they are in effect told, "We don't have enough for ourselves—and as for you—solve your own little problems!" No doubt irritated and sputtering, the five stomp off to beg, borrow or buy a bit of oil. Everyone knows everyone in such villages, so acquiring a little oil from someone is not a problem—even in the middle of the night.

In the meantime, the groom and his new bride arrive and the entire crowd sweeps into the house and the door is shut. After all, it *is* the middle of the night.

In the final scene at the end of the story (7b) the shortsighted crowd of five women finally acquire some oil, get their lamps working again and arrive back at the house. "Sir/Lord! Open to us!" they shout through the door. "Sorry," replies the groom, "I don't think I know you."[4]

As is often the case, the reader of the parable is left hanging. Does the bridegroom relent and let them in or not? The listener/reader is not told. The locked door is what they deserve. We do not know what they receive when the conversation is over. In the Middle East the word *no* is never an answer, rather it is a pause in the negotiations. The reader has to finish the play. What then is the story all about?

SUMMARY: THE PARABLE OF THE WISE AND FOOLISH YOUNG WOMEN

Granting the inevitable fusion of good ethics and good theology, on the *ethical* level Jesus appears to be saying four things:

First, the *place of women*. Equality between men and women was important to Jesus. This could have been a parable about ten young men. The previous story in Matthew's Gospel (24:45-51) is an account of a master and two male servants, one noble and the other ignoble. By contrast this story is about women, not men, and there are ten of them, not two. Why so?

Thoughtful answers to both questions come from the great Syrian Orthodox monk, scholar, physician and poet, Ibn al-Tayyib, of the eleventh century. In his commentary on this text he points out that in the Gospels, the church is always feminine: the bride of Christ is the mother of us all. Thus it is appropriate that Jesus has here chosen women to act the part of the membership of the church, both wise and foolish.

Ibn al-Tayyib then reminds his readers that it took ten Jewish males to form a

---

[4]This final scene may or may not be added by the church and not traceable to the historical Jesus. Unless one is seeking a canon within a canon such speculation is interesting but not helpful for an understanding of the text as it presents itself to the reader.

company for the celebration of the Passover, and he claims that ten males were required for a valid wedding ceremony. Thereby this parable has ten women.[5] Ibn al-Tayyib implies that by choosing ten women, Jesus is trying to compensate for the gender gap in the religious culture of his day. The worth of women is clearly affirmed by the composition of the story.

Second, there is the question of *borrowed resources*. The faithful borrow many things from each other. But they cannot borrow their own preparations for the coming of the kingdom. Commitment and the discipleship that follows can be neither loaned nor borrowed. Each believer must participate in the kingdom with his or her own resources.

Third, is the *long haul*. Life in the kingdom of God requires commitment to the long haul. Advanced planning is necessary and reserves must be on hand. There is neither instant discipleship nor instant maturation in the fullness of the kingdom. The wise, thoughtful women knew it might be a long night and prepared accordingly.

Fourth are the *reactions to failure*. When things go wrong, due to poor judgment and other inadequacies, the resulting problems cannot be solved by shouting orders at neighbors and at the Lord in the manner exhibited by the foolish women. When short of oil they screamed at their friends, *"Give us some oil!"* When they arrived late and found the door of the house locked they cried to the bridegroom, *"Lord! Lord! Open the door!"*

This will not do. These five women are like the rich man in the story of Lazarus, who mistreated Lazarus day after day. They both died and the rich man found himself in hell while Lazarus was taken by the angels to the side of Abraham. The rich man then began giving orders. He commanded Abraham to send Lazarus down with a drink of water because he (the rich man) was thirsty. When that did not work, he made a second demand, which was, "Send Lazarus to my brothers to warn them." The rich man expected Abraham to carry out these orders. Lazarus was expected to jump at the chance of becoming either a table waiter or a messenger boy for the very man who had neglected him for years! In the kingdom of God, barking orders at others is not an acceptable way to try to solve problems created by our inadequacies.

But there is a more distinctively *theological level* to the story as well. On that level Jesus appears also to be saying four things:

1. There is Jesus' *disappointment at the lack of readiness* to receive the kingdom

---

[5]Ibn al-Tayyib, *Tafsir al-Mashriqi*, ed. Yusif Manqariyos (Egypt: Al-Tawfiq Press, 1907), 1:390-91.

when it arrives. In his ministry, Jesus inaugurated the kingdom of God and was disappointed that many around him, who had been waiting for the revelation of that kingdom, were not prepared for it when it arrived. Anna and Simeon, Nicodemus and the disciples were mostly ready. The high priestly guild, Jesus' hometown and many of the Pharisees were not. The shepherds were ready. Herod was not. The wise men were ready. The soldiers at his birth were not. The reality of Jesus' disappointments appears in this parable.

2. There is a *challenge and a warning* related to his second coming. The story clearly looks forward to the consummation of all things when the Messiah of God comes to his own and his own receive him at the marriage supper of the Lamb. He knows full well that some who come to the banquet, and are deliberately waiting for his arrival, will not be ready when he appears. For each believer, on a personal level, that meeting with the Lord will occur at the time of death. Thus the parable holds an existential challenge for all.

3. The kingdom has *a door that can and does close*. For all who are committed to the host of the banquet, the door to the banquet is open. But near the end of the parable that door is closed. Jesus' parable places limits to the Roman sacred cow of inclusiveness that wandered the streets of Rome and now traverses the byways of contemporary Western culture. As Allison and Davies have written, "The foolish virgins, who stand for unfaithful disciples, reveal that religious failure will suffer eschatological punishment."[6]

4. This parable is a warning that the time of the *arrival of the bridegroom is unknown* and that speculation regarding the hour is pointless. The enormous amount of energy that in certain Christian circles is poured into such speculation is here declared misguided. For "of that day or that hour no one knows" (Mk 13:32).

5. Finally there is *Christology*. The parable also provides information about the person of Jesus.

Jesus is the returning bridegroom who will arrive joyfully at the end of the age, extend a warm welcome to all the guests who have patiently remained in waiting for his coming, and are duly prepared for his arrival.

Blessed are those whose lamps are faithfully kept burning as they watch and wait for his appearance.

---

[6]Davies, *Gospel According to Saint Matthew*, 3:392.

PART SIX

Parables of Jesus

21

Introduction to the Parables

VERY EARLY IN THE LIFE OF THE CHURCH outsiders saw Christians drawing their faith from parables. One of these witnesses was Galen, the most famous medical doctor of the second century. He was also the first pagan to say positive things about Christians. Around A.D. 140 he wrote:

> Most people are unable to follow a demonstrative argument consecutively; hence they need parables, and benefit from them . . . just as now we see the people called Christians drawing their faith from parables [and miracles] and yet sometimes acting in the same way [as those who philosophize] . . . and in their keen pursuit of justice, have attained a pitch not inferior to that of genuine philosophers.[1]

In later centuries parables became a source for Christian *life* (ethics) but not Christian *faith* (theology). It is instructive to note that in the second century Galen saw Christians building their *faith* on parables. How did parables lose their status as a source of the Christian faith?

Today, Jesus is naturally seen by Christians as the Son of God and Savior of the world. The New Testament also presents him as the perfect example of love and an effective storyteller for simple folk. But have we thought of him as a serious *theologian?*

Jesus was a *metaphorical* theologian. That is, his primary method of creating meaning was through metaphor, simile, parable and dramatic action rather than through logic and reasoning. He created meaning like a dramatist and a poet rather than like a philosopher.

THEOLOGY: CONCEPTUAL AND METAPHORICAL

In the Western tradition serious theology has almost always been constructed from ideas held together by logic. In such a world the more intelligent the theo-

---

[1]This is from Galen's lost summary of Plato's *Republic,* preserved in Arabic quotations. The above text is quoted from James Stevenson, ed., *A New Eusebius* (London: SPCK, 1957), p. 133.

logian, the more abstract he or she usually becomes, and the more difficult it is for the average person to understand what is being said. Paul works with ideas *and* metaphors. In the West we have tended to emphasize his concepts and sideline his metaphors. By so doing we have made him fit into our world of conceptual theologians.

In contrast, the popular perception of Jesus is that of a village rustic creating folktales for fishermen and farmers. But when examined with care, his parables are serious theology, and Jesus emerges as an astute theologian. He is, as noted, primarily a *metaphorical* rather than a *conceptual* theologian.

What precisely is a metaphorical theologian? Consider the following. We know that God is Spirit and is neither male nor female. Yet in the Scriptures we are told that the believer is "born of God" (1 Jn 3:9). Here John uses female language to describe the relationship between God and believers. Similarly, when Jesus addressed God as "Father," he used a male metaphor/title to help us understand the nature of God. Scripture uses male and female images to enrich our understanding of God, who is Spirit and thereby beyond male and female.

A metaphor communicates in ways that rational arguments cannot. Pictures easily trump but do not replace abstract reasoning. A powerful television image communicates meaning that a thousand words cannot express. When used in theology to create meaning, the parable challenges the listener in ways that abstract statements of truth cannot approach. Yet the two are often linked, and both are critical to the task of theology.

Theologians often use "illustrations" to infuse energy and clarification into their abstract reflections. Illustrations are frequently "the sugar-coating on the theological pill," as T. W. Manson so aptly stated.[2] A metaphor, however, is *not* an illustration of an idea; it is a mode of theological discourse. The metaphor does more than explain meaning, it creates meaning. *A parable is an extended metaphor* and as such it is *not a delivery system for an idea* but a house in which the reader/listener is invited to take up residence.

The listener/reader of the parable is encouraged to examine the human predicament through the worldview created by the parable. The casing is all that remains after a shell is fired. Its only purpose is to drive the shell in the direction of the target. It is easy to think of a parable in the same way and understand it as a good way to "launch" an idea. Once the idea is "on its way" the parable can be discarded. But this is not so. If the parable is a house in which the listener/reader is invited

---

[2]T. W. Manson, *The Teaching of Jesus* (1937; reprint, London: SCM, 1964), p. 73.

to take up residence, then that person is urged by the parable to look on the world through the windows of that residence. Such is the reality of the parables created by Jesus of Nazareth, a reality that causes a special problem.

If theology is built on logic and reasoning, then all one needs to understand that theology is a clear mind and a will to work hard. But if, for Jesus, stories and dramatic actions are the language of theology, then the culture of the storyteller is crucial. Our task includes the responsibility of trying to understand the metaphors and stories from and about Jesus in the light of the culture of which he was a part.

UNLOCKING METAPHORS

To unlock the secrets of these metaphors, there are a few simple yet far-reaching challenges.

The first is to realize the importance of the task. It is easy to ignore historical questions. Granted, anyone can read the Bible and be blessed by that reading, just as anyone can listen to a Bach cantata and be moved. But at the same time, the trained ear will hear more and be moved on a deeper level by the same music.

One ploy often used to escape the hard work of attempting to discover what Jesus was saying to his audience is to affirm the "universal appeal" of his parables. Every culture has loving fathers, rebellious sons and self-righteous older brothers, and many, directly or indirectly, assume that the parable of the prodigal son needs no special cultural glasses. It is universal in its appeal. Up to a point this is true. But in the Middle East when a young man asks for his inheritance while his father is still alive his request means, "Dad, why don't you drop dead." The father is expected to get angry, slap the boy across the face and drive him out of the house. None of these things happens in the parable. By the time we process the significance of these three bits of cultural insight, the parable exhibits new meanings that otherwise would be missed.

The second challenge is to realize the historical nature of the Word of God. The Bible for Christians is not *just* the Word of God. Rather, it is the Word of God spoken through people in history. Those people and that history cannot be ignored without missing the speaker or writer's intentions and creating our own substitutes for them. Historical interpretation is the key to unlocking the vault that contains the gold of theological meaning. Without that key the gold turns to brass. It is helpful to note that this is true of all significant literature.

How is President Lincoln's Gettysburg address to be understood today? That speech was a turning point in American history because of the meaning it created in the middle of an identity-forming Civil War ("War Between the States"? or

"The Great Rebellion"? or perhaps "The War of Northern Aggression"?). Each American brings his or her own history and experience to a study of that war. In spite of that, anyone who ignores the context of the war and the battle of Gettysburg cannot understand Lincoln's speech. In like manner, it is critical to interpret the parables of Jesus within his own world. Only then can we grasp the meaning created by them. The question becomes, How much meaning?

The third challenge is to distinguish what meaning or meanings can be attributed legitimately to the parables. For many centuries allegory reigned supreme as a method of interpretation, and the fatted calf in the parable of the prodigal son became a symbol for Christ because the calf was killed. Through allegory, interpreters were able to locate their favorite ideas almost anywhere, and confusion and finally meaninglessness conquered. This is probably why parables ceased to be sources for Christian faith and were limited to ethics. The Latin proverb reads, "Theologia parabolica non est theologia argumentativa."[3]

In reaction to the fanciful exaggerations that the allegorical method produced in past centuries, across the twentieth century there was a stream of scholarship that argued for "one point per parable."[4] Others allowed for several themes in a parable. The purpose was to protect interpretation from adding meanings to the text that could not have occurred to Jesus or his audience. But if a parable is part of a larger worldview, and if it is "a house in which we are invited to take up residence," then the dweller in that house can look out on the world from different windows. The house has a variety of rooms. If the great parable of the prodigal son has "only one point," which shall we choose? Should the interpreter choose "the nature of the fatherhood of God," "an understanding of sin," "self-righteousness that rejects others," "the nature of true repentance," "joy in community" or "finding the lost"? All of these theological themes are undeniably present in the story and together form a whole that I have called "the theological cluster." Each part of that cluster is in creative relationship to the other parts. The meaning of each can only be understood fully within the cluster formed by the entire parable. The content of the cluster must be controlled and limited by what Jesus' original audience could have understood.

When the Pharisees sat together and reflected on what Jesus was talking about in a particular parable, what ideas were available to them? There may be one or more. The themes that comprise the theological cluster of a parable must grow out

---

[3]Martin Scharlemann, *Proclaiming the Parables* (Saint Louis: Concordia Publishing, 1963), p. 30.
[4]For a detailed review of the history of Western interpretation of the parables see Craig L. Blomberg, *Interpreting the Parables* (Downers Grove, Ill.: InterVarsity Press, 1990), pp. 29-167.

of the world in which the parable was told and first heard. But should such a principle be strictly applied?

A great work of art has a life of its own. The viewer of that art brings his or her own life and experience to the moment of encounter with the work. Michelangelo's statue of Moses leaps beyond the world of sixteenth-century Italy and becomes "the angry man of God." Yet there need to be limits to what can legitimately be found in a story. One of the island cultures of the Pacific glorifies the cleverness of the deceiver. People of that culture read the story of the passion of Jesus and the hero of the story becomes Judas. Jesus turns into the duped fool. In the West some have found Marxism or Freudianism or Existentialism in the parables of Jesus. Postmodernism is selected by others as the appropriate lens through which to study the parables. Such interpretations could not have been imagined by Jesus or his audience. Additionally, whatever the interpreter finds in a parable needs to be evaluated in the light of the life and witness of Jesus. All fair-minded reviewers appropriately extend such a courtesy to any modern author. Can't the same courtesy be offered to Jesus? Such a discipline keeps one within the "critical realism" that N. T. Wright eloquently presents as a starting point for New Testament interpretation.[5]

SUMMARY: INTRODUCTION TO THE PARABLES

Finally, the question is not, Where are you on the ladder? but Did you get there by climbing or falling? All of us have limited intellectual and spiritual resources as we approach "the mind of Christ" in the parables. Each of us is aware of great interpreters who are so far ahead of us that they are nearly out of sight. Others known to us may not have had the opportunity to learn what we have learned. This perspective is shared by the greatest scholar and the simplest believer. All readers of Jesus' parables are challenged to do the best they can with what they have and not despair at the ignorance or achievements of others.

Simply stated, our task is to stand at the back of the audience around Jesus and listen to what he is saying to them. Only through that discipline can we discover what he is saying to any age, including our own. Authentic simplicity can be found the other side of complexity. The theological and ethical House of the Parables of Jesus awaits. May all enter with great expectations!

---

[5]N. T. Wright, *The New Testament and the People of God* (Minneapolis: Augsburg/Fortress, 1996), pp. 32-37, 61-64.

22

The Parable of the Good Samaritan

LUKE 10:25-37

THE PARABLE OF THE GOOD SAMARITAN is famous for its ethics, and rightly so. This chapter will also look at the theology and Christology contained within it. First is the dialogue setting in which the parable appears.[1]

DIALOGUE

Like a diamond in a gold ring, this parable is set in two rounds of dialogue between Jesus and a specialist in the religious law (a "lawyer"). If the story is removed from that dialogue, significant aspects of the parable are missed. The interpreter is not a "disembodied eye," as Lesslie Newbigin has observed, looking down on the world from 100,000 miles in space. Rather, every interpreter is influenced by his or her country's language, culture, history, economics, politics and military. The authors of the Gospels have given us the parables of Jesus in first-century settings. To strip away those settings is to substitute our own. Luke presents his readers with two rounds of a dialogue. The first round is shown in figure 22.1.

Initially, the lawyer asks a question (1). Jesus does not answer but puts his own question to the lawyer (2). The lawyer then answers Jesus' question, and finally Jesus responds to the lawyer's query. In short, the lawyer asks, "What must I *do* to inherit eternal *life?*" Jesus does not reply but asks, "What about the law?" The lawyer responds, "You must love God and your neighbor." Jesus concludes this opening interchange with, "If you *do this*, you will *live*." This section of the dialogue opens and closes with "do" and "live."

Jesus and the lawyer then engage in a second round of dialogue. Again, the lawyer begins with a question that is actually a follow-up of his original query. This

---

[1]For an earlier discussion of this parable see Kenneth E. Bailey, *Poet and Peasant*, in *Poet and Peasant and Through Peasant Eyes* (Grand Rapids: Eerdmans, 1980), pp. 33-54.

And behold, a lawyer stood up to put him to the test, saying,

1. "Teacher, what shall I *do*
   to inherit eternal *life*?"   LAWYER: Question 1

2.   He said to him, "What is written in the law?   JESUS: Question 2
      How do you read?"

3.   And he answered, "You shall love the Lord your God
      with all your heart, and with all your soul,   LAWYER: Answer to 2
      and with all your strength, and with all your mind;
      and your neighbor as yourself."

4. And he said to him, "You have answered right;   JESUS: Answer to 1
   do this, and you will *live*."

Figure 22.1. First dialogue (Lk 10:25-28)

He, desiring to *justify himself*, said to Jesus,

5. "And who is my neighbor?"   LAWYER: Question 3

6.   Jesus replied, "A certain man went down from
      Jerusalem to Jericho..." [the parable follows]
      "Which of these three became a neighbor?"   JESUS: Question 4

7.   Lawyer:
      "The one who showed mercy on him."   LAWYER: Answer to 4

8. Jesus:
   "*Go* and continue *doing* likewise."   JESUS: Answer to 3

Figure 22.2. Second dialogue (Lk 10:29-30; 36-37)

second exchange follows the same form of question (3), question (4), answer to 4, and finally reply to 3. The bare bones of this second round of dialogue are illustrated in figure 22.2.

The lawyer opens with a question (3). Jesus does not directly answer that question but chooses to tell a story, at the end of which he asks a question (4), which is, "Which of these three *became a neighbor?*" The story serves to introduce the fourth question. The lawyer answers Jesus' question (4), and Jesus' final comment is a response to the lawyer's question (3). Both rounds in this dialogue focus on the question, "What must *I do* to inherit eternal *life?*" The parable functions within this debate composed of four questions and four answers.

In Middle Eastern traditional culture the teacher sits and the student shows respect for the teacher by standing to recite. But in this instance the lawyer *stands* in order to *test* the teacher. ("Teacher" is Luke's word for rabbi.) As Ibrahim Saʿid of Egypt notes in his Arabic commentary on this parable, there is a built-in deception. He is standing to ask a question, like a humble student trying to learn something, but his purpose is to test/examine the teacher.[2]

Ibn al-Tayyib has an extended discussion of this opening exchange between Jesus and the lawyer. He notes that the lawyer did not ask, "How can I obey God," which is the natural question for a religious lawyer to ask, but, "How can I inherit eternal life?" Ibn al-Tayyib offers two explanations for the lawyer's special interest. He suggests, "The first is that it was the custom of the Savior of all to teach those who came to him, indeed, those who were drawn to him, on the subject of eternal life." Second is that the lawyer imagined he could trap Jesus by means of his answer and then take even some trivial word and shape it into evidence that Jesus' enemies could fashion into a denial of the validity of the law of Moses.[3]

Ibn al-Tayyib argues that Jesus' refusal to give a direct answer to the lawyer's question is because Jesus understands what the lawyer is trying to do. Jesus obliges the lawyer to expose his own views on the law of Moses. His methodology was to invoke the lawyer's reaction to a related question and then use that response to answer the original question.

Actually, the lawyer's original question is flawed. What can anyone *do* to inherit *anything?* Inheritance, by its very nature, is a gift from one family member (or friend) to another. If you are born into a family, or perhaps adopted into it, then you can inherit. Inheritance is not payment for services rendered. The questioner in this story is a religious lawyer who is fully aware of such things.

On the other hand, this kind of discussion regarding eternal life was taking place among the rabbis in the first century.[4] In keeping with that debate, Jesus asks the lawyer what he thinks about the topic. The lawyer responds with a summary of Jesus' view, which was "love God and love your neighbor." Had he heard Jesus present this summary of the law on some previous occasion? Perhaps. In any case, some first-century rabbis had their own summaries of the law.

A "heathen" approached the famous Rabbi Shammai shortly before the time of Jesus, stood on one foot and said, "Teach me the whole Law while I stand on one

---

[2]Ibrahim Saʿid, *Sharh Bisharat Luqa* (Beirut: Middle East Council of Churches, 1970), p. 276.
[3]Ibn al-Tayyib, *Tafsir al-Mashriqi,* ed. Yusif Manqariyos (Egypt: Al-Tawfiq Press, 1907), 2:177-78.
[4]Babylonian Talmud, *Berakot* 28b, ʾAbot de Rabbi Nathan, 25b2, *Pesahim,* 113a.

foot." Shammai got angry and drove him away. The man then went to Rabbi Hillel, the founder of the other famous rabbinic school of the first century, and posed the same challenge. Hillel responded, "What is hateful to you, do not do to your neighbor: that is the whole Torah, while the rest is the commentary thereof; go and learn it."[5] This is easily recognized as a negative form of the Golden Rule. Jesus apparently took Hillel's reply and turned it into a positive.[6]

The lawyer may have quoted Jesus' summary of the law in order to hear what Jesus would say. Notice, however, that this summary contains two parts: "love God" and "love your neighbor." The two parts come from the Old Testament; the commandment to "love your neighbor" occurs in Leviticus 19:18, while the injunction to "love God" appears in Deuteronomy 6:5. One would expect such Scripture quotations to follow the canonical order. Instead, Jesus placed "love God" before the commandment to "love your neighbor." The order is important. Experience dictates that it is very hard to love the unlovely neighbor until the disciple's heart is filled with the love of God, which provides the energy and motivation necessary for the arduous task of loving the neighbor. Often the motives of the one who serves are misunderstood by the recipient of that love, who then responds with hostility rather than gratitude. If the one who serves is hoping to be sustained by the responses received, and if the expected responses are not forthcoming, that person may well give up in frustration and disappointment. But if costly acts of love are extended to others out of gratitude for the love of God, then the believer is sustained by the unwavering love of God toward him or her.

In summary, the lawyer quotes Jesus' synopsis of the law (Mt 7:12; Lk 6:31). Jesus tells the lawyer, "Fine, follow your own advice. Live up to these standards and you will indeed inherit eternal life." To inherit eternal life, all he must do is to consistently practice unqualified love for God and his neighbor.

Is Jesus thereby saying that salvation can be earned? Indeed, anyone who can meet such a standard does not need grace. But the standard is to love God unfailingly with all one's heart, mind, soul and strength, and consistently love the neighbor as much as the self. As Paul enunciates, the problem is not the law, the problem is that we cannot keep it (Rom 7:13-20). Here the standard set by Jesus eludes our finest efforts. To put it another way, the lawyer asks, "What must I *do* in order

---

[5]Babylonian Talmud, *Šabbat* 31a.

[6]The positive form of the Golden Rule appears in *The Testament of the Twelve Patriarchs* in the *Testament of Issachar* 7:6, *Testament of Zebulon* 5:1 and *Testament of Dan* 5:3. This pre-Christian document, however, has Christian additions to it and these may be among them. In any case, as Davies and Allison note, the truth of this teaching "did not necessarily hinge upon its novelty" (*Gospel According to Saint Matthew*, 1:688).

to inherit eternal *life?*" Jesus replies, "You must jump over this ten foot fence!" The lawyer should be able to see that he cannot jump that high and that he has thereby asked the wrong question. But he fails this expectation.

Instead, he repeats his question in a different form. He apparently says to himself, "So, I must love God and my neighbor to earn my salvation. Fine, what I need now is a few definitions. To love God is to keep the law. I already know that. What I need is some clarification of *exactly* who is and who is not my neighbor. Once I have clarification on this point I can proceed."

Luke (or the tradition given to him) helps us understand what is going through the lawyer's mind by including, "He, desiring to *justify himself*, asked, 'Who is my neighbor?'" To *be justified* is to be saved, and to be saved is to "inherit eternal life." To be justified, in biblical language, means to be granted the status of one whom God accepts as he stands before God. This fellow, desiring to *justify himself* is clearly a person who wants "to achieve acceptance before God on his own."

So he asks, "Who is my neighbor?" As a good first-century Jew, he expects Jesus to respond with a list that the lawyer hopes he can manage. The neighbor will naturally include his fellow Jew who keeps the law in a precise fashion. Gentiles are not neighbors and everyone knows God hates the Samaritans, so they certainly do not qualify as neighbors. After all, he could read Leviticus 19:18 which commands, "You shall not take vengeance or bear any grudge against the sons of your own people, but you shall love your neighbor as yourself: I am the LORD," and conclude that his neighbor was limited to "the sons of your own people." Such a reading would be easy even though inaccurate because the conclusion of the chapter commands: "The stranger who sojourns with you shall be to you as the native among you, and you shall love him as yourself; for you were strangers in the land of Egypt: I am the LORD your God" (Lev 19:34). The lawyer might have preferred Psalm 139:21-22 which reads:

> Do I not hate them that hate thee, O LORD?
> And do I not loathe them that rise up against thee?
> I hate them with perfect hatred;
> I count them my enemies.

The tendency to read Scripture selectively is an old problem. With a careful line drawn between those who are and those who are not his neighbors, the lawyer would be equipped to earn his way to eternal life.

How would Jesus define "the neighbor" for the lawyer? Would it be, "The son of your own house?" Or will he choose, "The stranger who sojourns with you?" In either case, on the basis of these texts, the lawyer could hardly have imagined anything beyond "my family" and "the stranger who lives in my town."

SEVEN SCENES OF THE GOOD SAMARITAN

Jesus responds to the lawyer's question by creating the classical story of the good Samaritan.

Ibn al-Tayyib has a long discussion of whether the parable is built on an historical incident or whether it is fiction. He grants that the message of the parable is the same either way, but at the same time he tells a story he heard from the Jewish community in southern Iraq in the eleventh century. The story is set in the aftermath of 2 Kings 17:24-38. In that text the King of Assyria brings foreign tribes to live in Samaria who do not "fear the LORD." The Lord sends lions to eat the people, and the King of Assyria responds by returning "priests whom they had carried away" to teach the people about the "god of the land." The project was only partially successful. The story told to Ibn al-Tayyib builds on the fall-out of that partial success. It reads:

> The children of Israel say: When the priest [of 2 Kings 17:24-38] came and taught the people how to fear the Lord, the lions were cut off from them, but after some time, they returned [to their old ways] and the lions returned. When this happened, the priest and the Levite who was with him fled, escaping it all. At that time there was a Jew who worked in a vineyard. That man took his pay and traveled from Jerusalem to Jericho. On the way he met a group of men from one of the tribes with whom Moses and Joshua, the son of Nun had fought. The group attacked him to exact blood vengeance *[thar]*. They beat him, took his clothes and left him with barely a breath remaining, that is, as one dead. The priest passed by ignoring him, as did the Levite. Then it happened that a Babylonian was traveling from Jerusalem and when he saw him he had mercy on him and felt compassion for him. So he took out some wine and some oil and bound up his wounds. When the wounded man could not move, that is, because he did not have the strength to walk, he placed him on his own riding animal and took him to a hotel in Jericho. There he commended him to the owner of the hotel and gave the wounded man two denars for the expenses of his journey and said if the situation required more than two denars, "When I come back I will give you more." This story then became a rebuke to the sons of Israel and spread throughout the land and the man who carried out this noble deed was called "Samaritan" because he was from the protectors, that is from among the guards [police] of Samaria.[7]

It is curious that Ibn al-Tayyib recounts this as a Jewish story told by the Baby-

---

[7]Ibn al-Tayyib, *Tafsir al-Mashriqi*, 2:180-81.

lonian Jewish community in Iraq in the eleventh century. He did not hear it as an Iraqi Christian story told about the Jews. The hero of the story is not a Jew, so it is impossible to imagine that the Jewish community invented the account to make their own people appear noble. Its Jewish connection with the account in 2 Kings emphasizes its Jewish roots. I can think of no reason for seeing the connection with 2 Kings as a Christian interpolation into the Old Testament record. Ibn al-Tayyib affirms that this story was used as evidence among commentators known to him who insisted that the parable of the good Samaritan was based on a historical incident. Ibn al-Tayyib concludes that whether it is creative fiction or historical incident, the parable has the same meaning.

Even if this story is a post-first-century legend influenced by the parable, it is of interest. For our purposes, it is important to observe that the wounded man was a Jew, blood vengeance was part of the story, and the hotel was in Jericho. Turning to the text with this Eastern story in mind, the parable falls into seven scenes that follow a time-honored model older than the writing prophets. I have named it The Prophetic Rhetorical Template. These scenes are shown in figure 22.3.

THE RHETORIC

Isaiah 28:14-18 and Psalm 23 are also prophetic rhetorical templates. There are seven scenes in all, seven being the perfect number. The climax is at the center, and the last three scenes are linked to the first three (in an inverted order). The parallels are strong and clear. In scene 1 the robbers take all the man's possessions, and in scene 7 the Samaritan pays for the man out of his own resources because the man has nothing. In scene 2 the priest fails to transport the wounded man to safety, and in scene 6 the Samaritan fulfills that costly act.   The Levite in scene 3 could at least have bound up the man's wounds, and in the matching scene 5 the Samaritan compensates for this failure. The center climax describes the Samaritan's compassion. These details reveal that the story is fashioned, in its present form, by a Jew, using Jewish rhetorical features and recorded for Jewish readers.

COMMENTARY

With the above parallels in mind, we turn to the seven scenes. First, scene 1.

1. A man was going down from Jerusalem to Jericho
   and he fell among *robbers*.   ROBBERS
   And they stripped him and beat him   Steal and Injure
   and departed, leaving him half dead.

1. A man was going down from Jerusalem to Jericho,	
and he fell among *robbers*.	ROBBERS
And they stripped him and beat him	Steal and Injure
and departed, leaving him half dead.	
2. Now by coincidence a certain *priest*	
was going down that road,	PRIEST
and when he saw him,	See
he passed by on the other side.	Do nothing
3. Likewise also a *Levite* came to that place,	LEVITE
and when he saw him,	See
he passed by on the other side.	Do nothing
4. And a certain *Samaritan*, traveling, came to him,	SAMARITAN
and when he saw him,	See and show
he had compassion on him.	compassion
5. He went to him,	TREAT WOUNDS
and bound up his wounds,	(The Levite's failure)
pouring on oil and wine.	
6. Then he put him on his own riding animal	TRANSPORT THE MAN
and led him (it) to the inn,	(The Priest's failure)
and took care of him.	
7. The next day he took out and gave	
two denarii to the manager and said,	SPEND MONEY ON HIM
"Take care of him, and whatever more you spend	(Compensating for the thieves)
I, on my return, will repay you."	
"Which of these three, do you think,	
proved neighbor to the man who fell among the robbers?"	
He said, "The one who showed mercy on him."	
And Jesus said to him, "Go and do likewise."	

Figure 22.3. The parable of the good Samaritan (Lk 10:25-37)

A gang of cutthroats "stripped him and beat him." Robbers in the Middle East are known to beat their victims only if they resist. It can be assumed, therefore, that this poor fellow made this mistake and consequently suffered a severe beating and was left naked and unconscious on the road from Jerusalem to Jericho. The wounded man is naturally assumed to be a Jew. The wounded man in Ibn al-Tayyib's story is a Jew. The significance of this detail is seen later. Scene 2 features the priest.

2. Now by coincidence a certain *priest*
   was going down that road,   PRIEST
   and when he saw him,   See
   he passed by on the other side.   Do nothing

The temple in Jerusalem was served by three classes of people. Priests comprised the first, the second was the Levites, and the third were laymen who helped with various aspects of the life of the temple.[8] All three are important to the story. The priest was on his way down the mountain from Jerusalem to Jericho. Many of the priests in the first century lived in Jericho. They would go up to Jerusalem for a two-week assignment and then return to their homes in Jericho. This priest fits easily into such a pattern and may well have been on his way home from the sacred precincts of the temple.

Priests were a hereditary guild and were known to be wealthy. Menahem Stern writes, "Towards the close of the Second Temple period, the priesthood constituted the prestigious and elite class in Jewish society."[9] As a person of means, the priest would not be hiking seventeen miles down the hill when he could easily afford to ride. A Middle Eastern listener to the story would assume that the rich priest was riding. He could well have transported the man to help.

Then, as now, various ethnic communities in the Middle East are identified by their clothes, their language or their accent. In the first century, Jewish scholars could speak Hebrew while peasants spoke Aramaic. Along the Phoenician coast, people still used the Phoenician language. Around the Sea of Galilee, Syriac was in use. The Greek cities naturally conversed in Greek, and tribesmen in the south spoke Arabic. Government officials would have known Latin.[10] Language, dress and accent—with these three ethnic and class markers it was easy to distinguish "them from us."

But the priest had a special problem. The wounded man beside the road was unconscious and stripped. If the victim was a fellow Jew, and especially a law-abiding Jew, the priest would have been responsible to reach out and help him. But this victim was naked and unconscious, so how could anyone be sure of his ethnic-linguistic identity?[11] No doubt, the priest wanted to do his duty under the law. But what was his duty?

---

[8]The Greek word *hypēretēs* means "servant, helper, assistant." This word often appears in connection with the temple and is translated "officer," "guard" or "servant" (Mt 26:58; Mk 14:54; Jn 7:32; 18:3, 18).

[9]Menahem Stern, "Aspects of Jewish Society: The Priesthood and Other Classes," in *The Jewish People in the First Century* (Philadelphia: Fortress, 1976), 2:582.

[10]Cf. Chaim Rabin, "Hebrew and Aramaic in the First Century," in *The Jewish People in the First Century* (Philadelphia: Fortress Press, 1976), pp. 1007-39.

[11]Even circumcision would not settle the matter for him. Samaritans and Egyptians were circumcised.

The wounded man could have been dead. If so the priest who approached him would become ceremonially defiled, and if defiled he would need to return to Jerusalem and undergo a week-long process of ceremonial purification. It would take some time to arrange such things. Meanwhile, he could not eat from the tithes or even collect them. The same ban would apply to his family and servants. Distribution to the poor would also have been impossible. What's more, the victim along the road might have been Egyptian, Greek, Syrian or Phoenician, in which case, the priest was not responsible under the law to do anything. If the priest approached the beaten man and touched him and the man later died, the priest would have been obliged to rend his robes, and in so doing would have violated laws against the destruction of valuable property. The poor priest did not have an easy time trying to determine his duty under the law. After deciding that his ceremonial purity was too important to risk he continued on his way.

The decision was freighted with danger. If the priest became defiled and tried to serve at the altar in a state of uncleanness, he could suffer the following fate: "his brethren the priests did not bring him to the court, but the young men among the priests took him outside the Temple Court and split open his brain with clubs."[12] Even the risk of being accused would be frightening.

Scene 3 introduces the Levite.

3. Likewise also a *Levite*	
came to that place,	LEVITE
and when he saw him,	See
he passed by on the other side.	Do nothing

The Levites functioned in the temple as assistants to the priests. This particular Levite probably knew that a priest was ahead of him on the road and may have been an assistant to that same priest. Since the priest had set a precedent, the Levite could pass by with an easy conscience. Should a mere Levite upstage a priest? Did the Levite think he understood the law better than the priest? Furthermore, the Levite might have to face that same priest in Jericho that night. Could the Levite ride into Jericho with a wounded man whom the priest, in obedience to his understanding of the law, had opted to ignore? Such an act would be an insult to the priest!

Scene 4 features the Samaritan.

4. And a certain *Samaritan*, traveling, came to him,	SAMARITAN
and when he saw him,	See
he had compassion on him.	Compassion

---

[12]Mishnah, *Sanhedrin* 9:6 (Danby, pp. 396-97).

Stories that establish a series also set a direction. If a contemporary story begins with a bishop and then introduces a priest, the third person in the story is expected to be a deacon. If a first-century Jewish story introduces a priest, then a Levite, the third person down the road is and should be a Jewish layman. But this is not what happens.

Scene 4 explodes in the faces of its listeners. The hero of the story is not a Jewish layman but a hated outsider. I doubt if settlers in the American West told stories in the nineteenth century with "a good Indian" as the hero of those tales. The wounded man in the Jewish story told by Ibn al-Tayyib was a Jew. Here the parable assumes the wounded man to be a Jew. It would have been more acceptable to the audience if Jesus had told a story about a good *Jew* who helped a wounded *Samaritan* on the way to Shechem. The Jewish audience might have managed to praise a "good Jew" even though he helped a hated Samaritan. It is, however, a different matter to tell a story about a good Samaritan who helps a wounded Jew, especially after the Jewish priest and Levite fail to turn aside to assist the unconscious stranger!

Unlike the two travelers on the road before him, the Samaritan is moved with compassion. The saving agent in the story breaks in from the outside, binds up the man's wounds, and pours oil and wine on them. Origen, Ambrose, Augustine and Ibn al-Tayyib all identify the Samaritan as a symbol for Jesus, and rightly so.[13] This identification is freighted with meaning:

5. He went to him,	TREAT WOUNDS
and bound up his wounds,	(The Levite's failure)
pouring on oil and wine.	

First aid must be administered before the man can be moved. Greek grammar allows for the binding of a wound and the pouring on of oil and wine to occur together. Syriac and Arabic versions of this text, following Semitic grammar, can only describe two actions: binding wounds and then pouring on oil and wine. Is this backward? Surely the Samaritan would first clean the wound with oil, then disinfect it with wine before finally binding it? But a deep cut is often bound before medication is poured onto the wound through the bandage. In the first century, oil and wine were sometimes mixed to form a medication for wounds. It is difficult to make a case for the significance of the order of the actions. What matters is that the Samaritan is using all his available resources (oil, wine, a cloth wrapping, riding animal, time, energy and money) to care for the wounded man. Ibn al-Tayyib comments:

---

[13]Arthur A. Just Jr., ed., *Luke,* Ancient Christian Commentary on Scripture (Downers Grove, Ill.: InterVarsity Press, 2003), pp. 179-81; Ibn al-Tayyib, *Tafsir al-Mashriqi,* 2:182.

Yes, indeed, love that fails to give money *[darahim]* as charity or as alms is common in the world, but heartfelt love that is free from the seeking of praise or honor and which is willing to endure distress, suffering and loss, in the path of good works, such as is set forth in this parable, is extraordinarily rare.[14]

Ibn al-Tayyib understands instinctively that the Samaritan is paying a high price to assist the wounded man.

6. Then he put him on his own riding animal	TRANSPORT THE MAN
and led him [it] to the inn,	(The Priest's failure)
and took care of him.	

The Samaritan then risks his life by transporting the wounded man to an inn within Jewish territory. Such inns were found in villages, not in the wilderness. There are no archaeological remains to indicate that there was an inn in the midst of the wilderness between Jerusalem and Jericho at the time of Jesus. The listener to the story would naturally expect the Samaritan to take the wounded man down to Jericho where an inn could be found, as Ibn al-Tayyib's story confirms.[15] The Samaritan is expected to unload the wounded man at the edge of Jericho and disappear. A Samaritan would not be safe in a Jewish town with a wounded Jew over the back of his riding animal. Community vengeance may be enacted against the Samaritan, even if he has saved the life of the Jew. I have read of and personally witnessed these grim realities in the Middle East.

7. The next day he took out and gave	
two denarii to the manager and said,	SPEND MONEY ON HIM
"Take care of him, and whatever	
more you spend	(Compensating for the thieves)
I, on my return, I will repay you."	

This last scene takes place the following day at the inn. Two denarii would have covered the bill for food and lodging for at least a week and perhaps two.[16] The overlooked reality of the Samaritan's final act is that he risks his life to care for this man in a Jewish inn. Putting the story into an American context around 1850, suppose a Native American found a cowboy with two arrows in his back, placed the cowboy on his horse and rode into Dodge City. After checking into a room over the saloon, the man spent the night taking care of the cowboy. How would the people of Dodge City react to the Native American the following morning

---

[14]Ibn al-Tayyib, *Tafsir al-Mashriqi*, 1:181.
[15]Ibn al-Tayyib specifically refers to the Samaritan taking the wounded man to Jericho.
[16]Arland J. Hultgren, *The Parables of Jesus* (Grand Rapids: Eerdmans, 2000), p. 99.

when he emerged from the saloon? Most Americans know that they would probably kill him even though he had helped a cowboy.

After the Samaritan paid his bill he had yet to escape the town. Was there a crowd awaiting him outside the inn? Was he beaten or killed? We do not know. The story is open-ended, and as with many of Jesus' parables the listener must supply the missing conclusion. Why did the Samaritan expose himself to potential violence?

At the time, people could be sold as slaves if they could not pay their debts. Jesus' parable of the unjust servant mentions this grim first-century reality (Mt 18:25). Any lodger in a commercial inn who could not pay his bill risked being sold as a slave by the innkeepers, who, in general, had bad reputations. This particular victim had nothing, not even clothes. The Samaritan was obliged to make a down payment and pledge himself to settle the final bill lest his rescue of the wounded man be in vain. Without such an extraordinary effort the Samaritan might as well have left the poor man to die in the wilderness.

In this parable the Samaritan extends a costly demonstration of unexpected love to the wounded man, and in the process Jesus again interprets the life-changing power of costly love that would climax at his cross.

The dialogue between Jesus and the lawyer concludes:

> "Which of these three, do you think
> proved neighbor to the man who fell among the robbers?"
>   He said, "The one who showed mercy on him."
>   And Jesus said to him, "*Go* and *do* likewise."

The lawyer's question, "Who is my neighbor?" is not answered. Instead, Jesus reflects on the larger question, "To whom must I *become* a neighbor?" The answer being: Anyone in need. At great cost, the Samaritan became a neighbor to the wounded man. The neighbor is the *Samaritan*, not the wounded man. In this connection Ibn al-Tayyib notes:

> We see that the lawyer does not want to openly praise the Samaritan and thus refers to him obliquely without naming him. This answer comes from his conscience, but he is fearful of Jewish attitudes (toward Samaritans) with which he was raised. And if it were not for this parable he would never concede that the Samaritan was a neighbor to the wounded man.[17]

Ibn al-Tayyib astutely observes that both Jesus and the lawyer identify the Samaritan as the one who becomes a neighbor even though it is not easy for the lawyer to do so in public.

---

[17]Ibn al-Tayyib, *Sharah al-Mashriqi*, 2:184.

On hearing the story the lawyer has a chance to see that he cannot justify himself (that is, earn eternal life), because what he is challenged to do is beyond his capacity. At the same time he and all readers of the parable, since its creation, are given a noble ethical model to imitate.

SUMMARY: THE PARABLE OF THE GOOD SAMARITAN

This parable contains both ethical and theological content. What are the "rooms in the house" that this parable creates? I would suggest the following:

1. *Eternal life—a gracious gift.* The lawyer is given a standard he cannot meet. In the process he has the opportunity to discover that he cannot earn eternal life, for it comes to him as a free gift.

2. *Becoming a neighbor.* The lawyer's question, "Who *is* my neighbor?" is the wrong query. He is challenged to ask, "To whom must I *become* a neighbor?" The parable replies, "Your neighbor is anyone in need, regardless of language, religion or ethnicity." Here compassion for the outsider has its finest expression in all Scripture. The ethical demands of this vision are limitless.

3. *The limits of the law.* Compassion reaches beyond the requirements of any law. The priest and the Levite cannot discover their duty solely by examining their code books.

4. *Racism.* The religious and racial attitudes of the community are under attack. The story could have been located in Samaria with a good Jew rescuing a wounded Samaritan. Instead, it is a hated Samaritan who (presumably) rescues a wounded Jew.

5. *Jesus the teacher.* Jesus' skills as a teacher emerge. He does not answer the man's questions but raises other questions, allowing the lawyer to answer his own queries. In the process the lawyer is challenged to expand his understanding of what faithfulness requires of him.

6. *Christology.* After the failure of the listeners' religious leaders, the saving agent breaks in from outside to save, disregarding the cost of that salvation. Jesus is talking about himself.

7. *The cross.* The good Samaritan offers a costly demonstration of unexpected love. He risks his life by transporting a wounded Jew into a Jewish town and spending the night there. The wounded man will never be the same again. Jesus is demonstrating a part of the meaning of his own passion.

23

The Parable of the Rich Fool

LUKE 12:13-21

THE DIVISION BETWEEN BODY AND SOUL, so familiar to the classical Greek world, was foreign to the Hebrew mind where the *nepeš* —the self, the whole person—was an undissolvable composite of body and spirit. Thus for Paul, resurrection included the resurrection of the body, which he defined as a "spiritual body" (1 Cor 15:44).

It follows that there is no "spiritual gospel" that can be endorsed in isolation from the reality of the physical world that God created, called "good" and into which he placed human beings. This combination of the spiritual and the physical and its relationship to God is at the heart of the teachings of Jesus. For example, the Lord's Prayer includes a request for the gift of bread.

In regard to material things, Jesus said more about money than he did about prayer. Whenever he discussed money, he did so with the assumption that all material things belong to God. "The earth is the LORD's and the fullness thereof" (Ps 24:1), wrote the psalmist. Does this mean that the right to private property is denied?

In biblical thought we are stewards of all our possessions and responsible to God for what we do with them. At the same time the New Testament affirms the legitimacy of private property. Peter confronted Ananias and Sapphira in Acts 5:1-11 because they falsely claimed to have dedicated their property to God when they had not done so. Their sin was their false claim, not their possession of property. Christians everywhere are called to be stewards of their private possessions and of the whole earth.

The parable of the rich fool (see figure 23.1) is one of our Lord's primary teachings on this subject. The story is about a man who failed to recognize that he was accountable to God for all he owned.[1]

---

[1]For a more detailed interpretation of this parable see Kenneth E. Bailey, *Through Peasant Eyes,* in *Poet and Peasant and Through Peasant Eyes* (Grand Rapids: Eerdmans, 1980), pp. 57-73.

0. One of the multitude said to him,   SETTING
   "Rabbi, bid my brother divide the inheritance with me."
   But he said to him,
   "Man, who made me a judge or divider over you?"
   And he said to them,   GENERAL PRINCIPLE

1. "Take heed, and beware of every kind of insatiable desire.
   For life for a person does not consist in the surpluses of his possessions."

2.   And he told this parable, saying,   GOODS GIVEN
      "There was a certain rich man
      whose land brought forth plenty.

3.   And he discussed with himself saying,   DIALOGUE WITH SELF
         'What shall I do,   (My Crop, Not Stored)
         for I have nowhere to store my crops?'

4.   And he said, 'I will do this:
            I will pull down my barns, and build larger ones;   SOLUTION (?)
            and I will store all my grain and my goods.   (More Storage)

5.   And I will say to myself, "Self!
         You have ample goods laid up for many years.   DIALOGUE WITH SELF
         Relax, eat, drink, and enjoy yourself."   (My Crop Stored)

6.   But God said to him, 'Fool!
      This night your life is required of you,   GOODS LEFT
      and what you have prepared, whose will these things be?'

7. So is he who lays up treasure for himself,   GENERAL PRINCIPLE
   and is not gathering riches for God."

Figure 23.1. The parable of the rich fool (Lk 12:13-21)

THE RHETORIC

The prophetic rhetorical template of seven inverted stanzas again appears. A general principle opens the story and a second such principle closes it. "Goods given" and "goods left behind" form a second envelope. Scenes 3 and 5 focus on two dialogues that the rich man has with himself.[2] The subject of the dialogues is the storing of the goods. In scene 3 they are not stored while scene 5 projects a future where they are all safely preserved. The middle (4) contains his awareness of his

---

[2]The Greek word here is *psychē* which translates the Hebrew *nepeš*, which means "the self," that is, the entire person—body and spirit.

relationship to his possessions. It is all about me! "My barns . . . my grain . . . my goods" make up the rich man's world. His game plan is to expand his storage facilities in order to preserve all his surpluses for himself.

The soliloquy in the center of the parable is a distinctive feature that appears elsewhere. This feature is used in the parable of the unjust steward (Lk 16:1-8) and twice in the double parable of the lost younger son (Lk 15:11-23) and the lost older son (Lk 15:24-32). The noble vineyard owner also engages in a soliloquy that appears in the center of his story (Lk 20:9-18). In all five cases, the center soliloquy, for better or for worse, is a critical turning point in the story. With these rhetorical features in mind, we turn to the parable itself.

COMMENTARY

As in the case of the parable of the good Samaritan, this parable has a narrative setting. The text is as follows:

> 0. One of the multitude said to him,   SETTING
> "Rabbi, bid my brother divide the inheritance with me."
> But he said to him,
> "Man, who made me a judge or divider over you?"
> And he said to them,   GENERAL PRINCIPLE

"Teacher" is Luke's word for rabbi. The man in the crowd assumed he was addressing a legal expert. However, he does not say to Jesus, "Rabbi Jesus, my brother and I are quarreling. There is danger lest our fight create a permanent break in our relationship and I am concerned. Would you listen to me and to him and reconcile us? I beg you, bring us together!" Instead he, in effect, says, "Jesus! Tell my brother that he is wrong and that he should give me my rights." The demand means that the split between the brothers has already taken place.

The assumptions behind such a request are clear. The father had died without an oral or written will. There was an estate that was held by the two brothers. According to the law of the times the inheritance could not be divided until the older brother agreed. The petitioner therefore must be the younger brother, who is ordering Jesus to press his older brother into making the division. Apparently, the older brother did not want this to happen. The issue was important. Justice is a critical part of life. The petitioner in the text cries out for justice in the division of land, an extremely sensitive and divisive issue in our increasingly crowded world.

Jesus is a reconciler of people, not a divider. He wants to bring people together, not finalize separations. This does not mean that Jesus is indifferent to cries for justice. In many parables and dramatic actions, he demonstrates compassion for the downtrodden, the oppressed and the outcasts. These accounts show his finely honed concern for social justice in the world in which he lived (see Lk 4:16-30). Specifically this parable reflects on the relationships between material possessions, God and justice.[3]

Judging the cause of justice. For Jesus "the cause" must come under judgment. Lesslie Newbigin in his book *The Open Secret* describes a theology of mission for our day. In his chapter on justice he writes, "All human causes are ambiguous and all human actions are involved in the illusions which are the product of our egotism." He continues:

> If we acknowledge the God of the Bible, we are committed to struggle for justice in society. Justice means giving to each his due. Our problem, as seen in the light of the gospel, is that each of us overestimates what is due him compared with what is due to his neighbor. If I do not acknowledge a justice which judges the justice for which I fight, I am an agent, not of justice, but of lawless tyranny.[4]

In the Middle East since World War I, many communities have struggled for numerous forms of justice. Often these communities express a consuming sense of self-righteousness. They insist that all that they are fighting for is justice. But generally they acknowledge no justice which judges their cause, and at the end of the day, often unseen by them, they appear to be fighting for the "lawless tyranny" of which Newbigin speaks.

When the prophet Habakkuk wrote about the coming of the Chaldeans, the most alarming thing he could say about them was, "Their justice and self-worth proceed from themselves" (Hab 1:7, my translation). What could be worse? Habakkuk saw that the Chaldeans confessed no God of justice who could judge them and their cause. Indeed, they alone decided what was just—and this disturbed the prophet deeply!

Another difficulty is that the person who fights for a just cause usually thinks that he or she is thereby a just person. Everything such a person does in fighting for that cause usually becomes right in her or his own eyes. Woe to those who fall under the sway of this kind of self-created justice. This parable presents a new perspective on the cry for justice.

In the story before us the petitioner has already decided what justice requires and wants the visiting rabbi to enforce the petitioner's view. How will Jesus respond?

First-century rabbis were experts in the law of Moses and spent their time giv-

---

[3]See Craig L. Blomberg, *Neither Poverty nor Riches* (Grand Rapids: Eerdmans, 1999).
[4]Lesslie Newbigin, *The Open Secret* (Grand Rapids: Eerdmans, 1999), p. 124.

ing legal rulings. There is the case of the famous Johanan Ben Zakki, a contemporary of Jesus, who moved from Galilee to Jerusalem because he wasn't hearing enough cases in the north. Not enough people were coming to him with precisely the kinds of concerns that this petitioner expresses. The petitioner hoped Rabbi Jesus would take his case.

Exodus 2:11-15 tells a story of Moses, who saw two of his fellow Hebrews fighting each other and tried to adjudicate. They rejected his intervention saying, "Who made you . . . a judge over us?" (v. 14). In this text, Jesus is *asked* to make a judgment, but refuses. He has a different agenda.

Jesus responds with the question, "Man, who made me a judge or divider over you?" He was concerned to heal relationships between people, and out of that healing they could deal with the issues that divided them. Throughout Jesus' ministry, no one succeeded in giving him the "right answer" and pressing him to accept it.

Jesus responds to the petitioner with the title "Man." In Middle Eastern speech this is a rough way to address a person. This phrase means, "I'm not going to use your name, and I'm not going to call you 'Friend.' I'll just call you, 'Man.' "[5] The language carries strong hints of displeasure.

Jesus continues with a call for a new vision of the problem. A wooden, literal translation reads:

1. Take heed and beware of every kind of insatiable desire.
   Because not out of the surpluses to anyone
   the life of him it is—
   out of his possessions.

Possessions are bonded to a deep, often irrational fear—the fear of one day not having enough. Regardless of how much wealth is squirreled away, this gnawing fear presses frail humans to acquire more. There is never quite enough because the insecurity within never dies.

This is the problem with insatiable desires, about which Jesus warns his listeners in the wisdom saying. *Life* is not available in the surpluses that these insatiable desires produce. In good Middle Eastern fashion Jesus follows this wisdom saying with a parable about surpluses. If God is the owner of all things material and people are only his stewards, what rights do they have to the surpluses that their desires often create? Well-known responses to surpluses include:

- Hide them.
- Flaunt them.

---

[5]The Arabic colloquial equivalents *ya rajil* and *ya zalami* have this meaning across the Middle East.

- Spend them on expensive vacations.
- Upgrade one's lifestyle and they will evaporate.
- Buy expensive toys and go in debt.
- Buy more insurance.
- Pretend you are poor and just scraping by.
- Use them to acquire power.

Christians are obliged, on the basis of this wisdom saying and the parable that follows it, to consider both insatiable desires and the material surpluses produced by hard work, bountiful nature, a shift in the "market" or the gifts of others.

The parable begins with:

2. And he told this parable, saying,   GOODS GIVEN
   "There was a certain rich man
   whose land brought forth plenty.

The man in the parable is already rich. Then his land produces a bumper crop. He did not work harder to produce this bounty; it is a gift of God. What will he do with the surpluses?

The text continues:

3. And he discussed with himself, saying,
   'What shall I do,   PROBLEM
   for I have nowhere to store my crops?'

Literally translated, the text says, he "dialogued with himself." This is a very sad scene. In the Middle East, village people make decisions about important topics after long discussions with their friends. Families, communities and villages are tightly knit together. Everybody's business is everybody else's business. Even trivial decisions are made after hours of discussion with family and friends. But this man appears to have no friends. He lives in isolation from the human family around him, and with an important decision to make the only person with whom he can have a dialogue is himself.

Throughout the world, from the great houses of Arabia to the palatial summer dwellings in the mountains of Lebanon, and from Europe to America, the more wealth people acquire, the farther they generally withdraw from their neighbors. Isaiah describes this dynamic as he writes:

Woe to those who join house to house,
who add field to field,
until there is no more room,

and you are made to dwell alone
in the midst of the land. (Is 5:8)

This is precisely what appears to have happened to this man. There is no one
around, and he can talk only to himself. Jesus' listeners would have envisioned this
type of a picture as the parable unfolded.

The rich man asks himself, "What shall I do?" He has no place to store his
abundance and displays no awareness that his bumper crop is a gift from God or
that he is responsible to use it as its owner might direct. He sees it as *his* crop.

Ambrose, the fourth-century Latin theologian, astutely observes, "The things
that we cannot take away with us are not ours. . . . Compassion alone follows us."[6]
Augustine, of North Africa, Ambrose's student, writes, "He did not realize that
the bellies of the poor were much safer storerooms than his barns."[7]

The rich man holds a different perspective. The climax in the middle of the
parable describes his decision to pull down his barns and build larger barns for his
bountiful harvest:

4. And he said, 'I will do this:
    I will pull down my barns, and build larger ones;   PLAN
    and I will store all my grain and my goods.   (Present)

There is no mention of his employees, who have done and will do the work.
Rather, he knows only *my* crop, *my* barn, *my* grain, *my* goods and *my* soul. At the
end of this self-centered litany he thinks, "I will say to *my* self/soul." The dialogue
with himself continues.

5. And I will say to my self, "Self!
    You have ample goods laid up for many years.   PLAN
    Relax, eat, drink, and enjoy yourself." '   (Future)

He has no cronies with whom to share his thoughts and ideas, and from
whom he can derive some wisdom. He is all alone. "Self," he continues, "you
have ample goods laid up for many years. Take your ease; eat, drink, and rejoice."
Assuming that "This is as good as it gets," he is pathetic in his isolation. His inspiration appears to come from a verse in Ecclesiastes that says: "And I commend enjoyment, for man has no good thing under the sun but to eat and drink,
and enjoy himself, for this will go with him in his toil through the days of life

---

[6]Ambrose, *Exposition of the Gospel of Luke*, Homily 7.122, quoted in *Luke*, Ancient Christian Commentary on Scripture, ed. Arthur J. Just (Downers Grove, Ill.: InterVarsity Press, 2003), p. 208.
[7]Augustine *Sermon* 36.9, quoted in *Luke*, Ancient Christian Commentary on Scripture, ed. Arthur J.
Just (Downers Grove, Ill.: InterVarsity Press, 2003), p. 208.

which God gives him under the sun" (Eccles 8:15).

This is a nice philosophy, but the Preacher of Ecclesiastes is aware that "the days of life" are a gift from God. Our rich man reflects no such awareness. He remembers the first part of this verse that tells him to "eat, and drink and enjoy himself." But he conveniently forgets the latter part that speaks of "the days of life *which God gives* him under the sun."

Ibn al-Tayyib, in commenting on the rich man's failing, makes the following observation:

> He imagines that a person created in the image of God can be fully satisfied with the food for the body, for he says "O Self, you have an abundance of goods, relax, eat etc." He imagines that the self is animal-like and that its highest pleasure and greatest form of satisfaction is eating and drinking.[8]

The Greek word here is *psychē*, which is often translated "soul," which in English carries the meaning of a spirit that can be separated from the body. But behind this Greek word is the Hebrew *nepeš*, which is used in Psalm 42:1-2:

> As a hart longs
> > for flowing streams,
> so longs my soul *[nepeš]*
> > for thee, O God.
> My soul *[nepeš]* thirsts for God,
> > for the living God.
> When shall I come and behold
> > the face of God?

The psalmist notes that the hart *thirsts* for water in the desert. In like manner his *nepeš thirsts for God*. Not so the rich fool whose *nepeš* is fully satisfied with food and drink. His problem is a radical misunderstanding of the nature of the self *(nepeš)* and a critical misjudgment in regard to what is needed to sustain the self. Augustine is famous for saying "My soul is restless until it rests in thee." This rich man's view is, "My soul is restless until I am assured of an over abundance of food and drink."

Suddenly the voice of God is heard on stage thundering:

6. But God said to him, "Fool!
   This night your soul is required of you,   GOODS LEFT
   and what you have prepared, whose will these things be?"

---

[8]Ibn al-Tayyib, *Tafsir al-Mashriqi*, ed. Yusif Manqariyos (Egypt: Al-Tawfiq Press, 1907), 2:213.

God announces that his life is forfeited. There is a subtle play on words in the Greek. The word translated "rejoice" is *euphrainō*. The word for fool in this text is *aphrōn*. The *phrōn* is related to the *diaphragm*. When you reach the point where you can relax with a great sigh of relief and expand your diaphragm you have "arrived"; you have achieved the state of *euphrainō*. Following the advice of the preacher in Ecclesiastes, this man believed he had reached that magical stage. Before him the "good days would roll" where he could eat, drink and *euphrainō* (expand the diaphragm), that is, "make merry." But God tells him that he is in reality *a-phrōn* (a fool). Literally, he was a person with no diaphragm left to expand. He was reduced to this sorry state because of his miscalculation that his true and only self could be fully sustained by adequate food and drink. His self/soul thirsted after expensive drinks, not God.

Suddenly he discovered that his soul/self/life was not his but was on loan from God, who could demand the return of that loan at any time. In the Greek text the phrase, "your soul/self *[nepeš]* is required of you," is the language of the return of a loan. This is one of the major, often hidden, truths of Scripture. Life is not a right but a gift—on loan. If God gives five days of life to a child, we mourn our losses and are grateful for those five days. We have no rights, neither for ten days nor for eighty years. Each day is a gift, and we praise God for what the song writer David Bailey calls "One more day."[9] The Lord's Prayer speaks to the same subject.

The man in the parable forgot all of this, and the preacher of Ecclesiastes did not help him, because the rich fool truncated the sentence he borrowed from that venerable text and thereby perverted its meaning.

The new question is, Who will acquire all of these possessions? It seems that the rich fool had not read the book of Ecclesiastes carefully. The preacher not only tells his readers to eat, drink and be merry during the limited days given by God, he also warns:

> I hated all my toil in which I had toiled under the sun, seeing that I must leave it to the man who will come after me; and who knows whether he will be a wise man or a fool? Yet he will be master of all for which I toiled and used my wisdom under the sun. (Eccles 2:18-19)

In the parable God reminds the rich fool of this other gem of wisdom from Ecclesiastes.

Returning to the petitioner before him, Jesus indirectly says, "Supposing you win your fight over the inheritance—what then? Look beyond your earthly life. To

---

[9]David M. Bailey, "One More Day," *Vista Point* (1997).

whom will all of your inheritance one day belong?

Jesus closes the dialogue with the second wisdom saying,

> 7. So is he who lays up treasure for himself,   GENERAL PRINCIPLE
>   and is not gathering riches for God.

The Greek verbs in this sentence can both be translated as actives. The one who continues to labor for self alone will fail to acquire wealth for God.

This young man is impelled to look at the problem of economic justice not from the point of view of "I want mine" and "Let's finalize the division between us." Jesus summons him to consider economic justice from the perspective of who really owns all of it. Jesus calls the petitioner to think along the following lines:

> Whether the inheritance is under my authority or that of my brother, both of us must recognize that all of it belongs to God. We are both responsible as stewards before God for our material possessions and for how we spend the days of our lives. Our wealth and our lives are on loan and both of us can destroy ourselves if we do not curb an innate insatiable desire for more.

What then can we conclude from the teachings of this parable?

SUMMARY: THE PARABLE OF THE RICH FOOL

1. A naked cry for justice, unqualified by any self-criticism, is not heeded by Jesus.

2. In case of a broken personal relationship Jesus refuses to answer a cry for justice when the answer contributes to finalizing the brokenness of that relationship. He did not come as a divider.

3. Jesus is concerned for needs, not simply earnings (cf. Mt 20:1-16). Here a self-centered cry for justice is understood by Jesus to be a symptom of a sickness. He refuses to answer the cry but rather strives to heal the condition that produced the cry.

4. Material possessions belong to God who gives them as gifts to humans. Sometimes those gifts are in the form of unearned surpluses of material things. The rich man in the parable assumed exclusive ownership of all his material possessions and with it the right to keep them for his private use. Sharing his wealth with those in need never occurred to him.

5. The rich fool failed to account for his mortality. He failed in securing both his life and his possessions.

6. Human life is on loan from God. It is a gift, not a right. The rich man assumed

he owned his soul/self. He discovered his mistake when God suddenly asked for the loan of his life to be returned.

7. The person who believes that security and the good life are to be found in the acquisition and storing of more and more possessions is sadly mistaken.

8. The voice of God de-absolutizes material possessions by reminding the rich man that he does not know and cannot control who will acquire power over his wealth. He may have a will, but when the dust settles, who, in the end, will own his wealth?

9. The abundant life is to be found in "treasuring up for God" rather than for self.

10. James talks of the rich man who will "fade away in the midst of his pursuits" (Jas 1:11). Jesus paints a parabolic picture of this precise phenomenon. The fool's wealth destroyed his capacity to maintain any abiding human relationships. He had no one with whom to share his soul/life/self. Worst of all, he did not know he had a problem.

11. In contrast to the psalmist, the rich fool misunderstood the nature of his own self/soul/life. He saw it as a type of body that could be fully nourished and sustained by food and drink.

24

The Parable of the Great Banquet

LUKE 14:15-24

THE PARABLE OF THE GREAT BANQUET expands one of the major biblical metaphors for the kingdom of God.[1] When Jesus approaches this subject, he participates in a conversation that had begun over seven hundred years earlier. The parable in this chapter is a scene from a much longer movie.

DINNER PARTY CONVERSATIONS

In the verses preceding this parable, Jesus instructs his listeners at dinner about invitations for banquets. He advises them to host those who cannot reciprocate with similar invitations. It is better to invite the needy, advises Jesus. Someone seated at this dinner responds with, "Blessed is he who shall eat bread in the kingdom of God."

The setting is authentically Middle Eastern. A traveling rabbi/preacher passes through a local village. The religious leaders invite the village guest to a meal during which they investigate his political and theological views. In this particular case Jesus is the guest and the person who makes the opening statement wants to invoke Jesus' views on the topic of the coming kingdom of God and the Messiah who is to inaugurate that kingdom. At the end of history the final fulfillment of that kingdom was understood to include a great banquet with the Messiah, known as "the messianic banquet." The person's outburst is a challenge for Jesus to express his views on that topic. Those around the table would expect Jesus to say something such as, "Oh, that we might keep the law in a precise fashion so that when that great day comes, we will be counted worthy to sit with the Messiah and all true believers at his banquet."

---

[1] For a more detailed discussion of this parable, see Kenneth E. Bailey, *Through Peasant Eyes*, in *Poet and Peasant and Through Peasant Eyes* (Grand Rapids: Eerdmans, 1980), pp. 88-113.

The reclining guests would then have nodded approvingly and thought to themselves, "Fine, he passed that exam. Now let's move on to the next topic." But Jesus responds with a very different view of the messianic banquet of the end times from the views current in the community.

MESSIANIC BANQUET

This seven-hundred-year-old conversation begins in Isaiah 25:6-9, where Isaiah dreams of a great banquet to be held at the end of history in which "the LORD of hosts" spreads the banquet and serves the food of kings. It will be held on the holy mountain of the Lord and the guests will include peoples from *all the Gentile nations*. Death will be at an end, tears will be wiped away, and it will be a glorious day of salvation.

In the sixth century B.C., the Jews trudged into exile in Babylon. A few decades later some of them and their descendants returned to Judea, but by that time their everyday language was Aramaic. As centuries passed, synagogues were built and in them the Scriptures were read in Hebrew and translated orally into Aramaic so that people could understand the readings. Around the time of Jesus, a written Aramaic translation of the Scriptures began to emerge, which turned out to be an expanded version much like *The Living Bible*. The translators took the liberty of adding extra words to the text in an attempt to explain what they understood the Hebrew to mean. The translation was called the Targum. Sometimes the translators took a great deal of freedom with the text. As a result the Targum is often helpful in discovering how people in the first century understood various biblical texts.

The Targum translation of Isaiah's great banquet is of special interest:

> Yahweh of hosts will make for all the peoples in this mountain a meal. And although they supposed it is an honor, it will be a shame for them and great plagues, plagues from which they will be unable to escape, plagues whereby they will come to their end.[2]

Apparently, Isaiah's vision gradually became so unpopular that it was totally rejected by the creators of the Targum.[3]

---

[2]Aramaic text from *The Bible in Aramaic*, vol. 3, *The Latter Prophets*, ed. Alexander Sperber (Leiden: E. J. Brill, 1962), pp. 47-48.

[3]A precise date for the composition of *The Isaiah Targum* cannot be determined. Bruce Chilton argues for an "interpretive ethos" that stretches from the first to the fourth centuries. Chilton notes, "The Targumic portrait of the Messiah as a prayerful teacher, not merely a victorious leader (cf. 52:13—53:12), may help to explain why some, at least, came to see the forceful rabbi from Nazareth in messianic terms" (*The Isaiah Targum*, trans. Bruce Chilton [Edinburgh, T & T Clark, 1987], p. xxvii).

About the same time a second-century B.C. document emerged called the book of *Enoch*. This book speaks of a great banquet with the Messiah and affirms that the Gentiles will be included. But the angel of death will be present and will use his sword to destroy those Gentiles. The banquet hall will run with blood and the believers will be obliged to wade through the gore to reach the banquet hall where they sit down with the Messiah![4] Obviously, the author of the book of *Enoch* was also determined to present a view categorically opposed to Isaiah's vision.

A third early voice on this subject emerged from the Qumran community, which wrote the Dead Sea Scrolls. That community was composed of pious Jews, presumably of the Essene branch of Judaism, and one of its scrolls, called *The Messianic Rule,* discusses the famous banquet. The Qumran community was certain that no Gentiles would be present. Only pious Jews who observed the law would be allowed to attend. The text says, "And then [the Mess]iah of Israel shall [come] and the chiefs of the [clans of Israel] shall sit before him, [each] in the order of his dignity, according to [his place] in their camps and marches."[5] Earlier in this same scroll the text affirms that no one can attend the banquet who is "smitten in his flesh, or paralyzed in his feet or hands, or lame, or blind or deaf or dumb or smitten in his flesh with a visible blemish."[6] Isaiah's beautiful vision, which saw faithful Jews and Gentiles coming together at God's invitation, goes badly awry in these three reinterpretations of the great banquet.

THE PARABLE

Jesus, however, had something very different to say about this anticipated celebration. Luke first addresses this subject in Luke 13:22-30. That text speaks of people coming from East and West and from North and South, eating at the same table with Abraham, Isaac, Jacob and the prophets. Some respectable religious types will be denied entrance because of their failures. Furthermore, the "last will be first, and some are first who will be last." So there will be surprises. In Luke 14:15-24 Jesus' parable of the great banquet appears. The story, illustrated in figure 24.1, unfolds in a series of distinct scenes.

---

[4] *I Enoch* 62:1-11.
[5] "The Messianic Rule (IQSa 2:11-22)," in *The Dead Sea Scrolls in English,* trans. Géza Vermes (Middlesex: Penguin Books, 1975), p. 121.
[6] "The Messianic Rule (IQSa 2:5-10)," in *The Dead Sea Scrolls in English,* trans. Géza Vermes (Middlesex: Penguin Books, 1975), p. 120.

And he said to him,
"A man once gave a great banquet,   GREAT BANQUET
and invited many.   Many Invited

1. And he sent his servant
   at the hour of the banquet to say, 'Come!   DO THIS
   Because all is now ready!'   Because of This
   But they all alike began to make excuses.   Excuses

2. The first said to him, 'I have bought a field,   I DID THIS
   and I must go out and see it;   I Must Do This
   I pray you, have me excused.'   Excuse Me

3. And another said, 'I have bought five yoke of oxen, I DID THIS
   and I go to test them.   I Must Do This
   I pray you, have me excused.'   Excuse Me

4. And another said, 'I have married a bride,   I DID THIS
   and therefore—   Thus I Must
   I cannot come.'   Not Come

5.   So the servant came and reported this to his master.
      Then the householder in anger said to his servant,
      'Go out quickly   ANGER
      into the streets and lanes of the city.   Turned Into
      Bring in the poor, maimed, blind, and lame.'   GRACE

6. And the servant said, 'Sir,   SERVANT
   what you commanded has been done,   I Went
   and still there is room.'   Not Yet Full

7. And the master said to the servant, 'Go out   MASTER—GO
   into the highways and hedges,   To Highways
   and compel people to enter,   FILL UP HOUSE
   that my house may be filled.'

   For I tell you [pl.],
   none of those men who were invited   THOSE INVITED
   shall taste my banquet."   Not Taste of My Banquet

Figure 24.1. The parable of the great banquet (Lk 14:15-24)

THE RHETORIC

Within the framework of an introduction and a conclusion, the parable falls into
seven stanzas, except that the oft-appearing inversion of scenes does not occur and
the seven scenes flow in a *straight line sequence*.

Some traces of the prophetic rhetorical template, however, are visible. Within the introduction and conclusion the familiar seven scenes appear. Furthermore, there is a critical turning point or climax near the center. In this case it is not in scene four but scene five, where the master "in anger" opts for grace rather than vengeance. Finally, the story breaks into two halves, with a climax near the center. This feature can be seen in the following abbreviation of the parable:

The first guest list and its aftermath (scenes 1-4) and
The master turns anger into grace (scene 5)
The second guest list and what develops from it (stanza 6-7)

This rhetorical form can be called a *modified prophetic rhetorical template*.

COMMENTARY

The story opens with

And he said to him,		
"A man once gave a great banquet,	GREAT BANQUET	
and invited many.	Many Invited	
1. And he sent his servant		
at the hour of the banquet to say, 'Come!	DO THIS	
Because all is now ready!'	Because of This	
But they all alike began to make excuses.	Excuses	

The introduction, "A man once gave a great banquet, and invited many," brings the reader/listener at once to the topic of the great banquet. In a traditional Middle Eastern village the host of a banquet invites a group of his friends. On the basis of the number of people who accept the invitation, he decides how much and what kind of meat he will serve. On the day of the banquet animals or fowl are butchered and the banquet prepared. When everything is ready the master will send his servant around the village with the classical phrase, "Please come, everything is ready." The language of the parable is still used today.

In contemporary Western society banquets usually have two invitations. The first is often made over the telephone. On the day of the dinner party the guests assemble and are seated until the magical moment when the host or hostess appears and announces, "The food is on the table. Please come in." Everyone proceeds without delay to the table and the meal begins.

Imagine a contemporary Western scene in which the guests arrive and are seated in the living room. When the food is ready the hostess invites the guests to take their places but, to the shock of all, they offer excuses and head for the door. One says, "I have to mow the lawn." The second blurts out, "I must feed the cat."

The third says, "There are bills on my desk waiting to be paid." And the three walk out the door!

Excuses

The text states:

2. The first said to him, 'I have bought a field,	I DID THIS
and I must go out and see it.	I Must Do This
I pray you, have me excused.'	Excuse Me
3. And another said, 'I have bought five yoke of oxen,	I DID THIS
and I go to test them.	I Must Do This
I pray you have me excused.'	Excuse Me
4. And another said, 'I have married a bride,	I DID THIS
and therefore—	Thus I Must
I cannot come.'	Not Come

Yesterday, the guests pledged themselves to attend the banquet. Today, after the food has been cooked, they offer excuses for not attending.

A pattern is observable from the first excuse:

1. I did X.

2. Therefore I have to do Y.

3. Please excuse me.

The first man says that (1) he has bought a field. Therefore (2), he must go see it. On that basis (3), he asks to be excused. On the surface this appears to be fairly genuine. But on examination that genuineness disappears. The Middle East contains a great deal of desert and little agricultural land. In most traditional villages, various pieces of cropland have place names. To buy or sell cropland is a long, exacting process that can stretch over months and even years. Before a farmer buys a piece of cropland he learns everything he can about it. He will be interested in the quality of the soil, its drainage and whether or not it faces the winter sun. This is critical because in the Eastern Mediterranean rain falls in winter when the sun is low. A field that does not face the sun cannot produce a good crop. He will examine the quality of the terraces (if it is terraced) and will inquire about its yield in recent years. If it is terraced, it will be important to inspect those terraces. Are there fruit trees on the property? If so how old are they? These and many other questions will be asked before the buyer even considers acquiring a piece of farmland.

The first guest says that he has *just bought a field*, which he must *now* inspect. The cultural equivalent would be a Westerner who calls his wife to tell her that he will be late for supper because he has just purchased a new house over the phone, and having signed the check now wants to drive across town and look at it! Such an excuse is absurd because house buyers inspect property with great care *before* considering a purchase.

In the Middle East if someone is invited to a nobleman's house, one accepts and attendance is expected. If at the last minute the guest decides not to attend, he or she must offer a plausible excuse. An implausible excuse is a deliberate public insult. Surely this is true in cultures the world over.

If the first guest wants to be believed, he will need to say something like:

> My dear friend, you know that I have been negotiating over X piece of ground for a long time. Just an hour ago the owner unexpectedly told me that we must settle the price tonight or he will sell it to someone else. I am *very sorry* that I cannot attend the banquet. This has come up without warning. I am sure you understand. Please accept my sincere apologies.

Such an excuse allows the host to save face, and the relationship between the two will not be severed. But the excuse offered by the first guest is a public insult to the host. The servant turns to the second guest.

If only one guest backs out, the banquet can proceed. But if there is collusion between the guests and they all withdraw, it will be clear that the guests intend to shut down the banquet. Notice that the first guest speaks to the servant as though he were addressing the master. The servant so totally represents the master that this kind of language is used.

The servant then approaches the second guest who also gives an excuse. He claims that he has bought no less than five yoke of oxen and that he must go test them. This alibi is more transparent than the excuse offered by the first guest. Every farmer knows that a yoke of oxen is worthless unless the two animals pull together. Not only that, but they must tire at the same speed. No farmer will even bid on a pair of oxen without testing them carefully.

The rhythm of the conversation with the first guest is maintained. The second guest claims that he has (1) just bought five yoke of oxen and (2) must now go test them. Could he (3) please be excused? The second guest also wants to insult the nobleman in public.

The third man's excuse is unspeakably offensive. He says that (1) he has married a wife and (2) therefore he cannot come. He does not even ask to be excused. Middle Eastern chivalry produces a dignified and respectful manner of talking about one's wife. This third guest is very rudely saying, "I have a woman in the back of the house, and I am busy with her. Don't expect me at your banquet. I am not coming." In the Babylonian Talmud, Rabbi Hanan ben Raba is reported to have said, "All know for what purpose a bride enters the bridal canopy, yet whoever speaks obscenely [thereof], even if a sentence of seventy years happiness had been sealed for him, it is reversed for evil."[7]

This guest will be home that night. His excuse is extremely rude and totally unacceptable. Ibn al-Tayyib comments on the three excuses by saying, "Here the master of the house became angry because he knew that the excuses were vain and the apologies were insults that demonstrated the hatred of the guests [for the house owner]."[8] After hearing his master insulted three times, the servant refuses to continue and returns to report what has happened.[9]

The Master's Reaction

The servant knows and the master quickly discovers that the guests' intent is to humiliate the host and prevent the banquet from taking place. On hearing the servant's report the master becomes angry! The question of the hour is: What will he do with this anger? The master's response is truly "amazing grace."

> 5. So the servant came and reported this to his master.
>   Then the householder in anger said to his servant,
>
> | | |
> |---|---|
> | 'Go out quickly | ANGER |
> | into the streets and lanes of the city. | Turned Into |
> | Bring in the poor, maimed, blind, and lame.' | GRACE |

Insult and injustice cause great anger. That anger generates enormous energy. One of the major contemporary issues is: What is to be done with the energy created by anger produced by injustice? The master has every right to retaliate with verbal insults or go beyond such insults and threaten some action that will punish these guests who have attacked his personal honor in public. He has every right to tell the servant, "These former friends have chosen to be my enemies. Go back to them and tell them that after these insults, *I declare myself free to take any action!*"

Such a reply would be a prelude to some form of retaliation. But this is not what happens. Rather, the master creates a new and unprecedented option. He chooses to *reprocess* his anger into grace. The same dramatic refusal to retaliate, along with

---

[7]Babylonian Talmud, Šabbat 33a.

[8]Ibn al-Tayyib, *Tafsir al-Mashriqi*, ed. Yusif Manqariyos (Egypt: Al-Tawfiq Press, 1907), 2:256.

[9]The rewrite of this parable that appears in *The Gospel of Thomas* (no. 64) softens all three excuses. The offensive natures of the three excuses is, for the most part, removed. It appears that the original was too shocking.

the choice to turn the energy of insult into grace, is seen in the center of the parable of the unjust vinedressers (Lk 20:9-18). There the owner could have gathered armed men and stormed the vineyard in a move to bring the murderous renters to justice. Instead, he opts for costly grace.

Here, the master uses the energy generated by the anger of injustice and orders his servant to go out into the lanes and streets of the city and bring in the poor, the maimed, the blind and the lame. These are the very people that the Qumran community had decided to bar from the messianic banquet. Jesus is referring to the outcasts within Israel, the "people of the land," the common people who heard him gladly. These folk are now welcomed into the banquet even though they are not worthy to be seated with such a noble host and the possibility of their repaying him with a similar banquet is out of the question.

The story continues:

6. And the servant said, 'Sir,	SERVANT
what you commanded has been done,	I Went
and still there is room.'	Not Yet Full
7. And the master said to the servant, 'Go out	MASTER—GO
into the highways and hedges,	To Highways
and compel people to enter,	FILL UP HOUSE
that my house may be filled.'	

A time lapse occurs. The servant extends the master's gracious invitation to the outcasts of the village. As they enter the banquet hall the servant notices that there are still empty seats. Energized by the process, he reports to the master, "Sir, . . . still there is room."

Only then does the master give the order for the servant to go beyond the village to the highways and hedges, and "Compel people to enter." This last command is an important aspect of the cultural dynamic of the story, which has been misunderstood and misused for centuries. Augustine of North Africa invited the Latin military to force the Donatist churches into the Latin fold on the basis of this text, and the Spanish Inquisition used this text to justify its brutalities. The point the master is making is that he knows how the strangers on the highways will respond.

When an outsider, with no social status, is invited to a banquet in the home of a nobleman, the outsider has a very hard time believing that he is really wanted. On first exposure, grace is unbelievable. The recipient of the invitation will at once feel, *They don't really want me. Impossible! Look at who I am. The intent*

of the invitation is to impress me with the nobility of the master, but the invitation itself
is not serious.

The messenger who delivers such an extraordinary invitation will need some special way to convince the outsiders that they are indeed invited and wanted. Understanding this, the master suggests, "When they are reluctant, grab them by the hand and drag them in if you have to. I want you, by all means, to convince them that the invitation is indeed serious and that they are genuinely welcome and wanted at my banquet.

Ibn al-Tayyib writes:

> "Oblige them to come in." This does not mean compulsion or force or persecution, but refers to the strength of the need for urgent solicitation, because those living outside the town see themselves as unworthy to enter into the places of the rich and eat banquets. Such outsiders need someone to confirm that there is indeed a welcome awaiting them there.[10]

It has long been affirmed that the third round of guests symbolizes the Gentiles, who during Jesus' lifetime had not been approached. In the parable this last command is given, but the story stops before it is carried out. The parable fits historically into the life and ministry of Jesus.

When Paul and his friends go to the Gentile world with the message of the gospel, they are fulfilling a vision verbalized by Isaiah (Is 49:6) and reaffirmed by Jesus in this parable and elsewhere.

At the end of the parable, the Greek text uses the plural form for "you." The final phrase reads,

For I tell you (pl.),	
none of those men who were invited	THOSE INVITED
shall taste my banquet.	Not Taste of My Banquet

Throughout the parable the master speaks (in the singular) to his servant. The phrase, "For I tell you" is plural. The speaker is no longer the master in the parable but Jesus addressing the guests with whom he is eating. For Jesus, the messianic banquet has begun and that great banquet is *his* banquet. The religious leaders listening to him are welcome, but if they refuse to attend, the banquet will proceed with the "people of the land," the outcasts of Israel and will eventually be extended to the Gentiles.

Isaiah projected a time in which "foreigners who join themselves to the LORD" will be welcome on "my holy mountain" and their offerings

---

[10]Ibn al-Tayyib, *Tafsir al Mashriqi*, 2:257.

will be accepted on my altar;
for my house shall be called a house of prayer
for all peoples.
Thus says the Lord GOD,
who gathers the outcasts of Israel,
I will gather yet others to him
besides those already gathered. (Is 56:6-8)

This text is on Jesus' mind as he approaches Jerusalem; indeed he quotes the first part when he cleanses the temple. In this parable it is more than background music. Isaiah's vision of salvation (Is 56:1) was for three types of people: The first were the pious of Israel (who are just and righteous [v. 2]). Second, the outcasts of Israel (the eunuchs [v. 3]). And finally, he will gather "others to him besides those already gathered" (Is 56:8).

The parable of the great banquet builds on Isaiah's vision by affirming all three stages of ingathering. By rejecting Jesus the religious leadership was unable to shut down "his banquet." Jesus proceeded without them. The outcasts of Israel were welcomed, and finally the parable projects a vision that included those living outside the community in the "highways and hedges."

The Eucharist can be understood as a foreshadowing of the great banquet. At communion, believers are invited, in the present, to participate in the messianic banquet of the end time. We remember the past, celebrate in the present and look forward to the marriage supper of the Lamb. The parable assures the faithful that they already have a place at that banquet.

SUMMARY: THE PARABLE OF THE GREAT BANQUET

1. *Christology.* Jesus is the unique agent of God calling for participation with him in the banquet of salvation promised by Isaiah 25:6-9.

2. *Excuses.* The excuses people offer for refusing his invitation are insulting and unacceptable.

3. *Anger, suffering and costly love.* The experiential realities of anger, suffering and costly love are linked in the response of the master who takes the pain of his anger and reprocesses it into grace. Part of the theology of the cross is at the heart of this transformation of anger into grace.

4. *Now and the not yet.* The great banquet is inaugurated yet looks to the future.

5. *Grace.* A genuine invitation is extended to unworthy types from within and without the community. Special pleading is mandated for those outsiders who

will have a hard time accepting the authenticity of an invitation to accept grace.

6. *Mission.* Someone must take the good news of the open banquet to outcasts within and beyond the community. The invitation is limitless. It includes Israel, outcasts within Israel and foreigners beyond Israel's bounds.

7. *Vision for proclamation.* The obedient servant becomes a witness for his master and takes the invitation to the outcasts. This action on his part widens his vision and excites him. In the process he notes the empty tables and starts to fill them. His participation as a messenger of the generous invitation creates its own new vision and the will to participate in fulfilling it. Only after the servant's report does the master give the final command to reach beyond the community with the same gracious invitation. Was the master waiting to give the servant the opportunity to share with him in broadening the mandate of the banquet? Did the master think to himself, *I will give my servant time to grow into my larger vision because only then will it be his vision as well?*

8. *Response to the invitation.* Those who hear the good news must accept and enter the banquet hall or reject and stand aloof. Participation is not possible at a distance.

9. *Judgment.* Judgment is self-imposed. Those who refuse the invitation cut themselves off from the fellowship of the host and his guests. They choose not to taste the banquet.

Let's keep the feast!

25

The Parable of the Two Builders

OF ALL JESUS' PARABLES THIS ONE perhaps more than others has been reduced to a simple children's story. Western English-speaking churches have a simple song fashioned from the words of the parable. The song begins, "A wise man built his house upon a rock" and continues with, "A foolish man built his house upon the sand." The tune concludes with, "So build your life on the Lord Jesus Christ." This song has contributed to the ingrained assumption in the subconscious of many English-speaking Christians that this parable is a folkloric children's story.[1] But dynamite comes in small packages, and in context this parable creates powerful theological meaning. It is not by accident that it appears at the end of the Sermon on the Mount in Matthew 7:24-27 and holds the same prominent position at the conclusion of the Sermon on the Plain in Luke 6:46-49. However one understands the composition of those two famous collections, this parable was selected for special prominence. The reasons for that need to be investigated. The text in Luke 6:46-49 is presented in figure 25.1 (see p. 322).

THE RHETORIC

The parable uses step parallelism as a rhetorical structure. Three themes appear:

1. Hear/do

2. Building a house

3. The storm/flood and its results

The story moves through these three themes with a man who builds *with* a foundation and then repeats the same sequence with a man who builds *without* a foundation. When step parallelism is used as a rhetorical structure, the climax ap-

---

[1]Generally, modern commentators either omit this parable or confine themselves to a few brief remarks on it.

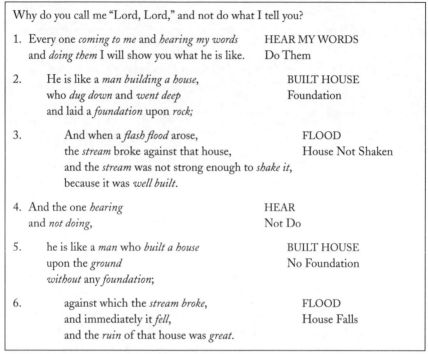

Figure 25.1. The parable of the two builders (Lk 6:46-49)

pears at the end of each series. This means that the storm and its effects on each of the houses form the climax of the parable.

COMMENTARY

The Gospels record this story in two different forms. In Matthew there is a comparison between a "wise man" who built on the "rock," and a "foolish man" who built on the "sand." In Luke, the issue is *foundation* versus *no foundation*. The version known and remembered across the church is the story in Matthew. The details of Luke's account are generally unnoticed. Yet the account in Luke has roots in a tradition that began with the prophet Isaiah. Luke's account is the focus of this chapter. The reasons for the differences between the two versions are beyond the scope of this brief study.

For the contemporary reader this parable has lost its initial impact. In the modern Western world a person who wants to build a house hires a backhoe to dig the foundation. Concrete for the foundation is delivered in a cement truck. Concrete blocks are lowered into the foundation with power equipment. Lumber and all building materials are delivered and unloaded with ease. Wall plaster comes in sheets and roofing in bundles, which are power-lifted onto the roof. The trusses are factory made to specification and are delivered and unloaded with power equipment. In spite of all this, building a house is still a strenuous task. By contrast, the time and energy required to build a house in ancient times was beyond anything builders in developed countries have experienced for centuries. The enormous effort required to build a house in the ancient world was more perfectly understood by Ibn al-Tayyib who began his reflections on this parable by saying, "Every Christian knows that building a house is not an easy endeavor. Rather it involves exhausting and frightening efforts, strenuous hardships, along with continuous and life threatening struggles."[2] Ibn al-Tayyib understood that in this parable Jesus was invoking a powerful metaphor. And there is more.

In Israel/Palestine villagers only build in the summer. The rains come in winter, and the ridge on which Jerusalem, Bethlehem and Hebron sit occasionally has snow. No one wants to build a stone house in winter. Summer provides dry, warm days suitable for building houses, but there is a down side. As mentioned in Leviticus, during the summer, the soil, with its high clay content, is "like bronze" (Lev 26:19 NIV).

It is easy to imagine a builder in summer, with little imagination or wisdom, thinking that he can build an adequate one-level house on hard clay. With his pick he tries digging and finds the ground is indeed "like bronze." The walls will not be more than seven feet high. It is hot. The idea of long days of backbreaking work under a hot, cloudless sky does not appeal to him. He opts to build his simple one- or two-room home on the hardened clay. The underlying rock is down there somewhere—it will all work out! He constructs a roof with a reasonable overhang and is pleased that he has managed to finish before the onset of the rains.

That winter, however, there is more rain than anyone can remember and the ground rapidly becomes soaked. A small runoff stream starts to flow down his street and the ground begins to turn into the consistency of chocolate pudding. The clay under the stone walls of his newly built house begins to settle and buckle as a result. The stones are uncut field stones. One stone after another pops out of the wall. A serious bulge develops in one wall. The bulge expands and finally gives way, bringing down the entire structure. First-century Middle Eastern villagers used mud for mortar.[3] If the wall is not built on the underlying rock, it will last

---

[2]Ibn al-Tayyib, *Tafsir al-Mashriqi*, ed. Yusif Manqariyos (Egypt: Al-Tawfiq Press, 1907), 2:118.

only as long as the ground under it remains dry and prevents settling. Such a scenario is believable and has happened.

The Friday, October 4, 1991, issue of the English-language weekly *In Jerusalem* (published in the Holy City) reported the collapse of an apartment complex in the Jerusalem suburb of Talpiot. The night of August 28, 1991, a third of the complex collapsed and twenty-eight families were forced to evacuate. After investigation it was discovered that a sewer line had leaked water under the collapsed third, which had been built on "loose soil" rather than "on the bedrock as is accepted practice." Interior walls buckled and a fourth floor bathtub fell into the third floor below it. "The destruction is massive and resembles that of a major earthquake" reads the report.[4] If the construction engineers had read Luke 6:46-49 before starting the building, they could have saved their company a great deal of money.

The prudent, hardworking builder knows better. In the Holy Land solid rock lies everywhere—just beneath the soil. If the builder plans a house in a valley, the earth and rubble may be ten or more feet deep. On the tops of the low hills the underlying rock is barely covered and often exposed. I have asked numerous village builders about the depth they must excavate to construct a stone house. The answer is always the same. They tell me they must dig "down to the rock." If that means one inch or ten feet, the principle remains the same. Building must be done *on the rock*.

But the parable of Jesus, as recorded in Luke's Gospel, is not a new set of images created by Jesus. Rather, these word pictures have a history that began with a parable dating from around 705 B.C. and is recorded in Isaiah 28:14-18. This text was examined in the introduction to this book, but for easy reference, I present it again (figure 25.2).

This example of what I have called the *prophetic rhetorical template* is as sophisticated and near perfect as any I have discovered in the entire Bible. There are seven inverted stanzas with a climax in the center. Stanzas 1 and 7 match each other with flawless precision. Inverted parallelism and step parallelism are woven together with great skill. The other matching stanzas are also finely crafted, and all of this was composed at the end of the eighth century B.C.[5] Why was such care given to the composition of this particular rhetorical piece?

Isaiah was addressing a nation facing an invasion. The dreaded Assyrian army

---

[3]In the first century, Roman builders had lime mortar, which was quite hard. Middle Eastern villagers traditionally used only mud for mortar.

[4]Gail Lichtman, "Improper Foundation Causes Building to Collapse in Talpiot," *In Jerusalem* 1, no. 18 (1991): 2.

[5]I have located seventeen cases of the use of this prophetic rhetorical template in Mark's Gospel alone.

Therefore *hear the word of the LORD*, you scoffers,
who *rule* this people *in Jerusalem*!

Because you have said,

1.	a. "We have made a *covenant with death*,	
	b. and *with Sheol we have an agreement*;	COVENANT MADE WITH
	c. when the *overwhelming scourge passes through*	Death, Sheol
	d. it will *not come to us;*	
2.	a. for we have made *lies* our *refuge*,	REFUGE
	b. and in *falsehood* we have *taken shelter*";	Shelter made
	therefore thus says the Lord GOD,	
3.	"Behold, I am laying in *Zion* for a *foundation*	BUILDING
	a *stone*, a *tested stone*,	Material
	a *precious cornerstone*, a sure *foundation:*	
4.	'He who *believes* [in it—LXX]	INSCRIPTION
	will *not be shaken.*'	
5.	And I will make *justice the line*,	BUILDING
	and *righteousness* the plummet;	Tools
6.	a. and *hail* will *sweep away the refuge of lies*,	REFUGE
	b. and *waters* will *overwhelm the shelter.*"	Shelter destroyed
7.	a. Then *your covenant with death* will be *annulled*,	
	b. and your *agreement with Sheol* will *not stand;*	COVENANT ANNULLED WITH
	c. when the *overwhelming scourge passes through*	Death, Sheol
	d. you will be *beaten down by it.*	

Figure 25.2. Isaiah's parable of the two builders (Is 28:14-18)

was approaching Israel and on the way was grinding up one little nation after another. The leadership of Israel had formed a mutual defense coalition with the Egyptians and felt confident that when the Assyrians arrived the Egyptian army would appear and save them. Isaiah was sure that their agreement with Egypt was worthless. The prophet delivered a stinging rebuke to the leadership in Jerusalem in the form of this parable. But along with that rebuke, he projected a hopeful future. The parable showcases two buildings: one is built and is doomed to fall. The other is only a future promise.

The Egyptians' entire worldview centered on death and the worship of the gods that governed death. In the opening stanza (1) Isaiah voices the confidence of his leaders who "have a covenant with death" (read: Egypt), and that they will be saved from the Assyrians as a result of that covenant. In stanza 7, Isaiah carefully composes a matching stanza that declares the total worthlessness of their covenant.

In stanza 2 Isaiah mocks the people by telling them that they have constructed a *refuge* and a *shelter* out of *lies*. In stanza 6 he predicts that a great storm will strike the *refuge/shelter* that they have built and will *destroy* it.

But all is not lost. The future is bright. God has not abandoned them, and one day he will lay "in Zion . . . a tested, . . . precious cornerstone, of a sure foundation" (3) and the one "who believes [in it] will not be shaken" (4). The building tools for the new building, to be constructed on that foundation, will be *justice* and *righteousness* (5).

To summarize, Isaiah had no confidence in the building they had built (the agreement with Egypt) and predicted that a great storm was on its way (Assyria). That storm would destroy their building, but in the future God would lay a new cornerstone in Zion that would be a sure foundation for a new building. The foundation would not be an ordinary rock but a gemstone. What happened to this dramatic parable?

Skipping ahead six hundred years we come to the writings of the Qumran community in the Jordan valley. These writings reflected Isaiah's parable, and in a document titled *Rule of the Community* the scribes wrote:

> In the Council of the Community there shall be twelve men and three Priests, perfectly versed in all that is revealed of the Law, whose works shall be truth, righteousness, justice, lovingkindness, and humility. . . . When these are in Israel, it shall be that tried wall, that precious corner-stone, whose foundations shall neither rock nor sway in their place.[6]

The pious of Qumran liked Isaiah's parable and claimed its promise for themselves. Their goal was to have a council of twelve men and three priests who knew the Law and had an impeccable record of good works. In their view once these fifteen men were in place, the great promise of God in the parable of Isaiah 28:14-18 would be fulfilled. Isaiah's promise was very real to them and they saw the possibility of its fulfillment within the walls of their settlement next to the Dead Sea. The authorities in Jerusalem, however, held a different view.

The Mishnah says, "After the ark was taken away a stone remained there from the time of the early prophets, and it was called 'sheteyah' [the foundation]. It was higher than the ground by three fingerbreadths. On this he used to place the fire-pan."[7]

---

[6]"The Community Rule," in *The Dead Sea Scrolls in English*, trans. Géza Vermes (Middlesex: Penguin Books, 1975), p. 85.
[7]Mishnah, *Mo'ed Yoma* 5:2 (Danby, p. 167).

This text discusses the ritual of the high priest in the temple in Jerusalem on the great Day of Atonement. In the middle of a twelve-hour liturgy on that solemn day, the high priest would enter the holy of holies carrying a large pan of burning charcoal covered with incense. In the center of the holy of holies there was a stone slightly elevated from the rest of the floor. On that stone he would "place the fire-pan." The stone was called "the foundation."

We are not told why this stone was given its name. No early Jewish commentary on Isaiah exists, but an educated guess can be built on what we know. For the Jews of the second temple the center of the holy of holies, with its raised stone, was the most sacred spot in the world, and that stone was "in Zion" at the center of the temple complex. Later Jewish reflection decided that the whole world was created from that sacred stone.[8] It appears that said stone at the center of the holy of holies was understood to be the fulfillment of Isaiah's promise that one day God would place a *precious stone*, a sure foundation in Zion. The Qumran community claimed that its fifteen righteous men would constitute the promised foundation. The temple leadership claimed the same promise for the central stone of its temple and called it "the foundation." The average Jew, loyal to the temple in the time of Jesus, surely knew that the authorities had named a raised stone in the center of the holy of holies "the foundation." It is also natural to assume that the complex of buildings around it, with its sacrificial system and rituals, was understood to be built on the foundation promised by Isaiah.

In such a world Jesus stood up and offered a third understanding of the way Isaiah's promise was being fulfilled. "To hear and to do my words," said Jesus, was to build on "the foundation" that Isaiah promised. In short, Jesus was saying, "I am the foundation stone, I am the *Sheteyah*. Build on me and my words and you will not be shaken. Isaiah's parable of the destroyed building and the promised new foundation is not fulfilled in Qumran or the second temple, but in me and my words."

Contrasts and comparisons appear when the two accounts are examined.

COMPARISONS

1. Each parable has two houses.

2. The water/storm symbol appears in both.

3. The foundation is a critical topic in each parable.

4. In both, people are called to "hear the Word."

---

[8]Tosefta, *Mo'ed Kippurim* (= *Yoma*) 4:14, vol. 2, *Moed,* trans. Jacob Neusner (New York: Ktav, 1981), 2:198.

5. Each is best understood as addressed to the individual and to the nation.

   a. Isaiah calls on the people to hear the word in light of the coming of Sennacherib and the Assyrians (c. 702 B.C.).

   b. Jesus is seen to be calling the nation to a new foundation in light of the coming conflict with Rome.

COMMENTARY

1. In Isaiah 28 the house that falls is a completed dwelling. The second structure is only a promised future foundation. In Luke 6 both buildings are built in the present.

2. Isaiah 28 calls on the reader to "hear the Word of the Lord." Jesus calls on his listeners to "hear and do my word."

3. Isaiah criticizes faith in the wrong thing, in Egypt and its gods. Jesus criticizes those who "hear and do not do my words."

Joachim Jeremias writes:

> The parables which deal with the impending crises were each uttered in a particular concrete situation, a fact which is essential for their understanding. It is not their purpose to propound moral precepts, but to shock into realization of its danger a nation rushing upon its own destruction, and more especially its leaders, the theologians and priests. But above all they are a call to repentance.[9]

Clearly, the parable of Jesus borrows some elements from Isaiah and rejects or reshapes others. These elements of similarity and dissimilarity show that Jesus' parable is based on Isaiah's parable. Like Isaiah, Jesus knew that a great storm was on its way in the form of the Zealot nationalists who were gathering strength, and cut off from reality they thought they could fight Rome and win.[10] Jesus foresaw disaster and knew that they would fail. The glorious house built as a dwelling place for God would be destroyed by a great storm of war with Roman forces. But, as in the case with Isaiah, all was not lost. Jesus offered himself and his words as a new foundation on which a new temple was already built and thereby affirmed that God's presence was among them in that temple, which was his body.

Throughout the New Testament there is witness to the astounding fact that a person had replaced a building. In faith and baptism believers in Jesus Christ be-

---

[9]Joachim Jeremias, *The Parables of Jesus* (London: SCM, 1963), p. 169.
[10]Marten Hengel, *The Zealots* (Edinburgh: T & T Clark, 1989), pp. 76-145.

come part of that temple. Writing at a time in which the temple in Jerusalem was intact and functioning, Paul told the Corinthians, "Do you not know that you are God's temple and that God's Spirit dwells in you?" (1 Cor 3:16).

This was not a new idea; Paul was enlarging on what Jesus had already taught in this parable. Mark affirms that the Holy Spirit was given to Jesus at his baptism (Mk 1:9-11). In our present parable (Lk 6:46-49), Jesus affirms himself and his words to be a sure foundation that would survive the coming storm of war with the Romans. His prediction proved to be true. But as he composed this great parable, Jesus drew on a second stream of prophetic insight.

Ezekiel composed a parable about a singer and his song. He encased that parable within a discussion of those "who hear—but do not do." Ezekiel 33:29-33, shown in figure 25.3, reads:

1. Then they will *know* that *I am the LORD*	
when I have made the *land a desolation* and a *waste*	THEN THEY
because of all *their abominations*	Will Know
which they have committed.	
2. "As for you, son of man,	
your people who talk together about you	
by the walls and at the doors of the houses,	
say to one another,	
each to his brother,	HEAR
'*Come*, and hear what *the word* is	The Word
that comes forth *from the LORD*,'	
And they come to you as people come,	
and they sit before you *as my people*,	
and they *hear your words*	HEAR
but they will *not do them*.	Not Do
For with their lips *they show much love*,	
but their *heart* is set *on their gain*.	
3. And, lo, *you* are to them like *a love song*	
sung by a *beautiful voice*	PARABLE
with a *well-played instrument*.	
4. For they *hear your words*	HEAR
but they do *not do them*.	Not Do
5. When *this* comes—and come it will!	
Then *they will know*	THEN THEY
that *a prophet* has been *among them*.	Will Know

Figure 25.3. Ezekiel's parable of the love song (Ez 33:29-33)

Although not symmetrical, the "ring composition" of this parable is evident. The word *this* in 5 unmistakably refers back to the devastation described in stanza 1. The theme of "hear and not do" appears in stanzas 2 and 4. The climax is the parable of the singer of love songs in the center. Ezekiel's words of warning were apparently offered in love, but sadly all the people heard was a love song sung by a beautiful voice. They chose to listen to his words but not to act on them. Jesus selects the language of "hear and not do" from this rhetorical piece, adds the imagery of Isaiah's parable of the building and the storm, and produces the account before us. This combination of two prophetic streams is accomplished with great theological, historical and rhetorical skill. Such an understanding of Jesus' parable may explain why the text appears as the conclusion of both the Sermon on the Mount in Matthew and the Sermon on the Plain in Luke. Dynamite does indeed come in small packages. Cut off from its context in Jesus' world and from the parables of Isaiah and Ezekiel, this parable has often become no more than a simple admonition to hear and do the words of Jesus. Such a view is not wrong. But Jesus can be seen here as making one of the most astounding affirmations of his entire ministry. In Islamic terms he is the new *Kaaba*. In Christian and Jewish terms, he is the foundation stone in the holy of holies of the third temple.[11]

SUMMARY: THE PARABLE OF THE TWO BUILDERS

1. The *foundation* on the rock is the person and words of *Jesus*. The listener/reader is called on to hear and do those words and by so doing to build on that foundation.

2. *Hearing and doing* are compared to the energy of digging through hard clay to the rock, and with danger and extraordinary risk and effort proceeding to build a house on it.

3. The storm hits both houses. Faith in Jesus does not provide magical protection from the storms of life. Rather, the parable promises that the house on the foundation will withstand the storms.

4. The Christology of the passage appears on two levels.

   a. Isaiah urges his readers to hear the Word of the Lord. Jesus calls on his listeners to hear and do *his word*.

   b. *Jesus* is the new foundation promised by God in Isaiah (not the temple or

---

[11]Paul continues with this same imagery in 1 Cor 3:10-17.

the priests and elders of Qumran). Indeed, a person has replaced a building.

A courageous Messiah declares boldly who he is and invites his listeners to hear and do his words and thereby find meaning and security in "the third temple," which will survive the coming storm.

26

The Parable of the Unjust Steward

LUKE 16:1-8

BY THE FOURTH CENTURY THE PARABLES of the unjust steward and the prodigal son were separated by a chapter division. If the monks who established those divisions had kept the two parables in the same chapter, the entire history of the interpretation of Luke 16:1-8 would be different. The two parables have a significant number of parallels. Among these are:

1. Each has a noble master who demonstrates extraordinary grace to a wayward underling.

2. Both stories contain an ignoble son/steward who wastes the master's resources.

3. In each the wayward underling reaches a moment of truth regarding those losses.

4. In both cases the son/steward throws himself on the mercy of the noble master.

5. Both parables deal with broken trust and the problems resulting from it.

These parallels suggest that the parable of the unjust steward needs to be examined in the light of what precedes it.[1] I am convinced that this parable continues to discuss theological themes that appear in the parable of the prodigal son. The subject is God, sin, grace and salvation—not honesty in dealing with money. T. W. Manson feels that the parable of the unjust steward "may almost be regarded as an appendix to the parable of the Prodigal Son."[2]

A DISTURBING STORY

The parable of the unjust steward has always been disturbing. Preachers, writ-

---

[1]For a more detailed discussion of this parable see Kenneth E. Bailey, *Poet and Peasant,* in *Poet and Peasant and Through Peasant Eyes* (Grand Rapids: Eerdmans, 1980), pp. 86-109.
[2]T. W. Manson, *The Sayings of Jesus* (1937; reprint, London: SCM, 1964), p. 291.

ers, interpreters and teachers of the Bible often avoid it like the plague. Superficially, the parable appears to present a story of a steward who cheats his master and is commended by Jesus for being a liar and a thief. In the fourth century, Julian the apostate used this parable as a primary text claiming that the parable taught Jesus' followers to be liars and thieves, and that noble Romans should reject all such corrupting influences. The parable's text is displayed in figure 26.1.

---

1. There was a rich man who had a steward,   MASTER
   and charges were brought to him   STEWARD
   that he was wasting his goods.

2. And he called him and said to him,
   "What is this I hear about you?   LOSES
   Turn in the account of your stewardship,
   for you can no longer be steward."

3. And the steward said to himself,
   "What shall I do, because my master
   is taking the stewardship away from me?   LOSES
   I am not strong enough to dig.
   I am ashamed to beg.

4.   I know what I will do,
       so that when I am put out of the stewardship   A SOLUTION
       they may receive me into their own houses.   Identified

5. So, summoning his master's debtors one by one,
   he said to the first, "How much do you owe my master?"
   And he said, "A hundred measures of oil."   GAINS
   And he said to him, "Take your bill,
   and sit down quickly and write fifty."

6. Then he said to another, "And how much do you owe?"
   And he said, "A hundred measures of wheat."   GAINS
   And he said to him, "Take your bill and write eighty."

7. Then the master commended the dishonest steward MASTER
   for his prudence.   STEWARD

For the sons of this age are wiser in their own generation than the sons of light.

Figure 26.1. The parable of the unjust steward (Lk 16:1-8)

THE RHETORIC

The outline of the parable is a *modified prophetic rhetorical template*. The classic seven stanzas appear but the inversion of the scenes does not follow the common 1-2-3-4-3-2-1 format. Instead, the second and third stanzas are on the same subject as is the case with stanzas 5 and 6. The climax in the middle occurs where the steward finally figures out how to proceed with his crisis. As in any well-told story, the listeners are not given the game plan, it simply unfolds before them. The parable uses two scenes to describe the problem (2-3) and two matching scenes (5-6) provide the solution. In the last scene the steward is praised (by the master in the parable) after he has cheated his master once again, and the listener/reader must discover the reason for the commendation. The verses that follow in Luke 16:9-13 display their own inner integrity and are best understood as a new paragraph.[3]

COMMENTARY

This parable is deeply embedded in Middle Eastern traditional culture, and it is to that culture that interpreters must turn. How would Jesus' listeners have heard this parable? And how would they have responded to it? The first scene says,

1. There was a rich man who had a steward,   MASTER
   and charges were brought to him   STEWARD
   that he was wasting his goods.

A rich man had a steward and charges were made against the steward for wasting the rich man's goods. Who brought these charges? We are not told, but the natural assumption is that the master's friends in the community told him not to trust his steward. If the reports were from other servants, the master would investigate further. Clearly, the reports are from sources that the master instinctively considers reliable.

From the existence of these reports, the listener learns that the master is respected in the community. There is no hint of any criticism of his character. If he were a rascal, the community would not bother to report the steward's wrongful activities. The first line of the parable reveals three kinds of people: the steward, his master and the community. To grasp the parable's thrust, the character of each needs to be understood.

In this parable the community is just off stage but is still an important part of what happens on stage. In the parables of Jesus, when there are two major characters and one is ignoble, the other is always noble. Both are never evil. In this case,

---

[3]Bailey, *Poet and Peasant*, pp. 110-18.

the steward is a liar and thief, but there is no hint that the master is dishonest. The two of them are not partners in crime.

In addition, any interpreter must decide whether the story is about bankers or farmers. The language presupposes a farming scene. It focuses on rents to be paid by tenants in the form of agricultural produce. The Greek word *oikonomos* (steward) can mean a manager of a farm or a banker's agent. Middle Eastern Arabic, Syriac and Coptic versions, however, have consistently translated this key word as "estate manager" not "banker." The story proceeds:

2. And he called him and said to him,
   "What is this I hear about you?   LOSES
   Turn in the account of your stewardship,
   for you can no longer be steward."

After being informed of the steward's dishonesty, the owner summons the steward and asks, "What is this I hear about you?" This question is a classic opener for such a confrontation. As Ibn al-Tayyib notes, the master is not seeking information.[4] The steward does not know what information has reached the master, and if the former panics on hearing this question he will no doubt give the master a great deal of new information. But this particular steward is too clever. Indeed, he has probably used this same technique with other servants. He knows the game and refuses to play. He responds to a direct order with complete silence.

After a few tense moments, the master realizes that although he cannot extract any new information from the steward, he already has enough reliable information to fire him. Accordingly, the master continues with, "Turn in the account of your stewardship for you can no longer be steward." The Greek word translated "account" has a definite article attached to it which means "the account books." The steward is not asked to "balance the books" but to "turn them in." In short, he is fired on the spot.

Drawing on rabbinic sources, George Horowitz summarizes the laws governing a master and his agent and writes:

> The appointment and powers of the agent may be revoked at any time with or without good cause, and whatever the agent does after revocation is not binding on the principle. It takes effect, however, only from the time that it is brought home to the agent or the person with whom he is dealing.[5]

In the story the master fires the agent in person, and from that point onward

---

[4]Ibn al-Tayyib, *Tafsir al-Mashriqi*, ed. Yusif Manqariyos (Egypt: Al-Tawfiq Press, 1907), 2:281.
[5]George Horowitz, *The Spirit of Jewish Law* (New York: Central Book, 1953), p. 542.

everything the steward does is illegal and thereby not binding on the master. The steward must relinquish the account books because he no longer has any authority for the workings of the estate. Yet the account books represent power and they are still in his hands. From this point on in the story the steward is an ex-manager who has the books but has been fired. These two facts are critical to the rest of the parable.

What did Jesus' listeners expect the steward to do? In a traditional setting in the Middle East, any person in authority over others does not expect to dismiss an ordinary servant, let alone a manager, without days of negotiation. As a first response the steward could say, "Beloved Master, I have served you. My father served your father. My grandfather served your grandfather. Surely you are not going to trash this beautiful three-generational relationship over a little misunderstanding over money!" Or he may offer, "This really isn't my fault. I have done my best, but I do not have a thousand eyes. I cannot watch everything. The people I work with are thieves." A third alternative might be, "Bring in these liars who tell you I am stealing. Let me confront them, and we will see if the cowards have the courage to repeat these lies in front of me!"

These and other well-known ploys are available to the steward, but he employs none of them. The last of his options is to send his influential friends in the community to visit the master and plead his case. The steward does not try any of these ploys because he knows that with this master such maneuvers will achieve nothing. East and West, silence is consent and in this story silence is a confession of guilt. It is also a confession regarding the nature of the master, who cannot be manipulated or pressured. Observing this indirect confession and unexpected retreat is fundamental to a more accurate understanding of the story.

The steward's silent acceptance of dismissal is stunning. For decades I have both observed and questioned Middle Easterners in positions of authority and have never seen or heard of a case of an underling, when dismissed, walking out of the room without pleading to be reinstated. Such behavior is unimaginable. Its theological significance must not be overlooked. From Adam onward, sinners, when confronted by God, never successfully offer excuses for the evil they have done, but like Adam they often try.

THE STEWARD RESPONDS

3. And the steward said to himself,
   "What shall I do, because my master
   is taking the stewardship away from me?   LOSES

I am not strong enough to dig.
I am ashamed to beg.

The next scene is a monologue by the steward who has been fired, although no one knows his status save the master. On his way to collect the account books, the steward says to himself, "What shall I do, because my master is taking the stewardship away from me?" He ruminates, "I am not strong enough to dig." That means that he cannot work as a laborer in the fields. Farming involves digging, which is necessary in preparing the soil for a new crop. Narrow terraces and sharp corners cannot be plowed, they must be dug. To his credit he considers such a menial task while admitting his physical limitations. He continues, "I am ashamed to beg." Not every one is. In addition to his sense of personal honor, he knows that he lacks the qualifications for begging that the community accepts (blindness, a broken back, loss of a limb, etc.). In short, he has a few redeeming qualities, which include a realistic appraisal of himself and some residual personal honor.

In the middle of reflecting on his "outcast state"[6] the light suddenly dawns as a new idea comes to mind. His soliloquy continues:

4. I know what I will do,
        so that when I am put out of the stewardship   A SOLUTION
        they may receive me into their own houses.   Identified

His declared goal is to be received into someone else's house. This phrase is an idiom that appears in the work of Epictetus, a first-century Greek Stoic philosopher, and means "to get another job."[7] He wants to manage somebody's estate, but how can he achieve such a goal?

The steward knows that anything he does with regard to the affairs of the estate is formally illegal, but the rest of the staff is not yet aware that he has been fired. He was dismissed in private and the books are still in his possession—but that will change quickly because he has been ordered to turn them in. He discovers that he has one last ace that he can play and with daring proceeds to play it. If he is simply fired for corruption, no one will hire him. In effect he says, "I am not the only thief in town. I know what I must do in order to be able to land on my feet when this unpleasant matter is finalized, and everybody finds out that I am fired. I must arrange an occasion that will demonstrate my shrewdness and at the same time make me popular."

---

[6]William Shakespeare, *Sonnets*, 29.
[7]Epictetus, "Concerning Those Who Are in Dread of Want," *Discourses* 25.2, *The Book of Epictetus*, ed. T. W. Rolleston, trans. Elizabeth Carter (London: Ballantyne Press, n.d.), pp. 207-8.

Being a clever rascal he dreams up a cunning scheme. His plan unfolds in scenes 5 and 6:

5. So, summoning his master's debtors one by one,
    he said to the first, "How much do you owe my master?"
    And he said, "A hundred measures of oil."   GAINS
    And he said to him, "Take your bill,
    and sit down quickly and write fifty."

6. Then he said to another, "And how much do you owe?"
    And he said, "A hundred measures of wheat."   GAINS
    And he said to him, "Take your bill and write eighty."

Ibn al-Tayyib notes that sin begets sin. After the servant is caught stealing, he should repent and reform his life. Instead he decides to steal more.[8] Following his preconceived plan, he does not go to his master's debtors. He summons them to come to him and is careful to talk to them individually. Naturally the steward orders the servants to inform the debtors that he, the steward wants to see them. The servants obey the steward's commands because they think he is still in authority over them. The debtors receive their summons and respond by going to the steward's office. They would not dream of appearing if they knew that he had been fired from his post. The very fact that the servants are still taking orders from him confirms (for the debtors) that the steward is still in command.

It is not harvest time. The summons can only mean that the master has some important information he wants the steward to communicate to them. Delegating the making of important financial decisions to underlings is not an assumed part of Middle Eastern culture. The debtors are confident that the steward has a message for them from the master.

These are precisely the assumptions that the steward wants the wealthy debtors to bring with them. On the debtors' arrival, the steward conducts private interviews, not a group meeting. Private interviews can be tailored to fit the various individuals, while a group meeting might spin out of control. In a group meeting the debtors could react to each other, and the steward's influence would wane. He wants to maintain control. Furthermore, as Ibn al-Tayyib suggests, he wants them to record the gifts that (they think) he has arranged for them. Ibn al-Tayyib writes:

> "Take your bill, sit down quickly and write fifty." This means, "Sit down before my master takes the bills from me, and write fifty instead of one hundred. And as for the extra fifty, they will be divided between the two of us after this is all over." Note that

---

[8]Ibn al-Tayyib, *Tafsir al-Mishriqi*, 2:282.

this steward should have safeguarded the rights of his master, but rather he does that which causes half of the debt to be lost in order to win the debtor as a partner with him in embezzlement so that in the future the debtor cannot lodge a complaint against him with the master.[9]

The steward's plan is astute, and Ibn al-Tayyib's reflections are brilliant. In honor-shame cultures, such as in the Middle East, a clear distinction is made between "public propriety" and "private awareness." Public propriety preserves personal honor. As regards "public propriety" the debtor's public stance is, "I had no idea that the steward was fired!" Publicly he can claim, "I thought the reductions were authorized by the master." Without the possibility of "public propriety" the debtors will not cooperate. They want to continue to rent land from the master. Privately, the debtor can accept a little deal that will enrich both the steward and himself. Ibn Al-Tayyib understands perfectly how such things work. He notes astutely that by cooperating in such a scam the debtor is surrendering the possibility of going to the master and telling him what has happened. Each conversation is private, and without witnesses, who can prove what was said? The steward knows exactly what he is doing.

The reason for haste is obvious. These little deals will not be possible once the steward surrenders the books to the master.[10] Having been ordered to turn them in, he dare not delay more than an hour or two.

When the steward asks the first debtor, "How much do you owe my master?" he is not asking for information. A Middle Eastern estate manager has the accounts in his possession. The question is the opening move in the discussion between the steward and the debtor to insure that they agree on the amount of indebtedness. If the farmer quotes the same figure that is written on the steward's documents, they can proceed. If not, the figure will need to be debated. In a world where documentary evidence is limited, few people can read and oral tradition is honored, such niceties must be observed.

The debts and the reductions are enormous. Fifty measures of oil was worth about five hundred denarii, which was the wage for a farm worker for a year and a half. The second renter receives roughly the same reduction even though the percentage is different. It is in the steward's interest to have the debtors do the writing. He wants the changes in their handwriting recorded so that anyone looking at the accounts will recognize the handwriting and know that the renters have been contacted and have accepted in writing.

---

[9]Ibid., 2:283.

[10]Hultgren's discussion is excellent. He misses the fact, however, that all of this has to take place in an hour or two. See Hultgren, *Parables of Jesus*, p. 153.

Each debtor makes the suggested changes in his rental agreement and returns to the village to share the "public" good news with family and friends. As word spreads in the village a festive mood breaks out in celebration of the most generous man who ever rented land in the history of the village and in praise of his steward who convinced the master to make huge reductions in their rents.

When the interviews are finished, the steward gathers the recently altered accounts and with a cat-that-ate-the-canary smile surrenders them to the master. The master takes the accounts, notes the changes recorded in the handwritings of his closest business associates and quickly considers his options. He is faced with two choices.

First, legally he can go to the village and explain that the reductions were not authorized, the steward had been fired at the time he made them, indeed he had no legal right to do anything, and the original amounts must be paid in full. But such an action would turn the party in progress that was praising his generosity, into a gripe session attacking him as unreasonable and unfair. Or, second, the master can remain quiet, pay the price of this clever rascal's salvation and continue to enjoy his reputation as a generous man, which is enhanced by this ruse but not created by it. He *is* a generous man because he dismissed the steward but did not jail him. Furthermore, he could have sold the steward and his family as slaves to recoup his losses, yet he did not. His generous nature led him to refrain from both actions.

In the light of the extraordinary grace that he had just received, the steward decides to risk everything on one roll of the dice. He builds his ruse on the basis of his unshakable awareness of the generous nature of his master. He "sins that grace might abound." As we will see, he is *condemned* for his action and *praised* for his confidence in his master's gracious nature.

The steward succeeds. The community will discover the details and will be amazed at his intelligence and daring. They will not trust him but will nonetheless employ him on the basis that such a clever fellow "must work for *us* and not *them*." Abraham Lincoln wanted those in opposition to him to work for him, not for his opponents. He also wanted to keep them in sight and under close scrutiny. He knew that they had ability. In our parable, the community will employ the steward for the same reasons. (After all—he did make them a lot of money—but don't breathe a word!)

The master pays the price of the steward's salvation and commends him for his mental agility.

7. Then the master commended the dishonest steward   MASTER
    for his prudence.   STEWARD
    For the sons of this age are wiser in their own generation than the sons of light.

The steward and the master become the heroes of the community. Having procured a huge economic windfall for the village, the community will find a place where the steward can be employed—and watched!

The master congratulates the steward for his cleverness and for the backhanded compliment he gives his master. The entire scheme is built on the steward's complimentary evaluation of the nature of the master. T. W. Manson summarizes the master's attitude: "There is all the difference in the world between 'I applaud the dishonest steward because he acted cleverly' and 'I applaud the clever steward because he acted dishonestly.'" Manson continues, "we must take the purport of the [final] speech to be: 'This is a fraud; but it is a most ingenious fraud. The steward is a rascal; but he is a wonderfully clever rascal.'"[11]

The parable is a "Tom and Jerry" story. The little mouse matches wits with the big cat and wins. The parable is built on the psychology of an oppressed peasantry, such as is known to have existed in Galilee at the time of Jesus. The steward is a Robin Hood figure, a countercultural hero. But at the end of the story, Jesus calls him "a son of this age/world." He is smart enough to know that his only hope is to put his entire trust in the unqualified mercy of his generous master. His morals are deplorable. Nonetheless, Jesus wants "the sons of light" to use their intelligence, like the dishonest steward, and to trust completely in the mercy of God for their salvation. The prodigal son made a similar decision.

SUMMARY: THE PARABLE OF THE UNJUST STEWARD

1. *The nature of God.* God is a God of justice, mercy and great personal integrity (honor). His sense of justice leads him to dismiss the rascal. His mercy is demonstrated in the decision to dismiss the servant rather than sell or imprison him for his thefts. It also shows in agreeing to pay the price for the servant's salvation. His integrity appears vis-à-vis the community's high regard for him and in his final dealing with the steward.

2. *The exposure of sin and its condemnation.* The coming of the kingdom brings a crisis. The steward's sins are exposed. Because of the master's nature, excuses for failures will not avail and the steward offers none. He is condemned as a "son of the world/age" because of his lies and his deceptions.

3. *The insidious nature of sin.* Once caught, the steward should have repented, reformed his life and tried to make amends. He did not do so, choosing instead

---

[11]Manson, *Sayings of Jesus,* p. 292.

to steal from his master, but in a bolder and more aggressive fashion. Sin breeds more and greater sin.

4. *The steward's intelligent perception.* The steward is not commended for his ethics (he is a son of this age/world) but for his accurate perception of his master's nature. He correctly reads his master. The steward experiences extraordinary mercy at the beginning of the story. He opts to risk everything in the confidence that this mercy and generosity are at the core of his master's identity. If he is wrong, he will lose everything, including the freedom of his family. His judgment regarding his master is confirmed. Jesus longs for his disciples to have the same informed perception of God.

5. *The steward's willingness to act.* The steward has the courage to act on his deepest perceptions. It is a huge risk but one he takes.

Julian was wrong. Jesus does not teach his disciples to lie and cheat. Using the psychology of an oppressed peasantry, Jesus creates a parable with profound theological and ethical resonances.

27

The Parable of the Pharisee and the Tax Collector

LUKE 18:9-14

THE MORE FAMILIAR A PARABLE, the more it cries out to be rescued from the barnacles that have attached themselves to it over the centuries. In the popular mind, the parable of the Pharisee and the tax collector is a simple story about prayer. One man prays an arrogant prayer and is blamed for his attitudes. The other prays humbly and is praised for so doing. Too often the unconscious response becomes, *Thank God, we're not like that Pharisee!* But such a reaction demonstrates that we are indeed like him! How can this parable best be understood? Is it strictly about styles of prayer?

No doubt humility in prayer is at the heart of the story, but in his introduction Luke tells his readers that the main focus of the parable is righteousness and those who believe they can reach that pious goal by means of their own efforts. The rhetorical structure of Luke 18:9-14 is shown in figure 27.1 (see following page).

THE RHETORIC

Within the introduction and the conclusion lie six scenes. In the first (1) two men "go up" to the temple to pray, and in the last (6) the same two men "go down," but the tax collector is the center of attention and the Pharisee is dismissed as "that one" rather than being referred to as "the Pharisee."

The center is composed around an A-B, A-B structure. The reader is told how the Pharisee stands and prays, and is then informed about how the tax collector stands and prays.[1]

---

[1]This is revised from Kenneth E. Bailey, *Through Peasant Eyes,* in *Poet and Peasant and Through Peasant Eyes* (Grand Rapids: Eerdmans, 1980), p. 142.

He also told this parable to some who trusted   (Introduction)
in themselves that they were righteous and despised others:

1.   *"Two men went up* into the temple *to pray,*   TWO GO UP
     one a *Pharisee* and the other a *tax collector.*   Pharisee and Tax Collector

2.   a. The Pharisee *stood by himself*   PHARISEE
            thus praying,   (His Manner)

3.   b. 'God, I thank thee because I am not like other men,
               extortioners, unjust, adulterers,   PHARISEE
               or even like this tax collector.   (His Prayer)
               I fast twice a week.
               I give tithes of all that I possess.'

4.   a. but the tax collector, *standing far off,*   TAX COLLECTOR
            would not even lift up his eyes to heaven,   (His Manner)
            but he beat upon his chest saying,

5.   b. 'God! Make an *atonement* for me,   TAX COLLECTOR
               a sinner!'   (His Prayer)

6.   I tell you, he went down to his house   ONE JUSTIFIED
     made righteous, rather than that one.   One Marginalized

For every one who exalts himself will be humbled,   (Conclusion)
and he who humbles himself will be exalted.

Figure 27.1. The parable of the Pharisee and the tax collector (Lk 18:9-14)

COMMENTARY

The narrative introduction to this parable should be taken seriously. Granted, it is interpretive in nature and is not part of the parable itself. But to dismiss it is to reject this apostolic signpost of what the parable is about and substitute our own twenty-first-century assumptions regarding its focus. Luke says this parable was directed toward certain people who considered themselves righteous and despised others.

What does it mean to be a righteous person? In the Greek and Hellenistic world *dikaios* was a general term that applied to a person who was civilized and who observed custom and legal norms.[2] Generally speaking, these meanings have placed their stamp on the popular understanding of a "righteous person," even today. Such a person maintains an admirable standard of morality, obeys the law and is known as a "decent person." But the Greek New Testament's roots are in the Old Testament

---

[2]G. Schrenk, "δίκαιος," *Theological Dictionary of the New Testament*, 10 vols., ed. Gerhard Kittel and Gerhard Friedrich, trans. Geoffrey W. Bromiley (Grand Rapids: Eerdmans, 1964-76), 2:182.

Hebrew, where righteousness is of supreme importance. Gerhard von Rad writes:

> There is absolutely no concept in the Old Testament with so central a significance for all the relationships of human life as that of *sadaqa* (righteousness). It is the standard not only for man's relationship to God, but also for his relationships to his fellows, . . . it is even the standard for man's relationship to the animals and to his natural environment.[3]

The righteous person is not the one who observes a particular code of ethics but rather a person or community granted a special *relationship* of acceptance in the presence of God. That relationship is maintained by acting in loyalty to the giver of the unearned status. Thereby, God's ṣĕdāqôt (righteousnesses) "means his saving acts in history."[4] Von Rad continues, "from the earliest times onwards Israel celebrated Jahweh as the one who bestowed on his people the all-embracing gift of his righteousness. And this ṣĕdāqâ (righteousness) bestowed on Israel is always a saving gift."

This understanding of God's righteousness, given as a gift, is set forth in Micah 6:3-5 which reads:

> O my people, what have I done to you?
> In what have I wearied you? Answer me!
> For I brought you up from the land of Egypt,
> and redeemed you from the house of bondage;
> and I sent before you Moses,
> Aaron, and Miriam.
> O my people, remember what Balak king of Moab devised,
> and what Balaam the son of Beor answered him,
> and what happened from Shittim to Gilgal,
> that you may know the ṣĕdāqôt [righteousnesses] of the LORD."

In the Revised Standard Version the word ṣĕdāqôt (righteousnesses) is rightly translated "saving acts." The prophet reflects on what might be an appropriate response to these mighty saving acts and decides that even thousands of rams and ten thousands of rivers of oil would not be adequate. The answer is that the Lord himself has shown them what he requires, which is

> to do justice, and to love kindness,
> and to walk humbly with your God. (Mic 6:8)

Behind this parable is the rich heritage of God's gracious gifts of saving acts (righteousness) and the call for a reflective response to that grace. Many around

---

[3]Gerhard von Rad, *Old Testament Theology* (New York: Harper & Row, 1962), 1:370.
[4]Ibid., 1:372.

Jesus no doubt were faithful to this prophetic heritage. But Jesus was also faced with some "who trusted in/by themselves that they were righteous and despised others." Such types, in any age, feel that they have earned God's grace through meritorious works. Their "self-righteousness" naturally leads them to despise others who do not put forth such efforts. The real focus of the parable, therefore, is not humility in prayer but how we are justified/made righteous before God.

THE PARABLE

The story begins, "Two men went up into the temple to pray." In English, we commonly use the word *pray* to refer to private devotion and the word *worship* to refer to what a community does together. In Semitic speech, whether Aramaic, Hebrew, Syriac or Arabic, "to pray" is used for both. On Sundays, the Christian in the Arab world says to his friend, "I'm going to the church to pray," and the friend knows the speaker is on his way to attend public worship.

In the parable a place of public worship is mentioned specifically, and two men are on their way to pray *at the same time*. What type of worship service is assumed by such language?

The only daily service in the temple area was the atonement offerings that took place at dawn and again at three o'clock in the afternoon. Each service began outside the sanctuary at the great high altar with the sacrifice for the sins of Israel of a lamb whose blood was sprinkled on the altar, following a precise ritual. In the middle of the prayers there would be the sound of silver trumpets, the clanging of cymbals and the reading of a psalm. The officiating priest would then enter the outer part of the sanctuary where he would offer incense and trim the lamps. At that point, when the officiating priest disappeared into the building, those worshipers in attendance could offer their private prayers to God.[5] An example of this precise ritual appears in Luke 1:8, where Zechariah had the privilege of offering up the incense in the sanctuary. Verse 10 states, "At the time of the incense offering, the whole assembly of the people was *praying* outside" (my translation).

Many pious Jews who were not at the temple would offer their private prayers at the time of day when they knew the incense offering was being made in the temple. In this way they could participate even when they were not able to be present.[6] This particular service afforded the opportunity for what we today

---

[5]The details of this service are carefully explained in the Mishnah, *Tamid* (Danby, pp. 582-89). A convenient summary is found in Alfred Edersheim, "The Morning and the Evening Sacrifice," in *The Temple: It's Ministry and Services as They Were at the Time of Jesus Christ* (London: Religious Tract Society, n.d.), pp. 152-73.

[6]See Judith 9:1, where Judith offers her private prayers at that precise time.

would call both public worship and private prayer. It is for this service that the Pharisee and the tax collector "go up" to the temple. The language of the text and what is known of the twice daily atonement sacrifice in the second temple assume such a setting.

THE PHARISEE

The Pharisee now steps to the center of the stage. The New Revised Standard Version's translation of what transpires reads, "The Pharisee, *standing by himself,* was praying thus, . . ." Earlier translations often state, "The Pharisee stood and *prayed thus with himself.*" Does he stand by himself or pray to himself? The flow of the Greek sentence means that the New Revised Standard Version is correct—he is *standing by himself,* praying. This more accurate translation indicates that he stands apart from other people while he attends the temple service.[7] He stands by himself because he is a Pharisee who does not wish to be defiled by "the great un-washed," whom he considers unclean. If he touches the clothing of someone who is ceremonially unclean, he becomes defiled. He must, therefore, stand apart. Ibn al Tayyib notes that those who see themselves as righteous fail to reflect on "their sins of the heart in the presence of God."[8]

Because he stands by himself (not praying to himself) he may well be praying aloud, as was common Jewish custom.[9] Such a voiced prayer would provide a golden opportunity to offer some unsolicited ethical advice to the "unrighteous" around him who might not have another opportunity to observe a man of his stratospheric piety! Most of us in our spiritual journeys have, at some time or other, listened to a sermon hidden in a prayer.

Translations of the Pharisee's prayer commonly read, "I thank you, God, that I am not like other men." In both verses 9 and 10, the Greek word for "other men/people" probably refers to the "people of the land," the unrighteous commoners despised by those who strictly observed the law, like this Pharisee. But is what follows really a prayer?

Prayer, according to the piety of first-century Judaism, was of three types:

- confession of sin

- thanks for bounty received

- petitions for oneself and for others

---

[7]Ibn al-Tayyib affirms the presence of a community of worshipers. See Ibn al-Tayyib, *Tafsir al-Mashriqi,* ed. Yusif Manqariyos (Egypt: Al-Tawfiq Press, 1907), 2:315.
[8]Ibid., 2:314.
[9]I. Howard Marshall, *The Gospel of Luke* (Exeter, U.K.: Paternoster, 1978), p. 679.

The Pharisee's prayer does not fall into any of these categories. He is neither confessing his sins nor thanking God for God's gifts, and he does not make any requests for help. His public remarks are an attack on others clothed in self-advertisement. He tells God that he despises extortioners, the unjust, adulterers and tax collectors. Rather than comparing himself to God's expectations of him, he compares himself to others. Having given God a short list of his views of the unrighteous, he proceeds to enumerate his ethical accomplishments and announces proudly, "I fast twice a week. I give tithes of all that I possess."

The Pharisees thought of the law as a garden of flowers. To protect the garden and the flowers, they opted to build a fence around the law. That is, they felt obliged to go beyond the requirements of the law in order to insure that no part of it was violated. Without a fence around the garden, someone just *might* step on one of the flowers. The written law only required fasting on the annual Day of Atonement. The Pharisees, however, chose to fast two days before and two days after each of the three major feasts. That meant twelve days a year. But this pious man announces to God (and others) that he puts *a fence around the fence!* He fasts two days *every* week.

The faithful in the Old Testament were commanded to tithe their grain, oil and wine. In New Testament times the standard laid down by the rabbis was, "A general rule have they laid down about Tithes: whatsoever is used for food and is kept watch over and grows from the soil is liable to Tithes."[10] The Mishnah tractate *Maʿaserot* (tithes) spells out all the possible exceptions that make such a blanket ruling easier to fulfill. The discussion continues for pages. But this Pharisee makes no exceptions, claiming simply, "I tithe all that I possess." Surely those listening to his "ad" would be impressed by such a high standard of righteousness. What then of the despised tax collector standing at the back?

THE TAX COLLECTOR

Sensing his defiled ceremonial status, the tax collector chooses to stand apart from other worshipers attending the magnificent atonement sacrifice for the sins of Israel.

The accepted posture for prayer in the temple was to look down and keep one's arms crossed over the chest, like a servant before his master.[11] But the tax collector is so distraught over his sins that he beats his chest where his heart is located.

In the Middle East, generally speaking, women beat their chests, men do not. Occasionally, women at particularly tragic funerals beat their chests. In the Bible,

---

[10]Mishnah, *Maʿaserot* 1:1 (Danby, p. 66).
[11]Edersheim, *Temple, Its Ministry & Services*, p. 156.

the only other case of people beating their chests is at the cross when the crowds, deeply disturbed at what had taken place, beat their chests at the end of the day just after Jesus died (Lk 23:48). Presumably, on that occasion both men and women were involved. If it requires a scene as distressing as the crucifixion of Jesus to cause men and women to beat their chests, then clearly the tax collector of this parable is deeply distraught! The only time I have seen or known of Middle Eastern men beating their chests is at the Shiite Muslim yearly commemoration of the murder of Hussain, the founder of their community. What does the tax collector say as he engages in this extraordinary act?

English translations usually render the tax collector's speech with the words "God, be merciful to me, a sinner." But this text does not use the common Greek word for "mercy," which is *eleeō*. Instead, the verse presents the word *hilaskomai*. This great theological term means to "make an atonement." The classical Armenian translation made in the Middle East in the fourth century reads, "O God, make an atonement for me." A few verses later the blind man beside the road cries out to Jesus, "Jesus, Son of David have mercy on me *[eleēson me]*." The latter word, *eleeō*, appears in many Eucharistic liturgies. Because Luke is familiar with both words, it is natural to assume that the tax collector's request is different from the cry of the beggar.

There is no apparent reason to deny the word *hilaskomai* its full weight and translate the tax collector's request as, "O Lord, make an atonement for me."[12] Both the Pharisee and the tax collector are standing in front of the great high altar on which a lamb, without blemish, has just been sacrificed for the sins of Israel. The tax collector stands far off, apart from the worshipers gathered around the altar, and watches the sacrifice of the lamb. He listens to the blowing of the silver trumpets and the great clash of the cymbals, hears the reading of the psalm and watches the blood splashed on the sides of the altar. He sees the priest disappear inside the temple to offer incense before God. Shortly afterward, the priest reappears announcing that the sacrifice has been accepted and Israel's sins washed away by the atoning sacrifice of the lamb. The trumpets blow again, and the incense wafts to heaven. The great choir sings, and the tax collector, distraught and beating his chest, stands far off and cries out, "O Lord, make an atonement *for me*, a sinner!"

Jesus then declares, "I tell you, he went down to his house *made righteous/saved*, rather than that one." Going down from the temple, the Pharisee is downgraded from

---

[12]Craig L. Blomberg, *Interpreting the Parables* (Downers Grove, Ill.: InterVarsity Press, 1990), p. 258. Arland Hultgren notes the verb "to make an atonement" but feels that the passive tense drains that meaning out of the word. See Arland J. Hultgren, *The Parables of Jesus* (Grand Rapids: Eerdmans, 2000), p. 124.

"the Pharisee" and is referred to dismissively, as "that one." One man goes to the temple for worship confident that his pious achievements guarantee his status as one of the righteous. The tax collector, who feels that the lamb could not possibly have atoned for *his* sins, is the one whom Jesus pronounces *justified/accepted* in God's presence.

The Gospel of John intensifies the theology of this parable with Jesus' affirmation as "the Lamb of God, who takes away the sin of the world" (Jn 1:29). But here Jesus confirms the atonement sacrifice as being at the center of his theology.

The concluding statement at the end of the parable is:

For every one who exalts himself will be humbled,
and he who humbles himself will be exalted.

This wisdom saying appears in a variety of places in the Scriptures (Mt 18:4; 23:12; Lk 14:11; 1 Pet 5:6). The meaning is not so much related to humility or pride in human society, but before God, who throughout Scripture shows compassion to the meek and humble while rejecting the arrogant. God exalts the sinner in his presence through the atonement sacrifice.

Again and again in his teaching Jesus presents the theme of the "righteous," who do not sense their need for God's grace, and the "sinners" who yearn for that same grace. This parable is an important part of that larger collection of teachings on this subject. Sin for Jesus is not primarily a broken law but a broken relationship. The tax collector yearns to accept the gift of God's justification, while the Pharisee feels he has already earned it. As Joachim Jeremias has written regarding this parable, "Our passage shows . . . that the Pauline doctrine of justification has its roots in the teaching of Jesus."[13]

ISAIAH 66:1-6

There is, as well, another aspect of the parable that, to my knowledge, has not been considered. In his parables Jesus often adopts an Old Testament theme and develops it. The parable of the good Shepherd in Luke 15:4-7 can best be understood as a retelling of Psalm 23.[14] The parable of the prodigal son contains fifty-one points of similarity and contrast to the story of Jacob in Genesis 27:1—36:8.[15] The parable of the two builders in Luke 6:46-49 is profoundly related to Isaiah 28:14-18.[16] In like manner, this parable can be seen as having roots in Isaiah 66:1-6, the text of which is shown in figure 27.2.

[13]Joachim Jeremias, *The Parables of Jesus* (London: SCM, 1963), p. 114.
[14]Kenneth E. Bailey, *Finding the Lost: Cultural Keys to Luke 15* (St. Louis: Concordia Press, 1992), pp. 54-92.
[15]Kenneth E. Bailey, *Jacob and the Prodigal* (Downers Grove, Ill.: InterVarsity Press, 2003).
[16]See above part 6, chap. 26.

Thus says the L<small>ORD</small>:

1. "*Heaven* is my throne
       and the *earth is my footstool*;
   what is the house which you would *build for me*,   GOD REJECTS
       and what is the *place of my rest?*   The Temple
   All these things *my hand has made*,
       and so *all* these things *are mine*,
           says the L<small>ORD</small>.

2.   But this is *the man* to whom *I will look*,   I LOOK AT THE POOR
       he that is *poor* and *contrite in spirit*,   Trembling at My Word
       and *trembles at my word*.

3.   He who *slaughters an ox*
               is like him who *kills a man*;
           he who *sacrifices a lamb*,   PARABLES OF
               like him who *breaks a dog's neck*;   Sacrifices and
           he who presents a *cereal offering*,   Offerings
               like him who *offers swine's blood*;   As Evil
           he who makes a memorial offering of *frankincense*,
               like him who *blesses an idol*.

4.   These have *chosen* their *own ways*,
           and their soul *delights* in *their abominations*;
               I also will *choose affliction* for *them*,   THEY CHOSE EVIL
               and bring their *fears upon them*;   I Choose Judgment
               because, when *I called, no one answered*,   They Do Not Listen
               when *I spoke they did not listen*;   They Choose Evil
           but *they did* what was *evil in my eyes*,
           and *chose* that in which *I did not delight*."

5.   Hear *the word of the L<small>ORD</small>*,   YOU WHO
           you who *tremble at his word*:   Tremble at His Word
       "*Your brethren* who *hate you*
           and *cast you out* for *my name's sake*   YOUR OPPRESSORS
       have said, 'Let the L<small>ORD</small> be glorified,   Shall Be Shamed
           that we may see your joy';
           but it is *they who shall be put to shame*.

6. Hark, an uproar from the city!
   A voice from the temple!
   The *voice of the L<small>ORD</small>*,   GOD SPEAKS JUDGMENT
   rendering *recompense to his enemies!*"   From the Temple

Figure 27.2. Isaiah 66:1-6

RHETORICAL STYLE

Ring composition appears again. Three stanzas are presented before being re-peated backward. Specific references to the temple appear at the beginning (1) and at the end (6). The man who is "poor and contrite in spirit," who "trembles at my word" (2), is clearly the hero of this prophetic homily. That same person in stanza 5 is identified as hated and cast out "for my name's sake," and told that he will be vindicated. A blistering attack on the person who offers sacrifices appears in the climactic center in stanza 3, and in stanza 4 the reason for the attack is given: "be-cause, when I [God] called, no one answered."

The prophet's anger is triggered by the presence of "sacrament" without "word." The rituals are rejected if, "when I [God] called, no one answered," and "when I spoke they did not listen." In passing, it is worth noting that this passage is prominent elsewhere in the New Testament. Stanza 1 is quoted in Stephen's speech in Acts 7:49-50 and indirectly referenced in the Sermon on the Mount in Matthew 5:34-35. What of the relationship between this prophetic homily and the parable of the Pharisee and the tax collector?

ISAIAH 66 AND THE PARABLE

When compared to the parable of the Pharisee and the tax collector, the following similarities and differences between the two texts are apparent:

Similarities

1. Each is set in the temple.
2. Each deals with a person who is shut out.
3. In both, the person who is shut out is the hero of the story.
4. Both contain arrogant people who shut others out and feel that they are serv-ing God by so doing. Considerable self-righteousness is condemned in both accounts.
5. Each mentions sacrifices in the temple.
6. Each has a pious man in awe/fear before God (one trembles, the other beats his chest).
7. Each has an individual who chooses that in which *he delights* rather than choosing that which *pleases God*.
8. In both the sacrifice itself is not enough without a contrite spirit which in both cases is praised.
9. There is judgment in each.

Contrasts

1. Isaiah's language is extremely harsh. By comparison, the parable is much softer. Various voices in the contemporary scene have criticized the parable as being anti-Jewish.[17] But strangely, the same criticism is not leveled against Isaiah 66. Jesus appears to be saying, "Sacrament without word is inadequate. But Isaiah's imagery is too aggressive and must be replaced."

2. In Isaiah, sacrifices are not under attack but instead the inadequacies of the one who makes them are (stanza 3). The reason for this attack is specified in stanza 4 where Isaiah condemns the failure to hear and answer God. The apparent assumption is that the sacrifices are enough and that listening to and obeying the Word is unnecessary. Up to this point the two texts are similar. The difference between them is that in Isaiah the entire cult system is under discussion while the parable mentions only the atonement sacrifice.

3. Judgment is pronounced in each account. Yet this theme is dealt with differently in the two texts. Judgment in Isaiah is bold and harsh. The Pharisee is judged indirectly in that he goes down to his house unjustified. Judgment results from his own failures; not from an overt act of God to bring "recompense to his enemies."

Observing these similarities and differences it is possible to conclude that the parable is a brilliant update of the theological content of the prophetic homily of Isaiah 66 by means of selection, expansion and conversion into a parable by Jesus of Nazareth. Such comparisons allow us to see Jesus as an extremely intelligent, metaphorical theologian who was a master of the Hebrew Scriptures and who developed significant aspects of his theology from the roots of his own tradition.

By way of summarizing the parable and its parallels with Isaiah 66, the following points can be made:

SUMMARY: THE PHARISEE AND THE TAX COLLECTOR

1. *Righteousness.* A right relationship with God (righteousness) is a gift from God that comes through atonement and cannot be achieved by observance of the law alone.

2. *Atonement.* God's offered grace through sacrifice cannot be received by the worshiper who is arrogant, judgmental and self-satisfied.

---

[17]See B. B. Scott, *Hear Then the Parable* (Minneapolis: Fortress, 1989), pp. 93-98; Eta Linnemann, *Jesus of the Parables* (New York: Harper & Row, 1964), p. 58.

3. *A pattern for prayer.* Informing God in a self-congratulatory manner of one's "virtues" is not prayer. A humble yearning for God's unearned grace is an authentic aspect of genuine prayer. As Ibn al-Tayyib notes, the Pharisee talks as if there were no righteous person on earth as noble as he, while the tax collector prays as if there were no sinner on earth as evil as he.[18]

4. *The perversion of perception.* Self-righteousness distorts visions of self, God and the neighbor.

5. *The recipient of the sacraments.* Only those who sense their unworthiness in the presence of God's offered grace can approach God's holiness and appropriately receive that grace.

6. *The critical linking of Word and sacrament.* As in Isaiah 66:1-6, hearing the voice of God and obedience to that voice (Word) is linked to the sacraments. John 6:40, 54 make the same linkage. Whenever Word and sacrament are separated and one or the other is neglected, serious problems result.

---

[18]Ibn al-Tayyib, *Tafsir al-Mashriqi,* 2:315.

28

The Parable of the Compassionate Employer

MATTHEW 20:1-16

THIS PARABLE HAS LONG BEEN CALLED the parable of the workers in the vineyard. Such a title assumes that the workers are the focus of the parable. The same confusion reigns with the parable in Luke 15:11-32, which has traditionally been called the parable of the prodigal son, as if the wayward younger son were the central figure in the parable rather than the father. The central focus of this story is the amazing compassion and grace of the employer, rather than the employees. I prefer to call this story the parable of the compassionate employer, for throughout the day this vineyard owner demonstrates sensitivity and compassion for the unemployed. That deep concern is then augmented by his generosity at the end of the day. Ring composition is once again used in the construction of the parable, which can be seen in figure 28.1 (see following page).

THE RHETORIC

This parable uses the classical template of seven stanzas that exhibits ring composition. I have called this the *prophetic rhetorical template*. It was at least a thousand years old in the Hebrew tradition at the time this parable was told/written. The first three stanzas relate to the last three in an inverted manner and a special point of emphasis appears in the center.

Three huge surprises surface in the center (4). To the reader's shock, a steward suddenly walks on stage. The reader wonders why he was not involved all through the day. Second, the master opts to pay everyone a living wage, and finally, the master deliberately reverses the natural and expected order of payment.

The relationships between the center and the outside are strong and clear. The living wage was known to be one denarius per day, such as was offered in stanza 1.

For the kingdom of heaven is like

1. A *householder* who *went out early* in the morning
   to *hire laborers* for his vineyard.   AGREEMENT
   After agreeing with the laborers for a *denarius* a day,   Made
   he sent them into his vineyard.

2.   And *going out* about *the third hour*
       he *saw others* standing *unemployed* in the market place;
       and to them he said,   I GIVE
       "You go into the vineyard too,   Justice
       and *whatever is right/just* I will give you."
       So they went.
       Going out again about the *sixth hour*,
       and the *ninth hour* he did the same.

3.   And about the *eleventh hour he went out*
         and found *others standing*;
         and he said to them,   ELEVENTH
         "Why do you stand here *unemployed* all day?"   Hour
         They said to him,
         "Because no one has hired us."
         He said to them,
         "You go into the vineyard too."

4.   And when evening came,
           the *lord of the vineyard* said to his *steward*,   *THE*
           "Call the laborers and pay them—*the wage*,   *Wage*
           beginning with the last, up to the first!"

5.   And when those came   ELEVENTH
         who were hired about the *eleventh hour*   Hour
         each of them received a *denarius*.

6.   Now when *the first came*,
       they thought they would receive more;
       but each of them also received a denarius.
       And on receiving it they *grumbled* at the householder, saying,
       "These last worked only *one hour*,
       and you have made them equal to us   WHERE IS
       who have borne the burden of the day   Justice?
       and the *scorching heat*."

7. But he replied to one of them,
       "*Mister*, I am doing you *no injustice;*
         did you not agree with me for a denarius?
           Take *what belongs to you*, and leave.
             I choose to give to this last as I give to you.
           Am I not allowed to do what I *choose*   AGREEMENT
         with *what belongs to me*?   Kept
       Or is your eye evil
       because I am good?"
       So the last will be first, and the first last.

Figure 28.1. The parable of the compassionate employer (Mt 20:1-16)

The master's decision to pay that wage to all his workers appears in the center in stanza 4 and at the end in stanza 7, where he defends his grace-filled decision.

The final stanza is constructed with an additional example of ring composition. The matching themes are:

I do justice
  You agreed
    What belongs to you
      I am free to choose
    What belongs to me
  Your eye evil?
I am good

The rhetoric of this text includes a prophetic rhetorical template within a prophetic template.

This counterpoint, this enfolding of a rhetorical form within a larger rhetorical form, is as old as the Isaiah 28 passage examined in chapter 25. The structure of the final stanza argues for its place in the original composition of the text.

Serious reflection on the parable requires the reader to observe and contemplate the seven scenes, their inverted order, the threefold climax at the center and the special tie that unites the center to the introduction and the conclusion.

COMMENTARY

In the parable a vineyard owner rather oddly hires workers five different times in one day and as the sun sets pays them all the same wage. Those hired early in the morning complain and the owner (now called the "master") replies to their complaints. What is the story all about?

In its Middle Eastern setting, as a minidrama the parable is filled with questions, surprises and passions. But the ending is missing. Do the complaining employees obey the master's command by taking their pay and leaving, or do they opt to continue shouting at him demanding more? We are not told, just as we do not know what the older son will do at the conclusion of the parable of the prodigal son (Lk 15:24-31) or what will happen to the good Samaritan when he walks out of the inn (Lk 10:25-37).

The owner of a vineyard needs extra workers. Either the vines need pruning or it is harvest time. He heads for a special corner of the village market where those without steady work assemble each day hoping for a job—any job, even for a day.

This ancient custom survives to the present. I have observed it in a number of places in the Middle East. One of the most striking locations is just north of the

Damascus Gate in East Jerusalem. In quieter days, in the recent past, unemployed Palestinians gathered each morning at a spot on a major road. Employers, usually Israelis, would pull up in vans. As the vans approached, five to ten young men would rush into the street to see how many men the employer wanted, hoping to be selected. I usually looked the other way when I passed, trying not to think about the humiliation those young men suffered and the quiet desperation that their presence reflected.

Returning to the story, in the first scene the vineyard owner appears at the unemployment corner of the market, selects some workers and offers them the standard wage of one denarius for a day's work. The workers accept his proposal and head off to do the best they can in the hope that by the end of the day they will be hired for a second day or perhaps longer.

Halfway through the morning the owner returns to the market. He finds other unemployed men who are standing, not sitting. They are alert and eager, still hopeful that they will be chosen by someone, anyone. Those who stand, are somewhat like runners expectantly awaiting the start of a race. If a potential employer appears they will leap into the street and thus have a better chance of being hired.

The master makes a second selection, but does not quote a pay scale. He says only, "What is just/right *[dikaios]* I will pay you." The men trust him and accept his terms, no doubt rejoicing that they have escaped further public humiliation and that they will have something for their families at the end of the day. Clearly, the vineyard owner is respected in the community and trusted by the day laborers. But why is the vineyard owner there?

Surely a well-organized vineyard owner would know how much work needed to be completed that day and could figure out how many workers the task required. There is no hint in the story that this vineyard owner is young or inexperienced. Why then does he spend the day returning every three hours to the market to hire new staff? A variety of options has been suggested and are conveniently summarized by Arland Hultgren.[1] None of these options focus on what appears to me to be the master's driving motive—which is *compassion* for the unemployed. He saw many eager, unemployed men at the beginning of the day and selected some of them hoping, for their sakes, that the others would soon be engaged by someone else. Three hours later he decided to check to see what had happened. On arrival at the unemployment corner he found many still waiting, and the early morning scene was repeated. He selected a few and (presumably) offered some word of en-

---

[1]Arland J. Hultgren, *The Parables of Jesus* (Grand Rapids: Eerdmans, 2000), p. 37.

couragement to the others that they also would soon be selected. By noon he was confident that the rest would have found work or gone home, but he wanted to see for himself and so returned, only to find a sad crowd. He hired more men. By 3:00 p.m. his compassion compelled him to check the unemployment corner yet again in the hope that it would be empty. To the master's amazement and dismay it wasn't, so he hired a few more workers, perhaps to reward the raw courage of those who remained.

Each time the men are told (so the story affirms indirectly) that the master will be *just* with them as well. The question, What is justice? is thus raised three times in succession but not answered. What is justice for an unemployed man, eager to work, who does everything in his power to find a job? What about those who are willing to stand in a public place all day long and endure the humiliating (or pitying) glances of the financially secure?

Finally, one hour before sundown, the master returns to the market for a fifth time, where he finds some deeply depressed workers who have been standing *all day*. The master assumes that surely by an hour before sundown all the unemployed will have given up and returned home. (The Palestinian laborers outside the Damascus Gate are gone by noon.) What is the use of continuing to stand, eagerly awaiting what by then is surely a hopeless hope?

All that remains for the brave few left in the market is the humiliation of returning home to an anxious wife and hungry children with the bad news of another day of frustration and disappointment. Why had these last men not given up and left their place of public psychic torment?

When asked why they are still standing there, the unemployed have a simple answer: "No one has hired us!" That is, "We are eager to work, willing to work, ready to work, able to work and we will not give up! We will stand here until the light fades and go home in the dark if we have to."

The master does not say to them, "Here, each of you take a *denarius* and buy some food for your families!" He refuses to humiliate them further by placing them on relief. Instead, he gives them the one thing they so desperately want—a job. There is no promise to pay them anything, and yet they accompany him. They had watched him return to the market repeatedly throughout the day and understood instinctively why he was there. No doubt they sensed that he was responding compassionately to their public humiliation and their determination to maintain their self-worth in spite of that humiliation.

By the end of the day five different groups of workers are busily employed. The first group has a "contract." They were promised a specific amount—one denarius each for a day's work. During the day three other groups were promised an un-specified "justice" in the pay scale. The last group was promised nothing and no doubt wondered what they might receive. Perhaps they were on trial and the master would pay them nothing. They did not merely trust what the owner said (or didn't say), they trusted the man himself.

Suddenly, the first of three big surprises takes place. Amazingly, an estate manager walks on the stage! If such a person was on the owner's staff, why wasn't he doing the footwork at the market throughout the heat of the day? Why wasn't the manager left to do the managing?

The second surprise bursts immediately on the heels of the first. The owner, now called the master *(kyrios)*, tells the steward, "Call the workers and pay them *the wage.*" For a thousand years Arabic versions have preserved this precise language that appears in the original Greek text. The steward is instructed to pay "the wage," which is a full day's pay!

The third surprise has to do with the order of payment. Those who came last are paid first and receive a full day's wage. The order of payment is dictated by the master who must have important reasons for choosing it. He knows that this is not the natural order his "pay master" would select. If he paid the agreed upon denarius to the first group they would receive their wages and leave, proud of the fact that they worked for and received a full day's wages. Each group, in turn, would have been amazed at receiving the same wage and would have left, delighted beyond words. In short, such an order of payment would have left everyone pleased and there would have been no angry shouting around the steward's pay table. Why cause unnecessary trouble? Obviously, the master wants those who had worked all day to observe the grace that he extends to the others.

The reader can sense the rising tension in the first group as they observe what is happening with the other four categories of workers. They suffer a series of shocks. First, they see the "one hour workers" receive a full day's wages. Then they note that the "three hour workers" did not receive more. The same would happen with the "six hour workers" and they would grow agitated expecting that surely the "nine hour workers" would be given at least a 50 percent increase over the others. When it doesn't happen, their anxiety starts to turn to anger. The climax comes when they are paid and discover that they received what were promised, but no more!

"Equal pay for equal work" is a centuries-old understanding of justice. But that is not the issue here. This parable presents the overpaid, not the underpaid. The story focuses on an equation filled with amazing grace, which is resented by those who feel that they have earned their way to more. Finally, the spokesman for the twelve-hour workers voices their complaint.

"Not fair!" shouts the leader. "We should receive more." This is not the cry of the *underpaid*. No one is underpaid in this parable. The complaint is from the justly paid who cannot tolerate grace! "You have made them equal to us!" they shout angrily, like the older son complaining to his father about the grace given freely to the prodigal! "This unemployed scum—whom no one else would hire—you have made *equal to us*. We worked all day and endured its scorching heat and wind!"

To their market-oriented minds, their worth as human beings is directly related to how much they are paid. Grace is not only amazing, it is also—for certain types—*infuriating!*

The master addresses the angry workers' spokesman. He does not call him "friend" *(philos)* but rather *hetairos*, which was "a general form of address to someone whose name one does not know" and is a polite title for a stranger.[2] Early Arabic versions often translate this word, *ya sah*, which can be roughly translated, "You who are doing the shouting." The master's reply can be paraphrased:

> You have no complaint! Justice is served! I have given you what I agreed to pay you. You are free to do what you like with what is yours! And I am free to do what I like with what is mine! I *chose* to pay these men a living wage. You will be able to go home to your wives and children and proudly announce that you found work and have a full day's pay. I want these other men to be able to walk in the doors of their houses with the same joy in their hearts and the same money in their pockets. I want their children and wives to be as proud of them as yours are of you.
>
> So you worked through the heat of the day, did you? That's fine. And what do you think *I* was doing during the heat of the day? Enjoying a traditional siesta? I was on the road to and from the market—trying to demonstrate compassion to others who, like you, are in need of employment. I could have sent my manager to do this. I didn't! I went myself to demonstrate solidarity with the men and help alleviate their suffering. Why are you jealous of them and angry at me? You must understand that I am not only *just*—I am also *merciful* and *compassionate*, because mercy and compassion are a part of justice! Have you never read the servant songs of the prophet Isaiah?
>
> On what basis should the grace I show others irritate you? It appears that you do not care whether or not they can preserve their self-worth or feed their families. You want to take more for yourselves. I have chosen to give more of myself. You want to be richer at the end of the day. I have chosen to be poorer at the end of the day. Don't try to control me! Take your *just wage* and get out!

---

[2] W. Bauer, *A Greek-English Lexicon of the New Testament* (Chicago: University of Chicago Press, 1979), p. 314.

With the master's final speech the story abruptly stops. It does not end—it stops. Just as in the parables of the prodigal son, the good Samaritan and many other stories told by Jesus, time and again the audience is placed on the stage and all listeners must finish the drama in the nitty-gritty of their own lives.

The final wisdom saying at the end states, "The last will be first, and the first last," which reflects what has just happened in the story. This statement can be seen as a different form of the comment at the end of the parable of the lost sheep (Lk 15:4-7), which reads, "There will be more joy in heaven over one sinner who repents than over ninety-nine righteous who need no repentance." The lost sheep arrived home first!

ETHICS

Having looked at the story we must ask, Are there ethical implications that grow out of the parable? Yes there are.

In spite of discouragement and rejection, the workers in the market earnestly sought gainful employment using the only method available to them. The master's compassionate response is a model for all. He finds a way to respect the dignity of the workers, encourages rather than short-circuits their self-reliance and sees that their basic needs are met. He offers a hand up not a handout, and he tries deliberately to educate the entire workforce in these matters.

THEOLOGY

What of theology? Two comments are perhaps appropriate. First, the workers who complain have, for centuries, been identified as the Pharisees, whose community up to that time had spent decades defining and observing the law in a precise fashion. They saw Jesus welcoming into the kingdom of heaven those who had not spent their lives keeping the law and making such types equal to earnest law-keepers. The law-keepers are told, "They *are* equal to you—get used to it!"

Others have seen the parable pointing to those disciples of Jesus who believed in him at the beginning of his ministry and resented Jesus' welcome of others who joined him near the end. Are Peter, James and John equal in the kingdom of God to the blind beggar outside Jericho? As Ibn al-Tayyib wrote, in the eleventh century, "In the Gospel, salvation through Christ is open to both Simion who held the baby Jesus in the temple at the beginning of his life, and to the thief who believed at its end. He [Jesus] opens it to the believer who dies today [even] as he opened it to Abraham the friend of God."[3]

---

[3]Ibn al-Tayyib, *Tafsir al-Mashriqi,* ed. Yusif Manqariyos (Egypt: Al-Tawfiq Press, 1907), 1:328.

The second is that the complainers represent those who not only *obey* the will of God but who also seek to *dictate* God's will as regards others. Such types are not denied their promised rights. But they are told, "Take what is yours and go away." C. H. Dodd catches this aspect of the parable when he writes:

> The point of the story is that the employer, out of sheer generosity and compassion for the unemployed, pays as large a wage to those who have worked for one hour as to those who have worked all day. It is a striking picture of the divine generosity which gives without regard to the measures of strict justice. . . . Such is Jesus' retort to the complaints of the legally minded who caviled at him as the friend of publicans and sinners.[4]

CHRISTOLOGY

Finally, there is the question of Christology. Landowners in the Middle East are known traditionally to be gentlemen farmers. They hire others to work the land and appoint a foreman/steward to manage the estate. A traditional landowner may give his steward careful instructions in the morning and ask for a report at the end of the day. But to make the trek, in person, from the farm to the market and back five times in a single day is unheard of. That is the manager's job.

Against the expectations of his class, the master in this parable does not remain aloof. His compassion leads him to go to the hurting himself and thereby incarnate his deep concern as he demonstrates costly love to the "poor." Jesus is describing his own ministry. Bethlehem and Jerusalem join hands. Incarnation and atonement kiss each other. Self-giving takes on the form of offers of costly love.

SUMMARY: THE PARABLE OF THE COMPASSIONATE EMPLOYER

1. *Justice defined:* Justice is more than equal application of law. In this parable, justice includes respect for the dignity of those in need and a deep concern for their welfare.

2. *The compassionate employer:* The parable offers an example of an employer who has compassion for the unemployed and who shows amazing sensitivity to both their physical needs and self-respect.

3. *The Kingdom of Heaven described:* The Kingdom is where costly grace is offered to those who need it.

4. *A warning:* The parable offers a picture of those who seek to control the master's grace and to pressure him into denying grace to the needy who have done

---

[4]C. H. Dodd, *The Parables of the Kingdom* (New York: Scribner's, 1961), pp. 94-95.

their best. As the recipients of his displeasure, they are told to leave. Indeed, the first will be last!

5. *Christology:* The master expends extraordinary efforts to go where the needy seek him and to offer salvation to them. Incarnation and atonement meet. The "master" becomes the "Lord." Furthermore, the master had an employee. He could have sent his steward. Through the heat of the day he chose to go himself, again and again.

6. *Law and grace:* Jesus' opponents thought that God's grace should be uniquely available to the "righteous" who keep the law. Jesus was constantly welcoming sinners into fellowship with himself. Does God love both "sinners" and the "righteous" with the same love? He does.

7. *The missing ending:* The parable reaches a critical dramatic moment and stops. What is the response of the workers who are complaining? We are not told. The readers/listeners are challenged to find themselves in the story and to bring it to an appropriate conclusion in their own lives.

A summary of the entire parable might be

He comes to us where we live.
He loves us as we are.

Once more Jesus creates a "house" in which listeners/readers are invited to take residence as they make the worldview of the parable their own.

29

The Parable of the Serving Master

LUKE 12:35-38

BETHLEHEM AND JERUSALEM ARE ONLY seven miles apart. Bethlehem (incarnation) is just over the hill from Jerusalem (atonement). In the Apostles' Creed we recite:

born of the Virgin Mary, suffered under Pontius Pilate . . .

Only a comma separates the two. In 2 Corinthians 5:19 (NASB), Paul wrote:

God was in Christ   (Bethlehem and incarnation)
reconciling the world to himself.   (Jerusalem and atonement)

For Paul, incarnation flowed naturally and with no interruption into atonement. In Matthew 1:23, we read:

and his name shall be called Emmanuel, which means *God with us.*
    (Bethlehem and incarnation)

A few verses earlier the text says:

You shall call his name *Jesus, for he will save his people* from their sins.
    (Jerusalem and atonement)

Again and again throughout the New Testament these two themes, incarnation and atonement, are closely linked.

D. T. Niles of Sri Lanka wrote a Christmas hymn, a line from which states: "Christmas shines with Easter glory."[1] Indeed, it does, and the light of that glory appears in many places.

One of those places is in the parable of the serving master (Lk 12:35-39). The length of a parable does not determine its power. This deceptively simple parable is heavily freighted with rich theological content.

---

[1]D. T. Niles, "On a Day," *C.C.A. Hymnal* (Kyoto, Japan: Kawakita, 1974), no. 114.

THE RHETORIC

The parable is composed of three interlocking stanzas.[2] The first presents a pair of metaphorical pictures. The second stanza is created by splitting the first in two and placing new material in the middle between the two halves. The same rhetorical device occurs again in the final stanza, where an astonishing climax is added, once more in the middle. In its briefest outline this can be seen as follows:

Stanza 1
Servants prepared (waists belted)
Servants prepared (lamps burning)

Stanza 2
Servants alert
   Master comes
   Master comes
Servants alert

Stanza 3
Servants blessed
   Master comes/finds
      Master serves the servants
   Master comes/finds
Servants blessed

With this three-stanza outline in mind, the full text is shown in figure 29.1.

This remarkable rhetorical sequence can be compared to a hungry person who begins to construct a sandwich. The first task is to select two pieces of bread (i.e., stanza 1). The second task is to place two pieces of cheese between the two slices of bread (stanza 2). Not satisfied, the hungry person opens the sandwich again and adds pickles and ham in the center (stanza 3). Finally the sandwich is complete and ready to eat. This parable moves through a similar sequence of three stages of composition.

David Noel Freedman observes, "It is as though the poet deliberately split a bicolon or couplet, and inserted a variety of materials between the opening and closing halves of the unit to form a stanza."[3] This same style of "sandwich construction" is used in John 10:11-15 and is shown in figure 29.2.

Our reflection on the parable of the serving master needs to begin with a close

---

[2]The rhetorical form is briefly noted in Kenneth E. Bailey, *Through Peasant Eyes*, in *Poet and Peasant and Through Peasant Eyes* (Grand Rapids: Eerdmans, 1980), pp. 116-18.
[3]David N. Freedman, prolegomenon to George B. Gray, *The Forms of Hebrew Poetry* (New York: Ktav, 1972), p. xxxvi.

Stanza 1	
1. Let your *waist* be *girded*	SERVANT (prepared)
2. and your *lamps burning*,	SERVANT (prepared)
Stanza 2	
3. and be like *people* who are *expecting* their master	SERVANT (alert)
4. when he *withdraws* from the wedding banquet,	Master (comes)
5. so that when he *comes* and *knocks*,	Master (comes)
6. *immediately* they may *open* to him.	SERVANT (alert)
Stanza 3	
7. *Bless-ed* are those *slaves*	SLAVES—blessed
8. who *coming*, the *master finds* awake.	MASTER—comes/finds
9. *Amen*, I say to you, he *will gird himself*	
10. and cause *them to recline* [to eat],	MASTER
11. and *come to them* and *serve them*.	serves
12. If (in the second or third watch), he *comes* and *finds* thus,	MASTER—comes/finds
13. *bless-ed* are those *slaves*.	SLAVE—blessed

Figure 29.1. The parable of the self-emptying master: incarnation and atonement (Lk 12:35-38)

observation of the *rhetoric* of John's presentation of Jesus the good shepherd in John 10:11-15 (figure 29.2 on p. 368).

Our particular interest in the rhetoric of Jesus the good shepherd (in John) focuses on comparing stanzas 1 and 7 (see the following page). Stanza 1 presents two ideas which are turned into a "sandwich" in stanza 7. This is as follows:

1a. I am *the good shepherd*.   GOOD SHEPHERD
1b. The *good shepherd lays down his life for the sheep*

Stanza 7 reads:

7a. I am *the good shepherd*;   GOOD SHEPHERD
        I know my own and my own know me,
        as the Father knows me and I know the Father;
7b. and *I lay down my life for the sheep*.

Stanza 7 reuses the two lines of stanza one with almost identical wording but with new material in the center. Such a two-stage sandwich is rare. But the parable of the self-emptying master (Lk 12:35-38) is composed of a three-stage sandwich such as I have yet to find elsewhere in all of Scripture. It is the creation of a very sophisticated Jewish poetical mind.

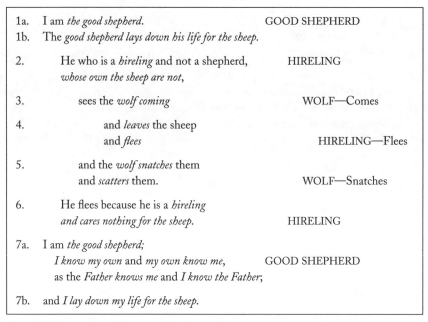

1a.	I am *the good shepherd.*	GOOD SHEPHERD
1b.	The *good shepherd lays down his life for the sheep.*	
2.	He who is a *hireling* and not a shepherd, *whose own the sheep are not,*	HIRELING
3.	sees the *wolf* coming	WOLF—Comes
4.	and *leaves* the sheep and *flees*	HIRELING—Flees
5.	and the *wolf snatches* them and *scatters* them.	WOLF—Snatches
6.	He flees because he is a *hireling* *and cares nothing for the sheep.*	HIRELING
7a.	I am *the good shepherd;* *I know my own* and *my own know me,* as the *Father knows me* and *I know the Father;*	GOOD SHEPHERD
7b.	and *I lay down my life for the sheep.*	

Figure 29.2. Jesus the good shepherd (Jn 10:11-15)

The parable also incorporates the number seven into its structure in two ways. First, the final stanza is composed of seven movements. That is, its structure is a mini *prophetic rhetorical template.* Second, if each of the two-line doublets is fused, the parable exhibits seven movements. These are:

1. Servants prepare
2. Servants wait
3. Master's return is anticipated
4. Servants counted blessed
5. Master returns
6. Master prepares to serve
7. Servants recline at table (to be served)

The climax of the whole is the center of the third stanza, where the master becomes a servant to serve his servants. With these finely crafted Jewish rhetorical features in mind, we turn to reflect on the parable.

COMMENTARY

The parable as a whole focuses on the *servant disciples* and the *serving master.* The model for servanthood is demonstrated by the master, and that model makes it abundantly clear that *serving* does not equal *servile*. One of the prayers in the Church of England liturgy says, "To serve you is perfect freedom."[4] The servant disciple chooses to serve through a free act of will (like the master) and that free act is not compromised by any degrading effects of servility.

Stanza 1

1. Let your *waist* be *girded*   SERVANT (prepared)
2. and your *lamps burning*,   SERVANT (prepared)

Two word pictures immediately appear. The servants are told to belt their robes and keep their lamps burning. The long robes of the Middle East (worn by both men and women) nearly touch the ground. They were and are worn without belts. The hot climate makes loose-fitting clothing the nearly universal preference. Any strenuous activity requires the wearer to tie a belt or rope around the waist to keep the bottom edge of the robe off the ground and out of the way. The Hebrews were instructed to tie up their robes on the eve of Passover in order to be ready to travel (Ex 12:11). Elijah belted himself in preparation for running before Ahab's chariot (1 Kings 18:46), and Jeremiah was told to do so as he took up his ministry to the nations (Jer 1:17). Cyril of Alexandria (fifth century) noted, "such as apply themselves to bodily labors, and are engaged in strenuous toil, have their loins girt."[5] Ibn al-Tayyib observes this practice in daily life around him and writes, "The person who wears a long robe, without a belt, is not equipped to travel or prepared to get to work."[6]

A similar idiom in contemporary English might be "to have one's boots on." The metaphor in the parable refers to servants who are fully prepared to carry out any order given by the master regardless of how strenuous it might be.[7]

Only those who have lived without electricity know how difficult it is to prepare and light a lamp after dark. The servant/disciple in this parable is told to have the lamps lit and to keep them lit regardless of how long the night. But why is the scene set at night?

The second stanza completes the picture by telling us that the master is at an evening wedding banquet.

---

[4] *The Alternative Service Book 1980* (Cambridge: Cambridge University Press, 1980), p. 59.
[5] Cyril of Alexandria, *Commentary on Luke*, Homily 92. Cf. St. Cyril of Alexandria, *Commentary on the Gospel of Saint Luke*, trans. R. Payne Smith (Studion, 1983), p. 370.
[6] Ibn al-Tayyib, *Tafsir al-Mashriqi*, ed. Yusif Manqariyos (Egypt: Al-Tawfiq Press, 1907), 2:217.
[7] Clerics and lay orders in the Catholic and Anglican traditions wear belted robes, a practice probably traceable to this text.

Stanza 2

3.	and be like *people* who are *expecting* their master	SERVANT (alert)
4.	when he *withdraws* from the wedding banquet,	MASTER (comes)
5.	so that when he *comes* and *knocks*,	MASTER (comes)
6.	*immediately* they may *open* to him.	SERVANT (alert)

This stanza gives the reasons why the servants need to be prepared. In this translation two key words appear that profoundly influence how the parable is understood. The English translation tradition has the servants "waiting" for the master who will "return" from the wedding banquet. Syriac and Arabic versions across the centuries have often chosen to describe servants who are "expecting" the master who will "withdraw" from the banquet in order to come to them. The Greek words allow for either translation.[8] The translator in each case must make a choice. "Waiting" is passive, like "waiting for a bus." But *"expecting* the movie to start" projects a different mood. *Expecting* denotes excitement and a dynamism that the first word lacks.

Furthermore, if the master "returns," the reader assumes that the wedding banquet is over and that all the guests, including the master, naturally return home. But if the master "withdraws" from the banquet, he is seen as "slipping out" while the banquet is still in progress and proceeding to his private quarters (perhaps in the same spacious residence). When we read "withdraws from the wedding banquet," we are immediately alerted to ask, Why is he withdrawing when the party is not over? Not until the third stanza is the amazing answer given.

Joseph Fitzmyer observes that the text literally says, "Whenever he breaks loose from the wedding celebrations."[9] It is this literal reading that the Arabic and Syriac versions have usually chosen. I find this translation more authentic to the larger world of New Testament images into which this parable must be placed. This often-neglected option brings added nuances to the story. If the master returns home after the party is over, then the reason for his return is obvious. The party is over—of course he returns home. But if he *withdraws* from the party while it is in full swing, the reader wants to know why is he doing so?

Furthermore the reader discovers that on arrival the master knocks. This is surprising! Only strangers knock on doors at night in the Middle East. The host in

---

[8]*Prosdechomai* can mean "expecting" (cf. Walter Bauer, *A Greek-English Lexicon of the New Testament,* trans. W. F. Arndt, F. W. Gingrich and F. W. Danker [Chicago: University of Chicago Press, 1979], p 712). *Analyō* can mean "depart from" or "withdraw" (cf. ibid., p. 57; H. G. Liddell and R. Scott, *A Greek-English Lexicon,* rev. H. S. Jones and R. McKenzie [Oxford: Oxford University Press, 1966], p. 112) (Syriac: *yiftar;* Arabic: *yinsarif min*).

[9]Joseph A. Fitzmyer, *The Gospel According to Luke (X-XXIV)* (New York: Doubleday, 1985), 2:988.

the parable of the friend at midnight in Luke's Gospel goes to his neighbor and *calls*, he does not knock (Lk 11:5-6). A knock will frighten his sleeping friend, while a recognizable voice calling, "Hey, Joe, it's me. Open the door" will assure those in the house that no foul play is afoot. The house owner will quickly open the door. Revelation 3:20 states: "Behold, I stand at the door and knock; if anyone *hears my voice* and opens the door, I will come in to him." The divine visitor knocks *and* calls. The house owner does not open to a knock but to a familiar voice. The hearing of the beloved voice inspires the opening of the locked door.

In the parable under discussion, the reader is stimulated to ask, Why is he knocking and not calling? Once it is evident that the master is "withdrawing from," not leaving, the banquet hall, it is clear that the wedding banquet is far from over. Before investigating why he left the party early we must ask why he knocked on his own door.

The most likely answer to why the master is knocking rather than calling is that he doesn't want his voice echoing through the residence.[10] Whispering cannot be heard through the door, but even a gentle knock at his door will be heard at once by his servants—if they are awake and alert. By knocking rather than calling, his voice will not echo through the house, announcing his absence from the wedding. As he knocks he fully expects his servants to open immediately, even at night! Clearly they are in a secure environment and the door is not an outside door. Why did he leave the party early? The final scene gives the following astounding answer.

Stanza 3

7.	Bless-ed are those slaves	SLAVES—blessed
8.	who coming, the master finds awake.	MASTER—Comes/Finds
9.	*Amen*, I say to you, he *will gird himself*	MASTER—Girds
10.	and cause *them to recline* [to eat],	SLAVES—Recline!
11.	and *come to them* and *serve them*.	MASTER—Serves
12.	If (in the second or third watch), he *comes* and *finds* thus,	MASTER—Comes/Finds
13.	*bless-ed* are those *slaves*.	SLAVE—blessed

This stanza identifies the servants as slaves. The residents of a wealthy estate, such as this parable envisions, were of different ranks. Among them in descending order were (1) the master, (2) the mistress and their children, (3) the steward, (4)

---

[10]Large homes all over the world have public and private quarters. A large banquet is naturally held in the public space of the great house. The master of the house has staff in his private quarters and can, if he chooses, slip out of a public banquet and withdraw to his private suite. This is the most likely picture this parable is painting.

the foremen, (5) the permanent hired staff, (6) the day laborers and finally at the bottom were (7) the slaves. Paul defined himself as "a slave of Jesus Christ" (Rom 1:1; Phil 1:1). The master is here seen dealing with the lowest of the low, which makes his actions all the more amazing and countercultural.

This scene opens and closes (stanzas 7 and 13) with the telling phrase "*bless-ed* are those slaves." The Greek word is *makarios*, which does not refer to a state of spirituality to be bestowed in the future but to a condition that already exists.[11] The meaning of this text is not: If these servants are awake and ready, their master will reward them with his blessing. Rather it says: Servants/slaves who have lamps lit, robes duly belted and are awake, eagerly expecting the arrival of the master, are already filled with the blessing of God and are a bless-ed presence in the household. The way they act is an expression of who they are, not an attempt to earn something they do not have.

Within the third stanza, there is a second envelope of meaning positioned inside the outer envelope. In stanzas 8 and 12 the master *comes* and *finds* the "bless-ed slaves" *awake*. Then, in stanza 12 a "footnote" appears. The two verbs *come* and *find* precisely match each other in 8 and 12, and each of the seven lines in stanza 3 is a single phrase or sentence. But in stanza 12 there is extra verbiage. The words "in the second or third watch" make this line extraordinarily long and without them stanza 12 is a precise parallel to stanza 8. The easiest way to understand this extra line is to read it as an expansion of the carefully worded original parable. This line tells the reader that the great coming of the Lord, which will bring in the messianic banquet of the end times, may be a while. Indeed, the master might come in the second watch (10 p.m. to 2 a.m.) or even during the third watch (2 a.m. to sunrise).[12] This extra note indicates that when Luke receives this account, it is already old enough to reflect both a parable of Jesus and a brief comment on that parable.[13] But the real surprise is in the center of the third stanza.

The master's final action is the climax of the entire parable. The servants have been waiting loyally *to serve him*. But on arrival he immediately turns to his bedroom and picks up a rope or belt, and to their utter amazement ties up his festive wedding garment. What is this? Is he going to scrub the floor? For the master to belt his robe in preparation for some lowly task is unthinkable! Servants, indeed, only lower-class servants and slaves, belt their robes.

No, the master is not going to scrub the floor, he is going *to become a servant*

---

[11]See the discussion in chap. 5 on the Beatitudes.

[12]The reference is Jewish, not Roman, in nature. The Jewish night watch was divided into three periods while the Roman custom was to have four watches in the night

[13]Or perhaps Luke adds this comment. Mark has a number of explanatory notes, such as Mk 7:3-4.

and serve them! This astonishing act is introduced by the rare (for Luke) phrase "Amen, I say to you." Whenever this phrase appears the reader is alerted to expect something astounding, and those expectations are realized. In this instance the master causes them to "recline" (in the *triclinium*). They cannot obey without protest, like Peter when Jesus washed his feet in the Upper Room (Jn 13:6-8). Good Middle Eastern servants "know their place" and would naturally put up considerable resistance to the very idea of reclining on the dining couch where the master with his family and guests eat their meals. The Talmud describes how a student of a rabbi should "honor the wise." One of the signs of this honoring was, "He must not sit in his accustomed place, speak in his stead or contradict his words."[14]

The master's acts represent a stunning reversal of roles. I know of no incident in contemporary life or in story out of the past in the Middle East where such an incredible reversal of status appears. Ibn al-Tayyib comments on this verse by saying, "Yes, the custom is that the master of the house serves his guests as did Abraham in Gen 18:7-8; but it is not the custom that the master serves his slaves!"[15]

Matta al-Miskin finds this scene even more amazing:

> The sacramental mystery of this verse is extremely deep. The one who stays awake refers to the person who enters into the realm of spiritual consciousness where a meeting with the Master is realized. This is where the slave ceases to be a slave and becomes a partner in love and a partner in glory. This is where those who are loved sit at the table of the one who loves. This is where one who loves is girded with glory and he sits and feeds them from his own body and gives them to drink from his cup. This is the fulfillment of a true promise given by the savior as a covenant which he resolutely took upon himself when he said, "I will not eat from this Passover meal except in the kingdom." This is where he shares with us his joy and his glory. The Christ fulfills this when he wills and chooses, and it is his pleasure to complete this in a sacramental mystery with those who stay awake, those whom the world has rejected and repudiated. He comes to them and wipes away the tears from their eyes and lets them taste his love in order that they might forget their suffering.[16]

I long for the day when the six large volumes of commentary on the Gospels by Matta al-Miskin are translated and published in English for the benefit of the world church. The spirituality of the modern desert fathers has a spirit-filled spokesman in this learned monk. The least we can say is that in the text under dis-

---

[14]Babylonian Talmud, *Derek Ereṣ Zuṭa* 58b(3).
[15]Ibn al-Tayyib, *Sharh al-Mashriqi*, 2:219.
[16]Matta al-Miskin, *al-Injil, bi-Hasab Bisharat al-Qiddis Luqa* (Cairo: Dayr al-Qiddis Anba Maqar, 1998), p. 528.

cussion the master offers his slaves a costly demonstration of unexpected love, and such demonstrations have incalculable life-changing power. How will these servants perceive and honor their master after this incident? What will this self-emptying love do to their sense of self-worth? Granted, this text offers a vision of the eschaton, but what effect does such a vision have on the reader of the text who is invited to contemplate such a future? For them, will not every day be brighter from now on? Furthermore, the Eucharist not only remembers the past and empowers the present, it also anticipates the future. The future here described includes a servant's wonder at being served by a loving master. The Eucharist can be seen as a foretaste of this future glorious event. In the present the participant in the Eucharist can be transformed and empowered by such a vision.

Incarnation (the master comes to them) and costly self-giving love (a part of atonement) meet in this parable. But picking up on a part of what Matta al-Miskin has written, more can be said.

If the servant/slaves are ordered to recline it is obvious that the master intends to serve them a meal. The purpose of reclining was to eat a meal. But what are they going to eat? What will the master serve his servants? The servants know he will dine sumptuously at the banquet and will not arrive home hungry. There is no food prepared in the kitchen. There is no hint that they have been asked to "have a little something ready" for him on his return, nor is there any suggestion that the master is scurrying around preparing a meal for them. They recline and he serves them with no apparent delay implied or stated. Matta al-Miskin understands the food and drink to be "the body of the Lord and his cup." The connection to the Eucharist is strong. But there is another way to understand the food offered. The natural assumption in the story, as a story, is that the master brings the food with him. What food? The obvious answer is: portions from the banquet itself.

The larger picture now begins to appear. In the middle of the wedding banquet the master remembers his house servants and, filling a tray with the best of the lavish feast before him, he slips out. He moves quickly to his private quarters in order that his staff might participate with him in the wedding banquet—and then proceeds *to serve them himself!* Is there any culture anywhere in the world where such a dramatic act is not a shock?

At this point the theological content of the parable moves dramatically beyond its "sister parable" in the account of the wise and foolish virgins in Matthew 25:1-13. A list of eight similar dramatic elements appear in each parable.[17] These similar-

---

[17]These are noted in chap. 20.

ities strongly suggest that the same mind created both parables. Serious reflection on the significance of these details goes beyond the scope of this chapter. I note this list to make the point that all of these items appear in each story, but the *serving master* is a unique, startling element in the Lucan account. Thus it is all the more amazing.

A second point of special emphasis in this parabolic gem is the fact that the master at the banquet does not send a waiter to carry out his will. He could easily have beckoned to one of those serving the banquet and ordered him to take a large tray of food over to his personal servants in the other wing of the house. Instead, he goes himself. For this master, sending a servant is simply not good enough. On arrival the incarnation of the big man comes to its climax as he dresses like a slave and serves his slaves with food from the great wedding feast.[18]

This parable, in spite of its drama, is often overlooked. Perhaps part of the reason for this neglect is the fact that its emphasis on servants expecting the return of their master goes against the grain of hyperactive contemporary Western culture. Slower-paced cultures of the Two-Thirds World, such as the world of Matta al-Miskin, see this parable in a different light. Yet this aspect of its message is there for all. Christians are called on to be faithful, not successful, and obedience is more important than production.

At the height of his literary and political career, John Milton gradually lost his eyesight. As the light faded, he composed a now famous poetic reflection on this parable. He wrote:

When I consider how my light is spent,
E're half my days, in this dark world and wide,
And that one Talent which is death to hide,
Lodg'd with me useless, though my Soul more bent
To serve wherewith my Maker, and present
My true account, lest he returning chide,
Doth God exact day-labour, light deny'd,
I fondly ask; But patience to prevent
That murmur, soon replies, God doth not need
Either man's work or his own gifts, who best
Bear his mild yoke, they serve him best, his State
Is Kingly, Thousands at his bidding speed
And post o're Land and Ocean without rest:
They also serve who only stand and wait.[19]

---

[18]This idea is close to Matta al-Miskin's thoughts on the matter as seen in the preceding quote.
[19]John Milton, "When I Consider How My Light Is Spent," *The Oxford Book of English Verse 1250-1918,* ed. A. Guiller-Couch (New York: Oxford University Press, 1940), p 352.

In a success-oriented competitive world, this parable and Milton's response to it deserve weighty contemplation.

From another angle, with Matta al-Miskin the candles on the communion table burn brightly in the back of my mind as I contemplate this parable's content. In this connection one's thoughts also turn to our Lord as he sets aside his garments, ties up his robe (not with a belt but with a towel) and washes the disciples' feet (John 13:1-18). Is that foot-washing scene best understood as partial enactment of the promise of this parable?[20]

SUMMARY: THE PARABLE OF THE SERVING MASTER

The following theological themes can be found in this parable:

1. *Discipleship/servanthood.* Discipleship (as with Paul) is defined as slavery to a self-sacrificing Master. At the same time the slave system is totally subverted. The Master's actions elevate servanthood to a self-emptying gift of costly love. By his actions we become his beloved friends and indeed his guests.

2. *Being versus doing.* Servanthood in this parable has to do with *being* more than *doing.* The servants are not commended for production but for being faithful, regardless of how long or dark the night.

3. *Prepared and alert.* Our lights do not burn out in that darkness. Our robes are tied up ready for travel or for any requested service. His agenda is our only agenda.

4. *Blessedness.* The faithful servant/slave is already a bless-ed presence in the household. The servant does not *become* bless-ed by serving or being served. She or he is already bless-ed and the Master confirms and rewards that bless-ed state by his actions.

5. *Leadership and the nature of the Master.* The Master exercises leadership through self-emptying servanthood. When he arrives he will dress himself like a slave, stand behind his reclining servants and serve them. This is so startling that it is introduced with the rare (for Luke) phrase, "Truly *[amēn]* I say to you . . ."

6. *Incarnation.* The Master does not send a tray of food over to his apartment for the staff. Instead, *he* goes to them and *himself* serves them portions of the wedding banquet.

7. *A costly demonstration of unexpected love (atonement).* The Master is not ex-

---

[20]Ibn al-Tayyib al-Mashriqi thinks it does (see *Tafsit al-Mashriqi,* 2:219).

pected to become a servant and humbly serve his slaves. To the amazement of all he chooses to do so. They can never be the same again.

8. *Eschatology.* The parable focuses on the parousia. At the same time, Cyril of Alexandria (fifth century) wrote regarding this text, "We must daily be prepared for our departure hence, and watch with unwinking eyes for our Master's nod."[21] Christ comes at the parousia. He also comes to each of us at the time of our death. We are called on to always be ready for his coming.

9. *Realized eschatology and the Eucharist.* In the footwashing drama (Jn 13:1-18) this parable's promise is partially fulfilled. The "not yet" of the parable becomes the "now" of the Upper Room. Both stories are about banquets. In each the Master becomes the slave. In both texts the disciple/slave is called bless-ed (*makarios*; cf. John 13:17). Every Eucharist is fellowship in the *present* with the Master, who *has* washed our feet and *will* cause us to recline while he serves us from the wedding banquet. Jesus is one who serves (Lk 22:27).

10. *Identity.* Identity and meaning are created by the metanarratives in which we find ourselves. In the parable the messianic wedding banquet is in progress. Our Master will leave that banquet and return to us at the time of his choosing. We expectantly await his coming. He will bring a portion of the banquet with him and serve it to us himself. Participation in this drama, that began with the ministry of Jesus and stretches to our death and to the eschaton, creates meaning and identity. This is who we are. Timothy Luke Johnson comments, "All of Christian existence . . . stands within an expectation. Its fulfillment may be sure, but its timing is unknown."[22]

11. *Timing.* A possible Lucan or pre-Lucan "footnote" affirms that the master's appearance may be some time in coming. This footnote also makes clear that Luke is presenting traditional material that he has not composed.

Incarnation and atonement, like righteousness and peace, kiss each other in so many ways, so many times and in so many places. They also come together in this simple parable of *the self-emptying master.*

---

[21]Cyril of Alexandria, *Commentary on the Gospel of Saint Luke,* p. 370, n. 2.
[22]Luke Timothy Johnson, *The Gospel of Luke* (Collegeville, Minn.: Liturgical Press, 1991), p. 205.

30

The Parable of Lazarus
and the Rich Man

LUKE 16:19-30

THE PARABLE OF LAZARUS AND THE RICH MAN (Lk 16:19-31) is often ignored. This may be due to uneasiness with the fact that the parable appears to be affirming a "reversal of roles" solution to the problem of "theodicy" (the justice of God). The story seems to be saying: Life is unfair. But, never mind, God will 'even things up' in the next life. Lazarus had a hard time here—and as a result he will enjoy good times in heaven. The rich man had a good life on earth and will therefore automatically spend eternity in hell. Put bluntly, the parable would then mean, If you are comfortable here, hell awaits you. If you are homeless here, heaven is guaranteed.

Indeed, there *are* stories like this from before and shortly after the time of Jesus,[1] but did Jesus endorse them? If so, most of the rest of the New Testament must be discarded. How then can this parable be viewed? What is it saying, and what is it not saying?

In the Middle East there is a huge corpus of pearly-gate stories that circulates orally. The "pearly gate" is reduced to "the gate of heaven," but St. Peter remains the gatekeeper even though the main characters are sometimes Moses, Jesus and Muhammad. These stories are usually humorous and often have nothing to do with the teller's understanding of eschatology. Frequently, they offer a political commentary on the ambiguities of public life in the Middle East. Somewhat similar stories are also found in the early Jewish tradition, such as the account of the two holy men in Ashkelon and Bar Maayan, the village tax collector.[2] In the light of this long Middle Eastern tradition, it is possible to suggest that the parable un-

---

[1]Jerusalem Talmud, *Hagigah* 2:2; *Ruth Rabbah* 3:3; Joachim Jeremias, *The Parables of Jesus* (London: SCM, 1963), p. 183.
[2]Jerusalem Talmud, *Hagigah* 2:2 and *Mo'ed Qatan* 20:57, trans. Jacob Neusner (Chicago: University Press, 1986).

der consideration is such a tale. Indeed, it bears many of the traditional marks of these stories (as I have known them). If the parable is a first-century "pearly gate story," its primary purpose is not to present fine points of Jesus' view of life after death. Jesus was no doubt opposing the Sadducees, who claimed that there was no resurrection from the dead. The Sadducees were wealthy, and the entire composition of the story appears to be a challenge to them.[3] In fact there is judgment after death, which is related to our earthly lifestyle. But the main point of the story can perhaps be stated differently.

A few verses before the parable of Lazarus there is a short poem on God and mammon (Lk 16:9-13).[4] The poem can be understood as an introduction to the parable. *Mammon* is an Aramaic word meaning "material possessions," "money" or "that which sustains life," and the poem says three things about mammon relevant to the parable.

First, Jesus says, "No servant can serve two masters. . . . You cannot serve God and mammon." The problem with material possessions is that they assume the characteristics of a personified force seeking mastery. They are necessary to sustain life and can be used to serve God, but the press for mastery is always there. This is probably why possessions are called *unrighteous* mammon. Mammon seeks to usurp God's place in human life. No one can *serve* both masters.

Second, Jesus asks the pointed question, "If you have not been faithful in unrighteous mammon, who will entrust the truth to you?" (Lk 16:11, my translation). This text exhibits a play on words in Aramaic, which was the language Jesus spoke at home. He says:

> If you have not been *amin* [faithful]
> in the unrighteous *mammon* [your material possessions]
> the *amuna* [the truth]
> who will *ja'min ith kun* [entrust to you].

The root *amn*, which appears in the word *amen*, is used here four times. It makes the point that anyone who cheats on his or her taxes will never understand the gospel. Those who have been unfaithful before God with material possessions cannot expect God to reveal his greater treasure to them, which is the truth of God.

Jesus' third point reinforces the second. He says, "If you have not been faithful in what is *another's*, what is *your own* who will give to you?" (Lk 16:12, my translation). All possessions belong to God because he created matter. Indeed, "The

---

[3]T. W. Manson makes a strong case for this view. See T. W. Manson, *The Sayings of Jesus* (1937; reprint, London: SCM, 1964), pp. 296-301.

[4]Kenneth E. Bailey, *Poet and Peasant*, in *Poet and Peasant and Through Peasant Eyes* (Grand Rapids: Eerdmans, 1980), pp. 110-18.

earth is the LORD's and the fullness thereof" (Ps 24:1). This basic biblical principle is foreign to the contemporary capitalist West. The car in the driveway, the
house I live in, the pen in my pocket, the watch on my wrist, the computer I use
to compose these reflections—all belong to God. I am merely a steward of them.
If all possessions belong to God, is there anything that is *really* mine/ours? There
is. The small part of God's truth that we manage to understand and struggle to live
out is truly ours, and we will "take it with us." God looks to see if his people are
faithful stewards of material possessions and then decides what he will reveal to
them of the "deep things of God" (1 Cor 2:10 NIV). The potential transforming
power of such a worldview is limitless.

This poem on money and God is followed by a reference to the Pharisees who
"were lovers of money" and who "lifted up their noses at him" (literal translation).
This is a gesture of disdain used across Palestine, Jordan, Syria and Lebanon.
"Scoffed" (RSV) and "ridiculed" (NRSV) are too strong. No words are involved. A
slight backward tilt of the head and a lifting of the eyebrows signal rejection laced
with condescension. Jesus' comments on money trigger this negative response.

With Luke 16:9-13 in mind as background, the reader of Luke's Gospel is presented with the parable of Lazarus and the rich man. It is as though Jesus says, "Now
I will tell you a story of two people; one served God and the other mammon."[5]

This parable is the third of a trilogy. In the first a *prodigal* wastes his *father's*
possessions (Lk 15:11-32). In the second a *dishonest steward* wastes his *master's*
possessions (Lk 16:1-8). And in the third, a *rich man* wastes his *own* possessions.
All three, properly understood, deal with the theme of salvation. This third parable is composed of two sections, each with its own rhetorical structure. Together
these can be seen in figure 30.1 (see following page).

THE RHETORIC

If the reader focuses on the two actors, the first four sections would be formatted
A B B A. The rich man is the subject in the first and the fourth and Lazarus appears in the two scenes in the middle. But an alternative focus is:

In Life: banquets
    and pain
In Death: a banquet
    and pain

---

[5]The reasons for the presence of Lk 16:16-18 between the poem on mammon and the parable have
thus far escaped me.

The Story

1. There was a *rich man*
   who dressed himself in *purple* and *fine linen*　　RICH MAN
   and *feasted sumptuously* every day.　　(In Life: banquets)

2.　At his gate a *poor man named Lazarus was laid*, full of sores,
   　who desired to be fed with what fell from the rich man's table.　LAZARUS
   　But [alla] the *dogs* came and licked his sores.　(In Life: pain)

3. The poor man died
   and was carried by the angels　　LAZARUS
   to Abraham's bosom.　　(In Death: a banquet)

4.　The rich man also died and was buried,
   　and in Hades, being in torment,
   　he lifted up his eyes, and saw Abraham far off　RICH MAN
   　and Lazarus in his bosom.　(In Death: pain)

The Dialogue

5. And he called out, "Father Abraham, have mercy upon me,
   and send Lazarus to dip the end of his finger in water
   and cool my tongue;　　RICH MAN (1)
   for I am in anguish in this flame."

6.　And Abraham said, "My dear son *[teknon], remember*
   　that in your *lifetime you received good things*,
   　and *Lazarus* in like manner *evil things;*　ABRAHAM (1)
   　and now he is *comforted* here,
   　and you are in *great pain.*
   　And besides all this, between us and you a great chasm has been fixed,
   　that *those who would pass from here to you cannot*
   　and none may cross from there to us."

7. And he said, "Then I beg you, father,
   send him to my father's house, for I have five brothers,　RICH MAN (2)
   to warn them, lest they also come into this place of torment."

8.　But Abraham said,
   　"They have Moses and the prophets;　ABRAHAM (2)
   　let them hear them."

9. And he said, "No, father Abraham;
   but if someone comes to them from the dead,　RICH MAN (3)
   they will repent."

10.　And he said to him,
   　"If Moses and the Prophets they do not hear,　ABRAHAM (3)
   　nor if one rises from the dead will they be convinced."

Figure 30.1. Lazarus and the rich man (Lk 16:19-30)

Granting that both rhetorical patterns are present in the text, the second appears to dominate the story, and thus I have chosen to format the text accordingly. Actually, there is a counterpoint. Both "tunes" are playing simultaneously.

The second half is a dialogue between the rich man and Abraham. The rich man makes three requests and Abraham responds to each of them.

COMMENTARY

1. There was a *rich man*
    who dressed himself in *purple* and *fine linen*   RICH MAN
    and *feasted sumptuously* every day.   (In Life: banquets)

The first scene is a brief yet brilliant picture of a self-indulgent rich man who cares for no one but himself. The verb tense used indicates that the rich man dressed himself (middle tense) *every day* in purple robes. He had other clothing. But purple cloth was extremely expensive, and only the truly wealthy could afford it. This man wanted to ensure that everyone knew he had money. Each day he was overpowered with the impulse to drive his "gold-plated Cadillac." In short he was a "clothes horse" with an inner need to constantly remind everyone of his wealth. He also wore "fine linen." The word in Greek is *bussos*, which transliterates the Hebrew word *butz*, which, in turn, refers to quality Egyptian cotton used for the best underwear.[6] There is light humor here. This man not only had expensive outer robes, but in case anyone was interested, he also wore fine quality underwear.

In addition to his purple robes and expensive underpinnings, the man feasted "sumptuously every day." He *did not, therefore, observe the sabbath.* His servants were never given a day of rest, and thereby he publicly violated the Ten Commandments every week. His self-indulgent lifestyle was more important to him than the law of God. The injustice he inflicted on his staff meant nothing to him. What of Lazarus?

2. At his gate a *poor man named Lazarus was laid*, full of sores,
    who desired to be fed with what fell from the rich man's table.   LAZARUS
    But [alla] the *dogs* came and licked his sores.   (In Life: pain)

Lying outside the gate of the rich man *was laid* a sick, hungry, neglected beggar. The poor man had a name, but why *this particular* name?

Lazarus is the only individual with a name in all Jesus' parables. Major characters move in and out of the parables but are not identified by name. The good Samaritan, the Pharisee, the father, the older son and the sower are anonymous. Laz-

---

[6]I. Howard Marshall, *The Gospel of Luke* (Exeter, U.K.: Paternoster, 1978), p. 635.

arus is the sole exception, and therefore his name must be significant.

The name Lazarus is a Hebrew word that means "the one whom God helps." Lazarus lay, day after day, at the rich man's gate and may have had a few scraps thrown to him, but was always hungry.[7] He was so sick he could not stand, and so poor he was reduced to begging. He appears to be a person whom God *did not help*.

I was a professor in a seminary in Beirut, Lebanon, from 1967 to 1984. The Lebanese Civil War raged for nine years of that period. A blind beggar stood at the gate of a Greek Orthodox Church near the apartment building where we lived. I passed him every day on the way to the seminary. He was a quiet, gentle man with a lovely face. He did not cry out in the traditional fashion of beggars. Instead, he had a small wooden box with a hinged glass top strapped to his shoulders and waist. It was filled with chewing gum because he was a "shopkeeper." I bought his Chicklets whenever I saw him, paid him double the price and then gave the gum to street children in the next block. He and I became friends. He insisted on imagining me and addressing me as "Mudir jamaa" (University Rector!). The war around us triggered horrible passions, but not in him. His quiet calm was never broken, regardless of the shells exploding nearby or the rattle of machine guns down the block. An inner peace radiated from him to all around.

His name was Abd al-Rahman (the servant of the Compassionate One). The Compassionate One naturally shows compassion. Did God show compassion to him? He was a blind beggar! How could he be blind and be called Abd al-Rahman? Was his name a cruel joke?

Lazarus "was laid" (passive) outside the rich man's gate. As he was too sick to walk, members of the community carried him to that gate every day and returned him to wherever he stayed each night. Ibn al-Tayyib writes, "And Lazarus, the poor (miserable) man was unable to move about and so was carried by his family and friends and placed at the door of the rich man."[8]

The community around Lazarus respected and cared for him as best it could. The only man in town with the resources necessary to meet his medical needs was the rich man, so members of the community carried him to the rich man's gate each day in the hope that the rich man or his guests would feel some compassion and give Lazarus something. The practice is common in the East. On Sunday morning beggars are usually gathered outside churches and at the doors of mosques for noon prayers each Friday.

---

[7]The verb *chortazō* can be translated he desired to "be fed" (RSV) or who longed to "satisfy his hunger" (NRSV). Both are legitimate translations.
[8]Ibn al-Tayyib, *Tafsir al-Mashriqi*, ed. Yusif Manqariyos (Egypt: Al-Tawfiq Press, 1907), 2:292.

The rich man had a gate to his property in addition to a door. There was, therefore, land, probably a garden, around his house with an ornamental gate that opened onto the street where Lazarus was laid by his friends.

Covered with sores, Lazarus was too weak to work or sit up, and he "desired to be fed" with what "fell from the rich man's table." The verb *desired* is used in Luke's Gospel for something a person wants but is unable to have. The prodigal son in Luke 15:16 desired to eat the pods he was feeding to the pigs, but did not have a stomach that could digest them. In the parable of Lazarus and the rich man food was thrown away in the rich man's house but it was not given to Lazarus.[9] As reference is made to leftovers from meals, a Middle Easterner immediately thinks of the estate's guard dogs, who are the natural recipients of the remnants of any meal.

This same scene appears in the account of Jesus and the Syro-Phoenician woman, near Tyre and Sidon (Mk 7:24-30). She pleads to be given the small pieces of bread,[10] which, after the meal, are thrown to the dogs. Lazarus longs for the remainders of the meal that "fall from the rich man's table." They were not given to him, but rather fed to the dogs. He may have been given a scrap or two, but never enough to be satisfied.

Lazarus was sick, hungry and covered with sores. But his deepest suffering was psychic. Traditional Middle Eastern villages are geographically tightly compacted. The gate at which Lazarus lay was certainly within easy earshot of the daily sumptuous banquets of the rich man. Only a few feet from Lazarus a group of overfed men reclined each day, while he lay hungry and in pain, listening to their conversation. Those same men passed him every day as they entered and left the rich man's house. They didn't need the food—he did. Help was always near at hand, yet withheld from him.

Having faced the beggars' gauntlet on numerous occasions for decades in the Middle East, I know something of the dynamics of the scene. It is easy to survive by developing compassion fatigue. Beggars are ever present. There are *so* many of them. One's resources are limited. Finally, one doesn't notice them anymore. Compassion fatigue becomes a way to cope and a strategy for survival. Perhaps this is what happened to the rich man.

A wealthy man who dressed in the most expensive robes available, had a banquet every day and lived on an estate with a walled garden would naturally keep

---

[9]Against Arland J. Hultgren, *The Parables of Jesus* (Grand Rapids: Eerdmans, 2000), p. 116.

[10]The Greek word used here (ψιχίων) is rightly translated *futayat* (small pieces) in Arabic. Middle Eastern bread breaks into small pieces but does not crumble. See Walter Bauer, *A Greek-English Lexicon of the New Testament*, trans. by W. F. Arndt, F. W. Gingrich and F. W. Danker (Chicago: University of Chicago Press, 1979), p. 893.

and feed vicious guard dogs to protect his property. Those dogs were fed, but Lazarus was not. One of the key features of the story here unfolds.

In reference to these dogs the text reads, "But *[alla]* the dogs came and licked his sores." The Greek word *alla* always indicates a contrast.[11] Invariably, the English language tradition has understood the dogs' actions to be in harmony with the cruelty of the rich man, and thus the Revised Standard Version translates the text as "*moreover* the dogs came and licked his sores," which indicates continuity with the rich man's behavior. The New Revised Standard Version and New International Version state, "even the dogs came," which also places the dogs on the side of Lazarus's tormenters. But for more than a thousand years most Arabic versions have accurately translated the Greek word *alla* as a contrast, and thereby emphasized that the dogs *were not* joining the rich man in tormenting Lazarus. This contrast is clear in the Greek text and is important to the story.

Dogs lick their own wounds. They lick people as a sign of affection. But more than this, recent scientific scholarship has identified that saliva contains "endogenous peptide antibiotics," which facilitate healing.[12] A dog's saliva contains such peptide antibiotics, and the ancients somehow discovered that if a dog licked wounds they would heal more rapidly.

In 1994 Professor Lawrence Stager of Harvard University discovered more than 1,300 dogs buried in ancient Ashkelon. The graves date from the fifth to the third centuries B.C. when Ashkelon was ruled by the Phoenicians. These animals were probably linked to a Phoenician healing cult. The dogs were, in all likelihood, trained to lick wounds or sores, whereupon a fee was paid to their owners. This may explain the background to Deuteronomy 23:18, which forbids the worshiper from bringing "the wages of a dog" into the house of the Lord.[13] Irrespective of healing or no healing, both the attitudes of the time against dogs and Lazarus's amazing friendship with them lead to comprehension and a discernable contrast. The rich man will *do nothing* for Lazarus, but these wild guard dogs, who attack all strangers, know that Lazarus is their friend and do what they can—they lick his sores. Lazarus lay each day in the heat and flies of the village street. The dogs gathered to help him.

---

[11]Ibid., p. 38.

[12]H. Mygind et al., "Plectasin Is a Peptide Antibiotic with Therapeutic Potential from a Saprophytic Fungus." *Nature* 437 (October 2005): pp. 975-80. I am indebted to Professor James R. Johnson of the University of the Sciences in Philadelphia for bringing this article to my attention.

[13]Lawrence E. Stager, "Why Were Hundreds of Dogs Buried at Ashkelon?" *Biblical Archaeology Review* 17, no. 3 (1991): 26-42; Lawrence E. Stager, "Ashkelon," in *The New Encyclopedia of Archaeological Excavations in the Holy Land,* 4 vols., ed. E. Stern (Jerusalem: Israel Exploration Society, 1993), 1:103-12.

Dogs in the Middle East are not pets. Elsewhere in Scripture they are always seen in a negative light (Is 56:10; 66:3; Phil 3:2; Rev 22:15) and often mentioned in connection with pigs (Is 66:3; 2 Pet 2:22). In the early Jewish tradition dogs were considered almost as unclean as pigs. The Mishnah notes, "None may rear swine anywhere. A man may not rear a dog unless it is kept bound by a chain."[14] Such dogs were kept as guard dogs. The dogs in this story may be wild street scavengers, but in that case the rich man's servants would have driven them away for the benefit of his guests.

This beautiful scene depicts a great deal about the person of Lazarus. He was kind, gentle and lived in quiet harmony with the animal world around him, regardless of the harshness of his environment. Many of the desert fathers exhibited this same harmony with wild animals. The traditional story of Jerome and the lion in the region of Bethlehem is one such example. St. Francis is said to have made friends with a wolf. Friendly lions attended the funeral of Paul the Hermit. Abba Macarius healed the blind pup of a hyena. John Climactus tells of a monk who reared a leopard by hand. Pachomius spoke of being carried across the Nile on the backs of crocodiles.[15] St. Cuthbert of England was saved from the incoming tide by sea lions. Historical or traditional, the list goes on and on, and begins notably with Jesus in the wilderness who "was with the wild beasts" (Mk 1:13). In this parable, with the briefest of strokes, Jesus paints a clear picture of Lazarus's gentle soul. He was a man at peace with himself—within his suffering—and managed to live in harmony even with the wild guard dogs around him. Did he sense that the dogs, like himself, were unjustly despised and ill-treated? The reader is not told. But there is much to ponder. Ibn al-Tayyib, the monk, biblical scholar and *medical doctor*, comments:

> I understand that the licking of Lazarus's sores gave him relief and eased his pain. This reminds us that the silent, unspeaking animals felt compassion for him and they helped him and cared for him more than the humans. He was naked *without medical attention other than what he received from the dogs*. This demonstrates that the rich man did not notice him or give him any attention at all. Thus when we compare the rich man's condition to that of Lazarus, we see that the first was clothed with purple and linen. The second was naked and covered with sores. The first luxuriated every day with a banquet while the second longed for scraps of bread. The first had many servants ready to satisfy all of his needs and the other had *no servants other than the dogs*.[16]

---

[14]Mishnah, *Baba Qamma* 7:7.
[15]Susan P. Bratton, "The Original Desert Solitaire: Early Christian Monasticism and Wilderness," *Environmental Ethics* 10, no. 1 (1988): 31-53; Helen Wadell, *Beasts and Saints* (London: Constable, 1949), pp. 17-23.
[16]Ibn al-Tayyib, *Tafsir al-Mashriqi*, 2:292-93 (italics added).

The parable continues:

3. The poor man died
   and was carried by the angels   LAZARUS
   to Abraham's bosom.   (In Death: a banquet)

Lazarus was too poor for a funeral, but angels transported him to heaven, where Abraham threw a party to welcome him.[17] Reclining in "Abraham's bosom" meant reclining on a U-shaped couch (triclinium) in the place of honor to Abraham's right. At the Last Supper John reclined "in/on the bosom of Jesus" (Jn 13:23). Such was the place reserved for Lazarus, beside Abraham. In his earthly life the rich man enjoyed sumptuous banquets every day. How will the rich man respond to a party/banquet in honor of Lazarus?

4. The rich man also died and was buried,
   and in Hades being in torment
   he lifted up his eyes and saw Abraham far off   RICH MAN
   and Lazarus in his bosom.   (In Death: pain)

Shortly thereafter the rich man died, was given a funeral and was buried. To no one's amazement the rich man found himself in Hades enduring its torments.[18] The dramatic tension between the rich man and Lazarus continues in the afterlife; a tension which is critical to what the parable is about. To the reader's surprise, the rich man recognizes Lazarus and knows his name. So, the rich man *knew* that Lazarus was at his gate and was acquainted with his desperate plight. Surely now the rich man, cast into Hades, seeing Lazarus honored by Abraham, will apologize to the former beggar and ask his forgiveness. The second half of the parable and its three-stage dialogue begins with a request from the rich man.

5. And he called out, "Father Abraham, have mercy upon me
   and send Lazarus to dip the end of his finger in water
   and cool my tongue   RICH MAN (1)
   for I am in anguish in this flame."

Amazingly, the rich man does not speak to Lazarus. The reader/listener is left to conclude that the rich man never talks to untouchables! Instead, he addresses Abraham, and what he says is revealing. He opens with, "Father Abraham, have mercy upon me."

The Semitic idiom says *"Abi* Abraham" (*my* father Abraham). All Syriac and Ar-

---

[17]This is the first time this idea appears in the Jewish tradition.
[18]If this is a "pearly gate" story, there is no need to ask how the dwellers of Hades can see what is taking place in heaven.

abic versions add the personal pronoun, which is implied but not stated in the Greek text. The rich man is playing his "racial card." He has the blood of Abraham in his veins, and Abraham is the patriarch of his clan. Matta al-Miskin notes that, after all, the rich man was circumcised, which would surely guarantee assistance from Abraham. It didn't.[19] Family is everything in the Middle East, and when in dire need one can always return to the family patriarch and throw oneself on his mercy because the patriarch is honor bound to offer help. This time it doesn't work.

The reader expects to find the rich man embarrassed to be talking with Abraham. But Abraham was a man of faith who went forth not knowing where he was going. He left his country, his father's house and his gods in costly obedience to the one true God who called him. Is the rich man, therefore, really a son of Abraham? Did he pay a price for obedience to the God of Abraham? The rich man evidences no such embarrassment.

After reminding Abraham of their family connection, the rich man verbalizes the traditional cry of the beggar, "Have mercy on me!" Two chapters later, in Luke's Gospel, this same cry appears in the mouth of the blind beggar beside the road (Lk 18:38). The rich man doesn't like beggars and obviously will not talk to them, his attitude being that if one feeds beggars they will return like stray dogs. Now he has become one of them. He longs to become "Lazarus" (the one whom God helps), but it is too late.

The rich man's first demand is unbelievable. When Lazarus was in pain, he was ignored *by the rich man*. Now the rich man is in pain and something must be done about it—immediately! After all, he is unaccustomed to such things. Instead of an apology he *demands services*, and from the very man he refused to help in spite of his great wealth! He wouldn't even give Lazarus some of his "dog food." He might as well have said, "Now that Lazarus is feeling better and is on his feet, I would like a few services. Given who I am, and he, being of the servant class, such service is expected. Send him down Abraham—and hurry up about it. Unlike Lazarus, I am not accustomed to discomfort!"

The person who works in a bakery cannot smell the fresh bread, and the clerk in a chocolate shop cannot smell the chocolate he or she sells. Even so with the pain of others: the rich man was oblivious both to what he did to Lazarus in the past and to what he wanted to do to him in the present. He saw Lazarus with his eyes but never with his heart. James has a few things to say about those who see the hungry and intone, "Go in peace, be warmed and filled" (Jas 2:16). Perhaps

---

[19]Matta al-Miskin, *al-Injil, bi-Hasab Bisharat al-Qiddis Luqa* (Cairo: Dayr al-Qiddis Anba Maqar, 1998), p. 592.

this is one of those cases where the parables of Jesus shine through the pages of the book of James?

The rich man played his cards instinctively. Had he absorbed the new realities of where he was and where Lazarus was, he could at least have pretended to "eat humble pie" and apologize to Lazarus in order to please Abraham. After all, Lazarus had become Abraham's guest of honor. It is in the rich man's interests to say something nice to Abraham's special guest. But the rich man cannot imagine a world where social stratifications do not apply. All he can think of is demanding help, even from the man he injured deeply.

Those who are listening to the parable are electrified! The tables are turned: Lazarus is in a position of power, reclining beside a man of great influence—no less than Abraham himself! How will Lazarus now respond to being treated as a servant and asked to relieve the pain of a man who unceasingly ignored his suffering? The listener/reader expects him to explode in rage and say something like:

> You half dead dog! I see you recognize my face and can call my name! You saw me outside your gate, but you did nothing to alleviate *my* pain. Your dogs were kind to me. They licked my wounds. But you—you no good scum of the earth—where were you when *I* needed your help? Now you want me to serve you? I can't believe it! Abraham! Leave this monstrous ego to fry in hell until the flesh falls off of his bones. He fed his dogs! He would not feed me. What he's now suffering is only half of what he deserves!

But Lazarus is quiet. This gentle, longsuffering man has no reservoir of anger ready to explode, no reflections on retaliation in the waking hours of the night, no score to settle and no vengeance to exact. Like Job he creates meaning by his response to what happens to him. Lazarus is a model of the mercy described by Jesus and recorded by Luke with the words: "But love your enemies, and do good, and lend, expecting nothing in return; and your reward will be great, and you will be sons of the Most High; for he is kind to the ungrateful and the selfish. Be merciful, even as your Father is merciful" (Lk 6:35-36). Lazarus is silent even as he was silent outside the rich man's gate.

In his matchless definition of Christian love *(agapē),* Paul provides a list of characteristics that are found in such love (1 Cor 13:4-7). The list begins with one form of patience *(makrothymia)* and ends with a second form of patience *(hypomonē).*

Makrothymia is a composite word consisting of *makran* (far away) and *thymos* (anger). As a single word *makrothymia* has to do with "putting one's anger far away." This is the patience of the powerful who are able to wreck vengeance on their enemies but choose to be patient and refrain from doing so. It is the patience of David standing over the sleeping body of Saul when Saul went to kill David (1

Sam 26:6-25). David could have opted for a "preemptive strike." Saul's only purpose in making that expedition was to kill David. David, with an aide, managed to penetrate Saul's camp in the night, and David's aide urged him to kill his sleeping enemy. But David exhibited *makrothymia* and stayed his hand.

The other form of patience, *hypomonē*, is also comprised of two Greek words. The first is the preposition *hypo* (under). The second is *monē*, which has to do with endurance. The person with *hypomonē* is willing to "remain under" great stress or suffering. The primary biblical example of this virtue is Mary standing silently at the cross and choosing to not walk away. She and her son exhibit *hypomonē*, usually translated "longsuffering." In this parable Lazarus exhibits both of these forms of patience. In his earthly life he had no complaints, he was longsuffering and full of *hypomonē*. When, in a position of power, at the side of Abraham, he demonstrates *makrothymia*, he puts his anger far away. Like Greek, Arabic has a word *(halim)* that describes this virtue precisely. American English has no such word.

Lazarus created meaning by what he chose not to do. He was quiet in his days of powerless suffering, and remained silent in his days of power as he listened to his former tormenter demand services from him. As the story continues all eyes are focused on Abraham to see how he will respond to this insensitive request.

> 6. And Abraham said, "My dear son *[teknon]*, *remember*
>   that in your lifetime *you received good things*,
>   and Lazarus in like manner *evil things*;   ABRAHAM (1)
>   and now he is *comforted* here, and you are in anguish.
>   And besides all this, between us and you a great chasm has been fixed
>   that *those who would pass from here to you cannot*,
>   and none may cross from there to us."

The rich man still fails to get the point, even though he is frying in hell. How can anyone respond adequately to such class pride? Abraham begins with the affectionate word *teknon* (my dear boy), rather than the more neutral *huios*. In the parable of the prodigal son, *teknon* is on the lips of the father when the older son insults his father in public by refusing to enter the banquet hall and greet his father's guests. The father humiliates himself publicly, walks out to his older son and addresses him as *teknon*. In this story Abraham does not deny that the rich man is a member of his extended family and addresses him in a kindly manner, irrespective of the rich man's insult to Abraham's guest and thereby to Abraham.

Abraham then voices the classical cry of the prophets as they call on wayward Israel to repent with the word *remember* (Mic 6:5). The rich man is called to remember four points:

1. You received good things   (the rich man—his extravagant life)
2. Lazarus, bad things   (Lazarus—his sickness and his neglect)
3. He is comforted   (Lazarus—in Abraham's bosom)
4. You are in anguish   (the rich man—in hell)

These four statements *exactly* match the four scenes in the earthly life of the two men as recorded in the first part of the parable and are in the same order. English translations often put the word *but* before the third statement. No contrast is indicated in the Greek text. Rather, continuity is expressed and should be translated "*and* he is comforted." Each of these four phrases is freighted with meaning.

Abraham begins with "you in your lifetime received good things." The verb is in the passive; the rich man neither earned nor deserved the good life he enjoyed; it was a gift. Such passives clearly refer to God. All the rich man's possessions, as well as his assumed good health, were free gifts from a bountiful God.

Abraham continues with the last three of the quartet:

and Lazarus in like manner *evil things*;
and now he is *comforted* here,
and you are in anguish.

These three phrases should be seen together. Lazarus is not described as *healed*, in which case his main problem would be his sores. Nor is he *well fed*, which would mean that his hunger was the focus of his suffering. But Abraham affirms that he was *comforted*, which demonstrates that outside the rich man's gate he was in anguish. It was his *psychic pain* that hurt the most. While reclining with Abraham he is *comforted*. Someone cares for him and does not leave him in earshot of banquets that produce garbage which he longs to eat but cannot because it is fed to the dogs. The key phrase "now he is comforted" emphasizes that the source of the most painful evil Lazarus endured was the treatment he received from the rich man. God gave good things to the rich man, and that same rich man in turn passed on evil things to Lazarus, lying helpless at his gate.[20]

Abraham then points out another problem and reveals a new and stunning surprise as he continues:

And besides all this, between us and you a great chasm has been fixed,
that *those who want to pass from here to you cannot*,
and none may cross from there to us.

The fact of a "great chasm" is easy to understand. But why does Abraham re-

---

[20]The reader can overhear the parable of the unforgiving servant who receives gifts from his master and then refuses to deal kindly with a fellow servant (Mt 18:23-35).

mind the rich man that "those who want to pass from here to you" cannot? Who, for heaven's sake, would want to journey from heaven to hell? Obviously, Abraham has a volunteer. There is only one other person on stage. Lazarus is whispering in Abraham's ear and saying something like, "Father Abraham, that's my old neighbor down there. We have known each other for years. Poor man—he is in such a fix. We have plenty of water here, and if it pleases you, I will be glad to take a glass down to him!"

More of Lazarus's nature is now revealed. His *makrothymia* motivates him on the deepest level of his being. He not only refrains from gloating over the rich man's well-deserved predicament but shows compassion for his fallen oppressor. Additionally, the rich man's speech is a broad hint that he would like to join those reclining at the banquet with Abraham. But it is too late; the one wanting to join Abraham's party cannot get there.

The rich man, in turn, responds. At this point in the conversation he has just received an order from the patriarch of the family to "remember" the good gifts that had been freely given to him. He chooses to disobey Abraham and changes the subject as he cries out:

7. And he said, "Then I beg you Father,
  send him to my father's house, for I have five brothers, RICH MAN (2)
  to warn them lest they also come into this place of torment."

Once again the rich man becomes a beggar. It is noble of him to show an interest in his brothers, but they are presumably of the same class in society that he enjoyed, and for him such people matter in the scheme of things, while the poor—like Lazarus—do not. If Lazarus cannot be used as a table waiter, he can surely be turned into an errand boy to serve the interests of his superiors, such as the rich man and his siblings. Once again, there is no hint of repentance before Abraham or of apology to Lazarus. The rich man's class-structured world is still intact.

Commentators have noted that the rich man's family was composed of six brothers (the number six being a symbol of evil). Had they accepted Lazarus as a brother, there would have been seven of them (the number of perfection).

8. But Abraham said,
  "They have Moses and the prophets;
  let them hear them."

It has been estimated that no more than 3 to 10 percent of the population in the first century were literate. The observant Jew could "hear" the Law and the prophets read in the synagogue. But the rich man was otherwise engaged on shabbot. He ordered a sumptuous banquet every day, so it was unlikely that he was familiar with the sacred writings of his community. The Law and the Prophets called for compassion for the poor, and the rich man's brothers could learn all they needed to know from the Scriptures. Besides, "to hear" in Semitic languages means "to listen and obey." The daily prayers opened with, "Hear, O Israel." If the rich man's brothers chose to worship and "hear" what was read to them from the Law and the Prophets, they would have had ample information to reform their lives. The request is declined. Yet the rich man, who is unaccustomed to anyone saying no to him, tries once more.

> 9. And he said, "No, Father Abraham;
>   but if someone comes to them from the dead,
>   they will repent."

The rich man contradicts and tries to correct Abraham as he would an inferior and in effect says to him, "No, you are mistaken!" Amazing! Furthermore, in the story, Lazarus was visible to the rich man beyond the grave. Indeed, Lazarus "appeared" to the rich man, but the latter did not repent. Instead, he began demanding services: waiter, messenger boy—whatever the rich man wanted, Lazarus was expected to comply immediately!

The rich man was not given a vision of Lazarus reclining "in the bosom of Abraham" at a party where he was also a guest. Instead, while frying in hell, he saw Lazarus enjoying a banquet at Abraham's side, and yet none of his attitudes changed! If the fires did not change the rich man, on what basis is there any hope that a vision or visitations would change his brothers?

Abraham concludes the conversation firmly with a terse statement:

> 10. And he said to him,
>   "If Moses and the prophets they do not hear,
>   nor if one rises from the dead will they be convinced."

The high priest had clear evidence that another man named Lazarus had been raised from the dead by Jesus. But the high priest did not repent; instead, news of that event solidified the high priest's determination to oppose Jesus (Jn 11:45-50).

It is good to seek historical evidence in matters of faith, but the deepest levels of some types of knowledge are not open to historical investigation. Neither the existence of God nor the fact that my family loves me can be demonstrated conclusively at the bar of historical research. I have a great deal of evidence for both facts, but at the end of the day a decision of faith is required, and as Lesslie Newbigin states repeatedly, all historical inquiry itself begins with "plausibility structures" in the mind that are themselves affirmations of faith.[21]

The parable invokes a realistic picture of too much of the world where the divide between the rich and the poor reflects gross injustice. Such things should not be. The sensitive listener/reader is encouraged and stimulated to create a just society in which adequate care is extended to the poor.

SUMMARY: THE PARABLE OF LAZARUS AND THE RICH MAN

This parable contains an embarrassment of theological riches. The primary focus is not on "reversal of roles" but on answering the question, How are we to respond to the grace and pain of life? In the process of presenting this theme the parable deals with the following ideas:

1. *The question is not Why? but What now?* The events of our lives have meaning. We access or fail to access that meaning by the way in which we *respond* to those events. What we *do* with the good gifts and the pain of life is what matters. The rich man responded to the good things given to him with self-indulgence, indifference to the needs of others, arrogance and class pride. Lazarus responded to his pain with patience, longsuffering, gentleness and implied forgiveness. He made friends with the wild dogs and inevitably showed gratitude to his friends in the community who carried him each day to the rich man's gate.

2. *Who is Elʿazar* (the one whom God helps)? From Lazarus's response to *suffering* in this life and his implied forgiveness of the rich man in the next life, it is clear that God was with him and helped him all the way. Only with divine help is such a response possible. He was indeed *Elʿazar* (Lazarus). In life the rich man refused God's help. He had money and managed his affairs alone. In hell, he begged to become "the one whom God helps," but it was too late.

3. *Repentance after death.* There is no opportunity for repentance after this life. Call upon God while God is near. Now is the only acceptable time.

4. *Pride of race.* The rich man was a member of the family of Abraham and could call him "Father Abraham." Yet even a family link to Abraham was not enough. Racism takes many forms. The rich man was infected by one of them. If anyone could claim privilege on the basis of racial connection, surely it was a son of Abraham. John the Baptist was faced with the same attitude. He cried out, "Do not begin to say to yourselves, 'We have Abraham as our father'; for

---

[21]Lesslie Newbigin, *Proper Confidence* (Grand Rapids: Eerdmans, 1995), and *The Gospel in a Pluralist Society* (Grand Rapids: Eerdmans, 1990).

I tell you, God is able from these stones to raise up children to Abraham" (Lk 3:8). Clearly, in the eyes of God no racial identity has any intrinsic merit.

5. *Compassion for the poor.* Lazarus has a name and becomes one of Abraham's guests. His neighbors, the wild dogs, the angels and Abraham love him and help him. He is the hero of the story, which rings with compassion for the poor.

6. *False formulas.* The formula "Wealth necessarily = God's blessing," and the related formula "Suffering always = You must have sinned," are both *totally rejected.* The story depicts an arrogant, rich man whom God does not bless, and a humble, sick man whom dogs, humans, angels and Abraham love, serve and honor.

7. *The corrupting potential of wealth.* Wealth, be it little or much, is not condemned in Scripture. What is criticized is the failure to see that all material possessions belong to God. We are merely stewards of his treasures. The parable reflects the corrupting, blinding *potential* of wealth and is critical of the socially irresponsible wealthy. The rich man used his resources for his own self-indulgent living. He cared nothing about his God, his staff or the needy in his community. Even in hell he remained unrepentant and continued to see Lazarus as an inferior who should serve him as a waiter or an errand boy. Mammon had become his master.

8. *Mission at home.* Mission is found on our doorstep. Just as in the case of the rich man, compassion fatigue can prevent us seeing it.

9. *Eternal life.* There *is* life after death (against the Sadducees). Earthly life is related to it.

10. *Theodicy.* The question, Why did Lazarus suffer? is not answered fully. We are not told how or why Lazarus became ill. Life is not fair, yet Lazarus had no complaints. He was even more patient than Job. This story can rightly be called "The New Testament Job." Job was wealthy, lost all, suffered, was vindicated and in the end recovered and prospered. Lazarus died in the midst of his hunger, sores and anguish. This gentle, forgiving man was respected, loved and served by the community, the dogs, Abraham and the angels. The arrogant, self-indulgent, insensitive, racist rich man received his just rewards. The mystery of suffering is not fully revealed—but this story is a significant move beyond the book of Job.

11. *The call to repentance.* The only call to repentance offered us is the witness of Scripture. It is enough. God does not owe us a supernatural visitation.

12. *Social justice*. In the parable wealth is not distributed justly. Economic re-
    sources are wasted by the rich and powerful on themselves. The tears of the
    poor and powerless are ignored. Lazarus is obliged to wait for the next life to
    find comfort. The parable presents a realistic social picture; such things hap-
    pen. But the seeker after the kingdom of God "on earth" is stimulated to pro-
    mote the kind of economic equity that eliminates the suffering presented in
    this parable.

13. *Judgment*. Death is not the end. The rich man's failure to love God (he breaks
    the sabbath every week) and his neighbor (Lazarus) does not pass unnoticed.
    Bishop Allison has written, "there is a sentimental cruelty inherent in the idea
    of a 'manageable deity,' because it cuts out any hope of final justice. . . . Abra-
    ham Heschel teaches us that 'God is not indifferent to evil!'"[22] The rich man
    apparently thought he was.

14. *Historical verification and faith*. Historical proof of resurrection does not nec-
    essarily create faith. The rich man saw a resurrected Lazarus and failed to re-
    pent. To demand proof for great mysteries is to cheapen faith.

The focus of the parable is not on a form of justice that evens the score, but is
found in discovering the ways in which meaning is created by our responses to the
good gifts and the suffering that life brings to everyone. Lazarus's silences are eloquent beyond any words that he or we might use. As Plummer writes:

> The silence of Lazarus throughout the parable is very impressive. He never murmurs
> against God's distribution of wealth, nor against the rich man's abuse of it, in this
> world. And in Hades he neither exults over the change of relations between himself
> and Dives, nor protests against being asked to wait upon him in the place of torment,
> or to go errands for him to the visible world.[23]

He was indeed Lazarus—the one whom God helped.

---

[22]C. FitzSimons Allison, "Modernity or Christianity? John Spong's Culture of Disbelief," in *Can a Bishop Be Wrong?* ed. Peter C. Moore (Harrisburg, Penn.: Morehouse, 1998), p. 91.

[23]Alfred Plummer, *The Gospel According to S. Luke*, 5th ed., International Critical Commentary (1922; reprint, Edinburgh: T & T Clark, 1960), p. 392.

31

The Parable of the Pounds

OUR UNDERSTANDING OF SCRIPTURE must always be open to refinement. All interpretations of Scripture need to be *tentatively* final. They have to be final in the sense that obedience cannot wait for the disciple to read yet one more technical article in biblical studies. At the same time, all efforts in biblical interpretation are flawed. Our interpretation of Scripture, therefore, must never be closed to correction and revision.

One of the biblical stories that warrants a fresh look is the parable of the pounds. Lesslie Newbigin talks about the "plausibility structures" through which all of us see the world.[1] What he means is that each of us perceives reality through the lenses of our language, culture, history, politics, economic theories, religion and military. As Westerners, one of our lenses is capitalism. Does the parable of the pounds need to be liberated from the presuppositions of capitalism that perhaps have unconsciously influenced our translations and interpretations of this story?

With this question in mind the introduction to the parable, whether from Luke or his source, makes clear that some of Jesus' followers were apocalyptic enthusiasts. The story before the telling of this parable concludes with Jesus saying to Zacchaeus and his friends, "Today salvation has come to this house" (Lk 19:9). Jesus and his disciples were on their way to Jerusalem to celebrate Passover, which was a joyful recollection of political liberation from Egypt. The phrase "today salvation has come" is dripping with apocalyptic overtones. If salvation has come for a hated tax collector like Zacchaeus, it surely has arrived for the nation! Passover is the perfect time for "the day of the LORD" (Amos 5:18) to appear. The text states that Jesus taught this parable, "because they supposed that the kingdom of God was to appear immediately" (Lk 19:11).

---

[1]Lesslie Newbigin, *The Gospel in a Pluralist Society* (Grand Rapids: Eerdmans, 1990), pp. 64-65.

In every age (including our own) there are voices announcing that the end of all things is upon us. Such speculation provides a convenient escape valve from responsibilities in the present. If the end of the world is imminent, then there is no need to speak truth to power! Efforts to create a just society are pointless. Why work for peace and reconciliation? All things will soon be over. Energy spent to protect and preserve the natural world is in vain. The prayer, "Thy kingdom come . . . on earth" needs no commitment or response because the earth itself will soon pass away.

The New Testament presents three paradoxes on the subject of the coming of the kingdom of God. The kingdom *has come* in Jesus Christ and it is still *in the future*. The kingdom is *near* and yet *far off*. Followers of Jesus will *never know the timing* of the coming of the kingdom of God—and *here are its signs!*[2]

The parable before us discusses the kingdom of God and makes clear that its completion "is going to be a while." The text, with its rhetorical structure is shown in figure 31.1.

Herod the Great made a trip to Rome in 40 B.C. seeking a Roman appointment as king, and his son, Archelaus, made a similar journey in 4 B.C. to argue his case against his half-brother Antipas. Jesus used a political scene familiar to his audience as the background for this parable. As the story opens, a nobleman is giving a speech to his servants before he journeys "into a far country to receive for himself kingship and return." Obviously, the nobleman is confident that he will receive the kingship he seeks. Not everyone around him agrees. The speech and the setting require scrutiny.

The nobleman calls ten servants and gives each of them a pound (the equivalent of one hundred days' wages for a working man). Matta al-Miskin suggests that the talents themselves symbolize "Faith, hope and love, and are the vital components of the unearned salvation by grace that they had freely received."[3] The "pound" was clearly a free gift from a generous master to each of his servants. As the nobleman gives these gifts he tells them, "Engage in trade *[en ho]* I am coming back." The little used Greek expression *en ho* literally means "in which." It can also legitimately be translated "until," meaning, "Engage in trade *until* I return."[4] A third option is to read it as a causative and translate the sentence, "Engage in trade

[2]Werner G. Kümmel, *Promise and Fulfillment*, Studies in Biblical Theology 23 (Naperville: Alec R. Allenson, 1957).
[3]Matta al-Miskin, *al-Injil, bi-Hasab Bisharat al-Qiddis Luqa* (Cairo: Dayr al-Qiddis Anba Maqar, 1998), p. 634.
[4]Walter Bauer, *A Greek-English Lexicon of the New Testament*, trans. W. F. Arndt, F. W. Gingrich and F. W. Danker (Chicago: University of Chicago Press, 1979), p. 261.

1.	A *nobleman* went into a *far country* to receive for himself *kingship* and *return*. Calling ten of his servants he gave them ten pounds, and said to them, "Engage in trade/in a situation *in which I am coming back/because* I am coming back."	FAITHFULNESS
2.	But his *citizens hated him* and sent an *embassy after him*, saying, "*We do not want this . . .* to reign over us."	CONDEMNATION
3.	And he *returned*, having *received kingly power*, and he said to *call* to him those *servants* to whom he had *given the money*, that he might know *what business they had transacted*.	
4.	The *first* came before him saying, "*Lord!* *your pound* has made *ten more*."	FAITHFULNESS
5.	And he said to him, "*Well done, good servant!* Because in a *very little* you have been *faithful*, I appoint you in *authority over ten cities*."	RESULT
6.	And the *second*, came saying, "*Lord*, *your pound* has made *five pounds*."	FAITHFULNESS
7.	And he said to him, "I appoint you over *five cities!*"	RESULT
8.	Then *another* came, saying, "*Lord*, here is *your pound*, which I kept *stored in a rag*, for *I was afraid of you*,	UNFAITHFULNESS (What he did)
9.	because you are a *hard man*; you take *up what you did not lay down*, and *reap what you did not sow*."	THE SERVANT'S EVALUATION
10.	And he said to him, "*Out of your own mouth* I will *condemn* you, you *wicked* servant!	CONDEMNATION
11.	You *knew/experienced* that I was a *hard man*, *taking up what I did not lay down*, and *reaping what I did not sow*.	THE SERVANT'S EVALUATION
12.	Why then did you not *put my money in a bank*, and at my *coming* I should *collect* it with *interest?*"	UNFAITHFULNESS (What he should have done to be consistent)
13.	And he said to those standing by, "Take the *pound* from him, and give it to him who *has ten*." And they said to him, "*Lord*, he has *ten pounds*."	RESULT
14.	And I tell you, to *every one who has shall be given*; and from *him who has not*, what *he has* shall be *taken away*.	
15.	But as for those *enemies* of mine, who did not want me to reign over them, bring them here and *slay them before me*."	CONDEMNATION Announced

Figure 31.1. The parable of the nobleman in the far country (Lk 19:11-27)

because I am coming back." English language translations have chosen the second and rendered the text "Engage in trade *until* I return."

By turning *en ho* into a time reference (until), the whole point of the master's command becomes: "Get out there and do your best. You have limited time to prove yourself in the market place. On my return I expect profits! See how much money you can generate! Make hay while the sun shines!"

On returning, however, the master summons his servants and commends the first for being *faithful*, not *successful*. What is the master really seeking?

If *en ho* is read literally, the text can be translated, "Engage in trade in a situation in which I am coming back." This legitimate reading renders a significantly different understanding of the entire story. (If *en ho* is read as a causative and translated "because," the result is the same.) There were no stable political institutions across the Middle East at the time of Jesus. Transitions were (and are) times of great stress and uncertainty.[5] Imagine a scene where the Shah of Iran, in his last days in power, summons ten of his servants and tells them:

> I am going away to take a little vacation. I have $5,000 for each of you. I want you to open shops in downtown Teheran in my name! The sign on the shop will, of course, read, "His Majesty's Royal Rug (or whatever) Shop." Keep in mind that I *am* coming back! I know I have enemies. They will most likely follow me and try to destroy me. But never fear; I will prevail and return.

What will those servants do once they receive the money and the Shah leaves the country? The plot thickens with the very next phrase.

> 2. But his *citizens hated him* and sent an *embassy after him*,
>   saying, "*We do not want this . . .* to reign over us."   CONDEMNATION

Once again this text is my literal translation of the original. It means, "We do not want this [expletive deleted] to rule over us." During the American Civil War, every time the Northern Army lost a battle, investors withdrew large sums of money from the market. The price of gold went up, and the value of the new paper money, the green backs, went down. Many did not want Lincoln this . . . (gorilla, country bumpkin, hairy ape) to rule over them!

The story assumes that the servants in the parable know all about the delegation that followed the nobleman with the intention to undermine him at all costs. Even so, anyone who understands the total instability of the political milieu in which they live will bury the money and wait to see who wins the right to rule: the

---

[5]Stewart Perowne, *The Later Herods* (London: Hodder & Stoughton, 1958).

nobleman or his known enemies. Anyone who dared to start a business as the known friend of the absent nobleman would surely be circumspect and try to stay out of the public eye. Perhaps some form of underground operation would be the most prudent. All the "smart money" in town would be buried under the floor of a back room.

Such is the real world of this parable. King Herod's trip to Rome was successful; he received kingly power. His son Archelaus made the same trip and was banished. No one knows how such a perilous journey will end. The nobleman wants to know, "Are you willing to take the risk and openly declare yourselves to be my loyal servants (during my absence) in a world where many oppose me and my rule?"

It is amazing to note that after the reference to the determined enemies of the nobleman, the story continues almost as though those enemies did not exist. An elephant walks into the room and no one looks up. Matta al-Miskin makes reference to the servants who "struggled and endured hardships for the sake of the pounds that were given to them."[6] He writes out of the background of being part of a Christian island in the midst of a sea of Islam. He is thus sensitive to what it means to live in a world where the majority look at Jesus and say, "We do not want this . . . to rule over us." As the nobleman distributes gifts to his servants, he is in effect saying, "Once I return, having received kingly power, it will be easy to declare yourself publicly to be my loyal servants. I am more interested in how you conduct yourselves when I am absent and you have to pay a high price to openly identify yourself with me."

It has been my privilege to teach short courses for the Lutheran Church of Latvia. While I was at the Luther Academy in Riga, I observed the interviewing of new students for the academy. I asked the interviewing committee what kinds of questions they asked the applicants. They told me, "The most important question is, 'When were you baptized?' " And I asked, "Why is the date of baptism such an important question?" They answered, "If they were baptized during the period of Soviet rule, they risked their lives and compromised their futures by being baptized. But if they were baptized after liberation from the Soviets, we have many further questions to ask them about why they want to become pastors." In the parable the master challenges his servants to live boldly and publicly as his servants, using his resources, unafraid of his enemies, confident in the future as his future.

Throughout history various movements have disliked the Jesus they found in the pages of the Gospels and have created their own. The best known of these

---

[6]Matta al-Miskin, *al-Injil, bi-Hasab Bisharat al-Qiddis Luqa*, p. 634.

fabricators were the ancient Gnostics, who preferred philosophical speculation to historical revelation. They wanted and created a Jesus who told them to discover God within themselves. Others, called Docetists, did not want a Word that became flesh, so they created a "spiritual Word" that did not become flesh. With the rise of Islam a new Jesus was invented who claimed to be only a prophet bringing guidance and warning.[7] The persecuted church in many places in the majority world over the last two hundred years has been obliged to live out its life and witness in a world that despised Jesus and his message. The greatest challenge of the parable before us can be found in this crucial aspect of the story. The parable continues:

> 3. And he *returned,* having *received kingly power,*
>   and he said to *call* to him those *servants* to whom he had *given the money,*
>   that he might know *what business they had transacted.*

In the story the nobleman does receive kingly power and returns (in spite of the delegation that followed him and tried to prevent his enthronement). On arriving home he summons the ten servants a second time. He wants to know what *diepragmateusanto* (from *diapragmateuomai*)? This is the only appearance of this word in the Greek New Testament. Its primary meaning is "How much business has been transacted."[8] Bauer lists "How much *has been gained* by trading" as a second meaning. From the second century onward the Syriac and Coptic versions of this text have consistently chosen the first meaning. Most of the Arabic versions have done the same. The difference is critical. If the master wants to find out what has been gained by trading, he will ask some form of "Show me the money." But if he is asking, "How much business have you transacted?" he is seeking to discover the extent to which they have openly and publicly declared their loyalty to him during the risky period of his absence. A quick perusal of the account books will reveal the scope of the servants' public exposure as loyal servants of the absent nobleman. The primary meaning of this key word reinforces my suggested understanding of the master's original charge to the servants. Before the master departed, he challenged his servants to represent him publicly during the uncertain time of his absence, and assured them of his return. At his homecoming he wishes to check the extent of their obedience to his command.

---

[7] Tarif Khalidi, *The Muslim Jesus* (Cambridge, Mass.: Harvard University Press, 2001). This learned volume collects, translates and comments on 303 "sayings of Jesus" that appear in Muslim sources.
[8] Bauer, *Greek-English Lexicon,* p. 187.

A full ledger will reveal that the entire community knew the servant in question was his master's man. A nearly empty account book will witness to the servant's fear of showing public loyalty to him. Why has this key phrase usually been translated as, "How much did you gain by trading?" Has capitalism influenced the way Westerners have translated and understood this parable? Is the focus of the story on *profits,* or is it *faithfulness* to an unseen master in a hostile environment?

The conversation between the master and the first two servants unfolds as follows:

4. The *first* came before him saying, "*Lord!*   FAITHFULNESS
   your pound has made *ten more.*"

5. And he said to him, "*Well done, good servant!*
   Because in a *very little* you have been *faithful,*   RESULT
   I appoint you in *authority over ten cities.*"

6. And the *second* came, saying, "*Lord,*   FAITHFULNESS
   your pound has made *five pounds.*"

7. And he said to him,
   "I appoint you over *five cities!*"   RESULT

The faithful servants are the first to report. Each of them could have replied:

I had a good product.
I carried out careful market research.
I burned the candle at both ends.
I hired competent staff.
Here are the results: 1,000 percent profit on your investment.

Instead, the first reports, "Your pound produced ten pounds." That is, "Your gifts produced the fruit of our efforts." The master commends both servants for being faithful, not successful. Furthermore, their reward is greater responsibilities, not privileges. The first is given responsibilities over ten cities and the second over five.

In like manner Paul tells his readers:

I planted, Apollos watered.
But God gave the growth. . . .
And each shall receive his wages according to his labor. (1 Cor 3:6, 8)
[Not according to his production.]

This brings us to the dialogue with the third servant:

8. Then *another* came, saying, "*Lord,*
here is *your pound*, which I kept *stored in a rag;*
for *I was afraid of you,*
    UNFAITHFULNESS
(What he did)

9. because you are a *hard man;*
you take *up what you did not lay down,*
and *reap what you did not sow.*"
    THE SERVANT'S
EVALUATION

10. And he said to him, "*Out of your own mouth*
I will *condemn* you,
you *wicked* servant!
    CONDEMNATION

11. You *knew/experienced* that I was a *hard man,*
taking up what I did not lay down,
and *reaping what I did not sow.*
    THE SERVANT'S
EVALUATION

12. Why then did you not *put my money in a bank,*
and at my *coming*
I should *collect* it with *interest?*"
    UNFAITHFULNESS
(What he should have done
to be consistent)

The third servant claims to be afraid of his master! But he was more likely afraid lest the master not return, in which case he would have backed "the wrong horse!" As it turns out the horse he failed to back won the race! When caught flat-footed, how does he attempt to defend himself?

It is impossible to imagine that when the servant fails his master's test of faithfulness, he deliberately insults that same master. The intention of the servant's speech must be to compliment his master. But how can this be true when he tells the master to his face (in effect), "I see you as a thief." Can this be a compliment?

Such a label was indeed a compliment among the Gauls. Cicero, in *The Republic*, writes, "The Gauls think it disgraceful to grow grain by manual labor; and consequently they go forth armed and reap other men's fields."[9]

Returning to the Middle East, the same has been historically true of the Bedouins. If the master in the parable is a Bedouin raider chieftain, what the unfaithful servant says about him is a high compliment. For the Bedouins of the past the worth of a man was measured by his skill as a raider. Friends of mine have told me that Bedouin love songs are full of praise for the noble clan leader who can swoop down on unsuspecting encampments and capture all their supplies and camels.

The Babylonian Talmud records a story about King David that says:

A harp was hanging above David's bed. As soon as midnight arrived, a north wind

---

[9]Cicero *The Republic* 3.9.16.

came and blew upon it and it played of itself. He arose immediately and studied the Torah until the break of dawn. After the break of dawn the wise men of Israel came in to see him and said to him: Our lord, the King, Israel your people require sustenance! He said to them: Let them go out and make a living one from the other. They said to him: A handful cannot satisfy a lion, nor can a pit be filled up with its own clods. He said to them: Then go out in troops and attack [the enemy for plunder].[10]

King David is presented here as a pious man who studies the Torah from midnight until dawn and at the same time recommends plundering as an acceptable economic enterprise. In harmony with this story the unfaithful servant most certainly thinks he is offering his master a compliment. The servant describes his master as one who plunders his neighbors and is successful at it—he takes up what he does not lay down and reaps what he does not sow.

But if the master is a nobleman in a settled agricultural community, such language is an insult. Jesus and his disciples are from settled farming and fishing villages. Clearly, the unfaithful servant has critically misjudged his master. The *faithful* servants had no difficulty understanding their master's true nature. It was the *unfaithful* slave who completely misunderstood the big man, and in trying to compliment him the slave actually insults him. What is the master's response?

The master observed, "You knew me [i.e., you experienced me] as a hard man . . ." He does not admit that he *is* a hard man but says, "I understand that *you experienced me* as a hard man." The judgment he then passes on this unfaithful servant is that the servant is to be left with the twisted view of the master that was produced by the servant's unfaithfulness. The servant looks at the master through blue sunglasses created by his unfaithfulness. Looking through those glasses, the master (to him), appears blue. The master says, "My judgment against you is this: I will leave the blue sunglasses on your face. I will leave you with your self-created, distorted perceptions of my nature."

Speaking of God, Psalm 18:25-26 reads:

With the *loyal* thou dost show thyself *loyal;*
with the *blameless* man thou dost show thyself *blameless;*
with the *pure* thou dost show thyself *pure;*
and with the *crooked* thou dost show thyself *twisted.* (italics added)

This psalm goes beyond the parable. In this instance the psalmist understands that the communities' attitudes and ethical behavior influence God's revelation of

---

[10]Babylonian Talmud, *Berakot* 3b. This story is attributed to Simeon the Pious, a second- to third-century A.D. rabbi.

himself to it. The parable places the blame solely on the servant. The *servant's un-faithfulness* produces a twisted vision of the master. Both texts affirm that the way we live influences how we see God, which is the unfaithful servant's problem.

The nobleman also points out to the unfaithful servant that he is inconsistent. If the nobleman were indeed a robber baron, he would care nothing about the law and would be happy to have his money invested in a bank and receive the interest. Interest was forbidden in Jewish law. But if the nobleman was a robber he would not care.

His pound is given to the man with ten, and there are cries of, "It isn't fair." Jesus then affirms that the one who responds with faithfulness to gifts received will receive greater gifts. But the one who proves to be unfaithful will lose the very gift with which he began. The life of discipleship provides many examples of such truths.

The more problematic text is the last sentence. The opponents of the nobleman are "on stage" at the beginning of the drama. At its conclusion the master orders them to be killed. Perhaps this final word reflects a church looking backward to the fall of Jerusalem and struggling to make sense of its horrors.

In the text, however, that order is given but not carried out. The master's enemies are not on stage when the story stops. The parable does not end, it simply stops with a final scene missing. A better option is to see this command as a statement of what the enemies *deserve* and to remember that the text does not record what they *receive*. Abraham received an order from God to kill his son. A second later command canceled that order. What conclusions would a reader of Genesis come to about God if he or she read the account of the first order, did not read further and assumed that Isaac was killed? Many of the parables of Jesus are left open-ended. Does the older son agree to be reconciled with his father in the parable of the prodigal son? We do not know. Does the wounded man taken to the inn by the good Samaritan make it home? We are not told. Do the workers in the vineyard accept the master as a gracious man or do they persist with their cries of "It's not fair"? There is no answer. Here the master declares what his enemies deserve. The reader is not told what they receive. Yes, "The wages of sin is death" (Rom 6:23). The rest of the verse states, "but the free gift of God is eternal life in Christ Jesus our Lord." In the Middle East the word *no* is not an answer, it is merely a pause in the negotiations.

If a Westerner is told by his employer, "You're fired! Clear out your desk! I want you off of the property by 5 p.m. today!" the employee will understand that he or she is fired and start packing at once in preparation for departure at 5 p.m. A traditional Middle Easterner will listen to the same speech and conclude: "The master is clearly very upset! Hmm—I see that I have a long negotiating process ahead of me. I must seek help from my most influential friends. This is a very serious matter that requires immediate attention."

In this parable the master's command is an opening statement, no more. The story has no concluding scene and the reader is stimulated to reflect on the unfinished symphony that is the parable. At the beginning of the story the master gave his servants gifts that they neither earned nor in any way deserved. He demonstrated his generosity. That same generosity was again verified by the manner in which he treated his faithful servants on his return. He was even generous with the unfaithful servant, who had his pound taken from him but was not fined, punished or even dismissed. By this point in the story the master had demonstrated his generosity three times. As he arrives to settle with his aggressively active enemies, he publicly announces what they deserve. Everyone knows that this is the beginning of the process of dealing with them. What will the end of that process be? The wages of sin is death and . . . ? The reader/listener is called on to remember the master's nature and contemplate how such a master may complete his dealings with those who bitterly opposed him.

Another aspect of this command has to do with Luke's integrity. If the master's statement regarding his enemies is assumed to be his final word, then a serious question must be asked regarding Luke's view of Jesus. In Luke 6:35-36 Jesus teaches: "But love your enemies, and do good, and lend, expecting nothing in return; and your reward will be great, and you will be sons of the Most High; for he is kind to the ungrateful and the selfish. Be merciful, even as your Father is merciful."

If, in Luke's Gospel, Jesus calls on his disciples to love their enemies, is the command in Luke 6:36 flatly contradicted by the last scene in the parable? Is Luke critically damaging his own presentation of the person of Jesus? Or does our understanding of the parable's unfinished conclusion need to be reconsidered?

SUMMARY: THE PARABLE OF THE POUNDS

What theological and ethical content does this parable offer the reader?

The overall sweep of the story is a metanarrative into which the reader/listener is invited. Jesus, the nobleman, gives gifts to his disciples for them to use in his service. He anticipates returning to God and being enthroned. In God's good time he will return to his servants to deal with the faithful and the unfaithful. Judgment is pronounced against the master's determined enemies, but that judgment is not enacted. Within that overarching vision, a number of ethical and theological directions are given. Among these are the following:

1. The anticipated fullness of the coming of the kingdom of God is in the unknown future and "it will be a while."

2. Resources for fulfilling the master's commands are gifts for which the servants are accountable to the master.

3. The master's primary expectation from his servants is courageous public faithfulness to an unseen master in an environment where some are actively opposed to his rule.

4. Humility is appropriate in his service. The faithful servant tells the master, "Your pound has produced . . ." (rather than, "My hard work has achieved . . .").

5. The reward for faithfulness is greater responsibilities. The servant whose pound produced ten was not given a generous pension, a paid vacation or a villa on the sea. He was appointed ruler over ten cities.

6. A static preservation of God's gifts is to betray the one who gives them. The servant who hid his pound was not dismissed but instead judged unfaithful, and in the end the gift was taken from him.

7. Unfaithfulness distorted the disobedient servant's vision of his master. This led him to radically misjudge his master's nature.

8. The master's judgment on the unfaithful servant was to leave him with distorted perceptions of the master (created by his unfaithfulness).

9. Conscious, active, determined opposition to the master is taken very seriously. His servants are told what those enemies deserve. The reader is not told what happens to them.

10. Jesus is clearly the generous master who expects loyalty from his followers, and in his own good time he will make an accounting with them, to the joy of some and the disappointment of others. He demonstrates his generosity by passing out unearned pounds, by his generous rewards to faithful servants and his choice to not punish or dismiss the unfaithful slave. Even his judgment on his enemies is announced but not carried out.

The parable leaves many loose ends. How will those appointed to rule over multiple cities manage? Does the unfaithful servant learn his lesson and repent? How will the enemies respond to the failure of their attack on the nobleman? What, in the end, will the master do with his determined enemies? The parable provides no answers to these questions. Important theological and ethical directions, however, are delineated and clarified for the readers of the text in any age.

A British journalist once asked Mother Teresa how she kept going, knowing that she could never meet the needs of all the dying in the streets of Calcutta. She replied, "I am not called to be successful; I'm called to be faithful." (Very bad capitalism! Don't invest in her company.)

32

The Parable of the Noble Vineyard Owner and His Son

LUKE 20:9-18

THIS PARABLE IS OFTEN CALLED "the parable of the wicked vinedress-ers," which assumes that the renters are the major players in the drama.[1] But in its cultural context the vineyard owner is clearly the hero of the story. He exhibits *makro-thymia*. This rich word refers to a person in a position of power who can exact ven-geance on his enemies but chooses not to do so. That is (literally) "he puts his an-ger far away." In this parable the vineyard owner opts for total vulnerability in the face of violence. English has no single word for this virtue. Greek *(makrothymia)* and Arabic *(halim)* have such words. Patience, longsuffering, risk-taking, compas-sion and self-emptying together describe the vineyard owner. I have reluctantly chosen *noble* as the best word available. The goal is to find a word that describes the virtue of David standing over the sleeping body of King Saul. David, against the advice of his companion, stays his hand and spares the king's life even though Saul was seeking to kill David (1 Sam 26). David put his anger far away, as does the vineyard owner in this parable.

The setting of the parable, both in Luke and in Mark, is the account of the tri-umphal entry of Jesus into Jerusalem and the cleansing of the temple. The second of those events was a very serious matter for the temple authorities. Jesus clearly occupied the entire temple area for a few hours. Mark writes, "He would not allow any one to carry anything through the temple" (Mk 11:16). It seems that the pub-lic was using the temple area as a public thoroughfare. Jesus, with his supporters,

---

[1]The Greek word is *georgos*, which can mean "farmer," "tenant" or "vinedresser." They are renters and farmers. But their work is dressing vines. I have chosen "vinedressers." See Walter Bauer, *A Greek-English Lexicon of the New Testament*, trans. W. F. Arndt, F. W. Gingrich and F. W. Danker (Chicago: University of Chicago Press, 1979), p. 157.

blocked that unauthorized bypass, overturned the tables of the money changers and the seats of the merchants selling doves, driving out *both* sellers and buyers. This necessitated controlling the entire thirty-five acre complex. In the process, for that day, he shut down the afternoon sacrifice. At the end of the day, Jesus and his followers voluntarily withdrew. They had made their public statement. The new messianic King had claimed his own and had signaled the obsolescence and destruction of the temple, as argued by N. T. Wright.[2]

Middle Easterners have always taken their sacred sites very seriously, and it is not surprising that as a result of this action, "The chief priest and the scribes and the principal men of the people sought to destroy him" (Lk 19:47) but were frustrated in so doing because "the people hung upon his words" (v. 48). Jesus' actions were provocative in the extreme, and from that time onward he was only safe from arrest when protected by his extraordinary popularity. A reaction from the authorities was inevitable.

The first public response from the temple leaders, recorded in all three Synoptic Gospels, is the approach of a delegation of "chief priests and the scribes with the elders" (Lk 20:1). The Sanhedrin was composed of these three types of people, and the presence of all three in the delegation indicates the seriousness of their concerns. They wanted to know by what *authority* Jesus presumed to "do these things"? Jesus countered with a second question, which his challengers declined to answer. The debate closed with Jesus' reply, "Neither will I tell you by what authority I do these things" (Lk 20:8). He *will not answer* their question as to the source of his authority, but he will tell a story! The story he tells answers their question indirectly. To that parable we now turn.

Formatted along the lines of its rhetorical structure the text is shown in figure 32.1 (see following page).

THE RHETORIC

Briefly summarized, although asymmetrical, ring composition provides the following structure:

   a. The *vineyard* is *rented.*

   b.   The *servants* are *sent*
         and the vinedressers *treat them badly.*

   c.   The *owner* responds by sending his son
           alone and unarmed.

---

[2]N. T. Wright, *Jesus and the Victory of God* (Minneapolis: Fortress, 1996), pp. 414-21.

And he began to tell the people this parable:

1.	"A man *planted a vineyard,*	VINEYARD
	and let it out to vinedressers,	Rented
	and went into another country for a long time.	
2.	When the time came, he *sent a servant*	
	to the *tenants,*	
	that they should *give him*	SERVANT SENT
	some of the *fruit of the vineyard;*	And Beaten
	but the vinedressers beat him,	
	and *sent him away* empty-handed.	
3.	And he sent *another servant;*	
	him also they *beat*	SERVANTS SENT
	and *treated shamefully,*	Beaten and Shamed
	and *sent him away* empty-handed.	
4.	And he *sent* yet a *third;*	SERVANT SENT
	this one they *wounded*	And Wounded
	and *cast out.*	
5.	Then the *owner* of the vineyard said,	
	'What shall I do?	SON
	I will *send my beloved son;*	Sent
	it may be they will *feel shame* before him.'	
6.	But when the vinedressers saw him	
	they said to themselves,	
	'*This is the heir;*	SON SEEN
	let us *kill him,*	And Killed
	that *the inheritance may be ours.*'	
	And they *cast him out* of the vineyard	
	and *killed him.*	
7.	What then will the *owner* of the vineyard do to them?	
	He will come and *destroy those vinedressers,*	VINEYARD
	and *give the vineyard to others.*"	Transferred
	---------------------------------	--------------
8.	When they heard this,	LEADERS
	they said, "God forbid!"	Shocked
9.	But he looked at them and said,	
	"What then is written:	
	'The very stone which the builders rejected	JESUS and
	has become the head of the corner'?	Supporting Scriptures
	Every one who falls on that stone	
	will be broken to pieces;	
	but when it falls on any one	
	it will crush him."	

Figure 32.1. The parable of the noble vineyard owner and his son (Lk 20:9-18)

d.   The *son is seen*
    and the vinedressers *murder him.*

e.   The *vineyard* is *given* (rented) *to others.*

As usually happens when ring composition is employed, the climax of the story appears in the center. Traditionally, the story has been read as a straight-line sequence of events with the climax at the end. Thus the murder of the son and, even more, the transfer of the vineyard to others is seen as the central thrust of the story, and most likely that perception has led to the naming of the parable "the parable of the wicked vinedressers." But the decision made by the owner of the vineyard is *huge*, and that decision is indeed the climax of the parable. The closing stanza (7) reverses the first stanza (1). The customary seven stanzas appear. The climax in stanza 5 is in the exact center of the *drama* even though it is off center in the seven scenes.

Finally, the center soliloquy (or important speech) is a feature of a number of parables. The prodigal son has a soliloquy in the far country (Lk 15:17-19). The unjust steward makes such a speech on the way to pick up the accounts (Lk 16:3-4). The compassionate employer makes a critical speech in the center of his story (Mt 20:8) and the older son makes his self-revelatory speech in the middle of his scene (Lk 15:29-30). In each case these speeches are at the heart of the story and in the center of the rhetorical presentation of that parable.

Stanzas 2 through 4 are constructed carefully. Each of them begins with someone "sent," and each closes with the same messenger "sent away." All three are treated badly. As the renters' responses to the messengers grow *harsher*, the descriptions of their treatment become *briefer*. Six lines give way to four and finally to three. With these clear rhetorical features in mind, we turn to the story itself.[3]

COMMENTARY

The opening stanza reads:

1.   A man *planted a vineyard*   VINEYARD
    and let it out to vinedressers   Rented
    and went into another country for a long time.

The imagery has a classical ring. The Old Testament has few parables, but the "Song of the Vineyard" in Isaiah 5:1-6 is one of them. In that song/parable God plants a vineyard and spares no effort to see that it will produce good grapes, but,

---

[3]The same parable in Mk 12:1-12 has a great deal of extra verbiage, which would indicate that Luke's account is more primitive.

alas, it produces wild grapes. The vineyard owner judges the vineyard to be a failure and opts to tear it down. The symbols of the story are identified in the text, and the judgment made against the vineyard is extremely harsh. Those symbols need to be compared with the symbols in the parable before us. This appears in figure 32.2.

	Isaiah's Song of the Vineyard (and its allegorical symbols)	Jesus' Parable (and its allegorical symbols)
Owner	= the Lord of hosts	= God
Vineyard	= house of Israel	= Israel
Vines	= men of Judah	———
The benefits are anticipated from:	= the vineyard	= the renters
Expectations Consist of:	= good grape (justice and righteousness)	= part of the crop (??)
Yield	= wild grapes (bloodshed and a cry of pain)	= no share given to the owner and there are beatings, insults and bloodshed
Result	= vineyard is to be destroyed	= vinedressers to be replaced

Figure 32.2. Isaiah's song of the vineyard and Jesus' parable of the vineyard

The Isaiah parable contains both the parable *(māšāl)* and some extra information necessary for its interpretation *(nimšal)*. Jesus' parable, in like manner, provides both the parable and keys to its meaning.

In the Herodian period the wealthy often lived some distance from their estates.[4] Thereby the social setting of the parable was familiar to Jesus' listeners.

The Song of the Vineyard and the parable contain similar symbols. But there are important differences. Clearly Jesus is retelling and giving new shape to the story recorded in Isaiah. Mark's account of this same parable adds extra details that reinforce the connections between the two accounts (Mk 12:1).

Regarding the critical differences, in this first stanza of Jesus' parable the owner and builder of the vineyard lives some distance away, while in Isaiah's story the

[4]Yizhar Hirschfield, "A Country Gentleman's Estate: Unearthing the Splendors of Ramat Hanadiv," *Biblical Archeology Review* 31, no. 2 (2005): 18-31.

owner seems to be farming the vineyard himself. This change in the Isaiah parable makes it possible for Jesus to add the all important element of renters who refuse to pay the rent. Isaiah has no renters. Further comparisons will be noted.

Stanzas 2-4 read:

2. When the time came he *sent a servant*
    to the *tenants*,
        that they should *give him*   SERVANT SENT
        some of the *fruit of the vineyard;*   And Beaten
    but the *tenants* beat him,
  and *sent him away* empty-handed.

3. And he sent *another servant;*
    him also they *beat*   SERVANT SENT
    and *treated shamefully,*   Beaten and Shamed
  and *sent him away* empty-handed.

4. And he *sent* yet a *third;*   SERVANT SENT
    this one they *wounded*   And Wounded
  and *cast out.*

The traditional three scenes found in many stories appear here, and as usual there is progression. The first servant is beaten. The second is beaten and "treated shamefully." The third is "wounded and cast out." There is no doubt that these scenes invoke the fates of various prophets sent to Israel. Mark includes the killing of the latter servants.[5]

The shameful treatment of the second servant is a significant intensification of the ill-treatment of the servants. In the Middle East personal honor is held in extremely high esteem. The last servant is "wounded and cast out," which indicates that some physical violence was involved, not only as he arrived but also when he was expelled. The first two were simply "sent away." The third was "cast out."

How much violence and insult against his servants will the owner of the vineyard tolerate? What response is expected and what will the owner choose to do? The fifth scene provides an answer.

5. Then the *owner* of the vineyard said,
    'What shall I do?   SON
    I will *send my beloved son;*   SENT
    it may be they will *feel shame* before him.'

---

[5]For the killing of the prophets see Jer 26:20-21; 2 Chron 24:20-22; Mt 23:34-37; Lk 13:34. The extra verbiage in Mark's account indicates that Luke's telling of the story may be an older tradition.

The owner has the right to contact the authorities, who at his request will send a heavily armed company of trained men to storm the vineyard, arrest the violent men who have mistreated his servants and bring them to justice. The abusing of his servants is an insult to his person, and he is expected, indeed honor bound, to deal with the matter. No anger is mentioned, but it is assumed. The question is, what will he do with the anger generated by the injustice he and his servants have suffered?

In the rabbinic tradition there is a very interesting midrash on the story in Exodus of Moses and the ten plagues. In the midrash God's servant Moses is verbally slighted by Pharaoh and God responds. The text is as follows:

> For whose sake did God reveal Himself in Egypt? For the sake of Moses. R. Nissim illustrated by a parable of a priest who had an orchard of figs, in which there was an unclean field. When he wished to eat some of the figs, he told one of his men to go and say to the renter, "The owner of the orchard bids you bring him two figs." He went and told him; whereupon the tenant replied: "Who is this owner of the orchard? Go back to your work." Then the priest said: "I will go myself to the orchard." His men said: "Will you go to an unclean place?" He replied: "Even if there be there a hundred forms of uncleanness I will go, so that my messenger may not be put to shame."
>
> So when Israel was in Egypt, God said to Moses: "Come now therefore, and I will send thee unto Pharaoh" (Ex III, 10), so he went and was asked: "Who is the Lord, that I should hearken unto His voice? . . . I know not the Lord; get you unto your burdens." Then God said "I will Myself go to Egypt." . . . Whereupon His angels said: "Wilt Thou go to an unclean place?" The reply was: "Yes, so that My messenger Moses may not be put to shame."[6]

Rabbi Nissim studied in the famous rabbinic school of Sura in Baghdad and returned to follow his father in the rabbinate of Kairwan, Tunisia, where he died in 1040. Some of his writings were apparently in Arabic. He was culturally a Middle Easterner.

The reader of this midrash knows that when God says, "I will Myself go to Egypt," the purpose of his going was to carry out the tenth plague, which killed all the firstborn of Egypt. Rabbi Nissim reflects the very attitudes any Middle Eastern reader of Luke 20:9-18 expects from the owner of the vineyard when his servants are not merely put to shame by being dismissed in an off-handed way, but are insulted, beaten and thrown out three times in a row.

In short, if (according to Rabbi Nissim) God is willing to go to Egypt *in person*

---

[6]*Midrash Rabbah, Exodus.* Trans. H. Freedman, vol. 3 (London: Soncino, 1983), pp. 183-84.

and inflict the death of the firstborn on the Egyptians in response to a verbal slight received by his servant Moses, what violent acts will the vineyard owner (in Jesus' parable) perpetrate when a series of his servants is insulted and beaten? In Isaiah's parable God destroys the entire vineyard and his final word against it is, "I will also command the clouds / that they rain no rain upon it" (Is 5:6). The devastation of the vineyard is total! For the Egyptians the tenth plague was also devastating! How are we to understand the decisions made by the owner in Jesus' story?

In the parable of the great banquet (Lk 14:15-24) a wealthy man gives a great banquet and invites many. At the time of the banquet he sends his servant to the homes of the guests to tell them "Come; for all is ready," and one after another they refuse to attend, providing fabricated, paper-thin excuses that constitute insults hurled at the host.[7] After three such public insults to the host, the servant cannot endure more and returns to his master, who, on hearing of the nature of the refusals, gets angry! At that point the host of the banquet faces the same problem as the owner of the vineyard: what will he do with his anger? To the amazement of the reader, he reprocesses his anger into *grace*. He sends the servant out to invite the outcasts to his banquet!

In the parable before us, the owner of the vineyard must answer the same question: What is to be done with the anger generated by injustice? Will he allow his enemies to dictate the nature of his response? He is in a position of power. Retaliation is possible and expected. But is further violence the only answer?

Can this vineyard owner follow the same costly path that the master of the great banquet chose when he turned his anger into a gracious invitation to outcasts within and then beyond the community? We sense a painful pause in the middle of stanza 5, where the master says:

> What can I do?
>> (The owner experiences anger, frustration, pain, anguish, rejection, desire for
>> retributive justice and finally a costly peace out of which he chooses to act.)
> I will send my beloved son.

To the reader's total surprise the son is sent to the vineyard alone and unarmed. Esau took four hundred armed men with him to meet Jacob (Gen 33:1). But with recollections of the humiliation and suffering of his returning servants fresh in his mind, the noble owner decides to send his beloved son. That son journeys, with no escort, to meet the vicious men who were tensely awaiting his father's response

---

[7]See chap. 24; see also Kenneth E. Bailey, *Through Peasant Eyes*, in *Poet and Peasant and Through Peasant Eyes* (Grand Rapids: Eerdmans, 1980), pp. 88-99.

to their last outrage. On the part of the owner, is this sending of his son a case of outrageous stupidity?

In the concluding decades of the last century the late Hussein bin Talal was King of Jordan. Many unforgettable stories circulate orally around the Middle East about the king. I first heard the following account in Lebanon, and two decades later I was able to confirm it from a high-ranking American intelligence officer who was serving in Jordan at the time the incident took place. The story is as follows:

> One night in the early 1980s, the king was informed by his security police that a group of about seventy-five Jordanian army officers were at that very moment meeting in a nearby barracks plotting a military overthrow of the kingdom. The security officers requested permission to surround the barracks and arrest the plotters. After a somber pause the king refused and said, "Bring me a small helicopter." A helicopter was brought. The king climbed in with the pilot and himself flew to the barracks and landed on its flat roof. The king told the pilot, "If you hear gun shots, fly away at once without me."
>
> Unarmed, the king then walked down two flights of stairs and suddenly appeared in the room where the plotters were meeting and quietly said to them:
>
> > Gentlemen, it has come to my attention that you are meeting here tonight to finalize your plans to overthrow the government, take over the country and install a military dictator. If you do this, the army will break apart and the country will be plunged into civil war. Tens of thousands of innocent people will die. There is no need for this. Here I am! Kill me and proceed. That way, only one man will die.
>
> After a moment of stunned silence, the rebels as one, rushed forward to kiss the king's hand and feet and pledge loyalty to him for life.

King Hussein opted for total vulnerability. He acted nobly and by so doing he fanned into flame the dying embers of the rebels' sense of honor.

In the text before us, Jesus tells an autobiographical story about himself. The owner of the vineyard says (literally):

> I will send my beloved son;
> *perhaps they will feel shame* in his presence. (v. 13)

Like the army plotters before King Hussein, the vineyard owner's hope is that the violent men in the vineyard will sense the indescribable nobility of the owner who sends his beloved son alone and unarmed into the vineyard in response to the violent acts they had committed against the owner's servants. The story implies that if the renters accept the authority of the son and pay their rent, amnesty will apply. Such was the assumption of King Hussein's gesture. English language translations of verse 13 usually read, "It may be they will respect him" (RSV). What is transpiring in the story at this point is deeper and more profound than the question of respect. The owner is acting out of unspeakable nobility and he profoundly hopes that his choice of total vulnerability will awaken a long-forgotten sense of honor in the hearts of the violent men who are waiting in the vineyard. He is willing to take this risk. His servants had already been beaten and wounded. Yet, he will risk an even greater loss.

Most Arabic versions of the last thousand years have translated this key phrase literally with *yastahiyun minhu*[8] (they will feel shame in his presence). Retaliation is not the only way. The costly path of total vulnerability has the power to be as life-renewing as it was with King Hussein. The violent option would only trigger further violence.

Hussein risked death and achieved a resurrection. In a different way, at far greater cost, and on a different level, so did Jesus. The two stories end differently, but both climax with the total vulnerability that demands the offering of costly self-emptying love. Incarnation (born in a manger) can never be separated from atonement ("It is finished" and "he is risen"). The center of the parable is the center of the parable. The owner's unbelievable decision is truly earthshaking and deserves far deeper reflection than it has received.

How is the phrase "my beloved son" to be understood? In Psalm 2:7 the Lord tells the newly enthroned king of Israel, "You are my son, / today I have begotten you." The Messiah of Israel was to be such a king. There is no need to assume that the language of the vineyard owner/father in the parable could not have been used by Jesus but must reflect the theology of Paul a generation or more after the cross. A few days before Jesus told this parable, he had publicly affirmed his messianic identity in the dramatic act of the triumphal entry. This story affirms a great deal of what the reader of Luke's Gospel had already learned about the person of Jesus. The Father spoke at his baptism and on the mount of transfiguration regarding his "beloved/chosen son," paraphrasing the language of the first of the Servant Songs (Is 42:1). The language of the owner in the parable fits both the ministry of Jesus and the theology of the church after the resurrection.

The owner asks the resonant question, "What shall I do?" By means of his costly action he sends the ball into the court of the tenants, who, on seeing the son,

---

[8]Ibn al-'Assal, *The Four Gospels*, British Museum Oriental Manuscript No. 3382, 1252 A.D., folio no. 268 (Recto). Many other Arabic translations use the same word.

would have to ask the same question of themselves. The story continues:

6. But when the vinedressers saw him
   they said to themselves,
       'This is the heir;   SON SEEN
       let us *kill him,*   And Killed
       that *the inheritance may be ours.'*
   And they *cast him out* of the vineyard
   and *killed him.*

They drag the son outside the vineyard because if they kill him within the vineyard, their grapes will become defiled and thereby worthless.[9]

But far more important is the phrase *the inheritance will be ours.* What does this mean? On the story line there is a ruling in the Mishnah regarding "squatters rights" that reads: "Title by usucaption to houses, cisterns, trenches, vaults, dovecots, bath-houses, olive-presses, irrigated fields, and slaves, and aught that brings constant gain, is secured by occupation during three completed years."[10] This ruling places the parable in the Jewish world of Jesus. It also sheds light on the mentality of the renters in the story, who believe that if they can maintain physical possession for three years, they can secure ownership of the vineyard.

The reader's deepest concern at this point in the parable is to ask, does "the inheritance" mentioned refer to the land or the nation of Israel or the spiritual inheritance of Israel? The parable itself offers hints for an answer but no more. Related to this question is the identification of the "others" to whom the "vineyard" is to be given in stanza 7 (v. 16). *What* is to be given *to whom?*

Isaiah's parable is about the vineyard that is identified in the text as representing "the men of Israel." In that story the reader is told that the vineyard will be torn down (implying the coming destruction of the nation). But in Jesus' parable the renters are criticized, not the vineyard. The renters forgot that they were renters and began to assume that they were owners! Through the medium of this important story Jesus is expressing his understanding of the conflict between himself and the temple leadership, and voicing his criticism of them. This is confirmed by their concluding remark in Luke 20:19: "The scribes and the chief priests tried to lay hands on him at that very hour, but they feared the people; for they perceived that he had told this parable against them."

---

[9]Some have claimed that Luke places the murder of the son outside the vineyard in order to accommodate his telling of the parable to the fact that Jesus was killed outside the city. Such speculation is unnecessary when the potential defilement of the grapes is considered.

[10]Mishnah, *Baba Batra* 3.1 (Danby, p. 369).

After telling this parable, Jesus was still popular with the crowds, who knew he was not criticizing them or the nation as a whole. The parable was directed against "the scribes and the chief priests," and they knew it. Something is to be taken from them and given to others.

Arland Hultgren rejects the idea that the "others" are the Gentile church or the Christian community. He adds, "It is more fitting that the 'others' are a new or renewed leadership other than the Jerusalem leaders. If the parable is authentic, that could consist of the Twelve, Jesus and the Twelve, or at least a new leadership that God shall raise up that accepts the proclamation of Jesus."[11]

Jesus was not interested in starting a settler movement and controlling the land. Nor was he interested in becoming a new Herod the Great and ruling the nation. He was, however, keenly interested in the *heritage of Israel*. In commenting on the word *inheritance* in the light of the parable before us, Foerster writes:

> The inheritance is the kingdom of God. . . . When Jesus in His earthly lowliness describes Himself as υἱὸς καὶ κληρονόμος ["son and heir"], the concept of the kingdom of God and of the inheritance is freed from all earthly limitations and qualifications. The kingdom or inheritance is the new world in which God reigns alone and supreme.[12]

The psalmist wrote, "The lines have fallen for me in pleasant places; / yea, I have a goodly heritage" (Ps 16:6). My personal inheritance was very small. But my heritage through a British Church of England mother and an American Presbyterian father was and is enormous. Israel's high priestly establishment controlled an institution with a set of buildings. They also spoke for the heritage of Israel. In the first century the house of Annas, with his five sons (each of whom became high priests) and Caiaphas (his son-in-law), controlled the high priestly office for decades. They were no doubt confident that their administration would continue indefinitely. By means of his brief occupation of the temple area, Jesus challenged that assumption. He sensed their confidence that if they could just get rid of him, surely their ability to control the inheritance would not be challenged again. Jesus saw himself and his disciples as having the right to define what it meant to be faithful to the God of Abraham, Moses and the prophets, which was for him the inheritance that mattered. Worship in Jerusalem or on Mt. Gerizim was not critical. But worship in "spirit and in truth" was of ultimate significance (Jn 4:21-23).

The idea that "the inheritance" was far more than land and nation was well

---

[11]Arland J. Hultgren, *The Parables of Jesus* (Grand Rapids: Eerdmans, 2000), p. 360.
[12]Werner Foerster, "κληρονόμος," *Theological Dictionary of the New Testament*, 10 vols., ed. Gerhard Kittel and Gerhard Friedrich, trans. Geoffrey W. Bromiley (Grand Rapids: Eerdmans, 1964-1976), 3:782.

known in the centuries shortly before and after Jesus. First *Enoch* 40:9-10 speaks of "the hope of those who would inherit eternal life."[13] In Luke 10:25 a lawyer asks Jesus, "Teacher, what shall I do to inherit eternal life," and in Luke 18:18 a ruler asks the same question. Finally, late in the first century Rabbi Eliezer was asked by his disciples about how to "take possession of the life of the future world" (my translation).[14] The key word here is *hkz*, which is used in connection with "owning," "taking possession of" and "legally qualifying to acquire ownership."[15] Thus from at least the first century B.C. through the New Testament and on to the late first-century rabbis, the idea of "inheritance" is "often linked with the concept of eternal life."[16]

King Hussein of Jordan was prepared to die. The beloved son in the parable knew what had happened to the other servants and clearly understood how the confrontation might end. Luke records three occasions when Jesus predicted his own death. So in the parable the vinedressers continued to act as though they were owners and not renters, and proceeded to kill the son. What would the vineyard owner now do?

7. What then will the *owner* of the vineyard do to them?
   He will come and *destroy those vinedressers*,   VINEYARD
   and *give the vineyard to others*."   Transferred

   ---------------------------------   -------------------

8. When they heard this,   LEADERS
      they said, "God forbid!"   Shocked

9. But he looked at them and said,
      "What then is written:
      'The very stone which the builders rejected   JESUS and
         has become the head of the corner'?   Supporting Scriptures
      Every one who falls on that stone
         will be broken to pieces;
      but when it falls on any one
         it will crush him.'"

Time and again the prophets of Israel spoke of the coming destruction of the nation. In the song of the vineyard, Isaiah projected the destruction of the vine-

[13] *1 Enoch*, in *The Old Testament Pseudepigrapha*, trans. E. Isaac, ed. J. H. Charlesworth (New York: Doubleday, 1983), 1:32.
[14] Babylonian Talmud, *Berakot* 28b.
[15] Marcus Jastrow, *A Dictionary of the Targumim, the Talmud Babli and Yerushalmi, and the Midrashic Literature* (New York: Padres, 1950), 1:398.
[16] I. Howard Marshall, *The Gospel of Luke* (Exeter: Paternoster, 1978), p. 442.

yard long before Jerusalem fell. But the parable of Jesus is much milder than its prototype. The vineyard is not criticized or in any way threatened. The *renters* are the problem, and thus Jesus' prophecy is directed against the temple leadership, not against the nation, which deserves better shepherds.

Naturally, the audience (which is composed of representatives of the temple leadership) gasped and said, "God forbid!" Jesus replied with a parable about a stone that appears in the center of Psalm 118:19-28. Why that particular passage, and why the parable/metaphor of the stone?

Psalm 118:19-28 contains a series of striking features that appear in the triumphal entry. These include:

1   a procession going up to and through the gates of the temple

2. the cry "Hosanna"

3. the affirmation, "Blessed be he who enters in the name of the LORD"

4. the carrying of branches in the procession

In the middle of verses that describe the festive procession lies the parable of the stone that is rejected and then endorsed as the "chief cornerstone." The text says:

> The stone which the builders rejected
> has become the chief cornerstone. (Ps 118:22)

Thoughtful observers of the triumphal entry could hardly miss the connections between the procession described in Psalm 118:19-28 and the special features of the parade taking place before their eyes. It is impossible to observe that connection without reflecting on the parable of the stone that is at the center of that same passage (Ps 118:22).

Furthermore, during the triumphal entry Jesus defends his followers before the Pharisees by saying to them, "I tell you, if these [disciples] were silent, the very *stones* would cry out" (Lk 19:40). What stones? we ask. Was he thinking about the great stones in the temple buildings and about the stone of the parable in Psalm 118 that was rejected and then became the chief cornerstone? Perhaps with this in mind, it is easy to see Jesus invoking this same parable of the stone the following day and applying it to himself.

There may be a Hebrew word play in the parable (the *māšāl*) and the dialogue that follows it (the *nimšal*). The Hebrew word *ben* means "son." *Eben* in Hebrew is a "stone." The *'eben* (stone) that was rejected is the *ben* (son) of the parable.[17] If this suggestion is given credence, Psalm 118:19-28 as a whole was fresh in the minds

---

[17]Hultgren notes that this word play is available in Hebrew but not Aramaic (Hultgren, *Parables of Jesus*, p. 363).

of everyone, due to the recent triumphal entry that appears to follow its outline.

To this is added a quote from Isaiah 8:14, where the reader is told that God will become both a "sanctuary" and "a stone of offense" to Israel. Echoes of Simeon's blessing in Luke 2:34 can be heard where Simeon declared, "Behold, this child is set for the fall and rising of many in Israel."

But the larger question raised by the Isaiah 8:14 quotation is: Did Jesus take a biblical text that referred to God and apply it to himself?

The late distinguished Israeli professor of New Testament, David Flusser, published a brief article comparing Jesus and Hillel. The title of the article is "Hillel's Self-Awareness and Jesus."[18] Flusser's argument is that Hillel, the great rabbi who lived one generation before Jesus, had high self-esteem and he quoted Scripture texts about God and applied them to himself. Flusser's point is that it is no longer possible to affirm that "a high self-esteem, both with regard to one's personal and one's religious standing, did not exist in Judaism of the Second Temple period."[19] In addition to Hillel, argues Flusser, the Teacher of Righteousness in the Qumran community also had an elevated self-awareness.

When the Gospels record Jesus applying such texts as Isaiah 8:14 to himself, he can be seen to be in the same theological pond as Hillel and the Teacher of Righteousness. In reflecting on Flusser's thesis, it appears to me that the difference between Jesus and Hillel is that Hillel's students did not think he was serious, but the disciples of Jesus were convinced that Jesus meant it—and that it was true.

In any case, the judgment affirmed at the conclusion to the parable is a far milder prophetic word than the devastation announced in the parable of Isaiah 5.

In this parable Jesus offers grace and judgment, themes that recur in his teachings. In the parable of the great banquet, grace is extended to the unworthy, and at the end of the day those who rejected the nobleman's banquet and who brought judgment on themselves were shut out (Lk 14:24). In the parable of the talents, grace was extended to all the servants, even to the one who was unfaithful, and yet those who flatly refused the master were confronted with what they deserved (Lk 19:27). In the parable of the fig tree (Lk 13:6-9), the unfruitful tree was the recipient of extraordinary grace and the option of judgment remained (Lk 13:9).

To summarize this great parable is nearly impossible. It opens avenues of thought and action that lead in many directions. The following can be considered.

---

[18]David Flusser, "Hillel's Self-Awareness and Jesus," *Judaism and the Origins of Christianity* (Jerusalem: Magnes Press, 1988), pp. 509-14.
[19]Ibid., p. 509.

SUMMARY: THE PARABLE OF THE NOBLE VINEYARD OWNER

1. *Incarnation and atonement.* These two great themes meet in this parable. God sent his beloved son alone into the vineyard where his servants had been beaten, insulted, injured (Mk: killed) and thrown out. The parable exposes God's willingness to give himself through his son, in total vulnerability, in order to win his people back to himself. The incarnation is affirmed and the cross foreseen. Herod's will was carried out on Golgotha. The short-term result of the offer of love is the death of the son. The parable stimulates the mind to reflect on the long-term effects of the self-emptying act of the owner and his beloved son.

2. *Christology.* Jesus is in the line of the prophets and is also the beloved son. The prophetic tradition comes to its climax in him. He is the agent through whom the ultimate appeal of costly love is made. He is sent into the world to call all his people, particularly opponents, to be reconciled to his Father. Language that describes God in the Old Testament is quoted and applied to Jesus (Ps 118:22; Is 8:14-15).

3. *The reprocessing of anger into grace.* The vineyard owner does not respond to the renters with force or violence. Rather he chooses incarnation with its total vulnerability. To do this he must reprocess his anger into a costly demonstration of unexpected love/grace. That incarnation implies forgiveness for those who accept his offer of love.

4. *The leadership of the vineyard of God (cf. Is 5:1-5).* The vinedressers were renters, not owners. They forgot that fact and began acting on the assumption of "squatter's rights." They imagined that if they controlled the vineyard long enough, and if they could "create facts on the ground" by killing the son, the vineyard would become theirs. They were mistaken. Followers of Jesus in every age are reminded that they do not own "the inheritance" and that they cannot keep its fruits for their own exclusive use. Any attempt to do so will take them down a path that unites them with the vinedressers. The fruits of the vineyard must be offered to its owner. The renters are challenged to offer obedience to the beloved son.

5. *The nature of the fruits of the vineyard that are due to God.* In Isaiah 5:7 these fruits are identified as "justice and righteousness." In Jesus' parable the same identifications are implied, yet the details are left to the imagination of the reader/listener.

6. *The nature of the inheritance.* The violent renters murder the son hoping to gain

"the inheritance." Jesus is not interested in possessing or controlling the land or the "temple made with hands." But all through his ministry he is very interested in the theological and ethical heritage of Abraham, Moses and the prophets. Who has the right to claim that heritage and distill meaning from it for the present and the future? Jesus claims that right and is willing to die exercising and fulfilling it.

7. *The depth of sin.* The depth of sin knows no shame. The vinedressers respond to the owner's costly love by murdering his son.

8. *Vindication.* The stone (Jesus) rejected (by the temple leadership) has become the chief cornerstone. The rights of the messianic king that were affirmed in the triumphal entry are here repeated and clarified. At the time of the telling of this parable Jesus was already the "head of the corner." That role was confirmed by resurrection.

9. *Judgment.* Judgment in the parable focuses on the temple leaders and their demise, not on the people. The multitude hears the telling of the parable and continues to support and protect Jesus. The judgment is much milder than the song of the vineyard (Is 5:1-7). The vineyard is not destroyed, rather a change to more faithful leadership is promised. Grace is free and abounding, but, as in other parables, judgment does not evaporate as a result.

Bibliography

Abuna, Albert. *Adab al-Lugha al-Aramiyah* (Literature of the Aramaic language). Beirut: Starko Press, 1980.

Achtemeier, Paul J. *The Inspiration of Scripture: Problems and Proposals*. Philadelphia: Westminster Press, 1980.

Alfeyev, Hilarion. *The Spiritual World of Isaac the Syrian*. Kalamazoo, Mich.: Cistercian Publications, 2000.

Allison, C. FitzSimons. "Modernity or Christianity? John Spong's Culture of Disbelief." In *Can A Bishop Be Wrong?* Edited by Peter C. Moore. Harrisburg, Penn.: Morehouse, 1998.

The Alternative Service Book 1980. Cambridge: Cambridge University Press, 1980.

Arberry, Arthur J. *The Koran Interpreted*. 2 vols. New York: Macmillan, 1955.

Bailey, David M. *Vista Point*. (1997) <www.davidmbailey.com>.

Bailey, Kenneth E. *Poet and Peasant and Through Peasant Eyes*. Grand Rapids: Eerdmans, 1980.

———. "The Structure of I Corinthians and Paul's Theological Method With Special Reference to 4:17." *Novum Testamentum* 15 (1983).

———. *The Cross and the Prodigal*. Downers Grove, Ill.: InterVarsity Press, 2005.

———. *Finding the Lost: Cultural Keys to Luke 15*. St. Louis: Concordia Press, 1992.

———. "Hibat Allah Ibn al-'Assal and His Arabic Thirteenth Century Critical Edition of the Gospels." *Theological Review* (Beirut), 1 (1978).

———. *Jacob and the Prodigal*. Downers Grove, Ill.: InterVarsity Press, 2003.

———. "The Manger and the Inn: The Cultural Background of Luke 2:7." *Theological Review* (Beirut) 2 (1979).

———. *Open Hearts in Bethlehem*. Louisville: Westminster/John Knox, 2005. (A Christmas musical drama.)

———. "The Song of Mary: Vision of a New Exodus (Luke 1:46-55)." *Theological Review* 2, no. 1 (1979): 29-35.

———. "Women in Ben Sirach and in the New Testament." *For Me to Live: Essays in Honor of James Leon Kelso*. Edited by R. A. Coughenour. Cleveland: Dinnon/Liederbach, 1972.

———. "Women in the New Testament: A Middle Eastern Cultural View." *Theology Matters*. Blacksburg, Va.: Presbyterians for Faith, Family and Ministry, 2000.

Barrett, C. K. *The Gospel According to St John*. London: SPCK, 1960.

Barth, Markus. *Ephesians*. Anchor Bible 34A. New York: Doubleday, 1974.

Batey, Richard A. *Jesus & the Forgotten City: New Light on Sepphoris and the Urban World of Jesus*. Grand Rapids: Baker, 1991.

Bauckham, Richard. *Jesus and the Eyewitnesses: The Gospels as Eyewitness Testimony*. Grand Rapids: Eerdmans, 2006.

Bauer, Walter. *A Greek-English Lexicon of the New Testament*. Translated and adapted by W. F. Arndt, F. W. Gingrich and F. W. Danker. Chicago: University of Chicago Press, 1979.

Beasley-Murray, George R. *John*. Word Biblical Commentary 26. Waco, Tex.: Word, 1987.

Bishop, E. F. F. *Jesus of Palestine*. London: Lutterworth, 1955.

Blomberg, Craig L. *Neither Poverty nor Riches: A Biblical Theology of Material Possessions*. Grand Rapids: Eerdmans, 1999.

Bonhoeffer, Dietrich. *Life Together*. New York: Harper, 1954.

———. *Meditations on the Cross*. Edited by Manfred Weber. Louisville: Westminster John Knox, 1998.

Bratton, Susan P. "The Original Desert Solitaire: Early Christian Monasticism and Wilderness." *Environmental Ethics* 10, no. 1 (1988).

Brown, Raymond E. *The Birth of the Messiah: A Commentary on the Infancy Narratives in Matthew and Luke*. London: Geoffrey Chapman, 1977.

———. *The Gospel According to John*. Anchor Bible. 2 vols. Garden City, N.Y.: Doubleday, 1966.

Brooten, Bernadette. "Junia . . . Outstanding Among the Apostles (Romans 16:7)." *Women Priests: A Catholic Commentary on the Vatican Declaration*. Edited by L. Swidler and A. Swidler. New York: Paulist, 1977.

Bruce, F. F. *The Gospel of John*. Grand Rapids: Eerdmans, 1983.

Bultmann, Rudolf. *The Gospel of John*. Philadelphia: Westminster, 1971.

———. *Theology of the New Testament*. 2 vols. New York: Scribner, 1955.

Burkitt, F. Crawford. *Evangelion Da-Mepharreshe*. 2 vols. Cambridge: Cambridge University Press, 1904.

Burge, Gary. *John*. NIV Application Commentary. Grand Rapids: Zondervan, 2000.

Calvin, John. *The Epistles of Paul the Apostle to the Romans and to the Thessalonians*. Translated by R. Mackenzie. Grand Rapids: Eerdmans, 1976.

———. *A Harmony of the Gospels, Matthew, Mark and Luke, I*. Translated by A. W. Morrison. Grand Rapids: Eerdmans, 1972.

Charlesworth, J. H., Editor. *The Old Testament Pseudepigrapha*. 2 vols. New York: Doubleday, 1983.

Christie, William M. "Sea of Galilee." In *A Dictionary of Christ and the Gospels*. 2 vols. Edited by James Hastings (Edinburgh: T & T Clark, 1908).

Chrysostom, John. *Homilies on Galatians, Ephesians, Philippians, Colossians, Thessalonians, Timothy, Titus, and Philemon.* Edited by Philip Schaff. Nicene and Post-Nicene Fathers 12. Grand Rapids: Eerdmans, 1979.

Cicero. *The Republic.* Translated by C. W. Keyes. Cambridge, Mass.: Harvard University Press, 1970.

Coughenour, Robert A., ed. *For Me to Live: Essays in Honor of James Leon Kelso.* Cleveland: Dillon/Liederbach, 1972.

Cranfield, C. E. B. *Romans: A Shorter Commentary.* Grand Rapids: Eerdmans, 1985.

Cullman, Oscar. "Infancy Gospels." In *New Testament Apocrypha.* Edited by W. Schneemelcher. 2 vols. Philadelphia: Westminster Press, 1963.

Cyril of Alexandria. *Commentary on the Gospel of Saint Luke.* Translated by R. Payne Smith. n.c.: Studion, 1983.

Daniélou, Jean. "The Ebionites." *The Theology of Jewish Christianity.* Philadelphia: Westminster Press, 1964.

Davies, W. D., and Dale C. Allison Jr. *The Gospel According to Saint Matthew.* 3 vols. New York: T & T Clark, 1988.

Davis, Burke. *To Appomattox: Nine April Days, 1985.* New York: Popular Library, 1960.

Derrett, J. D. M. "Law in the New Testament: The Parable of the Prodigal Son." *New Testament Studies* 14 (1967).

Dewey, J. *Markan Public Debate: Literary Technique, Concentric Structure and Theology in Mark 2:1-3:6.* Chico, Calif.: Scholars Press, 1980.

Dodd, C. H. *The Interpretation of the Fourth Gospel.* Cambridge: Cambridge University Press, 1965.

———. *The Parables of the Kingdom.* New York: Scribner's, 1961.

Dunn, James D. G. *The Parting of the Ways (Between Christianity and Judaism and Their Significance for the Character of Christianity).* London: SCM, 1991.

———. *Romans.* Vol. 2. Waco, Tex.: Word, 1990.

Edersheim, A. *The Temple: It's Ministry and Services as They Were at the Time of Jesus Christ.* London: Religious Tract Society, n.d.

Eisenman, R. H., and M. Wise. *The Dead Sea Scrolls Uncovered.* Rockport, Mass.: Element, 1992.

Ellis, E. E. "The Authorship of the Pastorals: A Resume and Assessment of Recent Trends." *Paul and His Recent Interpreters.* Eerdmans: Grand Rapids, 1979.

Elton, Lord. *Gordon of Khartoum.* New York: Knopf, 1955.

Ephrem the Syrian: Hymns. Translated by Kathleen E. McVey. New York: Paulist, 1989.

Epictetus. *The Book of Epictetus: Being the Enchiridion Together with Chapters from the Discourses and Selections from the Fragments of Epictetus.* Edited by W. Rolleston, translated by Elizabeth Carter. London: Ballantyne Press, n.d.

Eusebius. *The History of the Church.* Translated by G. A. Williamson. Baltimore: Penguin Books, 1965.

Fitzmyer, J. A. *The Gospel According to Luke (I-IX)*. New York: Doubleday, 1981.

―――. *The Gospel According to Luke (X-XXIV)*. New York: Doubleday, 1985.

Flusser, David. *Judaism and the Origins of Christianity*. Jerusalem: Magnes Press, 1988.

Freedman, David N. "Prolegomenon." In *The Forms of Hebrew Poetry*, by George B. Gray. New York: Ktav, 1972.

Gibson, M. D., ed. *An Arabic Version of the Epistles of St. Paul to the Romans, Corinthians, Galatians, with part of the Epistle to the Ephesians from a Ninth Century Ms. in the Convent of St Catherine on Mount Sinai*. Studia Sinaitica 2. London: Cambridge University Press, 1894.

Godet, Frédéric Louis. *Commentary on the Gospel of John*. 2 vols. 1893. Reprint, Grand Rapids: Zondervan, 1969.

Goodwin, Jan. *The Price of Honor*. Boston: Little, Brown, 1994.

Graf, Georg. *Geschichte der christichen arabischen Literatur*. 5 vols. Studie Testi 113, 133, 146, 147, 172. Vatican City: Biblioteca Apostolica Vaticana, 1944-1953.

Green, Joel B. *The Gospel of Luke*. Grand Rapids: Eerdmans, 1997.

Gray, George B. *The Forms of Hebrew Poetry*. New York: Ktav, 1972.

Guidi, I. "Le traduzione degle Evangelli in arabo e in ethopico." *Tipografia della Reale Accademia dei Lincei*, vol. CCLXXV, 1888.

Hamilton, V. P. "Marriage (OT and ANE)." In *The Anchor Bible Dictionary*. Edited by D. N. Freedman et al. Vol. 4. New York: Doubleday, 1992.

Hastings, James. *A Dictionary of Christ and the Gospels*. 2 vols. Edinburgh: T & T Clark, 1908.

Hauck, Friedrich, and G. Bertram. "μακάριος." *Theological Dictionary of the New Testament* 4:362-70. Edited by Gerhard Kittel and Gerhard Friedrich. Translated by Geoffrey W. Bromiley. Grand Rapids: Eerdmans, 1967.

Hauptman, J. "Images of Women in the Talmud." *Religion and Sexism: Images of Women in the Jewish and Christian Traditions*. Edited by Rosemary R. Ruether. New York: Simon & Schuster, 1974.

Hedrick, Charles W. *Parables as Poetic Fictions*. Peabody, Mass.: Hendrickson, 1994.

Hengel, Martin. *The Zealots: Investigations into the Jewish Freedom Movement in the Period from Herod I Until 70 A.D.* Edinburgh: T & T Clark, 1989.

Hertz, Joseph H. *The Authorized Daily Prayer Book*. New York: Bloch, 1979.

Hirschfield, Yizhar, with M. F. Vamosh. "A Country Gentleman's Estate: Unearthing the Splendors of Ramat Hanadiv." *Biblical Archaeology Review* 31 March/April (2005).

Horowitz, George. *The Spirit of Jewish Law*. New York: Central Book, 1953.

Hoskyns, E. C. *The Fourth Gospel*. Edited by F. N. Davey. London: Faber & Faber, 1947.

Hultgren, Arland J. *The Parables of Jesus*. Grand Rapids: Eerdmans, 2000.

Ibn al-'Assal. *The Four Gospels* (Arabic). British Museum Oriental Manuscript no. 3382. 1252 A.D.

Ibn al-Tayyib al-Mashriqi, Abdallah. *Tafsir al-Mashriqi*. Edited by Yusif Manqariyos. Two vols. Egypt: al-Tawfiq Press, 1907. An Arabic commentary on the four Gospels by Abdallah Ibn al-Tayyib al-Mashriqi, Arabic, originally composed in the 11th century.

Ibn al-Salibi. *Kitab al-Durr al-Farid fi tafsir al-Ahad al-Jadid* (The book of rare pearls of interpretation of the New Testament). Cairo: n.p., 1914. Originally composed in Syriac in the 13th century.

The Isaiah Targum, The Aramaic Bible II. Translated by Bruce D. Chilton. Edinburgh: T & T Clark, 1987.

Jastrow, Marcus. *A Dictionary of the Targumim, the Talmud Babli and Yerushalmi, and the Midrashic Literature.* 2 vols. New York: Padres, 1950.

Jeremias, Joachim. *Jerusalem in the Time of Jesus.* Philadelphia: Fortress, 1967.

———. *Jesus' Promise to the Nations.* Studies in Biblical Theology 24. Naperville, Ill.: Alec R. Allenson, 1958.

———. *The Lord's Prayer.* Philadelphia: Fortress, 1969.

———. *The Parables of Jesus.* London: SCM, 1963.

———. *The Prayers of Jesus.* Philadelphia: Fortress, 1978.

Jerusalem Talmud, Hagigah and Moed Qatan. Translated by Jacob Neusner. Chicago: University Press, 1986.

Johnson, Luke Timothy. *The Gospel of Luke.* Collegeville, Minn.: Liturgical Press, 1991.

Just, Arthur A., ed. *Luke.* Ancient Christian Commentary on Scripture. Downers Grove, Ill.: InterVarsity Press, 2003.

Justin Martyr. *Selections from Justin Martyr's Dialogue with Trypho, a Jew.* Translated and edited by R. P. C. Hanson. London: Lutterworth, 1963.

Khalidi, Tarif. *The Muslim Jesus: Sayings and Stories in Islamic Literature.* Cambridge, Mass.: Harvard University Press, 2001.

Kierkegaard, Søren. *Fear and Trembling.* Translated by Walter Lowrie. New York: Doubleday Anchor Books, 1954.

Kittel, Gerhard, and Gerhard Friedrich. *Theological Dictionary of the New Testament.* 10 vols. Grand Rapids: Eerdmans, 1964-1976.

Kopp, Clemens. *The Holy Places of the Gospels.* New York: Herder & Herder, 1963.

Kuhn, Karl G., and Otto Procksch. "ἅγιος." In *Theological Dictionary of the New Testament* 1:88-115. Edited by Gerhard Kittel and Gerhard Friedrich. Translated by Geoffrey W. Bromiley. Grand Rapids: Eerdmans, 1964.

Kümmel, Werner Georg. *Promise and Fulfillment: The Eschatological Message of Jesus.* Studies in Biblical Theology 23. Naperville: Alec R. Allenson, 1957.

La Sor, William S. "Artemis." In *The International Standard Bible Encyclopedia.* Vol. 1. Revised. Edited by G. W. Bromley. Grand Rapids: Eerdmans, 1979.

Ladd, George E. *Jesus and the Kingdom: The Eschatology of Biblical Realism.* Waco, Tex.: Word, 1970.

Lauterbach, Jacob Z., tr. *Mekhilta of de-Rabbi Ishmael.* 3 vols. Philadelphia: Jewish Publication of America, 1976.

Liddell, H. G., and R. Scott. *A Greek-English Lexicon*. Revised by H. S. Jones and R. Mc-Kenzie. Oxford: Oxford University Press, 1966.

Lindars, Barnabas. *The Gospel of John*. In New Century Bible. London: Oliphants, 1972.

Linnemann, Eta. *Jesus of the Parables*. New York: Harper & Row, 1964.

Maalouf, Tony. *Arabs in the Shadow of Israel*. Grand Rapids: Kregel, 2003.

Manson, T. W. *The Sayings of Jesus*. 1937. Reprint, London: SCM, 1964, c. 1937.

———. *The Teaching of Jesus*. Cambridge: Cambridge University Press, 1955.

Marmardji, A. S., ed. *Diatessaron de Tataien*. Beyrouth: Imprimerie Catholique, 1935.

Marshall, I. Howard. *The Gospel of Luke: A Commentary on the Greek Text*. Exeter: Paternoster, 1978.

Matta al-Miskin. *al-Injil, bi-Hasab Bisharat al-Qiddis Luqa* (The Gospel according to saint Luke). Cairo: Dayr al-Qiddis Anba Maqar, 1998.

———. *al-Injil, bi-Hasab al-Qiddis Yuhanna* (The Gospel according to Saint John). 2 vols. Cairo: Dayr al-Qiddis Anba Maqar, 1990.

McVey, Kathleen, tr. *Ephrem the Syrian: Hymns*. New York: Paulist, 1989.

Metzger, Bruce M. *A Textual Commentary on the Greek New Testament*. London: United Bible Societies, 1971.

Meyers, Eric M., and J. F. Strange. *Archaeology, the Rabbis & Early Christianity*. London: SCM Press, 1981.

Michel, Otto. "τελώνης." *Theological Dictionary of the New Testament* 8:88-105. Edited by Gerhard Kittel and Gerhard Friedrich. Translated by Geoffrey W. Bromiley. Grand Rapids: Eerdmans, 1972.

Midrash Rabbah, Song of Songs. Translated by M. Simon. New York: Soncino Press, 1983.

The Mishnah. Edited and translated by Herbert Danby. Oxford: Oxford University Press, 1980.

Moore, George Foot. *Judaism in the First Centuries of the Christian Era*. 2 vols. New York: Schocken, 1971.

Mygind, H., Micheal Zasloff and others. "Plectasin Is a Peptide Antibiotic with Therapeutic Potential from a Saprophytic Fungus." *Nature*, October 2005, 437: 975-980.

Neusner, Jacob. *The Tosefta*. Vol. 2, *Moed*. New York: Ktav, 1981.

Newbigin, Lesslie. *The Gospel in a Pluralistic Society*. Grand Rapids: Eerdmans, 1990.

———. *The Light Has Come: An Exposition of the Fourth Gospel*. Grand Rapids: Eerdmans, 1982.

———. *The Open Secret*. Grand Rapids: Eerdmans, 1979.

———. *Proper Confidence*. Grand Rapids: Eerdmans, 1995.

———. *Sin and Salvation*. Philadelphia: Westminster Press, 1956.

Niles, Daniel T. *C.C.A. Hymnal*. Kyoto, Japan: Kawakita, 1974.

———. *Upon the Earth*. London: Lutterworth, 1962.

———. *This Jesus . . . Whereof We Are Witnesses*. Philadelphia: Westminster Press, 1965.

Nolland, John. *Luke*. Word Biblical Commentary. 3 vols. Dallas: Word, 1989-1993.

Nouwen, Henri J. M. *The Return of the Prodigal Son.* New York: Doubleday, 1992.

Novum Testamentum Domini Nostri Jesu Christi, Versio Arabica. Translated by J. Dawud. Mosul, Iraq: Typis Fratrum Praedictorum, 1899.

The Oxford Book of English Verse 1250-1918. Edited by A. Guiller-Couch. New York: Oxford University Press, 1940.

Perowne, Stewart. *The Later Herods: The Political Background of the New Testament.* London: Hodder & Stoughton, 1958.

————. *The Life and Times of Herod the Great.* London: Hodder & Stoughton, 1957.

Plummer, Alfred. *The Gospel According to St. John.* Cambridge Greek Testament for Schools and Colleges. Cambridge: Cambridge University Press, 1982.

————. *Gospel According to S. Luke.* 5th ed. International Critical Commentary. 1922. Reprint, Edinburgh: T & T Clark, 1960.

Rabin, Chaim. "Hebrew and Aramaic in the First Century." In *The Jewish People in the First Century.* Vol. 2. Philadelphia: Fortress Press, 1976.

Rad, Gerhard von. *Old Testament Theology.* 2 vols. New York: Harper & Row, 1962.

Ringsdorf, Karl Heinrich. "ἀπόστολος." *Theological Dictionary of the New Testament* 1:407-47. Edited by Gerhard Kittel and Gerhard Friedrich. Translated by Geoffrey W. Bromiley. Grand Rapids: Eerdmans, 1964.

Safrai, S., and Menahem Stern, eds. *The Jewish People in the First Century.* Vol. 2. Philadelphia: Fortress, 1976.

Sa'id, Ibraham. *Sharh Bisharat Yuhanna* (Commentary on the Gospel of John). Cairo: Dar al-Thaqafa, n.d.

————. *Sharh Bisharat Luqa* (Commentary on the Gospel of Luke). Beirut: Middle East Council of Churches, 1970.

Sanneh, Lamin. *Translating the Message: The Missionary Impact on Culture.* Maryknoll, N.Y.: Orbis, 1989.

Sasse, Hermann. "γῆ." In *Theological Dictionary of the New Testament* 1:677-81. Edited by Gerhard Kittel and Gerhard Friedrich. Translated by Geoffrey W. Bromiley. Grand Rapids: Eerdmans, 1964.

Scharlemann, Martin H. *Proclaiming the Parables.* Saint Louis: Concordia, 1963.

Schneemelcher, Wilhelm, and Edgar Hennecke, eds. *New Testament Apocrypha.* Vol. 1. Philadelphia: Westminster Press, 1963.

Schrenk, G. "δίκη, δίκαιος, δικαιοσύνη." In *Theological Dictionary of the New Testament* 2. Edited by Gerhard Kittel and Gerhard Friedrich. Translated by Geoffrey W. Bromiley. Grand Rapids: Eerdmans, 1964.

Scott, B. B. *Hear Then the Parable.* Minneapolis: Fortress, 1989.

Shahid, Irfan. *Byzantium and the Arabs in the Fourth Century.* Washington, D.C.: Dumbarton Oaks Research Library and Collection, 1984.

Sperber, Alexander, ed. *The Bible in Aramaic.* Vol. 3, *The Latter Prophets.* Leiden: E. J. Brill, 1962.

Mt. Sinai Arabic Codex 151. Vol. 1, *Pauline Epistles.* Translated and edited by H. Staal. Corpus Scriptorum Christianorum Orientalium, Scriptores Arabici Tomus 40. Lovanii: A. E. Peeters, 1983.

Stager, Lawrence E. "Why Were Hundreds of Dogs Buried at Ashkelon?" in *Biblical Archaeology Review* 17 no. 3 (1991): 26-42.

———. "Ashkelon." In *The New Encyclopedia of Archaeological Excavations in the Holy Land.* Edited by E. Stern. 4 vols. Jerusalem: Israel Exploration Society, 1993.

Stendahl, Krister. *The Bible and the Role of Women.* Philadelphia: Fortress, 1966.

Stern, M. "Aspects of Jewish Society: The Priesthood and other Classes." In *The Jewish People in the First Century.* Vol. 2. Philadelphia: Fortress, 1976.

Stevenson, James, ed. *A New Eusebius.* London: SPCK, 1957.

Suetonius. *The Twelve Caesars.* Translated by Robert Graves. London: Penguin Books, 1979.

Swidler, Leonard. *Biblical Affirmations of Women.* Philadelphia: Westminster Press, 1979.

The Talmud of the Land of Israel. Translated by Jacob Neusner. Hagigah and Moed Qatan 20. Chicago: University of Chicago Press, 1986.

Temple, William. *The Church Looks Forward.* London: Macmillan, 1944.

———. *Nature, Man and God.* London: Macmillan, 1953.

———. *Readings in St. John's Gospel.* 1st and 2nd ser. London: Macmillan, 1955.

Teresa, Mother. *The Joy in Loving.* Compiled by J. Chaliha and E. Le Joly. New York: Viking/Penguin, 1997.

Thompson, William. *The Land and the Book.* 2 vols. New York: Harper & Brothers, 1871.

Trimingham, J. Spener. *Christianity Among the Arabs in Pre-Islamic Times.* London: Longmans, 1979.

Tutu, Desmond M. *Hope and Suffering: Sermons and Speeches.* Grand Rapids: Eerdmans, 1984.

van der Post, Laurens. *Venture to the Interior.* Middlesex: Penguin Books, 1957.

Vatican Arabic MSS #95, The Four Gospels. Unpublished manuscript.

Vatican Arabic Ms. No. 13, The New Testament (8th/9th centuries). Unpublished manuscript.

The Dead Sea Scrolls in English. Translated by Géza Vermes. Middlesex: Penguin Books, 1975.

Viviano, Benedict. *The Kingdom of God in History.* Wilmington, Del.: Michael Glazier, 1988.

Wadell, Helen. *Beasts and Saints.* London: Constable, 1949.

Wehr, Hans. *A Dictionary of Modern Written Arabic.* Edited by J. M. Cowan. Ithaca, N.Y.: Cornell University Press, 1961.

Werblowsky, R. J. Zei, and G. Wigoder, eds. *The Encyclopedia of the Jewish Religion.* New York: Adama Books, 1987.

Westcott, B. F. *The Gospel According to St. John.* 1908. Reprint, Ann Arbor, Mich.: Baker, 1980.

Whiston, William. *The Works of Josephus.* Rev. ed. Peabody, Mass.: Hendrickson, 1987.

Whitacre, Rodney A. *John.* IVP New Testament Commentary. Downers Grove, Ill.: Inter-Varsity Press, 1999.

White, R. C. *Lincoln's Greatest Speech: The Second Inaugural.* New York: Simon & Schuster, 2002.

Wise, O. M., and J. D. Tabor. "The Messiah at Qumran." *Biblical Archaeology Review* 18, no. 6 (1992): 60-65.

Zerwick, Max, and Mary Grosvenor. *A Grammatical Analysis of the Greek New Testament.* Rev. ed. Rome: Biblical Institute Press, 1981.

INDEX OF FIGURES

Scripture Index

ALSO FROM KENNETH E. BAILEY

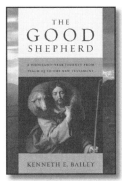

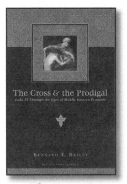

**The Cross &
the Prodigal**
978-0-8308-3281-1

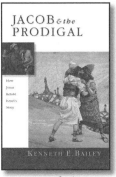

**The Good
Shepherd**
978-0-8308-4063-2

**Jacob &
the Prodigal**
978-0-8308-2727-5

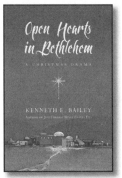

**Open Hearts
in Bethlehem**
978-0-8308-3757-1

**Paul Through
Mediterranean Eyes**
978-0-8308-3934-6